Curatopia

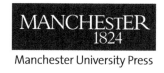

Manchester University Press

Curatopia

Museums and the future of curatorship

**EDITED BY PHILIPP SCHORCH
AND CONAL McCARTHY**

Manchester University Press

Copyright © Manchester University Press 2019

While copyright in the volume as a whole is vested in Manchester University Press, copyright in individual chapters belongs to their respective authors, and no chapter may be reproduced wholly or in part without the express permission in writing of both author and publisher.

Published by Manchester University Press
Altrincham Street, Manchester M1 7JA

www.manchesteruniversitypress.co.uk

British Library Cataloguing-in-Publication Data
A catalogue record for this book is available from the British Library

ISBN   978 1 5261 1819 6   hardback

First published 2019

The publisher has no responsibility for the persistence or accuracy of URLs for any external or third-party internet websites referred to in this book, and does not guarantee that any content on such websites is, or will remain, accurate or appropriate.

Typeset by Servis Filmsetting Ltd, Stockport, Cheshire
Printed in Great Britain by TJ International Ltd, Padstow

Contents

List of figures

Notes on contributors

James Clifford has written influential historical and literary critiques of anthropological representation, travel writing, museum practices and indigeneity: *Writing Culture, the Poetics and Politics of Ethnography*, co-edited with George Marcus (1986); *The Predicament of Culture* (1988); *Routes* (1997); *Returns: Becoming Indigenous in the 21st Century* (2013).

Eveline Dürr is Professor at the Department for Social and Cultural Anthropology, Ludwig-Maximilians-Universität, Munich, Germany. She has conducted fieldwork in Mexico, the USA, Aotearoa New Zealand and Germany, and her publications reflect her interests in urban anthropology, spatiality, material culture, environment and globalisation, taking into consideration the historical trajectories that have formed present conditions.

Larissa Förster is a researcher at the Centre for Anthropological Research on Museums and Heritage in Berlin, Germany (www.carmah.berlin/), and a representative of the Working Group on Museums of the German Anthropological Association. She has co-curated major exhibitions at the Rautenstrauch-Joest-Museum in Cologne, Germany (*Namibia – Deutschland: Eine geteilte Geschichte*; *Afropolis: City, Media, Art*). Her research centres on museums and (post)colonialism.

Ivan Gaskell is Professor of Cultural History and Museum Studies at Bard Graduate Center, New York, USA. He is the author or editor of twelve books, most recently *Tangible Things: Making History through Objects* (2015). He is a Permanent Senior Fellow of the Advanced Study Institute of the Georg-August University, Göttingen, Germany.

Viv Golding is Emeritus Associate Professor at the University of Leicester's School of Museum Studies. In 2013, Viv co-edited (with Wayne Modest) *Museums and Communities: Curators, Collections and Collaboration*. Since her academic research relates closely to international museum practice, she was elected President of ICME (The International Council of Museums of Ethnography) in 2013 and 2016.

Arapata Hakiwai is the Kaihautū (Māori co-leader) of the Museum of New Zealand Te Papa Tongarewa (Te Papa). Arapata has a PhD in Museum and Heritage Studies from Victoria University of Wellington, Aotearoa New Zealand, and has extensive museum experience at the national museum for over twenty years in various positions.

Vilsoni Hereniko is a professor, filmmaker and playwright at the University of Hawai'i, USA. He is best known for *The Land Has Eyes*, a narrative feature film that premiered at the Sundance Film Festival, and the books *Female Clowns and Power in Rotuma* (1995) and *Inside Out: Literature, Cultural Politics, and Identity in the New Pacific* (1999).

Noelle M.K.Y. Kahanu is a Native Hawaiian writer, artist, curator and film-maker with fifteen years of programme and exhibition experience at Bishop Museum, Honolulu, including serving on the project teams for the renovations of the Hawaiian Hall (2009), Pacific Hall (2013) and the exhibition, *E Kū ana ka paia* (2010). She is an assistant specialist at the Department of American Studies, University of Hawai'i.

Bronwyn Labrum is Head of New Zealand and Pacific Cultures at the Museum of New Zealand Te Papa Tongarewa. As well as working as a curator of history and textiles, she has been a university lecturer in programmes of history, design, and visual and material culture.

Billie Lythberg is Senior Research Fellow at the University of Auckland. She explores Indigenous economies and aesthetics, and has collaborated with Māori and Pacific artists, academics and communities towards co-developed research, co-authored publications, co-curated exhibitions, and projects of artistic and economic revitalisation. She has a particular passion for eighteenth-century Māori and Tongan artefacts, and the economic and political objectives their transactions were harnessed to.

Sharon Macdonald is Anniversary Professor in the Department of Sociology at the University of York, UK, where she directs the Profusion theme of *Heritage Futures*. She is also Alexander von Humboldt Professor in the Institute of European Ethnology, Humboldt-Universität zu Berlin, Germany, where she directs the Centre for Anthropological Research on Museums and Heritage.

Sean Mallon is of Samoan and Irish descent, and lives in Wellington, Aotearoa New Zealand. Since 1992, he has worked at the Museum of New Zealand Te Papa Tongarewa in collection management, education and curatorial roles. He is currently Senior Curator Pacific Cultures.

Conal McCarthy is Director of the Museum and Heritage Studies programme at Victoria University of Wellington, Aotearoa New Zealand. His recent books include *Museum Practice* (2015), *From Colonial Gothic to Māori Renaissance: Essays in memory of Jonathan Mane-Wheoki* (2017) and *Te Papa: Reinventing New Zealand's National Museum 1998–2018* (2018).

Wayne Modest is Head of the Research Center for Material Culture, the research institute of the Tropenmuseum, Museum Volkenkunde, Afrika Museum and the Wereldmuseum in the Netherlands. He is also Professor of Material Culture and Critical Heritage Studies at the VU University, Amsterdam, Netherlands. His recent publications include 'Anxious Politics in the European City', together with Anouk de Koning, in *Patterns of Prejudice*, 50:2 (2016).

Jennie Morgan is Research Fellow in the Department of Sociology at the University of York, UK, where she works on the Profusion theme of *Heritage Futures*. She is also Lecturer in Heritage at the University of Stirling, UK, where she is affiliated with the Centre for Environment, Heritage and Policy.

Moana Nepia is a Māori visual and performing artist, choreographer, dancer, video artist, curator, writer and assistant professor at University of Hawaiʻi's Center for Pacific Islands Studies, USA, and arts editor for the journal *The Contemporary Pacific*. Past projects include performances for the 2017 Honolulu Biennial, PQ15 with Carol Brown and Dorita Hannah, and the 2012 Auckland Triennial with Kō Nakajima and Kentaro Taki.

Wayne Ngata is Raukura/Chief Advisor Te Ao Māori, Ministry of Education Te Tāhuhu o te Mātauranga, Wellington, Aotearoa New Zealand. He is an advocate for Māori advancement through education in the Māori language, and the reconnection with relocated taonga. He is also a supporter of traditional navigation and waka hourua voyaging with related peoples in Te Moananui-a-Kiwa (the Pacific Ocean) as a means of rebuilding traditional knowledge platforms.

Bryony Onciul is a Senior Lecturer in Public History, University of Exeter, UK. She researches Indigenous heritage, decolonising museology, reconciliation and climate change in Canada, the UK and Oceania. Bryony is Chair of ACHS UK Chapter; author of *Museums, Heritage and Indigenous Voice: Decolonising Engagement*; and lead editor of *Engaging Heritage, Engaging Communities*.

Ruth B. Phillips is Canada Research Professor and is Professor of Art History at Carleton University, Ottawa, Canada. Her research focuses on the Indigenous arts of North America and critical museology. She has served as Director of the University of British Columbia Museum of Anthropology and President of the International Committee on the History of Art.

Amiria Salmond's research interests include Māori weaving, artefact-oriented ethnography, cultural and intellectual property, digital taonga and the 'ontological turn' in social anthropology. A former curator at the Museum of Archaeology and Anthropology, University of Cambridge, UK, she has also curated and designed exhibitions at the Tairāwhiti Museum in Gisborne, Aotearoa New Zealand.

Jette Sandahl was the founding director for the Women's Museum of Denmark and the National Museum of World Culture in Sweden. She served as Director of Exhibitions and Public Programmes at the National Museum of Denmark, as Director Experience at the Museum of New Zealand Te Papa Tongarewa and as Director of the Museum of Copenhagen, Denmark.

Philipp Schorch is Head of Research, State Ethnographic Collections of Saxony, Germany. He has held fellowships at Deakin University, Australia, the Institute of Advanced Study, Georg-August-University Göttingen, and Ludwig-Maximilians-Universität, Munich (Marie Curie, European Commission), Germany. Philipp is co-editor of the volume *Transpacific Americas: Encounters and Engagements between the Americas and the South Pacific* (2016).

Anthony Alan Shelton is Director of the Museum of Anthropology and Professor of Art History, Visual Art and Theory at the University of British Columbia, Vancouver, Canada. His publications include *Art, Anthropology and Aesthetics* (1992), *Heaven, Hell and Somewhere In-Between: Portuguese Popular Art and Culture* (2015) and *From Carnival to Lucha Libre: Mexican Masks and Devotions* (2017).

Paul Tapsell was formerly Chair of Māori Studies at the University of Otago, Dunedin, Aotearoa New Zealand. His Māori ancestry originates in the central North Island, and his research interests include the role of cultural heritage and museums in nation states. His academic and curatorial outputs expand on engagements at Rotorua Museum (curator), Pitt Rivers Museum, Oxford (doctoral research), UK, and Auckland War Memorial Museum (Director Māori), Aotearoa New Zealand.

Hilke Thode-Arora, a German social-cultural anthropologist, is the curator for the Pacific collections at the Museum Fünf Kontinente in Munich, Germany. She specialises in inter-ethnic relations and ethnic identities, material culture and the history of museum collections, and her research projects have included long-term fieldwork in Aotearoa New Zealand, Samoa and Niue.

Nicholas Thomas is Director of the Museum of Archaeology and Anthropology in Cambridge, UK. His books on colonial history, encounter, art and material culture include *The Return of Curiosity: What Museums Are Good for in the Twenty-First Century* (2016).

Friedrich von Bose is Curator at Humboldt University of Berlin, Germany, where he is preparing the university's exhibition space in the future Humboldt Forum. In 2015–2016, he was a member of the planning committee for the City Museum of Stuttgart, Germany. For his PhD, he undertook a multi-year ethnographic study of the Humboldt Forum's planning process (published 2016).

Ian Wedde is based in Auckland, Aotearoa New Zealand. He was Head of Art and Visual Culture at the Museum of New Zealand Te Papa Tongarewa 1994–2004 and established and taught a postgraduate curatorial practice course at the University of Auckland 2011–2013. His most recent publication is *Get a Move On* (2017).

Andrea Witcomb is Professor in Cultural Heritage and Museum Studies at Deakin University, Melbourne, Australia. Her work engages with the ways in which museums and heritage sites interpret difficult histories and facilitate cross-cultural encounters. She is also co-leading, with Alistair Patterson, a project on the history of collecting practices in Western Australia.

Acknowledgements

This volume is the outcome of two events, a conference held at the Ludwig-Maximilians-Universität, Munich, Germany, in 2015 and a seminar at Victoria University of Wellington, Aotearoa New Zealand, in 2011. The book was nurtured by the lively discussions spurred by papers presented and benefited from the ongoing intellectual engagement with conference participants as well as other authors we commissioned. It is, therefore, the product of the associated scholarly network, including university academics, museum professionals and community leaders, who are devoted to (re) thinking curatorship for the museums of the future.

We are indebted to a range of institutions and organisations that facilitated the realisation of the conference, seminar and book with their generous funding. We wish to thank the Goethe-Institut, the Ludwig-Maximilians-Universität, Munich (LMU), the Department für Kulturwissenschaften and the Institut für Ethnologie at the LMU for their financial and logistical support. Further funding was received from the European Union's H2020 Research and Innovation Programme under the Marie Sklodowska-Curie Grant Agreement No. 659660 awarded to co-editor Philipp Schorch. The Faculty of Humanities and Social Sciences at Victoria University of Wellington, and the Canadian High Commission, Wellington, deserve thanks for their research grants which supported the hosting of the seminar, associated travel and editorial assistance. We also would like to express our appreciation to the anonymous reviewers who assisted us with their critical comments and reflections on the manuscript.

In addition, we are grateful for the efforts of our student assistants who worked with us to organise and run the conference, and our editorial assistants, who helped with copyediting and finalising the manuscript: many thanks to Sasha Gora and Susette Goldsmith. Finally, we would both like to extend our heartfelt thanks to our partners, Eliza and Bronwyn, who put up with us while we were completing this project.

Philipp Schorch and Conal McCarthy
October 2017

Note on the text

In this book, when using the general category of 'Indigenous', we have used upper case, on a par with other conventional markers such as 'Western', and observe the use of capitals in reference to specific Indigenous peoples: Indigenous Australians, Native Americans, Māori, Samoan and so on. In order to avoid 'othering' Indigenous languages, we have italicised Indigenous words only on the first use in the main text; thereafter they are treated the same as words in English. Some of these words have different meanings and interpretations so we have left it to the author's discretion as to the translation.

We follow the convention in current New Zealand English of using macrons for Māori words to indicate a double vowel. However, Māori words in the titles of books, organisations and so on, and in historical archival sources and texts have been left in their original form. While the country remains formally 'New Zealand', we use the double appellation Aotearoa New Zealand where appropriate to reflect increasing formal use of this term. In the use of Pacific languages, we observe the glottal stop with appropriate diacritical marks, for example, in Samoan, the apostrophe *fa'a Samoa* (the Samoan way), and, in Hawaiian and Tongan, the reverse apostrophe e.g. *'akau* or stave club. Hawaiian words thus incorporate both the *'okina* (glottal stop) and the *kahakō* (macron). We also acknowledge hən̓q̓əmin̓əm̓ or the Musqueam language of British Columbia by using the word for the village and exhibition – c̓əsnaʔəm – and recognising that there are no capitals in this language.

Introduction: conceptualising Curatopia

Philipp Schorch, Conal McCarthy and Eveline Dürr

In Aotearoa New Zealand, bilingual museum titles reflect the Indigenous view of the world. Their Māori names liken museums to hills, caves, store houses and, commonly, to canoes (*waka*), either literally or figuratively through the image of a treasure box or carved vessel containing precious objects.[1] In other contexts, the word 'waka' can refer to the crews of, and those descended from, ancestral voyaging canoes, a flock of birds in flight and, today, to cars and other forms of transport. Nearly a century ago, Māori leaders used the same imagery in engagement with museum anthropology, as seen in the seal of the Board of Maori Ethnological Research showing a waka under sail. They urged their people to load on board this waka the 'precious freight/heritage' (*ngā morehu taonga*) of their ancestors, so that it could be preserved and disseminated 'for all the world to see'.[2] (See Figure 0.1.)[3]

These images of mobility are in contrast with those associated with the history of European museums which have been critiqued as static mausoleums devoted to the preservation of the past. This is prominently displayed in Michel Foucault's notion of heterotopias, in which he contrasts the 'museum' as an 'immobile place' with the 'ship' as 'the greatest reserve of the imagination'.[4] In this introduction to *Curatopia*, we reimagine the museum *as* ship, and explore the ways in which the associated practice of curating can be turned around to face the future, as the crew of the waka navigate the ocean before them.

This book brings together curators, scholars and critics from a range of fields in international institutions to engage in debates about curatorial histories, theories and practices. Old models of the curator as scholar connoisseur have been discredited, while new types – curator as entrepreneur, facilitator, artist, activist etc. – need more testing. As museums continue to change in the twenty-first century, the 'figure of the curator'[5] appears to be in flux. What is the future of curatorial practice? Is there a vision for an ideal curatorial model, an imagined future that we might call a 'curatopia'?[6] Would this take the form of a utopia or even a dystopia? We see in the plurality of approaches evident in this collection a curatorial 'heterotopia' emerging.[7] It is this new, critical but ethical approach to curating that we set out to describe in this volume.

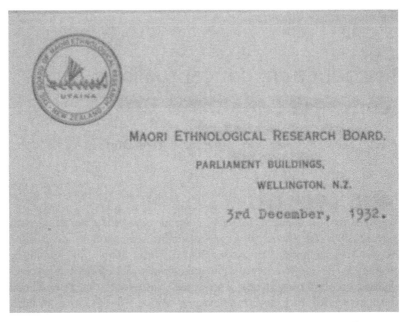

0.1 The seal of the Board of Maori Ethnological Research, Wellington, New Zealand, showing an ocean-going waka (canoe) under sail. This seal was used on all Board correspondence from its establishment in 1923.

Other questions have to do with the current vogue for curators as co-creators, in the service of cultural diversity, social inclusion and non-Western museology.[8] How can we historicise, theorise and ethnographically analyse museums as profoundly cross-cultural spaces, and study curatorship as an inherently cross-cultural method that requires dialogical translation and interpretative reciprocity? By addressing this challenge, the collection sets out to give co-curation a different and more substantial quality, imbuing it with conceptual and methodological rigour, in contrast to critiques that dismiss it as a shallow political gesture.[9] *Curatopia* explores the ways in which the mutual, asymmetrical relations underpinning global, scientific entanglements of the past can be transformed into more reciprocal, symmetrical forms of cross-cultural curatorship in the present. We argue that this is the most meaningful direction for curating in museums today.

In this opening provocation, we survey critical perspectives on curating in general. In the first historical part of the proposed line of inquiry, we follow others to suggest that the 'European Enlightenment' should not be understood as a sovereign and autonomous Europe-bound achievement.[10] Given the emerging mutual dependence of scientific travel practices, materialities, and academic disciplines in the eighteenth century, it can be argued instead that the encounter with Pacific people, among others, and their material manifestations in objects, had a significant influence on the development of new ideas, such as the Enlightenment,[11] an intersection of global encounters and European knowledge practices.[12] In other words, the Enlightenment should not be seen as a singular event originating in some (European) centre and radiating out into the global peripheries, rather it was a 'process of global circulation, translation, and transnational co-production'.[13] Since the same epoch in the eighteenth century, anthropology (and anthropological curatorship) has developed through scientific exploration and colonial expansion beyond Europe, as well as the establishment of ethnographic collections and museums in Europe, thus institutionalising and materialising the global circulation, translation and co-production of ideas.

Anthropological curatorship then and now can be understood as a mobile, cross-cultural form of knowledge production. We believe that what is needed today is a form of curating enacted not only through its analytical focus on cross-cultural action, traffic and appropriation but also at the level of method, interpretation and representation of the curatorial inquiry itself.[14] To address the second part of the proposed line of inquiry, and to shape *Curatopia* in more reciprocal, symmetrical forms, we explore how the relationships between Indigenous people in North America and the Pacific, collections in Euro-American institutions and curatorial knowledge in museums globally can be (re)conceptualised. How can we address the persistent problem that the majority of museological interventions produce and represent Indigenous visual and material cultures through the imposition of alien categories such as 'art' and 'artefact'? How can Indigenous histories, theories and practices drive their own visual language, representational mode, and thematic and spatial enactment through curatorial interventions in museum collections and exhibitions? We are accustomed to curators from 'the West' talking about objects and collections from 'the rest' of the world, but what happens when Indigenous curators interpret their own cultures using native and tribal frameworks? And what can European curators learn from this? On the analytical plane, we are accustomed to French and German social theory being exported into Anglophone museum and curatorial studies, but the ways in which Indigenous philosophies and ideas travel and speak back suggest that we can more effectively address the globalised world we inhabit and consider museums for what they are: profoundly cross-cultural spaces.

This volume follows these lines of enquiry by assessing the current state of play in curatorship, reviewing models and approaches operating in various museums, galleries and cultural organisations around the world, and debating emerging concerns, challenges and opportunities. The subject areas range over Native and tribal cultures, anthropology, art, history and philosophy. In some cases, authors look beyond Indigenous topics to consider how collecting, exhibiting and research in former settler colonies have developed in response to, or alongside, Indigenous people and culture; and/ or discuss the implications of these developments for European institutions. The volume is international in scope and covers three broad regions – Europe, North America and the Pacific.

Chapters are grouped by regions for several reasons. The Eurocentric projection of anthropological or curatorial imaginations has come under intense pressure while (post)colonial renegotiations in North America and the Pacific have initiated dramatic changes to anthropology through Indigenous knowledge practices including curatorship.[15] The book creates a dialogue between those situations, enabling Indigenous perspectives from North America and the Pacific to directly intervene in European debates and institutions that hold material traces from these regions and their Indigenous inhabitants. While chapters are grouped by region, thematic layers across the chapters show how these regions are relationally constituted, demonstrating that cross-Indigenous initiatives and networks are indeed global in reach. This becomes obvious, for instance, when exploring the manifold linkages across the Pacific and the Americas in both the past and the present. We do not conceptualise these as two separate regions, but instead emphasise the Transpacific as a relational space so that the dynamic character of locations and their entanglements is foregrounded.[16] In this vein, most, if not all, chapters in this volume resist conventional territorial boundaries, which reflects what museum objects, collections and exhibitions inevitably do: they circulate, and in the process become translated and co-produced.

The book is itself the product of a scholarly network that radiates out in different directions and on several levels. It is the result of two events, a conference held at the Ludwig-Maximilians-Universität, Munich, Germany, in

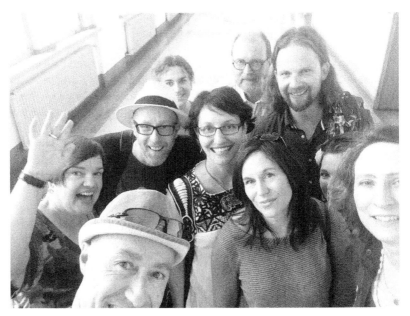

0.2 Delegates at the Curatopia conference, Munich, Germany, July 2015. They include, from left to right: Bronwyn Labrum, Paul Tapsell, Conal McCarthy, Billie Lythberg, Amiria Salmond, Ivan Gaskell, Philipp Schorch and Larissa Förster.

2015 (see Figure 0.2), and a seminar at Victoria University of Wellington in Aotearoa New Zealand in 2011. The contributors are leading and emerging scholars and practitioners in their respective fields. Furthermore, all contributors have worked in and with universities *and* museums, often in curatorial roles, and are therefore well positioned to enrich the dialogue between academia and the professional museum world. In this introduction, we refrain from the common trope of summarising and pre-interpreting individual contributions. Rather, we allow *Curatopia* to gradually unfold, seeing it as our task here, first, to situate it, then, second, to suggest how to study and enact it and, finally, to extend an invitation to (re)imagine and (re-)enact it.

Situating Curatopia

In this section, we consider how curators and curating have been and are being transformed, situating this museological practice against the background from which it can be studied, imagined and enacted. Since the late twentieth century, curating seems to be everywhere. Indeed, one might argue that we already live in a kind of curatopia. The *New York Times* art critic Michael Brenson calls the 1990s 'the age of the curator';[17] Paul O'Neill refers to the 'curatorial turn';[18] and David Balzar claims that 'curationism' has taken over the world and everything in it.[19] Much of the confusion that surrounds curatorship has to do with what Hans-Ulrich Obrist has called 'the amnesia of curatorial history'.[20] As with museums, curating is a modern, European invention with long historical roots.[21] By the twentieth century, the 'grey' literature of manuals, policies and other professional documents tells us that a museum curator was expected to acquire, research and manage collections, including their preservation (what we now call conservation), and, by extension, exhibitions (though these were in the main permanent displays).[22] But after the Second World War, the expansion of the number and type of museums brought diversification, specialisation and professionalisation with new roles such as collection managers and conservators taking over some curatorial duties, while the development of temporary exhibitions became more of a focus.[23]

Histories of curatorship tend to suggest a 'pendulum swing' during the last century going back and forth between scholarship and collections on the one hand, and exhibitions and the public experience on the other.[24] In the last thirty years, to put it simply, curatorial practice has changed 'from caring to creating'.[25] Moving beyond collection care, various new models of 'curator as' have proliferated which emphasise their creative agency: curator as exhibition-maker, project manager, producer, artist and many more.[26] 'The field of curating itself has changed from one of strict and specialised connoisseurship of individuals and their oeuvres,' writes Sarah Cook, 'to one that … has more to do with public service, diplomatic management, and cutting-edge knowledge of the problems at play in contemporary society'.[27]

The age of the Internet from the late 1990s seems to promise democratised access to museum collections, and the opportunity for everyone to become their own curator.[28] In Beryl Graham and Sarah Cook's *Rethinking Curating*,[29] they challenge art curators to take account of distributive and participatory systems, and hybrid and collaborative ways of working, characteristic of a digital and networked world.[30] Whether or not this access has been realised, the apparent flattening and democratising of an activity once confined to academic specialists is often greeted with alarm by 'traditional' curators and with joy by advocates of new media.[31] There has consequently been much lament from conservative critics at the apparent 'erosion' of curatorial control in the face of the now not-so-new museology.[32]

By the 2000s, there was an explosion of books, seminars and courses on curatorial practice, mostly dealing with the contemporary visual arts (which is not the focus of this book).[33] If technological issues such as those above are mainly articulated in the visual arts, in the writing by or on curators of history, anthropology, science and popular culture, external social factors are grappled with in fruitful ways which, we believe, look ahead to new curatopian futures.[34] In anthropology and natural history museums, perhaps most closely associated with the legacy of colonialism, curators have struggled since the 1980s to reconcile tensions of race, identity, conflict and change.[35] Objects collected from colonised people were often alienated from their original contexts and reassembled in the museum, reflecting the widespread desire to 'grasp the world' and control its resources.[36] However, we argue that the postcolonial critique of anthropology and museums overlooks a long and fruitful history of engagement by Native and tribal people,[37] failing to engage meaningfully with Indigenous scholars, concepts and frameworks.[38] We look to work on colonial museums which figures them as *relational* entities interconnected with networks of institutions and processes, and objects as active things.[39]

While we have to be aware of the shortcomings of much work that rather glibly puts an optimistic spin on the difficult work of community engagement and collaboration,[40] in recent years there has been much impressive research showing how curators, particularly in former colonies, have attempted to work in dialogue with Indigenous people, in what has often been called co-curation.[41] In Canada in the 1980s, for example, the controversy over the Glenbow Museum exhibition *The Spirit Sings* wrenched curators from their museal enclave and plunged them into the midst of a changing society, transforming their practice in the process.[42] Earlier curators might have viewed their work as 'isolated academic inquiry', writes Phaedra Livingstone, but this event 'rendered such a stance untenable'. From then on, many curators in Canadian history and anthropology museums 'began to see themselves as public intellectuals whose work had relevance and repercussions for the living communities that were represented in exhibitions'.[43] Laura Peers and Alison Brown, in an important survey published in 2003, refer to the emerging collaborative approach as the 'new curatorial praxis'.[44] As the anthropologist Christina Kreps has argued, these engagements with Indigenous people and material culture put curating into cross-cultural dialogue, which 'invariably entails viewing curatorial work as a continuing social process, and the acknowledgement of the social and cultural dimensions of peoples' relationships to objects'. Usefully for this volume, Kreps theorises 'curation as social practice and part of continuing social processes'.[45]

Studying Curatopia

Decolonisation in former European colonies, as seen above in North America and the Pacific, has brought about dramatic changes to museums and anthropological practices. Indigenous curators drawing on Indigenous ontological perspectives have reshaped collecting, exhibiting, fieldwork and research (often conducted in partnership with nearby communities). However, the danger persists that some so-called ethnographic objects in European museums remain largely disconnected from the distant cultural environments of their Indigenous producers and sources.[46] We believe that the problem is even deeper. Apart from the claims for moral redress, political concessions and legal reparations, which tend to dominate museological discussions, the issue is essentially methodological.[47]

It seems to us that anthropology does offer tools and methods that can critically analyse, revise and galvanise curatorial theory and practice. The historical gap between the university and the museum is closing up; museums are re-engaging with anthropology, and curators employing its methods to reform their practice. The key concerns of this book – historicising, theorising and ethnographically analysing museums as cross-cultural spaces, and curatorship as a cross-cultural method – are of mutual benefit for both museums and universities. Acts of translation across social worlds have always been at the centre of anthropological research, including not only semantics and cultural concepts but also gesture and performance. Translation can be seen as a world-making process, in which realms of experience are brought together. These processes are always embedded in particular social contexts. Thus, the act of translating is imbued with power and legitimacy. Further, when we conceptualise translation not only as a method but also as a social practice, translation itself comes under scrutiny.[48]

While the notion of culture as a preset entity is now conceptualised as a dynamic and constantly changing phenomenon, we suggest placing more emphasis on the ways in which 'culture' becomes 'alive', hence how it is enacted and performed. The performative act shifts attention from the (postmodern) preoccupation with representation to practices through which meaning in the social world is actively constituted. We argue that both notions, enactment and performativity, can help us better understand the figure of the curator in his or her role of (re)constructing or creating culture in terms of a meaning-maker and relationship-creator.

As this book conceives of museums as spaces of cross-cultural encounters, it is worth investigating the various ways in which these take shape and evolve. How can theories on, and empirical findings of, cross-cultural encounters advance our understanding of the interactions at work in museums? Cosmopolitan and transcultural approaches come to mind, challenging dualities and dichotomies, and stressing by contrast entanglement and overlap – e.g. the permeability of cultural boundaries, which are in a constant state of flux and allow for appropriation and adoption of new cultural forms. However, we take issue with the idea that cross-cultural encounters are, per se, something positive, or 'useful' in order to widen one's own horizon or to lay the ground for a better understanding of the 'other'. More often than not, cross-cultural encounters cause friction, further essentialising otherness and difference while idealising one's own cultural grounding. The task at stake is to investigate empirically the mechanisms that trigger different responses to face-to-face encounters and ask which theoretical conclusions, and practical – or, in a museum context, applicable – consequences can be drawn from these empirical findings.

Another important issue often addressed in museum contexts is questions of power and ownership of both objects and intangible treasures, and their 'correct' or adequate forms of representation, documentation and storage. We regard the quest for symmetrical relationships as an aporia, or even a utopia, that will hardly ever exist. Consequently, we suggest asking how hierarchy and authority are exercised and negotiated, how uneven power relations are installed and legitimised, and how they are challenged, appropriated and dealt with in subversive ways.

Further, we understand that with an eye to the so-called material turn and impulses from science and technology studies, evident in more recent work on museums, a strong focus was placed on the relationship between the curator and the object, or the space between them. However, we consider also the wider material structure in this interplay, that is, to include the structural framework in which museum processes are embedded and shaped. In this vein, it is worth studying which opportunities and challenges arise in specific social settings, such as the materiality of the museum building itself, and more specifically the spatial layout of the exhibition halls, the available budget and the institutional and wider political agendas. We could think along these lines about the practicalities of constraints and opportunities alike.

Another important impulse to be followed would be curatorial engagements with new (social) media, asking how physical materiality is transformed into the virtual presence of an object, and how virtuality changes and affects materiality. In which ways does the virtual go beyond, or complement, approaches that are currently widely discussed in the context of the so-called material turn and new material culture studies, along with ontological questions?[49] This might be of particular relevance with regard to one of the key questions addressed in this volume, that is, how can objects and concepts be translated or transformed through curatorial work?

We do not mean to suggest that there is one single answer to these questions, nor do we think that they are all and always equally relevant. Indeed, curators are not the only staff in contemporary museums involved with collections and exhibitions. But we do feel that these questions might be useful tools to think through the topics explored in this book from a theoretical, yet empirically grounded and historically informed angle. These debates should be coupled with the visitors' engagements with exhibitions. While many exhibitions present themselves to the visitors' eyes as coherent 'finished' and 'polished' projects, this might hinder the understanding of the complex processes that take place in order to create this exhibitionary product, ready for experience and consumption. The curator as key actor often remains unknown to the wider public, as do the sometimes years-long preparations on many scales that precede the opening of an exhibition.

The same holds true for conceptual debates that are brought up in the process of exhibiting, when key approaches are shifted, adjusted, dropped or reinstalled in this negotiation process. Further, probably only a few visitors are aware of the wide range of actors who are involved in different phases of the exhibition process, ranging from scholars to carpenters, designers to concierges, security staff to insurance personnel. It is interesting to understand what kind of negotiation processes are shaping the relationships between these heterogeneous actors and how their power structure affects discourses and practices regarding intra- and inter-community relationships, including what has come to be called 'source communities'. A further layer of management that is barely made transparent is the negotiation with regard to the geographical scope and spatial array of an exhibition. What kinds of networks exist between museums that ultimately facilitate or hinder the exchange of objects? Where are the objects from, where and in which contexts have they already been on display and where do they travel to next? How are tours arranged and secured, and which actors meet in the context of these itineraries, accompanying the objects and thus expanding networks and social relationships?[50]

We are of course aware of the fact that all these questions cannot be addressed in every exhibition – this would be an exhibition project in its own right. But it should be possible to include some of these aspects so as to make the processes behind the scenes more transparent and understandable to the visitor, and thus make knowledge that is evident to the expert, but not necessarily for the wider public, more inclusive and participatory. The great promise of museums, to us, has always been the potential for 'making things public'[51] by revealing the contested processes leading to the definition of categories and the interpretation of cultural worlds, and by giving 'faces' to decisions and public expression to controversies, in short, by conceptualising exhibitions as *processes* to be revealed rather than *products* to be presented and experienced.[52]

It is one thing to reflect on our own intentions when developing, curating, interpreting and designing an exhibition, but another to analyse its reception in terms of intended and unintended consequences. What effects do exhibits have on the audience, and who are the visitors?[53] The classification 'visitor' most likely comprises an enormous range and is hard to pin down as a social category. And what about the inclusion of individuals who are not intellectuals and cosmopolitan travellers but rather the socially disadvantaged, with Indigenous or other affiliations? What would they make out of the term *Curatopia* or other intellectual concepts that are foreign to their vocabulary? There might be a risk that we actually produce new 'elite' discourses in the context of cutting-edge curatorial thinking, thus actually losing the connection to 'non-elite' audiences.

Re-enacting Curatopia

The variety of disciplines, approaches and contexts in which curatorial work is practised today calls for an interdisciplinary framework which is not confined to specific media or collections. We propose that curation needs to develop its own theories and methods in a wider range of disciplinary settings and kinds of museums, in particular by drawing on specific, local, social and historical conditions, including Indigenous epistemologies and ontologies. Curators need varied, flexible, and practice-based frameworks for curating in a wider range of fields – anthropology, history, science, contemporary media and so on.

If curatorial or museum studies and anthropology lack Indigenous voices and perspectives, then the research feeding into this book, tapping a rich vein of contemporary Indigenous scholarship, offers much to think about, and to put into practice. This research shows clearly, if ever evidence were needed, not only that Indigenous curators themselves are aware of the global issues discussed in this Introduction but that in their practices they are pushing the boundaries and exploring new territory, decolonising and Indigenising curatorship in the process and lighting the way to a courageous future for museums.[54] As can be seen in the chapters that follow, they are working across diverse collections, and working with and for their people as well as scholarly research through collections and exhibitions. They are actively embracing digital technology, and ethnography/anthropology, and using it as a tool, despite all the detritus of colonialism and a history of strained relationships between museums, anthropology and Native people.[55] These Indigenous curators are also interested in social history and are collecting contemporary culture in a lively dialogue with young Indigenous audiences. Lastly, they are engaging with the natural environment, and issues such as climate change, not just objects in museums. Above all, even when they are dealing with the past, they bring it into the present and future.[56]

This is not to deny individual agendas and interests, or to draw an idealised picture. Importantly, what we see in the practice of these Indigenous curators is a realistically utopian 'curatorial dreaming',[57] a conviction in the role of the curator and a concrete, ethical sense of value and mission for the museum. This brings us back to the title of this book, a word that postmodern scepticism and postcolonial critique might frown on – *Curatopia* – but which our dire current situation demands: a commitment to cultural futures. After decades of suspicion about grand narratives and universality, which rightly drew attention to the limits of Western paradigms, it is time to move beyond the postmodern/postcolonial impasse and imagine a museum curatorship that deals not just with the past, and the present, but also the future.

In pursuit of this aim, we offer in this volume building blocks towards *Curatopia*, an ideal of socially and politically engaged, interdisciplinary, and radically cross-cultural curatorial practice. Curatorship as cross-cultural translation makes sense, however, only if we do not commit the 'the basic error of the translator', which, according to Walter Benjamin, 'is that he [or she] preserves the state in which his [or her] own language happens to be instead of allowing his [or her] language to be powerfully affected by the foreign tongue'.[58] Instead, Benjamin rightly insists, 'he [or she] must expand and deepen his [or her] language by means of the foreign language',[59] which is not confined to the linguistic domain but includes visual and 'thing languages'[60] among others. Curatorship thus faces the constant challenge of engaging with the effects and opportunities as well as the limits and risks of dialogical translation through mutual transformation. On the historical level, colonialism has neither been complete in the past nor completed in the present – it is not an event but a process. In curatorship, then, we cannot escape the constant dialectical effort to consciously 'inhabit histories'[61] while being placed into histories, that is – as Karl Marx famously noted – being thrown into 'circumstances' which are not 'self-selected' but are 'existing already, given and transmitted from the past'. There has to be a constant analytical movement between the 'here' and 'there', the 'now' and 'back then', to make sense of these 'messy entanglements'.[62]

On the theoretical and methodological level, such a dialectical effort requires a 'recursive anthropology'[63] which is not content with generating ethnographic evidence for pre-conceived ideas but allows different cultural worlds to 'dictate the terms of their own analysis'[64] while recursively reframing its own points of departure. That is, serious cross-cultural study searches for resonances between different culturally grounded analytical positions and their respective articulation and movement through a common sphere while opening spaces for dissonances,[65] which are provoked through the 'untranslatable'.[66] The nature of such curatorial inquiry is, like 'the very nature of exhibiting', of course, 'a contested terrain'.[67] Curatorial reciprocities/symmetries are never quite possible – but always worth striving for – through conscious attempts to produce heterotopian rather than hegemonic spaces.

We end by returning to our opening provocation to think of museums as moving vessels, inspired by the example of museums in Aotearoa New

Zealand which are figured as waka, vessels which move through time and space, joining and making worlds, people, ideas and things. Arapata Hakiwai, co-author of Chapter 13 in this book, works at the Museum of New Zealand Te Papa Tongarewa (which means a receptacle of treasured possessions). As the Māori co-director, he is the *Kaihautū*, or 'navigator' of the waka. Hakiwai's vision for Māori curatorship is to use the past as a resource to facilitate the future cultural development of *iwi* (tribes), working in partnership with those tribes.[68] He and his colleagues have answered the call, mentioned at the start of this introduction, to load the precious heritage of their ancestors on board their canoe, and to sail on into unknown seas. Curators everywhere in any museum can learn to do likewise, steering their craft, the museum, into the future, through storms and currents, keeping everybody on board, even when the seas are rough. As the proverb says: *He moana pukepuke e ekengia e te waka* / Mountainous seas can be negotiated by a canoe.[69]

Notes

1 Examples include the national museum (Museum of New Zealand / Te Papa Tongarewa), armed forces museums (National Museum of the Royal New Zealand Navy / Te Waka Huia o Te Taua Moana o Aotearoa) and regional museums (Golden Bay Museum / Te Waka Huia o Mohua). The 2017 national conference theme was *He Waka Eke Noa: Museums of Inclusion*. See www.nzmu seums.co.nz/. Accessed 15 March 2017.

2 See T.R. Balneavis, 'Te Poari Whakapapa: Board of Maori Ethnological Research', *Te Toa Takatini* (1 September 1924), p. 101; A. Ngata, 'He whakamarama/ Preface', in A. Ngata (ed.), *Nga moteatea: he maramara rere no nga waka maha. He mea kohikohi na A.T. Ngata / The Songs: Scattered Pieces from Many Canoe Areas Collected by A.T. Ngata. Part I*, trans. Pei Te Hurunui Jones (Wellington: The Polynesian Society, 1959/1928), p. xiv.

3 For an explanation of the image, see Ngata, 'He whakamarama/Preface', p. xiv.

4 M. Foucault, 'Of Other Spaces, Heterotopias', *Architecture, Mouvement, Continuité*, 5 (1984), 46–9.

5 P. Schorch, 'Assembling Communities: Curatorial Practices, Material Cultures, and Meanings', in B. Onciul, M.L. Stefano and S. Hawke (eds), *Engaging Heritage, Engaging Communities* (Woodbridge: Boydell and Brewer, 2017).

6 S.R. Butler and E. Lehrer, *Curatorial Dreams: Critics Imagine Exhibitions* (Montreal and Kingston: McGill-Queen's University Press, 2016).

7 Foucault, 'Of Other Spaces, Heterotopias'.

8 V. Golding and W. Modest (eds), *Museums and Communities: Curators, Collections and Collaboration* (London and New York: Bloomsbury, 2013).

9 S.R. Butler, 'Reflexive Museology: Lost and Found', in K. Message and A. Witcomb (eds), *The International Handbook of Museum Studies: Museum Theory: An Expanded Field* (Oxford and Boston: Wiley Blackwell, 2015), pp. 159–82. B. Lynch, 'The Hole in the Wall: Beyond Happiness Making in Museums', in Onciul, Stefano and Hawke (eds), *Engaging Heritage, Engaging Communities*, pp. 11–29.

10 S. Conrad, 'Enlightenment in Global History: A Historiographical Critique', *American Historical Review* (2012), 999–1027.

11 The 'discovery' of the Americas was key for the Enlightenment as it forced fundamental changes to European worldviews. One aspect of this was the question of whether Indigenous peoples have souls, that is, are human beings.

12 P. Schorch, C. McCarthy and A. Hakiwai, 'Globalizing Māori Museology: Reconceptualising Engagement, Knowledge and Virtuality through Mana Taonga', *Museum Anthropology*, 39:1 (2016), 48–69.

13 Conrad, 'Enlightenment in Global History'.

14 P. Schorch and A. Hakiwai, 'Mana Taonga and the Public Sphere: A Dialogue between Indigenous Practice and Western Theory', *International Journal of Cultural Studies*, 17:2 (2014), 191–205; P. Schorch and N.M.K.Y. Kahanu, 'Anthropology's Interlocutors: Hawai`i Speaking Back to Ethnographic Museums in Europe', *Zeitschrift für Kulturwissenschaften*, 1 (2015), 114–17.

15 M. Ames and M. McKenzie (eds), *Curatorship: Indigenous Perspectives in Postcolonial Societies* (Ottawa: Canadian Museum of Civilization, 1996). C. Kreps, *Liberating Culture: Cross-Cultural Perspectives on Museums, Curation, and Heritage Preservation, Museum Meanings* (London and New York: Routledge, 2003). J. Clifford, *Returns: Becoming Indigenous in the Twenty-First Century* (Cambridge, MA: Harvard University Press, 2013).

16 P. Schorch and E. Dürr, 'Transpacific Americas as Relational Space', in E. Dürr and P. Schorch (eds), *Transpacific Americas: Encounters and Engagements between the Americas and the South Pacific* (London and New York: Routledge, 2015), pp. xi–xxv.

17 P. Marincola, 'Introduction: Practice Makes Perfect', in P. Marincola (ed.), *Curating Now: Imaginative Practice/Public Responsibility* (Philadelphia: Philadelphia Exhibitions Initiative, 2001), p. 12.

18 P. O'Neill, 'The Curatorial Turn: From Practice to Discourse', in J. Rugg and M. Sedgwick (eds), *Issues in Curating Contemporary Art and Performance* (Bristol and Chicago: Intellect, 2007), pp. 13–28.

19 D. Balzar, *Curationism: How Curating Took Over the Art World and Everything Else* (London: Pluto Press, 2015).

20 H. Obrist quoted in Marincola, *Curating Now*, pp. 30–1.

21 See Oxford English Dictionary online: https://en.oxforddictionaries.com/defini tion/curator. Accessed 7 March 2017.

22 See for example J.M.A. Thompson (ed.), *Manual of Curatorship: A Guide to Museum Practice* (London: The Museums Association/Butterworths, 1984).

23 P. Boylan, 'The Museum Profession', in S. Macdonald (ed.), *A Companion to Museum Studies* (Malden, MA: Blackwell, 2006), pp. 415–30.

24 H. Norton-Westbrook, 'The Pendulum Swing: Curatorial Theory Past and Present', in C. McCarthy (ed.), *Museum Practice: The International Handbooks of Museum Studies*, vol. 2 (Oxford and Malden, MA, Wiley Blackwell, 2015), pp. 341–56.

25 K. Arnold, 'From Caring to Creating: Curators Change Their Spots', in McCarthy (ed.), *Museum Practice*, pp. 317–40; see also A. Harding (ed.), *Curating the Contemporary Art Museum and Beyond: Art and Design Profile no. 52* (London: Academy Group, 1997), p. 5.

26 P. O'Neill (ed.), *Curating Subjects* (London: De Appel, Centre for Contemporary Art, 2007), 13.

27 From S. Cook, 'Toward a Theory of the Practice of Curating New Media Art', in M. Townsend (ed.), *Beyond the Box: Diverging Curatorial Practices* (Banff, AB: Banff Centre Press, 2003), pp. 173–4.

28 M. Henning, *Museums, Media and Cultural Theory* (Maidenhead: Open University Press McGraw-Hill Education, 2006). Paul Crowther even calls for a 'postcuratorial' art: P. Crowther, 'Against Curatorial Imperialism: Merleau-Ponty and the Historicity of Art', in P. Smith and C. Wilde (eds), *A Companion to Art Theory* (Oxford and Malden, MA: Blackwell, 2002), pp. 477–86.

29 B. Graham and S. Cook, *Rethinking Curating: Art after New Media* (Cambridge, MA: MIT Press, 2010).

30 *Ibid.*, 10–11.

31 For an interesting view of this see N. Cummings, 'Everything', in Harding, *Curating the Contemporary Art Museum and Beyond*, pp. 13–16.

32 D. Stam, 'The Informed Muse: The Implications of "the new museology" for Museum Practice', in G. Corsane (ed.), *Heritage, Museums and Galleries: An Introductory Reader* (Oxford and New York: Routledge, 2005), pp. 54–70. K. Schubert, *The Curator's Egg: The Evolution of the Museum Concept from the French Revolution to the Present Day* (London: Ridinghouse, 3rd edn, 2009).

33 See Paul O'Neill's bibliography on his website *Curatorial Writing*: www.paulo neill.org.uk/curatorial/writing/. Accessed 15 January 2017.

34 C. Kreps, 'Non-Western Models of Museums and Curation in Cross-Cultural Perspective', in Macdonald (ed.), *A Companion to Museum Studies*, pp. 457–72.

35 I. Karp and S. Lavine (eds), *Exhibiting Cultures: The Poetics and Politics of Museum Display* (Washington, DC: Smithsonian Institution Press, 1991).

36 D. Preziosi and C. Farrago (eds), *Grasping the World: The Idea of the Museum* (Aldershot: Ashgate, 2004).

37 T. Bennett, R. Harrison, I. Jacknis, F. Cameron, B. Dibley, N. Dias and C. McCarthy, *Collecting, Ordering, Governing: Anthropology, Museums and Liberal Government* (Durham, NC: Duke University Press, 2017).

38 Schorch, McCarthy and Hakiwai, 'Globalizing Māori Museology'.

39 C. Gosden and F. Larson, *Knowing Things: Exploring the Collections at the Pitt Rivers Museum 1884–1945* (Oxford: Oxford University Press, 2007).

40 For a cautionary lesson, see B. Onciul, *Museums, Heritage and Indigenous Voice: Decolonising Engagement* (London and New York: Routledge, 2015).

41 R. Silverman (ed.), *Museum as Process: Translating Local and Global Knowledge* (London and New York: Routledge, 2015). Golding and Modest, *Museums and Communities*.

42 R.B. Phillips, *Museum Pieces: Towards the Indigenization of Canadian Museums* (Montreal and Kingston: McGill-Queen's University Press, 2011).

43 P. Livingstone 'Controversy as Catalyst: Administrative Framing, Public Perception and the Late 20th Century Exhibitionary Complex in Canada', in V. Gosselin and P. Livingstone (eds), *Museums and the Past: Constructing Historical Consciousness* (Vancouver and Toronto: University of British Columbia Press, 2016), p. 192.

44 L. Peers and A. Brown, *Museums and Source Communities: A Routledge Reader* (London and New York: Routledge, 2003), pp. 1–2, 531.

45 Kreps, 'Non-Western Models of Museums and Curation in Cross-Cultural Perspective', 469.

46 M. Horwood, 'Worlds Apart: Indigenous Re-engagement with Museum-held Heritage: A New Zealand–United Kingdom Case Study' (PhD dissertation, Victoria University, Wellington, 2015).

47 P. Schorch and N.M.K.Y. Kahanu, 'Forum as Laboratory: The Cross-Cultural Infrastructure of Ethnographic Knowledge and Material Potentialities', in *Prinzip Labor: Museumsexperimente im Humboldt Lab Dahlem* (Berlin: Nicolai, 2015), pp. 241–8.

48 W.F. Hanks, 'The Space of Translation', in W.F. Hanks and C. Severi (eds), *Translating Worlds. The Epistemological Space of Translation* (Chicago: HAU Books, 2015), pp. 21–49.

49 A. Salmond, 'Digital Subjects, Cultural Objects: Special Issue Introduction', *Journal of Material Culture*, 17:3 (2012), 229–44.

50 On this topic see L. Davidson, Museums and International Touring Exhibitions, blog, https://leedavidsonresearch.wordpress.com/author/leedavidsonnz/. Accessed 15 March 2017.

51 B. Latour and P. Weibel (eds), *Making Things Public: Atmospheres of Democracy* (Karlsruhe: ZKM, 2005).

52 P. Schorch, 'The "reflexive museum" – Opening the Doors to behind the Scenes', *Te Ara – Journal of Museums Aotearoa*, 33:1–2 (2009), 28–31; S. Macdonald and P. Basu (eds), *Exhibition Experiments* (Malden, MA: Blackwell, 2007).

53 L. Davidson, 'Visitor Studies: Towards a Culture of Reflective Practice and Critical Museology for the Visitor-Centred Museum', in *Museum Practice: International Handbooks of Museum Studies*, vol. 2 (Oxford and Malden, MA: Wiley Blackwell, 2015), pp. 503–28.

54 This research draws upon the dialogues recorded in 2011 in Wellington, in 2015 in Munich, and interviews with Māori curators conducted in 2016–2017: Huhana Smith, Paul Diamond, Anna Marie White, Awhina Tamarapa and Matariki Williams.

55 J. Clifford, *Returns: Becoming Indigenous in the Twenty-First Century* (Cambridge, MMA, and London: Harvard University Press, 2013).

56 See McCarthy, Hakiwai and Schorch, Chapter 13 below.

57 Butler and Lehrer, *Curatorial Dreams*, 2016.

58 W. Benjamin, 'The Task of the Translator', in M. Bullock and M.W. Jennings, *Walter Benjamin: Selected Writings Volume 1 1913–1926* (Cambridge, MA, and London: Harvard University Press, 1996), p. 262.

59 *Ibid.*

60 W. Benjamin, 'On Language as Such and on the Language of Man', in *One-Way Street and Other Writings: Walter Benjamin*, trans. by E. Jephcott and K. Shorter (London and New York: Verso Classics, 1997).

61 I. Wedde, 'Inside Job', in H. McNaughton and J. Newton (eds), *Figuring the Pacific: Aotearoa & Pacific Cultural Studies* (Christchurch: University of Canterbury Press, 2005).

62 A. Taku and M. Quanchi, *Messy Entanglements: The Papers of the 10th Pacific History Association Conference* (Tarawa: Kiribati Paperback, 1995).

63 A. Salmond, 'Transforming Translations (Part I): The Owner of These Bones', *HAU: Journal of Ethnographic Theory*, 3:3 (2013), 1–32.

64 A. Henare [Salmond], M. Holbraad and S. Wastell (eds), *Thinking Through Things: Theorising Artefacts Ethnographically* (London and New York: Routledge, 2007), p. 4.

65 Schorch and Kahanu, 'Forum as Laboratory'.

66 H.K. Bhabha, *The Location of Culture* (London and New York, Routledge, 1994).

67 Karp and Lavine, *Exhibiting Cultures: The Poetics and Politics of Museum Display*, 1.

68 Arapata Hakiwai, 'He mana taonga, he mana tangata: Māori Taonga and the Politics of Māori Tribal Identity and Development' (PhD thesis Museum and Heritage Studies, Victoria University, Wellington, 2014).

69 King Ihaka, 'Ngā whakatauki me ngā pepeha māori: Popular and Proverbial Saying of the Māori', *Te ao hou: The New World*, 2 (April 1958), 42.

EUROPE

 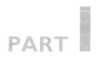

The museum as method (revisited)[1]

Nicholas Thomas

The spaces of, and between, museums and anthropology today are full of paradoxes. Museums cannot escape the association of anachronism, they connote colonial dustiness. Yet in the early twenty-first century they are probably more successful than ever before – they attract more visitors, they loom larger in cultural life and they are better resourced financially, in general, than they have been at any time in the past. This is true in Britain, notably because of the allocation of a share of national lottery proceeds (through the Heritage Lottery Fund) to museum redevelopment. Virtually all major, and many smaller, institutions have had significant extensions or improvements at some time over the last twenty years. In many other countries, too, museums and art institutions have, over recent decades, been the recipients of investment on a grand scale. National cultural and historical museums have received this support, in many cases, because what they now exhibit and affirm is multiculturalism, a civic project that is resonant of an anthropological legacy.

It is a commonplace of the history of anthropology that the academic discipline was once firmly based in the ethnographic museum, but moved steadily away from it with the ascendancy of sociological questions from the 1920s onward. Though the 1980s and 1990s saw a revival of debate around art and material culture, mainstream anthropology arguably continues to drift away from the museum as a research resource or site of analysis. The paradox here is that, at the same time, the public have come to know anthropology almost exclusively through the museum. Up to and during the 1960s and 1970s, anthropologists, such as Margaret Mead, enjoyed mass audiences, and Lévi-Strauss was required reading across the humanities, but anthropology books today are read mainly by anthropologists (there are, needless to say, distinguished exceptions). Similarly, in the 1970s and 1980s, ethnographic films were widely broadcast; but that television slot is now firmly occupied by so-called 'reality' programming, which is cheaper and more sensational. Hence anthropology is scarcely either read or watched by a broader public, but the numbers of visitors to both specifically anthropological collections and to survey museums that include extensive anthropological displays have risen very dramatically. The British Museum, which draws nearly six million people a year, is exceptional, but an institution such as the Pitt Rivers Museum, which thirty years ago was more a university facility than a genuinely public museum, can now attract around four hundred thousand.

Ethnographic collecting, collections and museums have been much debated, but the current 'success' of museums brings new questions into focus. Here I am not concerned with what lies behind the creation and resourcing of Museum of New Zealand Te Papa Tongarewa (Te Papa), the Musée du Quai Branly or the National Museum of Australia, the ascendancy of the British Museum, or museum-friendly policies on the part of governments and local authorities – though of course there is much to be said about new conceptions of culture and governance, and the growing preoccupation with tourism as a driver for urban regeneration and economic growth. I am interested, rather, in how we (curators of ethnographic collections) conceive of what we are doing, if our institutions are embedded less in academic anthropology and more in a domain of public engagement. Does anthropology remain the discipline that informs anthropological collections, to be in turn informed by them? What kinds of knowledge underpin the interpretation of collections, what methods does that interpretation involve, and what knowledge does it generate? And – to move from theory and research to public engagement – how in the early twenty-first century should anthropological collections be displayed, what stories should they tell, what questions should they raise?

These issues are related to, but somewhat different from, those that have been conspicuous in the museum studies literature over recent years. This literature has been broadly divided between studies that might be considered technical, which range from documentation through conservation and display to public education, and a more critical, historical and theoretical discourse. The critical discourse has tracked (and often lambasted) the project of colonial collecting, diagnosed museums as disciplinary formations in Foucault's terms, interrogated primitivist representation in display and otherwise explored the politics of institutions and exhibits.

If the issues that the critical discourse identified remain present, it makes a difference now that many of the poachers have turned gamekeepers. Critics, including Indigenous activists, have become curators, and the newer generation of curators have been trained by critics. A postcolonial understanding of the ethnographic museum has entered the mindset, not of the whole of the museum profession but of most of those who deal with ethnographic material, and contemporary native art. Hence, in many institutions, though certainly not universally, it is anticipated that originating communities are consulted around exhibition or research projects, they are indeed, increasingly, full collaborators. If this has become business as usual, that is surely positive, but it's perhaps also a sign that the issue of representation is no longer the right place to start from.

At one time, it was self-evident that a museum anthropologist used anthropology to contextualise and interpret museum collections – that anthropology was the discipline that 'went with' the anthropological collection. Yet the activity and method of museum work was, and is, profoundly different from that of the academic discipline. Broadly, the academic project begins with theories and questions that are brought, through research methods, to the analysis of a particular case. If, obviously, the museum worker carries conceptual baggage, the practical project tends to start from, and stop with, the object. (Objects are its 'stoppages', in Duchamp's and Gell's sense.) There is something to be gained, I argue, from reflecting on the simplest of practices, such as writing a label, that of course are not simple at all.

If the museum is not only an institution or a collection but also a method, a kind of activity, that activity has its moments. The moments we might reflect on are those of the discovery, the caption and the juxtaposition.

It goes without saying that curators choose or select objects for display (or for other purposes such as loan, publication, reproduction on a postcard or whatever) but these terms imply operations more rational than might be apt. 'Discovery' is more ambiguous; it often involves finding things that were not lost; identifying things that were known to others; or the disclosure of what was hidden or repressed. What needs to be considered is not the 'selection' of artefacts and artworks but their discovery, the encounter with arrays of objects and the destabilisation which that encounter may give rise to. For example, a search for a 'good' or 'representative' piece may put at risk one's sense of a genre or place. One may be distracted by another work, or by some aspect of the provenance or story of an object which is not good or not typical. This is in one sense entirely unremarkable, it is the contingency of dealing with things, but in another sense it represents a method, powerful because it is unpredictable.

To assert that there might be value in looking for, at or into things, in a manner only weakly guided by theory, or literally misguided, in the sense that direction given by theory is abandoned as things are encountered along the way, sounds like the affirmation of an antiquarian curiosity, an indiscriminate and eclectic form of knowledge, one surely long superseded by rigorous disciplines and critical theories. But there are two reasons why 'happening upon' things might have methodological potency. The first is that a preparedness to encounter things and consider them amounts to a responsiveness to forms of material evidence beneath or at odds with canonical ethnographies, national histories, reifications of local heritage – and subaltern narratives. In other words, 'happening upon' brings the question of 'what else is there?' to the fore. That question has confronted, and should continue to confront, claims about great art, cultural traditions, historical progress and celebrated acts of resistance.

Second, the antiquarianism which this discovery licenses is not that of George Eliot's Casaubon but of Sebald. Not the self-aggrandising accumulation of ancient citations or specimens, but a distracted meditation on larger histories of culture, empire, commerce and military enterprise, marked by madness, violence and loss, as well as more obscure personal projects, humanitarian missions and idiosyncratic inquiries. If this is an eclectic antiquarianism, it is one that throws wide open the questions of history – what, out of all that has happened in the past, are we to remember and consider significant? What presence, and what bearing do histories and their residues have, on our various lives?

If the moment of discovery gives us a good deal to think about, that thinking must be carefully and deliberately depleted in the act of captioning. By captioning I mean not only the literal composition of a line of text that might accompany an image or object but the business of description and the discursive contextualisation of any museum piece. There has been a great deal of circular argument about whether ethnographic artefacts should be described and presented as works of art or contextualised anthropologically (as though these were the only, and mutually exclusive, options). I am interested not in this sort of debate, but in the point that labelling or captioning, like discovery, involves a particular kind of research that turns on simple questions, such as 'What is it?' Is a certain object a decorated barkcloth or a painting? Is a shield a weapon? Is a toy canoe or a diminutive spirit house a model canoe or model house? Is a walking stick an orator's staff or a souvenir? Is a certain carving a spirit figure or a copy of a spirit figure commissioned by an ethnologist? The question is asked, only incidentally to get the answer right, for the particular piece. The method is the use of the object in the exploration of what these categories and distinctions might mean, where they come from, where they mislead, where they remain useful or unavoidable.

The moment of juxtaposition arises because objects are seldom exhibited on their own. Whatever 'it' may be, one has to ask what it goes with, what it may be placed in a series with or what it may be opposed to. Again, it goes without saying that a chronological ordering of works by a single artist or an assemblage representing a particular culture each asks objects to speak to different conventions. My interest is not in the burden these classificatory or narrative conventions carry but in the moment in which other possibilities are present, and the scope for the 'simple' question to become a question of itself. Can objects that belonged to the secret, esoteric, ritual life of mature men (please not 'of a community') be placed with quotidian tools? Where does difference become incommensurability? When is it wrong, and when might it be right, to put incommensurable things together?

If it has been taken for granted for several generations that the locus of innovation in disciplines such as anthropology has been 'theory', there is now scope to think differently and to revalue practices that appeared to be, but were actually never, sub-theoretical. This comment has not tried to map out in any rigorous way what an understanding of 'the museum as method' might entail. My general point is simply that one can work with contingencies, with the specific qualities and histories of artefacts and works of art, in ways that challenge many everyday or scholarly understandings of what things are and what they represent.

This work has diverse products, including cataloguing data made use of mainly by museum insiders. But among the most important are displays and exhibitions that make wider statements for diverse public audiences. In this context the question of how, today, ethnographic collections are to be shown and interpreted is in practice answered. In the UK, the most general response employs the 'world cultures' rubric. Material from diverse parts of the world presents diverse cultures side by side, not least in order to represent and affirm the cultural heritages of immigrant, ethnic minority, communities. At some level, there is no problem with this, it is broadly desirable, and to some extent anyway unavoidable – even a lightly contextualised array of material from around the world must in effect present and offer for comparison a set of 'world cultures'.

If, however, this is the primary paradigm, it may sell a collection short, and fail to capitalise on its most fertile associations and their salience to cultural and historical debate today. Anthropological collections are always also historical collections, they are the products of, the evidence for and maybe even the memorials to, entangled histories. In the Museum of Archaeology and Anthropology (MAA) in Cambridge, UK, important collections were made by explorers such as Cook and Vancouver, by the missionaries who followed them and sought actively to transform local ways of life, and by colonial administrators and travellers who, in some cases, saw themselves as part-time anthropologists.

For the most part twentieth-century additions to the collections were made by Cambridge fieldworkers. All of this material speaks to the history of empire, travel and exploration, to contacts that inaugurated colonial histories in Australia and Aotearoa New Zealand, to subsequent, enduringly contentious violence in, for example, Benin.

The collections bear witness, as well, to the formation of disciplines such as archaeology and anthropology, and to the emergence of influential ideas and arguments (such as those of Radcliffe-Brown in central Australia, Bateson in the Sepik, Fortes in Ghana and so forth), albeit through object transactions and fieldwork images often forgotten or suppressed in formal publications and at the level of theory.

Ethnographic collections may, as it were inadvertently, enable audiences to reinstate the 'co-evalness' that, Johannes Fabian has taught us, anthropological discourse chronically denied.

In the British context, anthropological collections speak not only of and to 'cultures' in various remote parts of the world, and to the 'cultures' of (for example) West African and South Asian immigrants, they also evoke engagements between the dominant (and itself heterogeneous) British population and the rest of the world over the last few hundred years. MAA in Cambridge is, as much as anything else, a museum of the formation of modern Britain, from a vantage point that may appear oblique, for those with a more traditional understanding of 'English' history, yet one that must also be considered fundamental, given the profoundly global character of British economy and society, from the seventeenth century onwards. Cook's

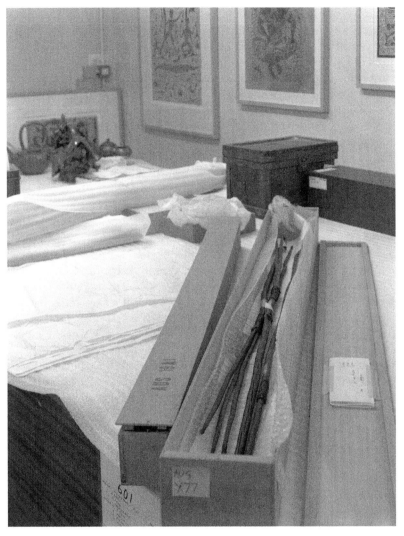

1.1 Mark Adams, *Gweagal Spears, Museum of Archaeology and Anthropology, Cambridge University, England.* 2002. C type print from 10 x 8 inch C41 negative.

Botany Bay spears belong, not only in a display dedicated to Aboriginal life, but with contemporaneous artefacts such as Gainsborough's *Blue Boy* and Sterne's *Tristram Shandy* – all three reflect aspects of a wealthy, experimental, dynamic and dangerous imperial society.

All good exhibitions should make material accessible at multiple levels, and it would be neither possible nor desirable to make the history of globalisation the sole or the predominant interpretative frame for anthropological displays at MAA or elsewhere. But it is worth considering how the histories of particular objects, of particular collections, and those of the institution as a whole could become lenses upon the much larger questions of

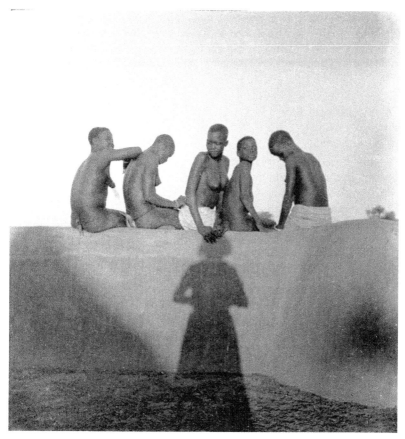

1.2 Five young Tallensi women, photograph by Sonia Fortes, Upper East Region, Ghana, January 1937. MAA N.102347.MF.

cross-cultural and colonial history. This would mean raising issues that are certainly difficult, from the point of view of the institution. Some members of the public assume that the material they encounter in ethnographic museums is essentially imperial loot. Although this is generally false, certain collections do include material seized in the aftermath of conflict, and the difficult histories of those collections, and the legacies of those histories, need to be acknowledged and explained.

Yet historically evocative displays would be provocative in other senses too. They would reveal empire, not just as dominance, not just as a one-way street, not as a set of wrongs that should or simply can be apologised for now. Objects such as gifts to missionaries, and novel, post-Christian forms such as Niue *hiapo* (tapa cloth) or Cook Islands and Tahitian *tivaevae/tivaivai* (quilt) demonstrate the complex creativity engendered by these global exchanges that have changed what was 'the West' as well as many other societies throughout the world. It is widely appreciated that museums work when they offer their audiences problems rather than solutions. It might be added that they work best when they allow their audiences to discover things, to be drawn into their unexpected, perhaps disturbing stories. Curiosity has a fraught history, but also an interesting future.

Postscript

In the early 1990s, during one of my first research visits to Aotearoa New Zealand, I was behind the scenes at the Auckland War Memorial Museum Tāmaki Paenga Hira, on my way to an appointment with one of the curators. As we ascended a staircase, I was surprised to encounter, on the broad landing, a group of Samoan women – sitting on pandanus mats, on the edges of steps, one or two on chairs, surrounded by bags and bundles of rolled and prepared leaves – engaged in conversation. A couple were actually weaving; others were drinking tea. They were there, presumably, in the context of some organised visit, and were making themselves comfortable in this improvised, interstitial way, I suppose, because there was no meeting room or workroom available. But if there was a straightforward explanation for the group's presence, I had a contrary sense that the women had somehow simply found their way into this part of the building, and were making the space their own, in an unselfconscious and unhurried way.

A few years later, I attended the 1996 meetings of the American Anthropological Association in San Francisco, in the somewhat uncomfortable and alienating environment of the downtown Hilton Hotel. Among the bewildering proliferation of sessions typical of such gatherings was one on museum themes, scheduled in a smaller meeting room. It was a pleasure to hear James Clifford talk about 'the museum as contact zone'. There were a few questions. We had not met before and chatted afterwards.

In hindsight, the presentation was a low-key outing for a paper that would, deservedly, go on to be influential. I took Clifford's point to be simple: whatever else they were, museums had become places of meeting and encounter. This was already true in many ways in many places – witness the ambiguity of what I had encountered in Auckland. Contacts were inevitably heterogeneous, some enormously rewarding, others tense, troubling, frustrating. In the twenty years since Clifford's presentation, the majority of museums with collections formerly or still called ethnographic have embraced the contact zone as an identity, some more carefully, consistently and effectively than others. In 'The Museum as Method' I suggested that engagement of this sort had become, in a good sense, business as usual. I was concerned to rearticulate its consideration with the practical and conceptual activity that constituted curatorial work.

What I intended was to signal that contact, collaboration, negotiation and partnership needed to be part of any museum's ongoing work. I did not intend to suggest that debate around the contact zone and its possible futures – imaginatively redefined by the editors and contributors to this book as 'curatopia' – was somehow over, neatly finished or resolved. Recent years have been marked by escalating contention around immigration, national narrative, identity, growing inequality and environmental futures. The multicultural values that museums of world cultures at least implicitly affirm are contested to an extent unprecedented in recent decades. Our ideally hushed conversations, in the company of artefacts, are sometimes drowned out by a political cacophony of categorical claims that refuse questioning, qualification or nuance, from 'A nation without borders is not a nation at all' (Trump) to 'Rhodes must fall' (student activists in Oxford and Cape Town).

There are two comments I would make on this new conjuncture, in the context of this impressive volume. The first is that curatorial authority is challenged, not only by 'communities'. If, in the 1980s and 1990s, commentators were preoccupied with a decolonisation of knowledge, that opening up was often facilitated and mediated by curators who revalued and repositioned their expertise. By now, increasing numbers of curators and museum professionals are, anyway, of Indigenous descent. The new issue is rather that museum restructuring has in too many places downgraded research-based curatorial practice. In many institutions, there is simply less expertise about collections, and less expertise to negotiate the challenges they raise, ranging from the complexities of provenance to ethical questions of access and interpretation. Collections cannot be sensitively and effectively activated if their liminal and sometimes difficult histories are inadequately understood. Partnerships between collections staff, university-based researchers and community members are now all the more critical to sustain understandings of the present and potential significances of remarkable expressions of past human creativity. But museums cannot mobilise those collaborations without some core, in-house capacity, which has in too many institutions been hollowed out as a result of both austerity and misguided approaches to museum management.

Secondly, we need a profoundly nuanced approach to the heterogeneity of material culture and interests in it, across milieux, communities and nations. This book is inspired particularly by Pacific and Māori perspectives on *taonga* (treasures) and their inspiring potential. But it is vital that we do not, in the manner of UNESCO, universalise particular forms of attachment to ancestral artefacts. Both within Oceania and comparatively, people's investments and disinvestments in things are manifold. Artefacts have telling capacities that both fall short of and exceed the double-edged narratives of belonging that are currently being reasserted so forcefully. We need to engage not only local perspectives but their diversity; we need to ask 'What else is there?' and confront uncomfortable issues about identity politics and postcolonial nations. And we cannot stop investigating Europe's difficult histories, and the difficult histories of collections and museums – that, however, have become fertile and revelatory in ways their makers never anticipated.

Note

1 This comment was written in November 2009, one of several invited opinion pieces commissioned by Chip Colwell-Chanthaphonh and Stephen Nash at the time they became joint editors of *Museum Anthropology*. Citations did not seem appropriate, though I am well aware of, and indebted to, a stimulating literature to which many colleagues have contributed. It may however be helpful to some readers if I make it explicit that I refer to Alfred Gell's discussion of Duchamp in *Art and Agency* (Oxford: Oxford University Press, 1998); to novels by W.G. Sebald including *Austerlitz* (London: Penguin, 2001); and Johannes Fabian's important *Time and the Other* (New York: Columbia University Press, 1983). I am grateful to Ruth Phillips, the editors of *Museum Anthropology* and their referees, and the editors of the present volume for their comments and their encouragement. Apart from the sentence at the end of the second paragraph, referring to the Pitt Rivers Museum, the text has not been updated or revised here; aspects of the argument were elaborated on in 'Global Reach', *Apollo* (April 2016), 30–4 (online version: 'We need ethnographic museums today – whatever you think of their history') and in *The Return of Curiosity: What Museums Are Good for in the Twenty-First Century* (London: Reaktion, and Chicago: University of Chicago Press, 2016).

2

What not to collect?
Post-connoisseurial dystopia
and the profusion of things

Sharon Macdonald and Jennie Morgan

Imagine a museum storeroom lined with shelves and racks. These are filled with boxes and objects, labelled by number and name. On one shelf sit a dozen or so radios, mainly from the 1950s, hefty things with dials and wood veneer. On another are six seemingly identical stoneware bedwarmers from the early twentieth century. A tall shelving unit is packed with ceramics – teacups, bowls, jugs, plates – and other, unidentifiable things. A bedframe leans against one of the few bare areas of wall; a butter churn stands on the floor at the end of an aisle. In a corner, two tables and a desk with a computer are piled high with paperwork, ring binders and yet more objects. A woman apologises when we enter: 'I'm so sorry about the state of this room. We're just in the process of trying to clear the megabacklog. Not that I can claim this is new – to be honest, it's always like this!' She gestures us to sit down and tells us about what she describes as 'my big headache':

> It's just so hard to know where to begin – and where to end. There's so much that we *could* collect and that we *could* display, so many stories that we *could* tell. Already, we have so much. Actually, we even have so much that we haven't fully catalogued or researched yet – our backlog is pretty scary, well, as you can see – those things on the tables over there waiting to be catalogued are just part of it. And don't even ask about digitisation. We are hardly alone in this. So many museums are in this position. Our storage is already filled to bursting point, so it is really hard to justify collecting more. But at the same time, we have a duty to future generations to actually try and show the way things are today. Are there ways of putting on the brakes and saying enough is enough? You want to know what we collect and why – and it's a good question. But to be quite honest, I think that sometimes it's more a matter of having to decide what not to collect – not that that makes it any easier.

The description and quotation above are fictional, in the sense that they are not literal descriptions or transcriptions (except in fragments) from a particular individual or any specific museum storeroom. They do, however, draw upon actual discussions that we have had, and speak in ways that we hope are true to the comments and feelings expressed by curators who we have met during our research fieldwork, and whom we quote directly in the rest of this chapter.[1]

That research field is museums, primarily those within the UK that have a remit to collect recent and/or contemporary everyday life. Our focus here is on what for many curators working in this context is a major challenge, and one that for some at least makes them feel that the role of curator has changed significantly from that of curators of a previous generation. The challenge is what to collect for the future, and how to cope with what has already been collected in the face of what is perceived as a proliferation of possibilities. While selecting what to preserve for the future can be said to have been a central task of curators of previous generations too – some would say this is the central role of curatorship – this, according to many curators of the contemporary everyday, no longer works, and can no longer work, as it once did. Unravelling the reasons for this and its implications for the changing figure of the curator is the aim of our chapter.

At issue, we maintain, is not just a practical challenge of the number of things that can potentially be collected and kept for future generations (though that is not irrelevant). Rather, we argue, our curator's predicament is also a function of shifts in ways of understanding the curatorial role; material culture and its value; and the relationship between curators, other people and things. Although our curator, and many like her, may sometimes feel the situation in which she works to be somewhat dystopian, this does not mean that she is, and others are, without utopian hopes and ideals. Indeed, the sense of dystopia is in part at least a function of utopian striving, sometimes for goals that, if not conflicting, do not always mesh seamlessly.

Profusion: politics, economics and (alternative) values

Our research is part of a larger project called *Heritage Futures*.[2] The theme on which we work is called 'Profusion'. It focuses on the apparent challenge of mass-production and mass-consumption for selecting what to keep for the future. How in the face of there being so many more things produced today — beginning with industrialisation and mass production, especially since the mid-nineteenth century, and then accelerated by post-Fordist production since the 1970s – is it decided what will be kept for the future? As research field sites within which to look at this challenge we focus on a selection of household practices and investigate museums that have a remit to acquire from the present and recent past. It is on our museum study that we draw in this chapter.

In setting up our research, we presumed that there was something specific and different about the challenge posed by so many things. Now, it might be contested that what makes it through one period of time to another has always entailed selection, some active, some accidental. There are always many more things that could have made it. While this is so, our reading of available scholarship suggests that there is something not just more acute but also more historically, culturally and experientially specific about the contemporary situation.[3] This is not, however, simply a reflex of mass-production and mass-consumption themselves. That is, there is more causing the headache than an increase in the sheer number and range of available things. Part of our aim, therefore, is to delve further into what is involved in what Elizabeth Chin has referred to as 'the growing sense of too muchness';[4] and to highlight 'profusion' in ways that go beyond quantitative understandings.

Certainly, as curators of the contemporary everyday explained to us, their difficulties over what to collect are aggravated *both* by the quantity and the constant production of new things (models of mobile phones were an example we encountered several times), and also by a 'lack of time perspective' as one put it, from which one can look back and make judgements. Here, the question of what was sufficient a difference to warrant collecting something was often raised: 'Every new model of the iPhone?' As another pointed out, what also makes the task for the curator of the contemporary everyday particularly difficult is that the range of possible things to collect has not yet been 'thinned down by the teeth of time' or by what another referred to as 'time sift'. 'I have this slight fear', we were told, 'that sometimes people think that any contemporary collecting is a gamble … You know, has this been tested by history and has it been found representative enough or vocal enough? Is it typical of its time?'[5]

Nevertheless, it should be emphasised that it is not only curators of the contemporary everyday who express concern about what to collect and who have mega-headaches over how much has already been collected and what to do with it. An international meeting of natural history museums in 1985, for example, described a dilemma of collections growing by about fifty million specimens per year.[6] This also serves to show that the perceived 'too-muchness problem' is not simply a reflex of mass-consumption, although it may relate to it in more complex ways. What we see more widely, however, is a growing discourse within museums and museum organisations about questions of what to collect in the face of an apparent glut of choice, and about how to deal with expanding numbers of objects in sometimes already full storage spaces.

Quite when the idea that museums might have a profusion problem began to be articulated is something that we are still investigating and intend to write about elsewhere. Our reading of available literatures and conversations with museum professionals indicate that – within the UK, at least – the problem seems to have been discussed and debated with particular intensity in the last two decades of the twentieth century.[7] In the UK, a 1989 report called *The Cost of Collecting*, commissioned by the Office of Arts and Libraries, was the source for the frequently quoted figure that 80 per cent of UK collections were in storage.[8] By 2003, the National Museums Directors' Conference could issue a report titled *Too Much Stuff?*[9] If that was not provocative enough, its subtitle, *Disposal from Museums*, referred to something that, as many curators have told us, was at that time 'something of a taboo' to even mention.

That there is an economic dimension to the sense of 'too-muchness' is undeniable. Looking at collections in terms of their 'cost', as the 1989 report, commissioned under the Thatcher government, was titled, was precisely the formulation that led to so much bandying about of the 80 per cent statistic (which later was revised upwards to 90 per cent). In theory, this statistic could have been used to praise the vast quantities of objects that museums care for – their extensive curatorial work behind the scenes. Instead, however, it has been almost invariably deployed in order to question the point of holding such collections. As the quote that opens *Too Much Stuff?* by David Rendel MP, put at the UK Government's Public Accounts Committee in 2001, shows, the implication of holding so much and not having it displayed was deemed to be a lack of proper public accountability: 'What percentage of the collection has not been on display during, say, the last ten years?'[10] Or similarly, as Jane Glaister, the Museums Association President from 2002 to 2004, stated in the *Collections for the Future* report: 'The cost of maintaining unused, stored collections must be taken into account and weighed against the benefits those "assets" could realise for the museum and its users'.[11] The problem, she concluded, was clear: 'too much unused stuff, draining resources'.[12] Trying to quantify this 'drain' has occurred as cost analyses have been carried out, such as one UK museum service calculating that building additional storage space costs £1,000 per square metre.[13] Such neo-liberal framing, which emphasises 'accountability' in primarily auditable economic terms, and which continually seeks ways of 'making effective' and 'increasing profit' according to such terms, has certainly also shaped the sense that museums have a profusion problem. Austerity politics, with its prioritising of cutting costs above all else, of 'lean efficiency', has sharpened this further.[14]

As important as audit culture and austerity politics have been in playing into senses of 'too muchness', however, they are not their sole cause. Moreover, how to understand the 'value' of collections is neither fully predetermined nor settled even within a broadly neo-liberal framework. Over the last decade especially, considerable effort has been made by cultural institutions to emphasise the value of collections – and indeed of culture more generally – in ways that go beyond their public display and calculability in terms of visitor numbers. While these are almost always still framed within an overall discourse of 'benefit', the attempt has been to go beyond narrowly economistic notions of 'value', sometimes by drawing on ideas of different kinds of 'capital'.[15] What is going on here, we suggest, is as much about revising and even subverting neo-liberal models as implementing them. There is considerable evidence of attempts to recognise and give priority to some of the many things that are valued in museums in practice – which usually includes expanding collections of objects – rather than simply adopting what is being imposed by the audit-minded. Put otherwise, our curator's headache is not simply a result of having been told to collect less or dispose of much of what she already has, or even the fact that she does not have more colleagues to help her. Let us look here, then, at what else, from our fieldwork so far, seems to be involved, before then considering what the implications of this might be for the utopian strivings of many curators of the contemporary everyday.

Collecting the everyday

Many curators stressed to us that they felt they were dealing with a problem 'that had built up over the years', or that was 'inherited', as they variously put it. It was a product of the way in which collecting had been carried out in the past. According to one social history curator, this had been done in a 'rescue' mode, in which curators had worried that things were being lost – especially when, say, companies or cottage industries were closing down – and 'just went in and gathered it up en masse'. She also referred to this as 'over-collecting' and said that it often resulted in 'lots of duplicates' or holding multiples of the same kind of thing. As she put it: 'Our collection was built up very rapidly in the 1980s and 1990s and it was driven by what was becoming available, rescuing things from firms that were closing, and so on. And now we're at a point where we have to take a step back and say, "okay, well what is actually important?"' Statements like these indicate curators not only grappling with the vast numbers of previously acquired objects but also thinking about what to tell with and through these collections.

Rescue or salvage collecting has been the source of many kinds of collections, including ethnographic as well as those of folk-life; and it reveals how collecting the contemporary everyday is so frequently understood as collecting what will very soon have vanished (even if this later proves not to be the case). Typical of such modes of collecting is the ambition to collect as much as possible from the way-of-life that is perceived to be disappearing, resulting in what one curator described to us as 'pretty indiscriminate' collecting, evident too in the use of terms such as 'gathering up' and 'salvage'. Although studies have shown that this kind of collecting often did in fact entail selection, not least by ignoring items deemed somehow inauthentic,[16] it was nevertheless seen as very different from a more connoisseurial mode of carefully planned and executed identification and acquisition of selected objects.

Also necessary to prompting this kind of collecting was the development of the idea that the stuff of everyday life was worth saving and putting into museums.[17] In the case of ethnographic collections, their perceived exoticness and the potential to understand very different ways of life provided motivation. So too for the case of folk-life collections, if on a lesser scale of difference. For many of the curators we met, however, it was predominantly ideas from social history, namely that museums should seek to represent 'ordinary people' and show 'everyday life,' rather than 'just the rich and famous' (as it was put to us), which also provided an impetus to collecting the contemporary everyday. While this sometimes led to rescue collecting, it also established a remit to document not just the exotic, the famous and the special but also more mundane and ubiquitous material culture. The lines between this and more folkloristic collecting are not always clear-cut, but what is often referred to as 'social history' collecting grew especially from the 1970s.[18] Once the remit is established, then, that the everyday, ordinary, and contemporary are worth collecting, the problems arise of just quite what this means in practice – especially in a context in which these things are not necessarily on the brink of extinction but are constantly being produced. Where does it end? What not to collect?

From type to story

Also aggravating the selection problem, as we have already noted, is the profusion of new things and of slight variations of models. The idea of being able to choose just one thing to illustrate a whole category – the notion of 'type' – is seen by curators as having become much more problematic today. 'Is it representative enough? Is it typical of its time? Will future generations want this one?' are questions that curators say that they ask, and struggle to answer. Partly, this is due to the issue of many variations of products, as in the much-used example of mobile phones, which often also claim technical innovation. Or to give an example from our opening quotation, from a curator with six stoneware bed-warmers on the shelf: to viewers such as us, the researchers, she said, these 'must look pretty much identical'. As she goes on to explain, they do 'in fact have various differences, especially different provenance and makers' marks'. So to take just one would obliterate what might be significant differences – differences that 'might be historically important'.

How 'historically important' is understood here tells us another reason why the idea of 'type' is not sufficient as a criterion for collecting the contemporary everyday. For history museums, type has often been less important than historical association with significant makers, individuals, places or events, the 'provenance' that so many curators mention. This usually produces singular objects, unique through their specific individualised associations. In social history approaches this is extended to a broader range of people and a more general way of life. This particular curator's expression of her task as 'representing how we live' articulates this, and, as she says, it sets up the problem of just what is 'representative'.

Perhaps surprisingly, however, this curator and many others with whom we spoke also complained that, despite the problems posed by the extent of collections, the collections also had 'gaps' or were 'uneven'. As one curator explained:

> We have really suffered from over-collecting of past curators in terms of people who have particular interests or even contacts, where it has meant that things have come into the collection that, perhaps, there's too much

of one thing in terms of it being over-represented to the detriment of other areas that may have been neglected.

Similarly, another told us how:

> You think about the things that people have collected and you think 'would I have collected those?' 'God, no, that doesn't tell the story in a way I want it to.' … I always joke about the spreadsheets. No one goes to a museum to see a spreadsheet. You just wouldn't go to look at that. It's not visual in the same way. But then loads of ephemera in the past, loads of stuff in the past just wasn't compelling. But it tells you about the time and what was important and what were priorities and what label was available and what the structures of power were. … Sometimes it's important to represent this story and it's important this story is told.

Even within profusion, then, there can be still be material lacunae, especially of things that were overlooked because they somehow did not seem 'compelling'. Many things, such as the spreadsheets (which this curator is actively trying to collect from organisations and individuals to represent working life) have not been noticed as worth collecting: even while, at the same time, numerous 'duplicates' built up elsewhere. For such curators, awareness of the risk of 'ephemera' being overlooked also contributes to their own concern to collect widely, so as not to be judged negatively by posterity, for having failed to collect what is later able to tell important stories about the current present.

The concern here is not only the potential lack of things capable of speaking about the contemporary, however. Curators also worry about whether 'the right kind of information' has also been collected. As many explained, in various words, this is 'a major problem' faced in dealing with 'backlogs' (as described in our opening quotation): 'we simply don't always know all that we want to, or that we should'. As one expanded 'sometimes all you have got is something like what it is made of – which you can see anyhow – and a rough date if you're lucky'. Moreover, information about how the thing came to be in the museum in the first place may have been misplaced, or never recorded.

Describing the problem in terms of 'mega-backlog', however, does not fully grasp what so many curators felt was absent in the documentation that surrounded the objects in their care. Here, the word that resonated through curators' verbal reflections – used at the end of the quote above – was 'stories'. This is a word that we have observed and commented upon previously in museum settings, and whose prevalence can also be seen in literature about museums.[19] Among our interlocutors, it was mostly used in an unmarked way, as a taken-for-granted or self-evident way of expressing the curatorial task. But it deserves note, for it is expressive of an important shift in the curatorial role and introduces another layer of profusion.

Curators' use of the term 'story' does not deny the importance in many museums of historical accuracy – as expressed by one museum worker who told us about the importance of telling 'authentic stories'. Conceptualising the curatorial task in terms of stories is recognised as working differently from more categorical or disciplinary modes of organising knowledge. Mark O'Neill, previous Head of Glasgow Museums, emphasised 'storytelling' as being at the heart of a major redevelopment of Kelvingrove Museum (2003–2006), a museum seen as path-breaking for its refusal to stay within conventional disciplinary categories.[20] He describes how the reorganisation of the museum was fuelled by curators being asked 'to suggest "the most interesting stories about the most interesting objects"',[21] a process that resulted initially in 'a list of about 200 potential stories'.[22] Although O'Neill argues that advantages of this approach are that it 'cut across disciplines, and … didn't require that gaps in the collection be filled with graphics, replicas, or mediocre objects',[23] it also necessarily meant that objects that did not have interesting stories would be even less likely to find a place on public display.

Also significant in the proliferation of the term 'story' is that it is so often used in the plural. This recognition that there are many different accounts of the past that might be told itself signals a museological approach to the past that understands this in terms of multiple players with different viewpoints – each of which might *tell* a different story. Significantly, and returning to the pointing out of perceived differences between what to us appeared to be similar stoneware bed-warmers, this curator also understands distinctions to arise from each holding the *potential* to tell many different future stories; stories that might emerge through further research, the possible roles they will play in exhibitions, or through the connections and links that might (even if quite unexpectedly) be made to other objects in the collection, not only by her but also by external experts and visitors.

Influenced by critical historical and museological approaches that question traditional typological and disciplinary classification and shaped by a politics that seeks to recover and introduce multiple and marginalised voices into museums, and often embraced with considerable enthusiasm and political commitment, the story emphasis, nevertheless, also contributes to our curator's profusion headache. Which objects should be collected to help ensure that stories can be told in the future? Is it possible that for some things a story might never be found? How is a curator to decide which stories are to be told? And is she or he even the person who should, or is able to, make such decisions?

Who decides, whose stories?

Such questions are undoubtedly ones with which many curators struggle, as we have found in our research. In response to a question about what she sees as her biggest challenge, one curator replied: 'The challenge is just the scope. … And the easiest thing to collect is everything. … It means so much to you to be able to tell different stories in a museum.' Yet even though 'collecting everything' – were this even possible – might seem to allow any stories to be told, it only does so if that collecting has been of the immaterial alongside the material; that of the kinds of rich contextual information we have flagged.

Compounding the dilemma here is the doubt expressed by some curators about their own authority to impose limits by making selections. They ask such questions as 'who can decide?', 'who can say?', 'how can we know what others will find interesting?', and 'how can we know what people in the future will want to know about us?' Again, one possible response to this has been to suggest ubiquitous collecting, as Neil Cossons, Director of London's Science Museum did – perhaps more as a thought-experiment than an actual proposal – back in 1992.[24] Take one of each new type of thing off the production-line, he suggested, and put it, nice and pristine, into 'a long shed' and then 'at intervals of 25, 50 or 75 years we'll open the door … and look at what we've got. And we'll throw some of it away.'[25] But as we have already noted, the idea that 'one of everything' be collected, as Cossons suggested, immediately raises the mobile phone dilemma outlined above, and is compounded by the potential limitlessness of accompanying information and stories. His idea of only collecting the brand new would mean that no stories of use would have accumulated. Such objects would lack just the kind of 'stories of use' and 'personal stories' that many curators said made them interesting. Nevertheless, the idea of trying to 'hold things for future generations, the next load of curators, to make the decision' was voiced by some with whom we spoke. But again, there was usually a quick realisation that this did not help to limit collecting in the present or its inevitable selectivity.

What we see here, then, is that a logic of recognising that future generations may have different interests – and the strong sense of responsibility towards such future generations – itself leads towards collecting as much as possible. In other words, particular curatorial logics, especially certain moralised assumptions about how it is proper to behave in relation to the future, generate dilemmas over how to set limits or decide what *not* to collect. The perception of profusion, then, is not only – and perhaps not even primarily – a consequence of neo-liberal evaluations in terms of 'value for money'. This does not mean, however, that these curatorial logics exist outside time. On the contrary, we have perceived a particular constellation that has emerged over time, with various impetuses. Moreover, it also involves a particular historiographic sensibility in which, rather than believing values to be universal and transcendent, the assumption is more relativist; that subsequent generations may want to tell different stories.

In addition to a temporal relativism, curators also speak of a relativism of social diversity. Most often, this is articulated in terms of different 'communities', that members will 'have their own stories' that they would want to see in the museum or collected for the future. The social history movement, which, as we have noted, was important in propelling the growth of contemporary everyday collecting, argued that museums and collections needed to rectify previous failures to represent the everyday life of the majority of the population, especially the working class and women. The remit was further expanded with the influence of identity politics, which argued for recognition of a wide range of what were at first often called 'minorities' and then, increasingly, 'communities', self-identifying or identifiable on bases such as sexuality, ethnicity and locality (though the last already had significant presence through village, town and city museums). All of this proliferated the range of those who curators of the contemporary everyday saw as potentially having their own stories to tell, through their own (even if mass-produced) objects. This set up a task for curators that one curator described as 'bringing in diversifying voices', or, in the case of her museum, 'to make sure our collections are as diverse as the city we live in'.

Social diversity – and the potential fragmentation within that – adds to the range of what needs to be collected.[26] Within the UK, this is typically framed through a discourse of museums as having the capacity to be agents for social change and/or inclusion.[27] The anxieties that curators express over the potential difference of perspective of future generations is reproduced here too in the form of anxiety over which identities should be represented and how they should find their way into the museum. It is also sometimes reflected in a commitment to representing as many differences as possible and finding ways of involving 'communities' in what might be included in the museum collection. Irit Rogoff refers to this as part of an 'additive mode at whose heart is a very old Enlightenment conceit that cultural institutions are universalist and infinitely expandable – they can stretch and expand to include every one of the excluded, elided and marginalized histories'.[28] In her view, this needs to be addressed through some kind of acceptance of limits and reduction, though quite what this might mean in practice is left unstated. One way would be through connoisseurial ideas of superior quality of some sort. Occasionally, we witnessed curators talking about their own selection of 'the best examples' of certain objects. Yet more often, curators expressed concern over how to find ways to 'allow new people and new ways of participating in collecting'.[29] As one curator said, when reflecting on contemporary interest in curation (and the proliferation of the word used in settings beyond the museum), 'Let's open it up! What I do, why couldn't somebody else think about what is important about their life and send it to me? They're the expert. I'm just going to help a museum process it'.

What we see here, then, is a significant shift in the role of the curator, away from being an expert in objects and more towards being a mediator between the museum and the many potential people and objects that the museum might include. As we discuss in the next section, the idea of the curator as a mediator – and a concomitant revision of the required expertise – has become widespread in these kinds of museums, and indeed in many others. In itself, however, it does not necessarily solve the profusion problem.[30]

Discussion: the curator as mediator

Curators of the contemporary everyday, and those working in museum organisations that interact with them, sometimes contrasted their roles with an imagined 'classical curator', what we are calling the connoisseurial curator. We should be wary, however, about setting this up as too strong an opposition. The connoisseurial curator who was fully confident of his (as the connoisseur is almost invariably imagined) superior, refined taste, which he exercised in the formation of highly selective collections, imagined as examples of universal, incontestable quality and value, may be something of a straw man. Its invocation by curators with whom we spoke was as much a way of explaining their own position and difficulties as a description of a singular state of affairs. Nevertheless, the idea that the curator nowadays is more likely to be an expert in mediating the relations between people and objects than an expert in the objects themselves is very prevalent. Curators today are more likely to be thought of as 'collaborators and brokers' rather than 'experts'.[31]

There are many factors involved in reshaping the role of the curator, and even sometimes displacing the curator altogether.[32] Here we have focused on how curatorship is reshaped for curators of the contemporary everyday as they deal with questions of what to collect, what to keep and, sometimes, what not to keep. As we have argued, the sense of facing an increasing profusion of things is experiential and cultural. This is not to say that it does not have a material realisation. There are many things that curators might collect. However, this perception of 'muchness' – and sometimes of 'too-muchness' – is not only created by a burgeoning material world. It is also a product of seeing more and more things, and more and more people, as deserving a place in museums. It is a product of museal logics in which 'value' has become considerably relativised. Not only does this mean that curators are reticent about claiming authority over what will be judged of value in the future, they also worry about this in the present. Increasingly, they see themselves as not having the authority to make such decisions but as needing to delegate to others who are seen as having greater rights to make them. In describing this state of affairs, our aim is not to judge it, though if pushed to do so we would broadly agree that it is a good thing, as do almost all of those with whom we have spoken. But what we also see, however, is that it autonomously propels more and more collecting. In itself, more and more collecting does not necessarily have to be seen as a bad thing. Yet we acknowledge the 'indigenous' perception of it as problematic – something that we were told again and again by curators who we met.[33]

In using the term indigenous we do so to point out that we are looking at a particular way of seeing the world that is rooted in particular locations, even if these cover a large and many-country area. The sense of need to save for the future, to 'represent' as much 'diversity' as possible, and to preserve both objects *and* stories, is part of a particular contemporary museological way of seeing that is neither historically nor spatially universal. In many ways, this is a utopian worldview; it is a hope for an impossible form of collecting. This impossibility is in part a function of economistic ways of looking at collections, which may be part of a new spirit of capitalism that financialises everything.[34] This way of seeing regards utopian, ubiquitous collecting as simply too expensive. And what is deemed too expensive is also, in this particular logic, regarded as irrational. Yet what we have heard in curators' own words, and seen in their struggles to tidy their desks and find space on their shelves for yet more things, is that the sense of too-muchness is not only generated by neo-liberal financialised models with their quests for efficiency. It is also a product of the limitlessness of politically, socially and materially utopian ideas that are as much about the operation of a world that evades and even defies the market. Here, we refer to our wider arguments, partly developed and to be further developed elsewhere, in which we suggest that museums and heritage are important alternative repositories of value from those of economistic systems.[35]

In *The Order of Things*, Foucault points out how sixteenth-century ideas of *resemblance* created a kind of limitless way of knowing that he describes as 'plethoric'.[36] That is, a way of seeing – and indeed of collecting – in which the search was for more and more resemblances, of many different kinds, inevitably resulting in an endless project that could never be contained. Although he saw this as an episteme that has largely been superseded, it seems to us that the curatorial dilemma that we have described here is rather similar. A quest to capture the everyday and ordinary, and social diversity, all in their detail, propels what, as mentioned above, Irit Rogoff calls 'the additive mode'. It leads to needing to collect more and more. This is, we believe, part of the 'structure of the space of possibilities' of which Manuel DeLanda, inspired by Gilles Deleuze, writes.[37] As with the assemblages that he discusses, what we are dealing with here is not just a set of ideas but a material-idea assemblage, with its own propulsions and effects. It is created and realised in shelves and shelves of stored objects, in expanding databases, in new work practices and in curatorial headaches.

To write that any utopia has a 'dark side' – a dystopia – would be simplistic. Nevertheless, the dystopian anxieties of curators whom we have met in our work can be seen in part at least as functions of their very admirable utopian ambitions. Perhaps here we could call for a pragmatic utopianism that argues for holding on to one's ideals but also being practical and realistic about achieving them. This indeed is something that we also witnessed underway within our fieldwork, with many meetings, proposals and creative ideas being devised to try to address the perceived profusion problem. Describing and discussing these would, however, be too much for one chapter.

Acknowledgements

This chapter draws on research undertaken for the Profusion theme of the *Heritage Futures* project. *Heritage Futures* is funded by a UK Arts and

Humanities Research Council (AHRC) 'Care for the Future: Thinking Forward through the Past' Theme Large Grant (AH/M004376/1), awarded to Rodney Harrison (Principal Investigator), Caitlin DeSilvey, Cornelius Holtorf, Sharon Macdonald (Co-Investigators), Antony Lyons (Senior Creative Fellow), Nadia Bartolini, Sarah May, Jennie Morgan and Sefryn Penrose (Postdoctoral Researchers). It receives generous additional support from its host universities and partner organisations. We thank our *Heritage Futures* colleagues for their ongoing support. In relation to this chapter, we especially thank the museum professionals who gave their time to collaborate with us, and particularly project partners Michael Turnpenny (York Museums Trust) and Gillian Greaves (Arts Council England, Yorkshire). Thanks are also due to Conal and Philipp, the Manchester University Press anonymous reviewers, and audiences in the Department of Sociology, University of York, and the Museums Lab in the Institute of European Ethnology, Humboldt University. Due to the profusion of great comments, some will have to wait to be taken up in future work.

Notes

1 We spoke to both male and female curators, and quotations included in this chapter are from both. The number of female respondents, however, substantially outweighed the number of male.

2 For more on *Heritage Futures* project funded by the UK's AHRC see https://heritage-futures.org. Accessed 1 December 2016.

3 For example, B. Czarniawska and O. Löfgren (eds), *Managing Overflow in Affluent Societies* (London: Routledge, 2012), and B. Czarniawska and O. Löfgren (eds), *Coping with Excess: How Organizations, Communities and Individuals Manage Overflows* (Cheltenham: Edward Elgar, 2013).

4 E. Chin, *My Life with Things: The Consumer Diaries* (Durham, NC: Duke University Press, 2016).

5 On contemporary collecting by Indigenous curators, see comments by Matariki Williams in McCarthy, Hakiwai and Schorch, Chapter 13 below.

6 J. Waddington and D.M. Rudkin (eds.), *Proceedings of the 1985 Workshop on Care and Maintenance of Natural History Collections* (Toronto: Royal Ontario Museum, 1985), https://archive.org/stream/proceedingsof19800work/proceedingsof19800work_djvu.txt. Accessed 30 November 2016.

7 S.J. Knell (ed.), *Museums and the Future of Collecting: Second Edition* (Aldershot: Ashgate, 2004).

8 B. Lord, G. Dexter and J. Nicks, *The Cost of Collecting: Collections Management in UK Museums* (London: Office of Arts and Libraries, 1989).

9 National Museum Directors' Conference, *Too Much Stuff? Disposal from Museums* (London: National Museum Directors' Conference, 2003).

10 *Ibid.*, 2.

11 H. Wilkinson, *Collections for the Future* (London: Museums Association, 2005).

12 *Ibid.*

13 Cited from Museums Association, *Collections … Love Museums*, www.museumsassociation.org/campaigns/love-museums/facts-and-figures. Accessed 20

November 2016. For a discussion of 'output analysis' see S. Weil, 'Creampuffs and Hardball: Are You Really Worth What You Cost or Just Merely Worthwhile?', in S. Weil, *A Cabinet of Curiosities: Inquiries into Museums and Their Prospects* (Washington, DC: Smithsonian Institution Press, 1995), pp. 33–8.

14 This is indicated, for example, through the annual UK-based surveys that the Museums Association has been undertaking since 2011 looking at the implications for museums of public funding cuts. The most recent report found that 'financially-motivated disposal looks set to rise', with 11 per cent of respondents considering this within the next year; that 'fundraising' and 'income generation' were top priorities for museums; and that some respondents were considering collections rationalisation to reduce storage costs. See Museums Association, *Cuts Survey 2015* (London: Museums Association, 2015), www.museumsassociation.org/campaigns/funding-cuts/cuts-survey. Accessed 30 November 2016.

15 See UK Arts Council, *The Value of the Arts and Culture to People and Society: An Evidence Review* (London: Arts Council, undated, c. 2014). This also summarises various earlier reports and studies. Economic value remains highly prized in this report but is also accompanied by other values, such as health and well-being, and society. Internationally, the 'Burra Charter', first developed in 1979 by Australia ICOMOS, to 'rank' the 'significance' or relative 'worth' of individual objects, or whole collections, has been influential in suggesting alternative notions of value.

16 J. Clifford, 'The Others: Beyond the "Salvage" Paradigm', *Third Text*, 3:6 (1989), 73–8.

17 S. Macdonald, 'Musealisation: Everyday Life, Temporality and Old Things', in S. Macdonald, *Memorylands: Heritage and Identity in Europe Today* (London: Routledge, 2013), ch. 6.

18 See S. Macdonald, 'Collecting Practices', in S. Macdonald (ed.), *A Companion to Museum Studies* (Oxford: Blackwell Publishing, 2006), pp. 81–97. On history curating, see also Labrum, Chapter 15 below.

19 For an ethnographic example, see L. Bedford, 'Storytelling: The Real Work of Museums', *Curator*, 44:1 (2001), 27–34. For a discussion on our own work, see S. Macdonald, 'A People's Story? Heritage, Identity and Authenticity', in C. Rojek and J. Urry (eds), *Touring Cultures. Transformations of Travel and Theory* (London: Routledge, 1997), pp. 155–75. Also J. Morgan, 'Change and Everyday Practice at the Museum: An Ethnographic Study' (PhD Thesis, University of Manchester, 2011).

20 M. O'Neill, 'Kelvingrove: Telling Stories in a Treasured Old/New Museum', *Curator*, 50:4 (2007), 379–99.

21 *Ibid.*, 385.

22 *Ibid.*, 386.

23 *Ibid.*, 385–6.

24 N. Cossons, 'Professionals and Museums 2. Rambling Reflections of a Museum Man', in P. Boylan (ed.), *Museums 2000. Politics, People, Professionals and Profit* (London: Routledge, 1992), pp. 117–26.

25 *Ibid.*, 123.

26 See ICOM, *Documenting Diversity: Collections, Catalogues and Context* conference report, 2015, http://network.icom.museum/cidoc/archives/past-conferences/2015-new-delhi/. Accessed 30 November 2016.

27 For example, R. Sandell, 'Museums as Agents of Social Inclusion', *Museum Management and Curatorship*, 17:4 (1998), 401–8, and R. Sandell, 'Social

Inclusion, the Museum and Dynamics of Sectoral Change', *Museum and Society*, 1:1 (2002), 45–62.

28 I. Rogoff, 'The Expanded Field', in J.-P. Martinon (ed.), *The Curatorial: A Philosophy of Curating* (London: Bloomsbury, 2013), pp. 41–8, 44.

29 See L. Meijer-van Mensch and E. Tietmeyer (eds), *Participative Strategies in Collecting the Present* (Berlin: Panama Verlag, 2013).

30 On co-curating see Mallon, Chapter 17 below.

31 N. Proctor, quoted in Meijer-van Mensch and Tietmeyer (eds), *Participative Strategies in Collecting the Present*, 10.

32 See M. Viau-Courville (ed.), 'Musées sans conservateurs/Museums without Curators', special issue of *Thema. La Revue des Musées de la Civilisation*, 4 (2016). See also Onciul, Chapter 10 below.

33 Here we use the word 'indigenous' as meaning the perception of those curators themselves – who in no sense would probably think of themselves as an Indigenous native or tribal group (with a politicised capital I).

34 L. Boltanski and E. Chiapello, 'The New Spirit of Capitalism', *International Journal of Politics, Culture and Society*, 18 (2005), 161–88.

35 For example, Macdonald, *Memorylands*.

36 M. Foucault, *The Order of Things: An Archaeology of the Human Sciences* (London: Routledge, [1966] 1989), p. 30.

37 M. DeLanda, *A New Philosophy of Society: Assemblage Theory and Social Complexity* (London: Continuum, 2006).

3

Concerning curatorial practice in ethnological museums: an epistemology of postcolonial debates

Larissa Förster and Friedrich von Bose

Debating ethnological museums in the German-speaking world[1]

Since the early 2000s, ethnological museums have come under increased scrutiny in the German-speaking world, as elsewhere.[2] While in North America, Australia and Aotearoa New Zealand they have had to confront and react to postcolonial critiques for much longer, colonial history has only comparatively recently started to enter public discourse and the politics of remembrance in Germany.[3] The critique of ethnological museums has also gained public attention increasingly, especially in the context of several large-scale museum openings, most recently the planning of the Humboldt Forum in Berlin, a new museum project, opening in late 2019, which will be housed in the reconstructed Berlin Palace on Museum Island. Nevertheless, the roots of the scholarly debate on 'de-colonising museums' in the German-speaking context can be traced back as early as the 1970s. It gained traction in the 1990s, when art historians and anthropologists paid ethnological museums more attention. Yet, the debate has only slowly begun to be reflected in the institutional context of the ethnological museum itself.

The transnational, often Anglophone debates about museums and postcoloniality have had a great impact in the German-speaking academic sphere. Critiques from anti-racist activists,[4] artists,[5] art historians[6] and others have fuelled the debate – in particular in Berlin, where the Humboldt Forum and its much-discussed historicist palace architecture have drawn attention and criticism from many professional fields and walks of life.[7] This has also happened against the background of a much broader discussion on the decolonisation of cityscapes and memory politics in public spaces.[8]

Since the early 2000s, we have seen a sharpening of postcolonial critiques centred on particular events and institutions. The Weltkulturen Museum in Frankfurt, under its director Clémentine Deliss (2010–2015), explicitly engaged in historical research related to the history of the institution.[9] The Museum of Cultures in Basel has adopted new ways of exhibiting that correspond with many of the critiques of traditional ethnographic displays, and which explicitly refuse to tell stories only about 'other cultures'.[10]

The Humboldt Lab Dahlem (2013–2015), installed as an experimental test run in support of the planning process for the Humboldt Forum, managed to involve many artists and critics who, together with the curatorial staff of the museums involved, have opened up new perspectives on how to critically and experimentally engage with the vast collections.[11] However, there have so far been only a few opportunities in which postcolonial critics, anthropologists, museum curators and educators could directly engage in an interdisciplinary discussion that goes beyond specific exhibition projects.

When we were invited to 'curate' a debate in the German journal *Zeitschrift für Kulturwissenschaften* (ZfK), a 'critical medium for discussion and controversy about "culture"',[12] we sought to address this paucity and create a platform for such an exchange between postcolonial critics from the visual arts and art history, and anthropologists working in and on museums. In the following, we want to take this debate as a starting point in order to reflect upon some of the more general problems surrounding ethnological museums in a German-speaking context. This is because some of the pitfalls and shortcomings of the discussion reflect the limitations of the current postcolonial debate on ethnological museums and of its 'dead ends' in general – in the German-speaking context, but possibly elsewhere as well. Therefore, we started to wonder how these limitations could be addressed explicitly in order to think about the future of ethnological museums. Our chapter, designed as a think piece rather than an epistemological analysis in the strict sense of the word, will therefore conclude by calling for a continuation of the debate in new and less limited ways.

Entering the controversy

To provide a glimpse of the dynamics of the debate in the German-speaking world, two significant yet contrasting arguments advanced during the course of the debate may be called to mind. In 2009, the art historian and museum theorist Nora Sternfeld accused the Musée du Quai Branly of what she called 'transformism', a strategy of co-opting criticism through engaging in a rhetoric of reflexivity without allowing for the revision of the underlying knowledge orders, such as the categorisations of objects which the institution employs and reproduces.[13] Her useful critique has been applied to other ethnological museums in Europe. But in a commentary published in 2013, the art curator and critic Vitus Weh regards the current wave of experimentation in ethnological museums as highly productive in terms of institutional self-reflexivity. He argues:

> Nowhere else are new interpretations, arrangements and educational formats sought with more intensity. And nowhere else are new approaches so fundamental … It is foreseeable that changes will be more extensive. At any rate, a differentiation is taking place in the area of ethnology that the standardised institutions of contemporary art can only dream of.[14]

Increased criticism has led to some ethnological museums making space for these debates within their own walls, as the examples mentioned above show. Nevertheless, occasions for in-depth, enduring and interdisciplinary dialogue have been very rare. Despite the broad range of people involved in projects like the Humboldt Lab Dahlem – in which cultural anthropologists talk to scholars from other disciplines, museum insiders converse with temporary curators or museum critics, museum theorists enter into dialogue with museum practitioners, and representatives from institutions engage with independent cultural workers or artists – they are still the exception. We believe what is lacking here is a fundamentally interdisciplinary and inter-institutional form of debate, a debate that may also be – or even needs to be – conflicting at times, as James Clifford suggested when introducing his notion of the contact zone.[15] In his seminal essay, Clifford argues that we should acknowledge the fundamentally conflict-laden character of museum work. By that, he implies, importantly, that museums are spaces of negotiation constituted by relations of power.

This applies equally, we argue, to the spaces where conversations about museums take place, and for the very practices employed in these spaces. They are, as Nora Sternfeld puts it, spaces where actors engage with each other under often unequal conditions.[16] Therefore, the debate needs not only to be interdisciplinary and challenging – we should also attend to the very parameters of how we engage in it, with whom and under which circumstances. This is because we can observe that the disciplinary and institutional divisions between the fields mentioned all too often prevent actors from a more fundamental mutual engagement. We consider this to be a result of what could be called *self-disciplining*: an acceptance of the very limits and boundaries that our respective disciplinary and institutional contexts impose upon us. We think that we should not accept these limits and boundaries, but rather make them visible, contest them and eventually transgress them.

The lack of a 'culture of debate' in the sense mentioned above, it seems, has its roots within the discipline of anthropology or ethnology, as well as in the reality of museum practice. To start with, direct criticism of each other's exhibitions, for example, is generally not very common, as Boris Wastiau, currently director of the Musée d'ethnographie de Genève, has pointed out.[17] This is particularly true for German-speaking ethnological museums, whose exhibitions rarely feature in reviews published in German journals of ethnology or social or cultural anthropology. Secondly, theoretical reflection on ethnological museums lacks institutionalisation in the German-speaking world. There are only two departments of social or cultural anthropology so far that have some continuity in thinking about the history and theory of ethnological collecting and exhibiting: the Institut für Empirische Kulturwissenschaft, Universität Tübingen (Institute of Historical and Cultural Anthropology), and the Institut für Europäische Ethnologie (Institute of European Ethnology), Humboldt-Universität zu Berlin, where the recently founded Centre for Anthropological Research on Museums and Heritage (CARMaH) can be seen as the first attempt to fill this gap in a more profound way. Partly as a consequence of this lack of academic institutionalisation, the most comprehensive historical studies of German ethnological museums published in the past decades came from Anglophone historians[18] and were only later complemented by important work from German scholars.[19]

Thirdly, and in spite of many individual links between museum and university staff, good and productive long-term relationships between museums and universities are not very common, and, moreover, museums and universities rarely co-operate on a longer-term basis.[20] These difficulties seem to persist beyond the discipline of anthropology or ethnology: discussants from different backgrounds apparently feel strong loyalties to their respective fields, which reduces the range of opinions and views that are talked about. Fears of being co-opted (or attacked, for that matter) pre-empt participation in cross-disciplinary events and foster partisan positions. This makes it difficult to open up new avenues of thinking.

Hence, by initiating a debate in a journal, our aim was to bring scholars from different fields together to discuss the changing landscape of ethnological museums in more depth. We invited the postcolonial art historian Christian Kravagna to write a critical essay about the current state of ethnological museums in the German-speaking sphere, writing from the perspective of one of its most prominent postcolonial critics, followed by four responses from the field of (international) social, cultural or museum anthropology, as well as the art field (Wolfgang Kaschuba, Barbara Plankensteiner, Peggy Buth, Philipp Schorch and Noelle Kahanu). In turn, Kravagna had the chance to respond. This format was used in *ZfK* in a very productive way to address recent and often controversial issues that spark an interdisciplinary theoretical debate.

Debates and their formats

Whereas many people, from both the academic and museum fields, saw the debate as fruitful, it may also be seen as indicative of some of the pitfalls of scholarly engagement. Firstly, some of the already-mentioned dichotomisations and antagonisms between museum insiders and outsiders, and between art history and ethnology, continue to structure the debate about ethnological museums. Loyalty to the discussants' constituencies continues to play a big role, and sometimes prevents scholars from exploring unorthodox arguments, or looking beyond established positions. Secondly, arguments often gravitate towards the issue of representation in museums. This made Schorch and Kahanu's contribution entitled 'Anthropology's Interlocutors: Hawai'i Speaking Back to Ethnographic Museums in Europe'[21] key to our debate in the *ZfK* because it went beyond the issue of representation and instead emphasised modes of co-creation, co-curation and intellectual reciprocity. Postcolonial museum critique, as much as it is able to critically reflect upon the process of self-fashioning in Europe and its museums, has yet to embrace more performative and praxiographic approaches. Thirdly, deconstructionist and historicising approaches can at times turn a blind eye to alternative intellectual traditions. A sole emphasis on the colonial dimensions of collections reduces ethnological museums to 'witnesses of colonial violence', displaces other layers of meaning and tends to ignore the agentive powers of collections, for example the ability of objects to act against the very academic and curatorial practices and institutional orders that they have been subjected to.[22] We regard this very resistant capability of collections as related to what this volume's editors have termed 'curatopian'.

Fourthly, in cross-disciplinary and inter-institutional contexts, ethnology or cultural or social anthropology often becomes the target of criticism – termed *Ethnologiekritik* (critique of ethnology) in postcolonial debates. What frequently slips out of sight, however, is anthropology's potential, as well as its own tradition, of critically reflecting on the politics and poetics of ethnography,[23] and hence also of ethnographic museum representation. Since the 'Writing Culture' debate,[24] originally inspired by post-structuralism and literary theory, the practice of ethnography and the specific positioning of ethnographers have been at the centre of self-reflexivity. However, the broad range of theoretical and methodical tools developed in scholarly work is only rarely employed in museum work. One reason may be the aforementioned gap between museums and universities in the field of anthropology or ethnology, as well as diverse preferences among different generations of curators. Another reason may be the culture of positivism in the museum field in which collections are often made to 'stand' for specific cultural contexts rather than to reveal a complex historical field of entanglement, appropriation and mutual dependency.

This brings us to our fifth point: the tendency of museums to incorporate critique without, however, fundamentally attending to its relevance for their own institutional status quo with regard to the politics of display, administrative structures and the museum's engagement with its manifold publics. Politicians as well as representatives of cultural institutions, for example of the Humboldt Forum, increasingly engage in a rhetoric that employs a decidedly postcolonial terminology, thereby mitigating the public demands of activists and scholars alike for critical scrutiny of the conventions guiding the practices of collecting and exhibiting – be they historical or contemporary – and opening up to claims for restitution.[25] As for the Humboldt Forum, terms such as 'dialogue of cultures', 'multiperspectivity', 'change of perspective' or, most recently, 'shared heritage', have gained increased importance in public pronouncements of what is to come in the reconstructed city palace.[26] Yet, the relevance of these terms and concepts in the history of anthropological theorising is barely made visible and reflected upon. When it comes to the much-emphasised collaboration with 'source communities', for example, we are still confronted with a museum politics according to which 'their' (the source communities') interpretative skills are supposed to enrich 'our' (the institution's) curatorial work in dealing with the collections in question, not to mention the problem of falling prey to an essentialist notion of 'voice' and 'perspective' that lies at the heart of the term 'source community'. By this, the concepts in question undergo a subtle shift in meaning: originally introduced into the debate about museums to interrogate and undermine the apparent certainties of 'self' and 'other', they are now used to repel the very criticisms that they sought to address in the first place. This is what Friedrich von Bose has termed 'strategic reflexivity'.[27]

Our sixth and last point concerns 'interdisciplinarity'. Barbara Plankensteiner, in her reply to Kravagna, pointedly argues that ethnological museums are not the only sites in the museum world that need to be decolonised. Objects from elsewhere have not only been *appropriated by* ethnological museums, but they have also been *relegated to* ethnological museums. As an important example, art museums have been historically complicit in creating dichotomies of 'self' and 'other' – in their own institutions, but also in regards to creating the category of 'ethnological' or 'ethnographic' and 'ethnological museum'. This argument speaks to the structural dimensions of the debate. The history of the institution of the museum, as we know it today, is a history of disciplining: of subjecting objects to certain categories, be they geographically defined or otherwise. 'European' and 'non-European' (or 'Western' and 'non-Western' for that matter), 'art' and 'anthropology': these categories seem to be so pervasive and self-evident that we all too often use them in a descriptive and uncritical way even in those debates that aim at deconstructing the very knowledge orders that are so intrinsically tied to them. The opposition between objects of nature and culture is equally contingent, as many important recent studies in the field of the history of science have pointed out.[28] In the critical debates about German (ethnological) museums, this distinction is only slowly, yet increasingly, being paid attention to. On the other hand, the museum has always been an institution of disciplining subjects. Barbara Kirshenblatt-Gimblett's call from twenty-five years ago seems to be as topical as ever: 'The first order of business is therefore to examine critically the conventions guiding ethnographic display, to explicate how displays constitute subjects and with what implications for those who see and those who are seen.'[29] Yet, this also equally accounts for any other museum type.

As is well known, collections (assembled by one individual or on an expedition) have often been distributed across various museums rather wildly and contingently: to ethnological museums, natural history museums, history museums, art museums, city museums and so forth. During their 'lives' as museum objects, they have often been moved several times from one institution to another. Much more critical attention should be paid to past and present *boundary work* in the museum world, concerning both disciplinary boundaries and geographical ones. We need to understand more thoroughly not only how classifications were established and demarcations made, why and by whom, but also how these created inclusions and exclusions. We should also consider the question: which theoretical, ideological, political or economic purposes did these classifications and demarcations serve – be it on an institutional or an individual level? Underlying purposes and interests are revealed even more clearly in moments when classifications were or are questioned, abandoned or overthrown.

In this sense, it is quite peculiar that even at a time of greater self-proclaimed reflexivity, many ethnological museums still chose to follow a mode of representation that separates the world into Europe and its 'Others' (i.e. 'non-Europe', 'extra-Europe') or into world regions and continents respectively. The recent wave of renaming through which, in one way or another, 'ethnological' is replaced by 'world' or 'world culture' does not seem to change the problem that Europe still serves as the unmarked and seemingly non-present signifier of 'the Rest'. The contingencies of these separations and the historical renegotiation of categories like (high) 'art' (popular) 'culture', 'folklore' and 'ethnology' can be seen in Berlin,[30] as well as in many other cities and institutions. On the other hand, the continuous pronouncement of a 'dialogue of cultures' by politicians and institutional representatives, much in common with a multiculturalist discourse, has never, at least in the German context, been accompanied by any real interest in the actual question of political participation. As Kravagna has rightly pointed out, scholars of migration have critiqued the discourse of diversity, tolerance and dialogue for more than twenty years as one that disguises, rather than addresses, questions of power relations.[31]

How to move on from here?

Taking the points sketched out above into consideration, what does this mean for the debate on decolonising ethnological museums in the future? We want to start by pointing to three questions that we think need to be asked in order to keep the conversation generative. Firstly, how much common ground do we actually need in order to discuss things in a productive way? Studies of museums have theorised how the site of an exhibition, its institutional setting, the curatorial voice, and the infrastructure and media employed in its production, all have an impact on the way in which visitors make sense of the 'content' and foster or impede certain perceptions and understandings. We need to continue the debate on decolonising ethnological museums (or, in fact, any museum) with the same sensibility in terms of *how* it is shaped by the sites, structures and media that constitute it. As a consequence, we might have to experiment with the formats through which we engage with each other so that they enable both constructive and conflictive – and in any case productive – dialogue. We see the *ZfK* debate as just one attempt, and certainly only a beginning.

Secondly, even though ethnological museums, of course, require a lot of critical scrutiny, we should at the same time think about what the decolonisation of art museums, history museums, natural history museums and city museums could and should mean and look like, and how we can better interweave the pertinent disciplines and their debates, like ethnology or anthropology, art history, natural history and local or urban history, in our theory and practice. A joint effort to address the issue of museological decolonisation from a multidisciplinary perspective seems indispensable if we want to go beyond mutual accusations. We suggest not only questioning our own and each other's constituencies, institutions and mechanisms of boundary work but having an *un-disciplinary*, maybe even *undisciplined* debate, a debate in which we do not accept the institutional distinctions and separations with which many of us have grown up professionally. In this context, the current celebration of early modern cabinets of curiosity in the disciplines of art, art history and the history of science deserves more attention. Admittedly, by focusing on the interdisciplinary, non-hierarchical, and experimental character of cabinets of curiosities, this celebration often overlooks their colonial and exoticist dimensions.[32] But nevertheless it points out the necessity to think and work with collections in a non-disciplinary – or indeed undisciplined – way.

Thirdly, in order to come back to one of the key questions of this volume: what does this mean for curatorial practice? We would like to argue for a curatorial practice that deliberately and systematically addresses and cuts across disciplinary boundaries and institutional logics of and in museums. In our understanding, the point is not so much to include, for example, African art works in art museums or contemporary art works in ethnological museums. Rather, the order of business should be to curate exhibitions and to engage in co-operation *across* institutional and disciplinary divides: to undermine and unmake these divisions; and by doing so, slowly but steadily, to call into question whether the museum as we know it does actually continue to make sense. We should therefore invest more in creating *undisciplined museums* that reassemble objects and collections of all kinds.

In this endeavour, we should remember that the history of collecting is as much a history of attempts at encyclopaedic collecting as it is of arbitrary and contingent collecting enterprises. If we dare to abandon the idea that curating exhibitions is about exhibiting one's treasures and representing one's own collections, we could more easily embrace a broader notion of exhibition-making: namely, *that exhibitions are above all a means of making an argument in three dimensions.*[33] Such a notion neither takes collections for granted nor elevates them as key, but rather emphasises that curators tell (hi)stories, describe and reflect upon perspectives and positions, and argue cases. Exhibitions not only assemble objects and texts, and use colour, light and other design elements – often used to construct a timeless order of things – but they also carefully lay out meanings and interpretations in space and inspire visitors to navigate these meanings in a time-based, subjective and situational manner. And they do many more things: they work through sensual and bodily experiences of different, not only visual kinds; they suggest or render impossible connections through overview, juxtaposition, focus, selectivity or obstruction of access; thereby, they explore and exploit the directionality and positionality of the visitor as well as of the curator; and finally they provoke the visitor's very visible – not only discursive – opposition to decisions made by curators: be it the visitors' dwelling on and returning to certain elements of the exhibition, or their turning away and leaving out other elements. Therefore, exhibitions have an incredible potential to make curators and visitors engage in a conversation.

This potential approach to curating as presenting an argument and enabling a conversation could also be used to set up a museum that is more willing to endure tensions and debates around its history, collections and activities. The audience of such a 'wild museum'[34] will no longer fall prey to an understanding of a bounded 'local audience' here and distant 'source communities' there. This museum will have an audience that radically cross-cuts such 'imagined communities'. We think that these three avenues – revising the formats of the debate, extending the debate towards other museum types and curating in systematic and radically cross-disciplinary and cross-institutional ways – could lead us further towards the goal of 'curatopia'.

Notes

1 We would like to thank the editors Philipp Schorch and Conal McCarthy for their many insightful comments and for thinking up such a great book project.
2 In Germany, the term *Ethnologie* is used synonymously for the English term (social or cultural) anthropology, while *Anthropologie* denotes physical or bio-anthropology. Only in recent years has *Anthropologie* also been adopted for cultural anthropology as, for example, in *Kulturanthropologie*, which is sometimes called *Europäische Ethnologie*. Similarly, ethnographic museums tend to label themselves 'ethnological' in the German-speaking context and thereby carry on the long history of *Völkerkunde* – as do many university departments. We have therefore chosen to use the terms 'ethnology' and 'ethnological' here when referring to social or cultural anthropology in the German-speaking world.
3 In this regard, two very significant dates were the years 2004, the centenary of the outbreak of the war of anti-colonial resistance in then German South West Africa (today Namibia), and 2005, the centenary of the outbreak of the Maji War in German East Africa. In these and subsequent years, scholars and activists initiated a series of events and publications that raised public awareness about Germany's colonial past. However, only in 2015 did the German government eventually acknowledge the colonial war in Namibia as genocide and took up negotiations with the Namibian government on material redress. In 2016, the Deutsches Historisches Museum (German Historical Museum) opened an exhibition entitled *German Colonialism: Fragments Past and Present*, which testifies to Germany's slow awakening from colonial 'amnesia', as Reinhart Kössler has termed it in *Negotiating the Past* (Windhoek: Gamsberg Macmillan, 2015). See also Stiftung Deutsches Historisches Museum, *German Colonialism: Fragments Past and Present* (Darmstadt: Konrad Theiss, 2016), and in particular Larissa Förster, 'Problematic Provenances', in *ibid*.
4 B. Kazeem, C. Martinz-Turek and N. Sternfeld (eds), *Das Unbehagen im Museum: Postkoloniale Museologien* (Vienna: Turia und Kant, 2009); Artefakte//

anti-humboldt (eds), 'Afterlives', special issue of *darkmatter Journal*, www.
darkmatter101.org; see also the website of the campaign *NoHumboldt21!*, www.
no-humboldt21.de/. Accessed 10 March 2017.

5 See, among others, Peggy Buth's work on Belgium's colonial legacy in the Congo
as presented at the Royal Museum of Central Africa in Tervuren: P. Buth, *Desire
in Representation: Travelling through the Musée Royale* (Berlin: argobooks,
2008), as well as several projects in the Humboldt Lab Dahlem, see Humboldt
Lab Dahlem (eds), *The Laboratory Principle: Museum Experiments in the
Humboldt Lab Dahlem* (Berlin: Nicolai, 2015).

6 S. Leeb, 'Contemporary Art and/in/versus/about the Ethnological Museum',
in *darkmatter Journal* 11 (2013) www.darkmatter101.org/. Accessed 10 March
2017. C. Kravagna, 'The Preserves of Colonialism: The World in the Museum',
EIPCP (2008), http://eipcp.net/transversal/0708/kravagna/en. Accessed 10
March 2017. V. Schmidt-Linsenhoff, 'Institutionelle Selbstkritik und visueller
Diskurs. Ästhetische Effekte in der Neuaufstellung des Rautenstrauch-Joest-
Museums', *Paideuma*, 60 (2014), 259–72.

7 For an ethnographic analysis of the Humboldt Forum's planning process, see
F. von Bose, *Das The Humboldt-Forum: Eine Ethnografie seiner Planung* (Berlin:
Kadmos, 2016). See also F. von Bose, 'The Making of Berlin's Humboldt-Forum:
Negotiating History and the Cultural Politics of Place', *Darkmatter* 11 (2013).
www.darkmatter101.org/site/. Accessed 10 March 2017.

8 S. Macdonald, *Memorylands: Heritage and Identity in Europe Today* (London
and New York: Routledge, 2013); M. Rothberg, *Multidirectional Memory:
Remembering the Holocaust in the Age of Decolonization* (Stanford: Stanford
University Press, 2009); K.E. Till, *The New Berlin: Memory, Politics, Place*
(Minneapolis: University of Minnesota Press, 2005).

9 This resulted in the exhibition *Foreign Exchange (Or the Stories You Wouldn't
Tell a Stranger)* (2014–2015), prior to which the museum organised several
'think tanks', gathering experts from around the world to discuss how to
best engage in a postcolonial dialogue and display politics. See C. Deliss and
Y. Mutumba (eds), *Foreign Exchange (Or the Stories You Wouldn't Tell a
Stranger)* (Zürich: Diaphanes, 2014).

10 The most far-reaching example may have been the exhibition *EigenSinn* (2011)
after the reopening of the Museum of Cultures, which explicitly turned the
museum into a space of reflection about ethnological categories (Museum der
Kulturen Basel 2011).

11 Humboldt Lab Dahlem, *The Laboratory Principle*; Bose, *Das Humboldt-Forum*.

12 For a description see www.transcript-verlag.de/zeitschriften/zfk-zeitschrift-
fuer-kulturwissenschaften. Accessed 15 January 2017. We would once again like
to thank the editors for inviting us to moderate the debate, as well as our guest
authors for taking part and discussing some of the issues we have touched upon
in this chapter.

13 N. Sternfeld, 'Erinnerung als Entledigung: Transformismus im Musée du Quai
Branly in Paris', in Sternfeld, Kazeem and Martinz-Turek (eds), *Das Unbehagen
im Museum*, pp. 61–75.

14 'Nirgends sonst wird so stark an Neubewertungen, an Neuordnungen und
an neuen Vermittlungsformaten gebastelt wie hier. Und nirgends sonst
sind die Neuansätze so tiefgreifend … Dass die Veränderungen deshalb
weiterreichen werden, ist bereits abzusehen. Zumindest ist derweil im Bereich
der "Völkerkunde" eine experimentelle Ausdifferenzierung im Gange, von der

die weitgehend standardisierten Institutionen der zeitgenössischen Kunst nur träumen können.' V. Weh, 'Die produktive Krise der Völkerkundemuseen', *Artmagazine*, 17 June 2013, www.artmagazine.cc/content69897.html. Accessed 10 March 2017.

15 J. Clifford, *Routes: Travel and Translation in the Late Twentieth Century* (Cambridge, MA: Harvard University Press, 1997), pp. 188–219.

16 N. Sternfeld, *Kontaktzonen der Geschichtsvermittlung. Transnationales Lernen über den Holocaust in der postnazistischen Migrationsgesellschaft* (Vienna: Zaglossus, 2013).

17 B. Wastiau, 'Comment: The Skeptical Commentator', *Museum Management and Curatorship*, 23:3 (2008), 220–3.

18 H.G. Penny and M. Bunzl (eds), *Worldly Provincialism: German Anthropology in the Age of Empire* (Ann Arbour: University of Michigan Press, 2003); H.G. Penny, *Objects of Culture: Ethnology and Ethnographic Museums in Imperial Germany* (Chapel Hill: University of North Carolina Press, 2002); Andrew Zimmerman, *Anthropology and Antihumanism in Imperial Germany* (Chicago: University of Chicago Press, 2001).

19 A. Laukötter, *Von der 'Kultur' zur 'Rasse' – vom Objekt zum Körper? Völkerkundemuseen und ihre Wissenschaften zu Beginn des 20. Jahrhunderts* (Bielefeld: transcript, 2007); B. Lange, *Echt, Unecht, Lebensecht: Menschenbilder im Umlauf* (Berlin: Kadmos Kulturverlag, 2006).

20 L. Förster, 'Öffentliche Kulturinstitution, internationale Forschungsstätte und postkoloniale Kontaktzone. Was ist ethno am ethnologischen Museum?', in T. Bierschenk, M. Krings and C. Lentz (eds), *Perspektivwechsel: Ethnologie im 21. Jahrhundert* (Berlin: Reimer, 2013), pp. 189–210. Cf. also M. Kraus and K. Noack (eds), *Quo vadis, Völkerkundemuseum? Aktuelle Debatten zu ethnologischen Sammlungen in Museen und Universitäten* (Bielefeld: transcript, 2014).

21 P. Schorch and N.M.K.Y. Kahanu, 'Anthropology's Interlocutors: Hawai'i Speaking Back to Ethnographic Museums in Europe', *Zeitschrift für Kulturwissenschaften*, 1 (2015), 110–13.

22 Recent attempts to institutionalise theoretical reflection on ethnographic collections like the Research Center for Material Culture in Leiden remind us of the diverse approaches to material culture that have been explored in the past three decades.

23 J. Clifford and G.E. Marcus (eds), *Writing Culture: The Poetics and Politics of Ethnography* (Berkeley: University of California Press, 1986); I. Karp and S.D. Lavine (eds), *Exhibiting Cultures: The Poetics and Politics of Museum Display* (Washington, DC: Smithsonian Institution, 1991); in the German-speaking context, see E. Berg and M. Fuchs (eds), *Kultur, soziale Praxis, Text: Die Krise der ethnographischen Repräsentation* (Frankfurt am Main: Suhrkamp, 1993).

24 See Clifford and Marcus, *Writing Culture*.

25 For a recent example see H. Parzinger, 'Geteiltes Erbe ist doppeltes Erbe', *Frankfurter Allgemeine Zeitung*, 241 (16 October 2015), 11.

26 On the contested phrase 'shared heritage', see Sandahl and Clifford, Chapters 5 and 7 below.

27 Von Bose, *Das Humboldt-Forum*, 233–60.

28 B. Latour, *Reassembling the Social: An Introduction to Actor-Network-Theory* (Oxford: Oxford University Press, 2005); T. Bennett and C. Healy (eds) *Assembling Culture* (London and New York: Routledge, 2011).

29 B. Kirshenblatt-Gimblett, 'Objects of Ethnography', in I. Karp and S.D. Lavine (eds), *Exhibiting Cultures: The Poetics and Politics of Museum Display* (Washington, DC: Smithsonian Institution, 1991), 386–443, 434.

30 S. Kamel, *Wege zur Vermittlung von Religionen in Berliner Museen. Black Kaaba meets White Cube* (Wiesbaden: VS Verlag für Sozialwissenschaften, 2004), 42f.

31 C. Kravagna, 'Vom ethnologischen Museum', 97.

32 D. Collet, *Die Welt in der Stube: Begegnungen mit Außereuropa in Kunstkammern der frühen Neuzeit* (Göttingen: Vandenhoeck & Ruprecht, 2007).

33 The notion of curating as 'making an argument in three-dimensional space' is based on one of the author's, Larissa Förster's, own experience and observations as a co-curator of two major temporary exhibitions that not only intended to cut across disciplines like anthropology and history, or anthropology and art, but that also addressed contested or much-debated subjects like colonialism and its memory, or African mega-cities and their 'informality'. See L. Förster, D. Henrichsen and M. Bollig (eds), *Namibia – Deutschland: Eine geteilte Geschichte. Widerstand, Gewalt, Erinnerung* (Munich: Edition Minerva, 2004), and K. Pinther, L. Förster and C. Hanussek (eds), *Afropolis: City, Media, Art* (Johannesburg: Jacana, 2011).

34 In her study of amateur museums, Angela Janelli uses the term 'wild museum' in a different sense: A. Janelli, *Wilde Museen: Zur Museologie des Amateurmuseums* (Bielefeld: transcript, 2012). See also Lythberg, Ngata and Salmond, Chapter 14 below.

4

Walking the fine line:
From Samoa with Love? at the
Museum Fünf Kontinente, Munich

Hilke Thode-Arora

This chapter explores the conceptual planning, the organisation and the reception of the exhibition *From Samoa with Love? Samoan Travellers in Germany, 1895–1911* at the Museum Fünf Kontinente in Munich, Germany, in 2014. It does so by taking into consideration competing obligations among the Samoan descendants and community, the responses of mainstream Munich museum visitors with no prior knowledge of *fa'a Samoa* (the Samoan way) and the expectations of the Bavarian government, who strictly controlled costs but wanted large audiences. Museums are not as free to create, or are as powerful, as is often assumed by outsiders and critics.[1] Being the curator responsible for this exhibition meant juggling positions, demands and interests in a setting affected by Samoan perspectives and claims, German audiences' pre-knowledge and viewing habits, structural constraints imposed by the Bavarian museum administration system, and even the Foreign Office and diplomatic agendas. Trying to meet these contradictory demands and to reconcile them with my own academic and ethical ideas of curatorship indeed meant walking a fine line, as the following personal account shows.

The background

Ethnic shows[2] were a widespread form of entertainment all over the Western(-dominated)[3] world in the late nineteenth and early twentieth centuries: non-European people were recruited to perform in Western spectacles in front of paying audiences and to show what were considered 'typical pursuits' of their cultures of origin. Several of these shows came from Samoa, and, for example, toured the United States, and there were three Samoan shows organised by two German brothers, that toured Germany and Central Europe. Ethnic shows are a very complex phenomenon incorporating a wide continuum of agency from forced to voluntary recruitment, from cruel treatment by the impresarios to professional showmanship and assertiveness on the side of the performers, from Western fantasies to non-European assertiveness and influence on what was presented to the

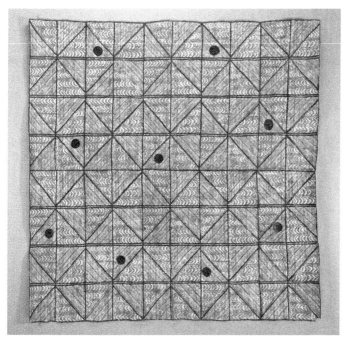

4.1 *Siapo*, 192 x 185 cm (MFK inv.-no. 10-345): one of the gifts Tamasese gave to Prince Regent Luitpold in October 1910. Museum Fünf Kontinente, Munich, Germany.

audiences.[4] In any case, however, ethnic shows are a highly sensitive and ethically charged subject which raises the question of whether an exhibition on this topic should be done at all, and, furthermore, how to deal with artefacts connected with the shows.

Two-thirds of the Samoan collections in the Museum Fünf Kontinente (Five Continents Museum) in Munich originate from the Marquardt brothers who were the impresarios of the three shows that toured Germany and Central Europe between 1895 and 1911. Fritz (1862–?) lived in Samoa with his Samoan-French wife Marie Denise Devère, and Carl (1860–1916) lived in Berlin and dealt in ethnographic objects that were supplied by his brother in Samoa. Part of the Samoan collection, in addition to the Marquardt pieces, is comprised of state gifts, which were presented to the Bavarian royal family by one of the most important high chiefs, Tupua Tamasese Lealofi. Tamasese, however, had come to Bavaria with one of these ethnic shows.

The research project

In a wider context, building on Jürgen Habermas, it could be argued that museums ought to be democratic, participatory spheres.[5] Ethnology-anthropology museums are, moreover, profoundly cross-cultural spaces, answering to Western and non-Western models and world views which attempt to classify and explain the world, but of course the Western academic worldview has been the dominant one, neglecting, if not excluding, Indigenous views.[6] It should be possible to reconcile Western academic criteria and the cultural sensitivities of the populations which museums work for, including source communities, as is the declared goal of the Jean-Marie-Tjibaou Cultural Centre in New Caledonia, for example.[7] Indeed, this is the aim of this chapter, and this volume.

My role in a three-year research project funded by the Fritz Thyssen Foundation was to contextualise the Samoan collection in Munich. Objects in all cultures, even in Europe with its concept of 'art for art's sake', embody wider social connections; it has been argued then that collecting is the result of relationships.[8] So, one of my aims from the beginning was not just to put the pieces in context in terms of their materials, how they were made and so forth, which are the basic tools of the museum anthropologist, but also to reconstruct and possibly renew the relationships underlying the group of objects now in Germany.

The research combined several approaches. The first step was the identification of Marquardt collections in other German museums, followed by a thorough inspection of every single piece and its documentation. The second step consisted of the careful reconstruction of the route and stops on the tour of the three ethnic shows from Samoa along with their available information. This proved to be time-consuming as it meant locating and working through archival material from most of the places where the tour stopped, consisting of hundreds of newspaper articles, correspondence, posters, historical photos and the like. As a next step, a deeper understanding was necessary of the historical setting in which the recruiting and touring of the ethnic shows took place, which meant working thoroughly through archival source material from the period that was spread across Berlin, Samoa and Aotearoa New Zealand. The Marquardt-organised Samoan shows toured Germany and Europe from 1895 to 1897, 1900 to 1901 and 1910 to 1911. This period covered the time of the tripartite government and the German colonial era in Western Samoa. In simplified terms,[9] these years were characterised by three powers – the United States, Great Britain and Germany – competing for influence over Samoa, which held true even after West Samoa became a German colony in 1900; while, on the Samoan side, the holders of the three highest titles and their followers were in competition with each other. In short, and again very simplified, terms, the Western and the Samoan powers strategically tried to take advantage of each other, and formed temporary and shifting alliances. As all three Samoa shows were organised by the Marquardt brothers, it was possible to compare them by tracing the links to the German and Samoan protagonists' interdependencies within the colonial networks in Berlin, the German, British and US American expatriate societies in Samoa, and Samoan society in the respective time periods.

While I was in the middle of the project and not yet thinking of an exhibition, and with all of this research and the wider theoretical debate[10] in mind, it became very clear to me that the Western perspectives on the Samoan ethnic shows, and on the artefacts that came to the Museum Fünf Kontinente through the Marquardt brothers and Tamasese, would just be one side of the story. Accordingly, in my last step, again in a long and thorough search for the pieces of the jigsaw puzzle that made up the sources, I managed to reconstruct the name of every single Samoan man, woman and child who had travelled to Germany between 1895 and 1911 with the Marquardt brothers, and to match these names with the faces in the historical photos of the show. This was the starting point in reconstructing their villages of origin and locating descendants in Samoa, Aotearoa New Zealand and Australia whom I could ask about Samoan perspectives. These conversations provoked a number of genealogical stories, oral history narratives of the Samoan travellers' lives before and after their participation in the tours, and their impressions while in Germany. There were also material reminiscences: travellers' graves which could still be located, or people depicted in photos of the historical ethnic show later appearing as elderly people in the family albums of their descendants.

In the European sources, mainly stemming from the late nineteenth and early twentieth centuries, artefacts were clearly seen as material specimens of Samoan cultural traits. Carl Marquardt had sales brochures printed and sent to the museums as potential buyers. He claimed that he could offer 'almost everything the Samoans of our time have ever produced' and that, upon request, he could provide 'additional pieces with different patterns'. In the brochures, the artefacts were divided into categories like 'fishing', 'barkcloth', 'wooden objects' and the like.[11] In essence, Carl Marquardt, as well as his museum customers, viewed the artefacts in terms of the paradigm espoused in nineteenth-century anthropology: that a culture could be fully grasped in its material and spiritual expressions. *Ethnographica* were thus seen as pieces of evidence for certain cultural aspects, and as being replaceable with other similar and equivalent samples.

As far as the ethnic shows were concerned (and this is the dominant discourse in academic circles even today), Western sources from the same period suggest that Samoan people were recruited to entertain German audiences and were meant to be impressed by Germany's military superiority – a perception of a very hierarchical power structure with dominant Western colonial powers on one end and dominated, if not oppressed, Samoans on the other. According to European, Australian and Samoan newspapers of the time, it was the Marquardts who recruited and took 'their' Samoans to Germany. The Marquardts tried to appeal to a German audience in terms of a romanticised and gendered image of the Pacific, as can be seen, for example, in posters and photos: the Samoan women, considered untainted by too many civilised constraints, as well as extremely beautiful and sensual from a Western male perspective, were the main attraction. This was also the way German audiences generally understood these shows, among them a number of artists[12] who got inspiration for their own works by admiring the Samoan belles.

The Samoan narratives, however, were very different. As descendants pointed out to me quite definitely, in all three ethnic shows there were persons of rank who travelled to Germany, for example in 1900 Te'o Tuvale (1855–1919) and in 1910 Tupua Tamasese Lealofi (1863–1915). Te'o and Tamasese, apparently like many Samoans, perceived the ethnic show tour as a kind of *malaga*,[13] or diplomatic visit. In Germany, the high chiefs did not of course participate in the performances, but supervised them. As persons of rank, they expected to meet German dignitaries and to engage with them in the exchange of gifts and other representational duties. Accordingly, although not given credit in the Western sources, it was not the Marquardts who in 1900 selected and recruited the participants, but Te'o himself: he chose a *taupou*, daughter of a holder of a high title who was versed in Samoan protocol, as well as talented singers and dancers, many yet untitled young men among them, who knew how to represent their culture. In 1910, Tamasese also carefully chose his entourage: he was accompanied by a number of good young dancers and singers from chiefly families and by Aiono, his oratory chief who had already held this position under Tamasese's father, the former title holder.

When rereading the European sources between the lines after receiving this information from the Samoan descendants, the Samoan perspective clearly made sense: Te'o and Tamasese gave official speeches, met many German dignitaries and exchanged gifts with them. One of these presents, obtained from Emperor Wilhelm II who received the Samoans in his castle, is still kept today as an heirloom in Te'o's family: a gold watch with the name *Te'o Tuvale* engraved on it. Tamasese met Prince Regent Luitpold and Prince Ludwig of Bavaria in Munich and exchanged presents with them. As the Museum Fünf Kontinente is the state museum of the Federal State of Bavaria, these gifts were given by the royal household to the museum. Contrary to the European notion of objects as specimens for Samoan cultural traits, and, apart from those objects either deliberately commissioned by or sold to Fritz Marquardt, the artefacts that high-ranking people gave away that ended up in museums were seen by Samoans as gifts in an exchange intended to create and validate important relations.

The exhibition: constraints and limitations

Although all Samoan descendants were adamant in stressing their ancestors' involvement, strategic planning and authority during their travels to Germany, the very idea of ethnic shows is tainted by a slightly undignified and primitivist overtone from a present-day Western perspective. Furthermore, in the case of Tamasese, it could be clearly shown that he had been lured to Germany under the false pretence of a diplomatic visit.[14] Although some of the damage done was partly repaired through his own initiative and that of German supporters, resulting in him giving political speeches, getting better living quarters for himself and his family, and meeting with dignitaries (including the German Emperor, as Tamasese had intended in the first place), yet this chapter of German–Samoan history clearly had its dubious side. Under these circumstances, and being such a sensitive issue, the first decision to be made in developing the exhibition was whether the findings of the research project should be highlighted and popularised in the form of a museum exhibition, or should rather be 'hidden' in a publication mostly accessible to academics and a few interested readers. My curatorial stance in this matter was that there is no justification in not acknowledging the wrongs of the past; on the contrary, making them public can be the first step for reconciliation and healing.

Before discussing the conceptual planning and involvement in the exhibition from the Samoan side, it ought to be reiterated that museums are more constrained in creating exhibitions than the literature often assumes; institutions and their personnel, even with the best intentions, have structural restrictions.[15] In the case of this exhibition, the two most obvious ones were time – only six months of preparation – and money: the Museum Fünf Kontinente had, and still has, a very limited annual budget of €90,000 from which *all* exhibition installations, lectures, festivals and events have to be funded. Finding a sponsor for additional funds was severely impeded by the time limit.

Another structural constraint is that the museum is located far away from the Pacific. In Munich, prior knowledge of the Pacific, let alone of fa'a Samoa, is not to be expected from the general public or regular museumgoers. Unlike, for example, the Museum of New Zealand Te Papa Tongarewa in Wellington, whose curatorial practices are informed on a daily base by nearby communities of Māori and Pacific people,[16] the Pacific hardly ever figures in German media. Furthermore, being so far away makes travelling to the Pacific too expensive and strenuous for most tourists; accordingly, only a tiny minority of Germans have ever been there or have had firsthand contact with Pacific people. A further impediment is to be found in the legal hierarchy of the museum's administrative structure within the Federal State of Bavaria, which means that the museum director reports directly to the government of Bavaria. The Bavarian Ministry of Culture basically expects the museum to create exhibitions that are attractive to the public and earn revenue from the entrance fees, but with low setup costs. It is forbidden to exceed the given budget, which has to be signed off for every single exhibition proposal submitted for approval. In the museum, there has to be a curator who works with the whole team, but who is individually held responsible by the museum director and the Bavarian government respectively. This was my role as a curator, which indeed meant walking a fine line. My challenge was to create an exhibition:

- that would bring Samoa and the history of the Samoan ethnic shows to German visitors who had no prior knowledge of Samoa or the Pacific

- that would be attractive for German and Samoan visitors alike, especially for the Samoan travellers' descendants
- that would be authorised by the Samoans involved, and which tackled a very sensitive historical issue
- that did not exceed the budget and time limits.

The exhibition: conceptual planning and organisation

An exhibition is a staging of ideas; it creates meaning and presents an argument.[17] Seeing museums as democratic and cross-cultural spaces in Habermas's sense,[18] the ideal situation would have been to have Samoan curators represent Samoan perspectives. One of the restraints that kept me and the team at the Museum Fünf Kontinente from doing this on a large-scale basis as much as we would have liked to was the limited time for planning the exhibition; applying to foundations who would have financed travel costs was just not possible in six months, nor could private sponsors be found. But even if this had been achievable, whom should we have invited? In Samoa, *matai*, the elected heads of extended families, are vested with the authority and prerogative of interpretation of genealogical issues. There were roughly seventy-five people who had come to Germany with the Samoan ethnic shows between 1895 and 1911,[19] and consequently this involved a considerable number of present-day matai descended from those people. Inviting just a few of them would have risked insulting the ones not asked. Genealogical interpretations are a highly complex issue in Samoa: as they form a way of legitimising access to land and other prerogatives, genealogies can be highly contested. Some parts of genealogical narratives are not shared with outsiders, or only on special occasions.

Competing versions of genealogies and narratives was a relevant concern prior to writing the book on the Samoan travellers and preparing the exhibition as well; the most complex case circled around the taupou in one of the shows. In each of the ethnic shows, there were several female travellers who were taupou in their respective villages. However, during the performances in Germany, only one of the women wore the regalia of a taupou and acted as one. While in two shows, even after more than one hundred years, it was very clear who the highest-ranking women were who would have acted as taupou, in one of the shows this became a contested issue during the research. The German sources gave only one name, which was supported by that woman's descendants in Samoa, but another family of descendants made the very plausible point that their grandmother was the daughter of a man with a very high chiefly title, and thus she, in their reading, must have been the taupou. None of the respective descendants could categorically identify one of the women in the ethnic show photos as their own ancestor. Both matai were adamant that the woman in taupou attire must be the one in question.

So then, what could a curator do to deal with these contending histories and sensitivities that were still an issue in the present day? The solution

I found with matai of both families was the following: the book and the exhibition gave both women's names as alternatives and possibilities and explained the reasons and sources for these claims. Furthermore, with the idea of reconciling Western and Samoan systems of knowledge as in the Tjibaou Cultural Centre previously mentioned, I made the offer to both families to bring in a well-known forensic specialist in Germany. This woman, whom I expected to be neutral as she lives so far away from the Southern Hemisphere, works on age-morphing photos of missing persons for the police. The idea was that she could compare the photos from the show of the young taupou with family photos, provided by the matai, of the respective women in old age. Both matai wanted this to happen, were reassured by my suggestion that the results would be just for them and me to know, and would not be published in the book or exhibition – in the end, this is what happened.

All the text about the people who had travelled to Germany with the ethnic shows was authorised by their descendants and/or the respective matai before I put it in the exhibition or published it in the book. Still, the question remained how to involve Samoan perspective without being able to invite the matai as co-curators. One of my ideas, which some of the matai warmly embraced, was to have them record a spoken commentary on their respective ancestors, which could be heard at an audio station in the exhibition. If a large number of matai could not be brought to Munich for practical reasons, what about inviting other guest curators, for example members of the Samoan diaspora communities? In all of Munich, however, there are only two Samoan sisters. They were involved in many stages of the exhibition, but are not descendants of the travellers. Furthermore, very early in the project I had got in touch with Samoan communities in Germany, Austria and Switzerland who engaged with and supported the exhibition in many different ways. Again, none of these people were the travellers' descendants, and the input they gave was concentrated on the opening of the exhibition and its supporting public programme while it was on display.

As it proved impossible in practice under the circumstances to invite all the matai speaking for the Samoan travellers and their descendants, another option was to look for Samoan authorities representing all of, or at least large parts of, the nation of Samoa. I went to great lengths to discuss the project with holders of the three highest Samoan titles, the Malietoa, Mata'afa and Tamasese title. Once we had received their backing and support, the ultimate official validation of the research project and exhibition came when the person with the highest political rank, the head of the State of Samoa (who is the present holder of the Tamasese title), graciously agreed to be the patron for the project and exhibition and timed his state visit to Germany so that he could open the exhibition in person. Tupua Tamasese Efi is also the grandson of Tupua Tamasese Lealofi, who came to Germany in 1910, and who had exchanged gifts with the Bavarian royal family, which now form parts of the Samoan collection in the Museum Fünf Kontinente. From the beginning, he had taken a keen interest in the project and exhibition.

Although neither Samoan dignitaries of the highest titles nor members of the Samoan diaspora in German-speaking countries nor matai who descended from the Samoan travellers actually came to Munich to act as guest curators, they still informed the exhibition in many ways, for example by suggesting what to stress in label texts on their ancestors, or how to counteract diplomatic regulations prescribed by the German Foreign Office during the exhibition opening.[20] To give a Samoan perspective even broader coverage, I invited an artist of Samoan background, Michel Tuffery, to create his own space in the exhibition, commenting on and speaking back to this episode of Samoan–German history. I got to know Michel Tuffery[21] during the research project as he addresses the German-Samoan colonial period in his art, especially in his *Siamani-Samoa* series, which is grounded in deep historical research on Samoan–German history. Furthermore, a few years earlier, Tuffery had visited the Museum Fünf Kontinente and taken a deep interest in the Marquardt collection from Samoa. In particular, the *selu* (combs) had inspired him to create his own defamiliarised version of combs, as well as a series of paintings that picked up on elements from historical photographs taken during colonial times. The combs, as well as the paintings of *Siamani-Samoa*, were enhanced with iconic animals, artefacts and buildings important in the Samoan and/or German contexts. Tuffery most graciously contributed his own exhibition *Siamani-Samoa* to *From Samoa with Love?* pro bono, otherwise his participation would not have been possible under the financial and time constraints. Yet, as indicated earlier when considering the option of inviting some matai instead of all matai, this was not met with positive reception everywhere: another artist of Samoan descent was unhappy about *not* having been invited as well, but the museum would simply not have been able to meet the expenses thereby incurred.

As he dealt mainly with Aotearoa New Zealand, Australian and Pacific audiences, it was hard in the beginning for Tuffery to appreciate that German audiences had mostly no prior knowledge about fa'a Samoa, tattooing or the kava ceremony, and their cultural significance. In guided tours for the press, an artist's talk in the museum, as well as in the book chapter on his art and in the exhibition texts, he explained his concepts in detail. Without this contextualisation, the symbolic clues in his work would have been lost on the overwhelmingly German audience. Participating in the spatial design of the exhibition, Tuffery opened up a number of visual axes and vistas, some of which we as the museum and design team had already planned, some of which we had not. His painted portraits of Tamasese, for example, would engage on a visual axis with Tamasese's historical portraits in photos or posters of the ethnic shows. The German visitors did not notice this unless it was pointed out to them. The exhibition had a number of Samoan visitors during the (European) summer months, however, and to them this hang was immediately understandable, as was, for example, the symbolism of the *manumea* bird.[22]

As for my own conceptual ideas as a curator, in order to make this exhibition a site of cultural mediation, I faced the double task of making

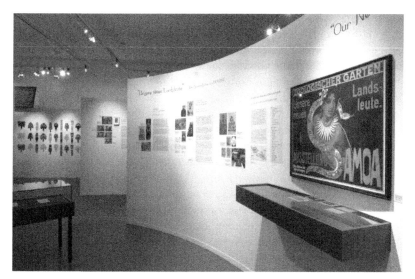

4.2 One of the vista axes in the exhibition *From Samoa with Love?*: Michel Tuffery's acrylic and wooden *selu* in the end part of the exhibition engaging with the section *Our new compatriots* on the 1900–1901 ethnic show travellers from Samoa. Museum Fünf Kontinente, Munich, Germany.

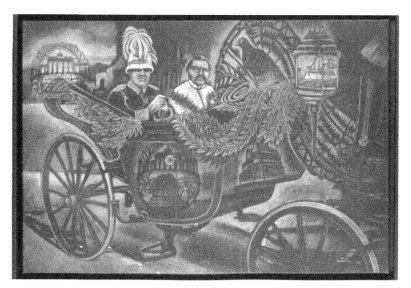

4.3 Michel Tuffery's art work *From Mulinu'u to Berlin*, defamiliarising a well-known historical photo of Tupua Tamasese Lealofi and Wilhelm Solf in a coach about to meet emperor Wilhelm: iconic buildings like the Brandenburg gate in Berlin and Tamasese's fale tele, the manumea and wooden selu, the emperor's yacht from the German-Samoan stamps and the German courthouse in Apia are interwoven with the original depiction; contrary to the historical photo, Tamasese has the 'ie toga (fine mats) with him which he is about to present to the emperor. Museum Fünf Kontinente, Munich, Germany.

the presentation acceptable for a Samoan audience, especially the descendants of the Samoan travellers, but also for a more or less unversed German audience who would need a lot of context and subtle guidance. There was another dilemma: many German visitors enjoy highly staged displays as a form of multi-sensory info-tainment, but this might have seemed disrespectful towards Samoan culture and risked association with stereotypes of the Pacific which are eternally caught in the ethnographic present. We addressed this problem by presenting a rather sober display in the section on fa'a Samoa, focusing on text and only a few exemplary key objects, such as a kava bowl or a *fue* (fly whisk) as indicators of rank and social structure. Photographs of today's modern Samoa and Samoan diaspora communities were grouped around this introductory display to counteract any images of a romanticised past. For the corresponding chapter in the book, I invited a high-ranking matai to write about fa'a Samoa. In the exhibition, the sections on the three ethnic shows were presented as a mixture of texts along with the artefacts proved to be directly connected with the respective show or its actors, as well as a great number of visual documents like historical photographs of the shows and their protagonists, posters, newspaper articles and the like. Scenography, however, was exclusively reserved for those sections which dealt with the European imagination: the section on ethnic shows as a phenomenon of late nineteenth and early twentieth centuries' exhibitionary business was designed as a ticket counter, modelled after historical photographs of the ticket counters at the shows, and an adjacent dark box-like chamber with dramatic light effects which could be imagined as a show room or stage. The section on European fantasies and their correlation

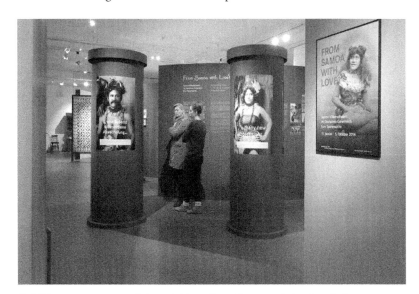

4.4 The entrance area of the exhibition *From Samoa with Love?* with the portraits of the travellers on Litfass-style columns. Museum Fünf Kontinente, Munich, Germany.

with the Samoa shows, mainly consisting of showcases and movable walls with texts, centred on a kitschy staged Pacific 'island' with artificial palm tree and deck chair which at the same time formed a rest area in the exhibition; historical German novels depicting a romantic Samoa, but also works by present-day Samoan writers, Albert Wendt and Sia Figiel among them, invited visitors to take a break and form their own pictures of German fantasies, as well as Samoan realities and perspectives.

To stress the Indigenous actor-centred approach of the project but simultaneously allude to the exoticising aspect of the spectacle, the entrance of the exhibition was half-blocked[23] by three round advertising pillars of the Litfass kind,[24] which were popular when ethnic shows were in full swing in Germany, and which are still used today. Each of them had a large portrait photograph of a different Samoan protagonist from the three different shows, and a quote in which he or she had commented on the trip to Germany according to the narratives passed on to the descendants. The exhibition was designed in a spiral form, forcing the visitor to pass the four outward sections on fa'a Samoa, colonial history, the Marquardt brothers and ethnic shows as a show-business phenomenon around 1900, formed by closely spaced movable walls and showcases, before moving into the wide inner space focusing on each of the three ethnic shows. The section on German fantasies, presenting works by late nineteenth-century and early twentieth-century writers and painters inspired by the Samoan shows, and the kitsch 'island', were in the centre of the spiral. Immediately adjacent, but with vistas and view axes through open spaces, was Tuffery's section which acted as the concluding commentary.

The exhibition: reception

The meeting between Tupua Tamasese Lealofi and Prince Regent Luitpold in 1910 took place at the fringes of the Oktoberfest where the ethnic show was performed; both dignitaries exchanged gifts, and the Samoan presents are part of the collection of the Museum Fünf Kontinente today. I felt that it was extremely important to admit, and reconcile, the dubious circumstances of Tamasese Lealofi's visit about one hundred years ago. Accordingly, apart from the government of Bavaria's official VIP programme, the museum team saw to it that Tamasese and present-day members of the Bavarian royal family would meet, this time under absolutely dignified circumstances. The contact was greatly facilitated by the present head of the royal family being a member of the Association of Friends of the Museum Fünf Kontinente. Visits with key players in Bavarian technology of potential interest for Samoa today, and with descendants of Germans important in Samoan–German history, also took place to the mutual satisfaction of the Samoan and German parties.

Apart from the Samoan delegation accompanying the head of state and members of the diaspora communities in German-speaking countries, a number of Samoan visitors, travelling in Europe to meet family or attend cultural and business events, attended the exhibition during its run (30 January – 30 November 2014). Word of the exhibition had already spread on the night of the opening through news and social media to the Southern Hemisphere, especially Samoa. Some matai sent Samoan relatives or trusted German friends to see for themselves and tell them about it. Most of the comments received from the Samoan side were favourable. A number of people commended what they termed the personal aspect of the display; in their opinion, having the names and villages of the travellers identified in the labels and historical photos stood out from other exhibitions with historical photographs from Samoa where this was not the case and which thus could not be linked to the Samoan present.

Criticism came especially from one matai, who in an exhibition text on the general colonial history of Samoa, in which his ancestor played an important role, would have liked me to have shown him to be of even greater political relevance. This was, however, counteracted by a descendant of a competing matai. The two matais' different views were again expressed at an international conference where I gave a talk on the exhibition, and where members of both of the extended families were present, culminating in finely tuned displays of their respective rank, but also avoidance of open conflict. On the other hand, some matai explicitly lauded the fact that I as a non-Samoan had curated this exhibition: in their view, I could strive for an impartiality that many Samoans, as part of contending title-holder factions, could not.

As a curatorial exercise, this show realised the claim that exhibitions ought to be understood as sites of cultural mediation, negotiating competing truths, and that they should even aim to be troubling by engaging with complexities, thus opening space for conversation and debate. This happened mainly through presenting Samoan perspectives to some parts of the German audience: in every single one of the many guided tours I took, the negotiating of competing Western and Samoan 'truths' during the travels of the ethnic shows, but even today, was an eye-opener to many viewers. On the other hand, there were clearly a number of German visitors who found it very troubling and irritating that Samoan travellers in the ethnic show were depicted as self-assertive actors and not as victims in a colonial situation.[25] To my great pleasure, the research project, book, and exhibition seem in many ways not to be the end, but just the beginning. There are a number of Samoan people who have seen the historical photographs in the book, discovered ancestors of their own among the travellers and are now sharing their stories beyond the book and exhibition.

Notes

1   C. McCarthy, *Exhibiting Māori: A History of Colonial Cultures of Display* (Oxford and New York: Berg, 2007); C. McCarthy, '"Our Works of Ancient Times":

History, Colonisation and Agency at the 1906–7 New Zealand International Exhibition', *Museum History Journal*, 2:2 (July 2009), 119–42.

2 I prefer the term 'ethnic shows' (*Völkerschauen*) to 'human zoos' – for example, Bancel, Nicolas, Blanchard, Pascal, Boetsch, Gilles, Deroo, Eric, Lemaire and Sandrine (eds), *Zoos Humains: De la Vénus hottentote aux Reality Shows* (Paris: La Découverte, 2002). Although a similar phenomenon also about *othering*, ethnic shows were different from freak shows where people were staged because of their *physical* difference. Ethnic shows, however, were much more about *cultural* differences, and always included a staged performance of cultural pursuits considered characteristic. Much more important though, the term 'human zoos' suggests a unilinear power relation and makes non-European ethnic show participants into victims, denying them any agency. Although most ethnic shows took place in a colonial setting of structural inequality, Indigenous agency in the sense of capacity to act and negotiate was definitely an important factor in many of them.

3 Also seen in British settler colonies, the New Zealand International Exhibition in Christchurch 1906–1907, for example.

4 See for example E. Ames, 'From the Exotic to the Everyday: The Ethnographic Exhibition in Germany', in V.R. Schwartz and J. Przyblyski (eds), *The Nineteenth Century Visual Culture Reader* (London and New York: Routledge, 2004); H. Thode-Arora, *Für fünfzig Pfennig um die Welt. Die Hagenbeckschen Völkerschauen* (Frankfurt and New York: Campus, 1989); H. Thode-Arora, 'Commercial Ethnographic Exhibitions in 19th and early 20th century Germany: Völkerschauen', in P. Poddar, R.S. Patke and L. Jensen (eds), *A Historical Companion to Postcolonial Literatures: Continental Europe and Its Empires* (Edinburgh: Edinburgh University Press, 2008); H. Thode-Arora, 'Exotic Humans on Display: Representations of Cultural Differences in German Ethnic Shows', in G. Mackenthun and S. Jobs (eds), *Embodiments of Cultural Encounters: Cultural Encounters and the Discourses of Scholarship* (Münster: Waxmann, 2011); H. Thode-Arora, *From Samoa with Love? Samoan Travellers in Germany, 1895–1911: Retracing the Footsteps* (Munich: Hirmer, 2014).

5 J. Habermas, *Strukturwandel der Öffentlichkeit: Untersuchungen zu einer Kategorie der bürgerlichen Gesellschaft* (Frankfurt: Suhrkamp, 1990); J. Habermas, *The Structural Transformation of the Public Sphere: An Inquiry into a Category of Bourgeois Society* (Cambridge, MA: MIT Press, 1989).

6 See for example P. Tapsell, *Waka Wairua – Imagining Another Way of Viewing Our Pacific*. Keynote Lecture, 21st annual conference 'Empires and Cultures of the Pacific', of the New Zealand Studies Association. Vienna, 2 July 2015.

7 See for example K. Message, 'Contested Sites of Identity and the Cult of the New: The Centre Cultural Tjibaou and the Constitution of Culture in New Caledonia', *ReCollections*, 1:1 (2006), 7–28.

8 See for example A. Gell, *Art and Agency. An Anthropological Theory* (Oxford: Oxford University Press, 1998); M. O'Hanlon and R.L. Welsch (eds), *Hunting the Gatherers: Ethnographic Collectors, Agents and Agency in Melanesia, 1870s–1930s* (New York: Berghahn, 2000); N. Thomas, *Entangled Objects: Exchange, Material Culture and Colonialism in the Pacific* (Cambridge, MA: Harvard University Press, 1991).

9 The literature on the colonial history of Samoa is vast. For a good general overview and further reading recommendations, see P. Hempenstall, 'Germany's Pacific Pearl', in Thode-Arora, *From Samoa with Love?*, pp. 27–45.

10 J. Barrett, *Museums and the Public Sphere* (Chichester: Wiley-Blackwell, 2011); I. Karp and S.D. Lavine (eds.), *Exhibiting Cultures: The Poetics and Politics of Museum Display* (Washington, DC, and London: Smithsonian Institution Press, 1991); S. Longair and J. McAleer (eds), *Curating Empire: Museums and the British Imperial Experience* (Manchester and New York: Manchester University Press, 2012).

11 C. Marquardt, *Verzeichnis einer ethnologischen Sammlung aus Samoa. Zusammengestellt in etwa zwanzig Jahren von Carl Marquardt* (Berlin: Dietrich Reimer, 1902), pp. 3, 15.

12 See for example the two literary pieces by the well-known German writer Joachim Ringelnatz, *Vergebens* (*In vain*) in his collections of novelettes and his youth memories – J. Ringelnatz, *Ein jeder lebt's. Novellen* (Munich: Albert Langen, 1913), pp. 26–31; J. Ringelnatz, *Mein Leben bis zum Kriege* (Berlin: Rowohlt, 1931), pp. 25, the theatre comedy *Die tanzende Samoanerin* (The dancing Samoan) by Maximilian Böttcher (Berlin: Kühling & Güttner, 1896) or the art works by member of the Berlin Academy of the Arts Nathaniel Sichel and members of the artist community Die Brücke like Ernst Ludwig Kirchner and Erich Heckel (cf. Thode-Arora, *From Samoa with Love?*, p. 204). Reportedly, other famous painters queued to immortalise the Samoans, Adolph Menzel, Reinhold Begas, Max Koner, Ludwig Knaus and possibly Paul Meyerheim among them (cf. Thode-Arora, *From Samoa with Love?*, p. 105); any works by them relating to the Samoans could not, however, be traced until now.

13 A *malaga* is a traditional journey of a chief with his entourage to another village or district; formal speeches as well as singing and dancing are part of the protocol.

14 See the reconstruction from the correspondence in Thode-Arora, *From Samoa with Love?*, pp. 139–41.

15 See McCarthy references in note 1.

16 See McCarthy, Hakiwai and Schorch, and Mallon, Chapters 13 and 17 below.

17 See Förster and von Bose, Chapter 3 above.

18 J. Habermas, *Strukturwandel der Öffentlichkeit: Untersuchungen zu einer Kategorie der bürgerlichen Gesellschaft* (Frankfurt: Suhrkamp, 1990), pp. 86–121.

19 The exact number of travellers in 1895–1897 is difficult to establish, as not all the people named in the programme brochure actually seem to have travelled. Cf. Thode-Arora, *From Samoa with Love?*, pp. 93–4.

20 One of the specifications was that the programme of the opening ought to be rigidly official, with only classical music, but no Samoan music or dance as these could give the impression of restaging an ethnic show today. On the day of the opening, a large group of Samoans from Germany, Austria and Switzerland arrived to honour the head of state as well as the Samoan delegation, and to show their support for the exhibition. When they heard of the restrictions, they decided to counteract with their own agenda. In order to not get the museum into trouble because of the state officials' specifications, my dialogue partners from the Samoan diaspora and I decided to have their own plans put into action immediately before and immediately after the actual opening: when the Samoan delegation entered the doors of the building, a row of Samoan ladies greeted them with *lei* of fresh flowers. After the last speech, before anyone left the auditorium to see the actual exhibition, the Samoan ladies started to sing hymns and other songs, moving many of the assembled Samoans and Germans to tears. In the exhibition, they again began to sing to honour the head of state.

As an answer, under the larger-than-life ethnic show photo of the head of state's grandparents and father, Tamasese's talking chief, quickly changing to the appropriate Samoan attire, responded with a speech and more songs, with other Samoans joining in. The Samoan reappropriation of the exhibition opening made a strong impression on many German guests and is still remembered.

21 Visit Michel Tuffery's website www.micheltuffery.co.nz/ for more information on his art and on his *Siamani-Samoa* series.

22 The *manumea* (tooth-billed pigeon, *Didunculus strigorostris*) is a bird endemic to Samoa. According to Samoan traditions and observation, if one bird is wounded, its partner will come to it, put its wing on it to protect it and not leave it, even if this is dangerous. Michel Tuffery metaphorically applies this relationship between the birds to the relationship between Germany and Samoa: in spite of everything bad that happened in colonial times, both needed and helped each other as well.

23 Because of this barrier, visitors were forced to engage with at least one of them before entering the exhibition.

24 Ernst Litfass (1816–1874) had invented the column-formed advertising pillar that became popular in Berlin in the 1850s, the time of emerging circus, music and show business, and later all over Germany. In German, these advertising pillars are still called *Litfaßsäulen* – Litfass columns – and widely used. Wilfried F. Schoeller, *Ernst Litfaß, der Reklamekönig* (Frankfurt: Schöffling, 2005).

25 I did not do a systematic documentation of this visitor experience. It occurred to me only after a number of guided tours that there seemed to be a pattern in the way visitors reacted: some became fidgety and nervous during the parts of the guided tour where I stressed Samoan agency; when I invited questions and comments afterwards, there would usually be quite an emotional, sometimes even aggressive outburst of the sort that (in spite of the evidence provided by my quoting Samoan informants) they could not believe what I said, or, in one case, what political agenda I had in stressing agency instead of victimisation. These were minority reactions, however, happening only now and then with one individual in the whole group. Most visitors seemed touched by the exhibition and marvelled at the Samoan agency which came as a completely unexpected eye-opener to them. This was evident after every single tour, when most of them did not disperse immediately afterwards but eagerly embraced the opportunity to talk longer.

5

Curating across the colonial divides

Jette Sandahl

Long live the excavation ban

Listen for a moment to the Swedish explorer Erland Nordenskiöld as he talks to himself, in 1902, in diaries and letters, in the tropical nights of Latin America:[1]

> When darkness falls, which it does swiftly in the tropics, we take our spades and go down the hillside. There is a terrible atmosphere over such a grave plundering at night time. Sometimes it is deadly quiet and in the humid heat half naked diggers work; sometimes someone throws in a raw joke to encourage himself and the others.

Well connected with powerful local European people as he was, he would still on occasion encounter the opposition of local authorities.

> I managed to negotiate freedom from customs, but those devils prohibited me from doing archaeological excavations. This is both illegal and scandalous and something I am not going to abide by. Any crook in this country can dig and sell the finds to traders in curiosities whereas a foreign archaeologist gets an excavation ban. It is absolutely crazy. A couple of days ago I galloped 7 Swedish miles to try to save a couple of settlements from pre-Hispanic times. Long live the excavation ban. In Bolivia things will be easier – I have good recommendations, and no one is going to thwart my research.

At times, but not always, he could count on relationships built up over different trips.

> I am very pleased with what has been accomplished so far. Due to our old acquaintance, they have shown me great trust and brought out several things that I have never seen in any collections from Chaco. [But] often one finds that the next area one wants to explore is closed for research. White people have attacked and murdered Indians, or less often, the opposite. Especially hard is it to come into contact with 'wild Indians'. Most often it is almost impossible to get anyone to accompany you on such a quest. If you are too few, you risk that your staff and carriers run off. If you are too many, then the Indians will take flight. They obviously cannot know that one's intentions are good.

He was driven, he wrote, 'almost sick with longing to come to the wild ones'.

> It will probably be my first excursion under which I will have to fight. It is rather improbable that the Siriono will receive me obligingly. I will do anything to enter into peaceful relations with these wild ones, who have so far been deadly enemies with white people. If all else fails, I will conquer a village with weapons in hand. For each object I steal, I intend to leave behind a present in the village.

Erland Nordenskiöld's private deliberations around the issues of collecting,[2] and exchange, morality and legality, allow a glimpse into the contradictions in values that underlay the appropriation and extraction of enormous cultural riches from one side of the Earth to the other. His faith in the supremacy of scientific research surpasses any other consideration or claim, and justifies his entitlement, at gunpoint or by any other means, to claim as his whatever he desires. Erland Nordenskiöld was the founding figure of the collections which, in the twentieth century, formed the core of the new Ethnographic Museum in Gothenburg, and which, at the beginning of the twenty-first century, as the challenges of globalisation and accelerated migration created a new political interest around the global collections, I and others were asked to transform into a museum of world cultures.

The principles behind the curatorial processes of this new Museum of World Culture constitute the primary case addressed in this chapter. In the shaping of the museum, I drew extensively on my experiences of, on one hand, having been part of creating, from scratch, the grassroots-based Women's Museum in Denmark, and, on the other, of having worked with the very established, high-quality ethnographic collections of the National Museum of Denmark. In both of these jobs I had taken inspiration from museums with strong community ties outside of Europe. The challenges, in a European museum context, of bridging the colonial divides and of decolonising traditional ethnographic collections drew me, in time, to work, and apprentice, at the Museum of New Zealand Te Papa Tongarewa (Te Papa), which forms another part of my personal background for the thinking that emerges in this chapter.

Being white is a moral choice

'Being white', said James Baldwin, is, 'absolutely, a moral choice (for there are no white people)'.[3]

Whiteness[4] jumps out of the pages of Erland Nordenskiöld's writings as it does from the ubiquitous hierarchies in the photographs from his travels, and as it does in the Declaration of the Importance and Value of Universal Collections,[5] published one hundred years later by a group of museums in Europe and the USA – an aggressively supremacist statement in defence of the rights of Western museums to exert continuous possession of these cultural heritage riches amassed from the rest of the world.

The document claims that collections 'acquired in earlier times must be viewed in the light of different sensitivities and values, reflective of that earlier era', and that these objects 'have become part of the museums that have cared for them, and by extension of the heritage of the nations which house them'. This assertion studiously ignores the resistance put up at the time of the appropriation, by individuals, local peoples, local authorities and national governments, and equally disregards the experience, learned through large-scale repatriation as that between the National Museum of Denmark and the National Museum of Greenland, that collections are more than abundant enough to be shared, without resulting in loss of knowledge or accessibility. Remarkable in its arrogant self-interest and casual divisiveness, the document pleads for 'a superior status, above morality and justice', to justify 'immunity from claims for repatriation of objects'.[6]

Repatriation, essential as this issue is, is only the tip of the iceberg, as Richard West Jr, founding director of the National Museum of the American Indian (NMAI), says.[7] It is shadowed by much wider and deeper divides around the issues of accountability, reparation and restitution. It is not so much about 'Erland Nordenskiöld raking in craniums as if they were potatoes', as one of his companions wrote,[8] as it is about where that leaves us now. It is not about changing the past or undoing history, as defenders of the status quo protest, but a question of seeking 'a correction of the present situation that no doubt has roots in the colonial past' and 'a modification of the present imbalance'.[9]

In the USA, the Native American Graves Protection and Repatriation Act (NAGPRA)[10] and the NMAI Act,[11] from 1990 and 1989 respectively, are meant to remediate 'the injustices of history' and establish a 'moral imperative that corrected vast wrongs committed during the nineteenth century'. The challenge to the traditional Western detachment of the objects from their original context had wide-ranging ethical and museological implications, not least in recognising the knowledge, expertise and legitimate authority of the people with an original cultural connection with the given objects.[12]

The Museum of New Zealand Te Papa Tongarewa Act from 1992 emphasises the ethnic and cultural diversity of the people of Aotearoa New Zealand and underscores the museum's responsibilities in regard to recognising 'the *mana* and significance of Māori, European, and other major traditions and cultural heritages', and in providing the means for every such culture to contribute effectively to the museum as a statement of Aotearoa New Zealand's identity.[13] In its practices, Te Papa formalised these values and principles in terms of consultation, participation, self-representation and shared authority, in terms of what is understood as valid knowledge and in terms of the role of communities in enhancing the care, understanding and interpretation of collections and *taonga*.

Decolonising a dwelling of demons[14]

The Museum of World Culture was thus created at the crossroads between two trends – a powerful White Western denial and disavowal of the implications of colonialism in museums, countered by a growing museological mobilisation and reinterpretation in countries or cultures outside of Europe, driven and supported by strong Indigenous pressure.

The troubled and fraught ethnographic collections, which were to form the basis for the new museum, could not, for me, just be curated into a new, shinier version of the traditional museum journey around the world, continent by continent. Decolonising museum curating involves decoding museum collections from the colonial meanings in which they have been embedded, in which they have been cut off, displaced and decontextualised from where they had once belonged, and in which they have been categorised, labelled[15] and transposed into the alien binary hierarchies of Western rationalism and the value systems of colonialism and imperialism. Two years of physical construction of a new museum building and new galleries were thus to be rooted in four years of systematic emotional and epistemological, personal and institutional self-reflection and reconstruction before the opening at the end of 2004.[16]

As national museums do, the new Museum of World Culture was to play its part in the building of national identity, positioning Sweden within an increasing global interdependence and interconnectivity, and contributing to cultural cohesion within the rapidly diversifying demographics. However, positioning the museum beyond the specifics of national or local politics, we – unusually for the time – embedded the purposes, visions and missions of the museum within the value systems of the Universal Declaration of Human Rights and the UNESCO Universal Declaration of Cultural Diversity.

Detailed mission statements described the museum's standpoints and methods within all the different strands of museum activities. Curatorial activities were thus governed, structured and informed by a shared framework of closely related and interdependent ethical, epistemological and museological principles. Two of these principles also set the museum apart from other European museums at the time. One was the fundamental curatorial point that both knower and knowledge are situated and positioned, which derived most strongly from within feminist epistemology.[17] The other was the commitment to the rights to self-representation, which was rooted both in a feminist context and in Indigenous-led revisions and reinventions of paradigms and practices to include or represent Indigenous worldviews and forms of knowledge.[18]

The principle of situated knowledge and the methodology of mobile positioning, shifting perspectives and a plurality of points of view were underpinned by the decision to shape and structure the museum through a series of concurrent, thematic special exhibitions, and thus avoid the unified worldview and grand totalising metanarratives of permanent galleries which

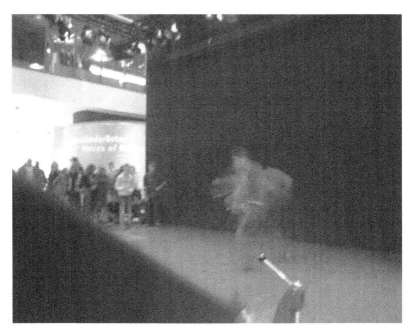

5.1 Hip hop jam on the stage in the exhibition *Horizons: Voices from a Global Africa* at the Museum of World Culture, Gothenburg, Sweden, 2005.

tend to legitimise historic power structures and hierarchies in museums. A principle of presenting peoples across the world as living cultures and as active historical subjects was behind a core strategy of supplementing and enhancing the museum's predominantly historic collections through extensive collaborations, as well as new collecting and loans from individuals, organisations and institutions with access to more current, substantive or meaningful objects.

Likewise, the complex principle of self-representation underscored the need for developing committed global partnerships with museums or similar institutions which, in continuity or discontinuity, may represent an original or primary authority over the relevant themes and collections. The exhibition *Horizons: Voices from a Global Africa* was thus developed in an intense, integrated process of institutional and individual co-creation and co-curation with, among others, national museums in Africa, local museums in the diasporic Caribbean, a group of local Gothenburg residents with cultural origins in the Africa Horn area, as well as with artists and other individuals from across Africa, the Caribbean and Europe. These processes spanned a continuum of collaborations. The National Museums of Kenya, for instance, conducted a model process of collecting and documenting contemporary urban life in a metropolis on behalf of the museum. The National Museum of Mali curated and lent the objects for a section on gender. A Haitian voodoo priest and musician collected objects and created photographic documentation of diasporic spiritual beliefs and practices. Other museums and artists lent individual objects and art works.

Supplementing the traditional ethnographic parameters of geography, nationality and ethnicity with contemporary trends of increased migration and cultural interaction, the museum conveyed a dynamic, future-oriented concept of intersecting, hybridising and fusing identities which are defined as much through age, gender, shared beliefs or lifestyles, shared political hopes and values as they are through ethnicity, nationality or primary languages.

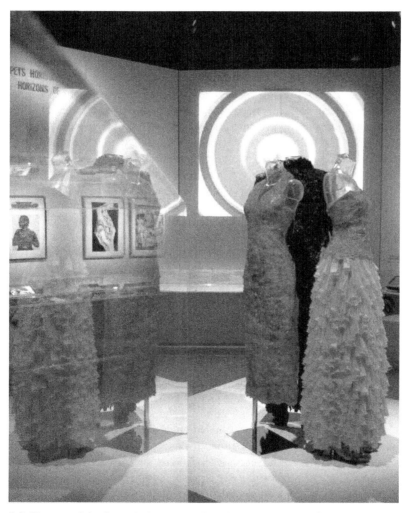

5.2 Photograph by Annie Leibovitz, condom dresses by Adriana Bernini, shadow theatre puppets from Java from the museum collection, South African memory boxes and body maps and the suggestive tunes of Russian Mumie Trolls music video, within the section called *Hope* in the exhibition *No Name Fever: HIV-Aids in the Age of Globalization* at the Museum of World Culture, Gothenburg, Sweden, 2005.

This contemporary approach to ethnography opened up themes like HIV-AIDS and human trafficking, which are global in character and scope, but act and manifest themselves in local, class and gender-specific ways, and which can only be adequately addressed within a profoundly interdisciplinary framework. The complexities and interconnectedness of contemporary society defy the boundaries and limitations of traditional museum divisions. In, for instance, the exhibition *No Name Fever: HIV-AIDS in the Age of Globalization*, a cacophony of material and immaterial objects, digital media, music, 'high' art and crafts objects, political documents, personal and therapeutic testimonies, blended with and confronted each other, while the curatorial voice splintered into thousands of different quotations, from people ill and dying, friends and relatives, politicians, physicians, priests, artists and political activists. Seven emotional themes, from desire and denial to fear, anger and grief, derived from the logic of the pandemic itself, created a shared structure for the whole, and provided a precarious but essential emotional balancing act of documenting societal and personal tragedy, while also celebrating and showcasing personal resilience, courage and solidarity.

While exhibitions like *No Name Fever* and *Trafficking* took their themes and content from urgent contemporary issues and were clearly not collection-based, they were none the less unequivocally object-based. Unexpected and emotionally challenging subjects such as slavery and the slave trade, HIV-AIDS and human trafficking, were sharpened by the irrefutability of objects as well as softened by their poetic beauty and by the beauty of the design language through which they were presented. *Horizons: Voices from a Global Africa* originated in and showcased the museum's very high-quality, but previously under-exhibited collections from the African continent, supplemented by extensive loans. The artist Fred Wilson's installation *Site Unseen: Dwelling of the Demons* drew solely on objects and photos from the museum's collections, creating a continuous red thread from outside the museum throughout the inside, questioning and demasking power, and reminding both staff and visitors of the underlying colonial histories and meanings.

Just as all exhibitions were object-based, they were also grounded in scholarship. Local, national and international academic specialists from within each theme were contracted to supplement the museum's own staff. To this academic expertise was added and included specialist knowledge that derives from a more personal, lived affiliation with a given theme. Curatorial teams behind each project were interdisciplinary, large and complex. They worked, with some variance, within a shared organisational model and method, and in close dialogue with the director and the museum leadership team. As a rule, each team was composed of a museological content expert, an educator with subject knowledge, a performing arts expert with subject knowledge, an architect, a communication person, a conservator and collection manager, and a maintenance person, all from in-house, joined by a representative for external partners, an external, often international, subject expert and an international architect.

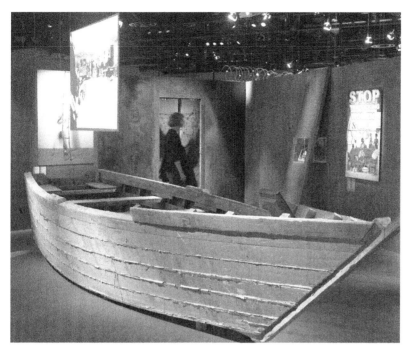

5.3 The patera was collected in 2005 by the Museum of World Culture, Gothenburg, Sweden, from the Southern coast of Spain to which it had carried people across from the North African coast. It is shown here as part of the exhibition *Trafficking.*

Following, again, the principle that knowledge is situated, and believing that recognition and identification play a role in fostering a sense of belonging with audiences and communities, a targeted approach to recruitment resulted in a perceptibly diverse staff, in terms of gender, ethnicity, race, sexual orientation and age. The composition of, not least, the educational staff, who performed all front-of-house functions, proved, I think, essential for the audience building and community building of the new museum.

In its first incarnation in 2005, the Museum of World Culture was a vibrant and rather magical place, diverse beyond anyone's expectation, inclusive in its somewhat funky, contemporary metropolitanism and internationalism, bringing together distant or antagonistic people who would not have met or interacted in any other space.

But 'the European vision of the world – or more precisely, perhaps the European vision of the universe, is a vision as remarkable for what it pretends to include as for what it remorselessly diminishes, demolishes, or leaves totally out of account', admonished James Baldwin.[19] The Museum of World Culture, and I, as the director of the museum, were no exceptions to this. We committed our share of cultural transgressions or cultural encroachments, and, while celebrating the achievements of the Museum of World Culture, I was also constantly made aware of our shortcomings. So

I went to work and apprentice at Te Papa, where Whiteness is not permitted to run rampant.

E Tū Ake: Māori Standing Strong

Te Papa's permanent galleries, from the museum's opening in 1998, have presented separate narratives between Māori and later settler cultures, pivoting around the 1840 Treaty of Waitangi. This exhibition layout interprets parallel universes through radically different languages – a mythological, immersive experience of Māori culture counterpointed by a humorous, jovial and rather deconstructed Pākehā tone of voice. A decade hence, however, the special touring exhibition from 2011, *E Tū Ake: Māori Standing Strong*, ventured across this divide into the interfaces, the interstices, the contact points, where the different cultures meet and have interacted.

E Tū Ake spanned a diverse range of materials, from highly prized taonga to everyday objects, and contemporary Māori visual culture.[20] It spoke from a concept of time in which the past is a tangible, guiding, ever-present now, and from which the protocols and customary thinking of the past inform and guide the actions of the present. It explores how the richness and multidimensionality of terms like mana, whakapapa and whenua allow for dynamic engagement on multiple levels simultaneously. The exhibition confronted, boldly, unflinchingly but graciously, the asymmetries of power and their concomitant economic, social and cultural conflicts, however painful these are and have been. Through its unique voices of self-representation and self-confident point of view, the exhibition demonstrated, vigorously, that Māori are not a people confined to an indefinite past. The concept of *rangatiratanga* or sovereignty in *E Tū Ake* drew the lines of continuity between

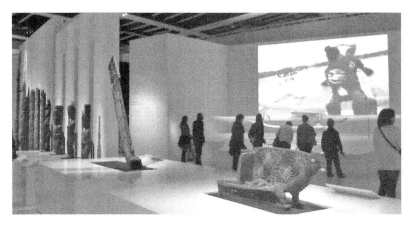

5.4 A contemporary waka ama (canoe) in the background seen in the context of precious taonga (treasures), from a war canoe in the foreground, in the exhibition *E Tū Ake* – as *Leurs trésors ont une âme* – at the Musée du Quai Branly, Paris, France, 2011.

ancient and current practices, and placed Māori people in a position of continuous historical agency, within which it is possible to remain embedded in
customary practices, while demanding participation, exerting influence or
even driving development in mainstream, contemporary society.

When *E Tū Ake* was shown at Quai Branly, Paris, France – titled *Leurs
trésors ont une âme* – Stephane Martin, president of the museum, surprisingly, at a scientific symposium, chose to draw attention to a critique of the
exhibition published in the *New York Times*. In a collective swipe at the
Quai Branly, Te Papa and the NMAI, the critic wrote off the exhibition and
Quai Branly's showing it as a 'curatorial abdication' done as an 'atonement
for colonial history'. There was, in the article, an underlying assumption of
a seemingly self-evident dichotomy between scholarship and Indigenous
voices. 'The Quai Branly has impressive research facilities: are they similarly
blinkered?' the critic asked rhetorically. In his disregard for Māori systems
of thought and knowledge, he chose to also overlook or discredit the PhD
of the chief curator of the exhibition, Huhana Smith, then Senior Curator
Mātauranga Māori at the national museum, and for that matter the doctor-
ates and other honours of many of the Māori voices quoted in the exhibition. He failed to grasp or acknowledge the potentials of belonging to, and
mastering, double systems of knowledge and worldviews.[21]

Were this critic a single erratic voice, one would laugh at the high-strung
pathos. But while recognising the need for extensive collaboration with,
in a broad sense, cultures of origin of the collections, European museums
have found it difficult to create and maintain this collaboration as long-
term, equal partnerships. At times, a radical rift is felt between European
museum traditions and the new, Indigenous-driven museums in other
parts of the world, like the NMAI, Te Papa or the National Museum of
Australia, carrying a – in professional circles often only whispered, hinted

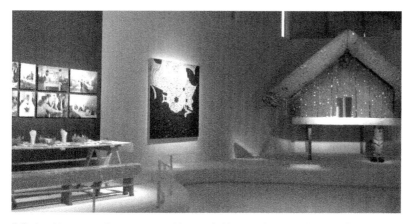

5.5 A table setting from a marae (the work *Nemesis*, by artist Reuben Patterson),
and a pātaka (food storehouse) all to be interpreted as commentary on the theme
of sustainability, in the exhibition *E Tū Ake* (as *Leurs trésors sont une âme*) at the
Musée du Quai Branly, Paris, France, 2011.

and intimated – delegitimisation of the epistemologies of Indigenous curating. The idea of Indigenous self-representation, and that of other oppressed groups, is not easily integrated into or absorbed within the framework of White Western interpretative monopoly and its foundation in the binary hierarchies of European scientific rationalism.[22]

They have forgotten the scale of the theft that enriched them[23]

Joe Horse Capture has criticised museums for their preference for sporadic, project-based and temporary partnerships over the knowledge, long-term backing and consent of a whole community. Museums tend to favour, he says, contributions from individual consultants, artists, writers and performers in roles that 'are secondary to the curatorial role in the exhibition, where the main ideas originate and reside'. He quotes his father, George Horse Capture Sr, saying that 'Native people do not need another exhibition about Native art organized by a non-Native person for a non-Native audience'. 'Where are all the Indians?' George Horse Capture asked, when he looked around the room at the people present to be part of the preparation of a large-scale Native American exhibition.[24]

Joe Horse Capture and George Horse Capture's critical statements resonate with my experience from being closely involved, during its formative years,[25] with the German Humboldt Forum, the largest-scale new museum and reinterpretation of ethnographic collections currently under development in Europe. The principle of self-representation never became a significant part or a driver of the discourse of the Humboldt Forum.

In the ICOM publication *Museums, Ethics and Cultural Heritage* from 2016, Richard West and Hermann Parzinger, Director General of the Stiftung Preussischer Kulturbesitz (SPK), the institution overseeing the Humboldt Forum, speak, in stark and disturbing contrast, from their anchoring in opposite cultural perspectives. For the SPK, the universalist aspirations from the *Declaration of the Importance and Value of Universal Collections* have remained essentially intact, when the organisation's position on the Museum Island is reiterated 'as the great vision of the nineteenth century', and Alexander von Humboldt is lauded as 'the second Columbus' and 'the scientific discoverer of Latin America'. Hermann Parzinger acknowledges that the ethnographic and Far East collections are 'to some extent associated with Germany's colonial history;. 'However, much more important for their emergence and development were Prussian-German scientific expeditions', he continues, as if these expeditions were not part of a colonial history, and as if, by definition, there could be no legal or ethical issues lingering after these scientific forages into other continents. Obscuring asymmetries of power, latent violence and dubious provenance in collecting processes, he cites the rule of 'partage', and underscores the importance that collections, from, for instance, the Near East, 'reached the museum legally following the legal regulations of the time'. 'Nevertheless', however, the organisation 'feels obliged to have the closest possible cooperation with the countries of origin, to preserve in the best sense of the word, a "shared heritage"'.[26]

When trusting, unequivocally, as do the SPK and its national government, the basic legitimacy of its ownership to the collections, then all decisions, definitions and interpretations of the scope, shapes and forms of this sharing will rest with the organisation.

But race is the child of racism, not the father[27]

In the USA, with increased pressure from underrepresented or misrepresented groups, and 'after Ferguson',[28] the issues of representation, racism and White supremacy are articulated with a new urgency in both academic and professional museum contexts. The American Anthropological Association (AAA) recognises that 'anthropology is the discipline that fostered and nurtured "scientific racism", a world view that transforms certain perceived differences into genetically determined inequality and provides a rationale for slavery, colonialism, segregation, eugenics, and terror', and encourages the interrogation of structural racism, also as it is manifested in this age of 'colour blindness'.[29] Studies and surveys conducted by the AAA have revealed anthropology as one of 'the least integrated disciplines', and documented the race avoidance, denial and marginalisation of scholars of colour enacted by anthropology departments, and the 'massive differences in perception of whether racism and white supremacy are at play'.[30] Within the USA (art) museum field, a report from 2015 highlighted the overrepresentation of non-Hispanic Whites in jobs associated with the intellectual and educational mission of museums, and the need for specific programmes to facilitate and encourage young people of colour into museum positions.[31] Likewise, the American Alliance of Museums has been under pressure to recognise 'the entrenched racism', to challenge and transform 'the institutional policies and systems that perpetuate structural racism and oppression in museums',[32] and open up a more active engagement with making questions of race central in institutional self-reflection.[33]

Epistemology of ignorance

In museums, as in life in general, the process of decolonisation is perceived almost solely as the need and responsibility of the colonised. While people of colour have grappled with the processes of oppression and of liberation, and with what these terms fully imply, the equivalent political, intellectual and emotional efforts have not been invested by White people.[34] The almost total silence or muteness around White privilege,[35] White supremacy, and racism in Europe, and the significant differences between White people and people of colour in how racism is perceived in, for instance, the USA, continue to beg for explanation.

Psychoanalytic traditions, reaching back to Sigmund Freud's statement that the 'unconscious is like an aboriginal population of the mind', have focused on how the figure of the Other functions as projection ground in the psyche of the White individual.[36] Toni Morrison speaks of racism as a distortion of the psyche, 'a profound neurosis that nobody examines for what it is',[37] while Frantz Fanon famously articulated how White people remain 'slaves to superiority'.[38] Within philosophy, efforts are made to understand 'reason's entanglement with social power' to 'provide a lens for the political values at work in our knowledge practices' and 'the role of power in the construction of what is known'. In racial oppression, the absent knowledge is actively produced, supported 'by a vast array of institutional systems', and the 'ignorance of injustice, cruelty, and suffering, such as contemporary white people's obliviousness to racism and white domination', serve to maintain White privilege and supremacy. The ironic result of the 'inverted epistemology' is 'that whites will in general be unable to understand the world that they themselves have made, and because they do not understand the racist world in which they live, white people are able to fully benefit from its racial hierarchies, ontologies and economies'.[39]

Nothing

'Nothing', said Malcolm X, as a response to a White woman who asked what she could do to further his cause. He then softened and continued that where White people had to work was with the racism in their own White communities.[40]

So, when White and European museum people, like me, advocate 'a continuous process of re-conciliation',[41] there is obviously an awareness that the colonial divides run deep and jarringly through the content, methods, staff and governance of museums, and will not be bridged by any one single effort, but will require continuous and painstaking effort by all partners.

But in these days of increasing global and intranational inequality, of sharpened economic contradictions and heightened social and cultural conflicts, when I hear myself reciting yet again, in conferences and in publications, the narrative of ground-breaking intercultural and cross-cultural projects accomplished by the different museum institutions with which I have been involved, and when I hear or read, for instance, the Humboldt Forum or Humboldt Lab reciting theirs, I find myself increasingly questioning the real status of these projects and wanting to gauge their token or symbolic character. Presented and viewed separately, each project sounds convincing, but viewed together and in the context of the total budget of a given museum or of the total budget of the museum sector, the sum remains small and the logic questionable.

Is it time for us to critically review the ways in which we, as museums, allocate our resources and examine how or whether our budgets reflect our rhetoric of inclusion, co-operation and partnerships as core business? Would an examination of the true proportions of our priorities reveal whether we are, indeed, deceiving and exonerating ourselves on these issues?[42] Do we all, as critics of the Humboldt Forum so polemically voiced it, live in a *Palast der Verlogenheit*, in a Palace of Mendacity?[43]

Slaves to superiority[44]

When disparate and distant relationships are recounted as close, when single events are presented as part of an all-encompassing strategy, when we discount our international advisory boards and dismiss the external experts who contradict us, when we think quotas for jobs are a bad idea, when ancient taboos seem to interest us more than current battles, when we ignore and reject as fringe the NGOs screaming oppression in our face, when we shrug away talk of colonialism as old-fashioned and theoretically passé, when we mute our critics by intimating that they are shrill, emotional, unstable, with a chip on their shoulder, when we pathologise opposition, when Whiteness jumps out of our larger than life self-portraits in our exhibitions – then could we recognise our unearned advantage and begin to reassess how privilege and supremacy act upon us, speak through us and interplay with our current political environment?

When climate change and geopolitics threaten the lives of people of our collections, when we watch with incredulity how Europe is about to come apart at the seams, in rising nationalism, xenophobia, barbed wire and a determined contempt for the weakest, when the USA implodes in mass shootings and potentiated racialised violence, when we manage to ignore the forty thousand people, half of them children, displaced every day, when our callousness grows to allow the roads of Europe to become roads to nowhere and the Mediterranean a mass-grave of drowned and murdered hopes, when the difference in which lives matter is increasingly pronounced – do we then examine the gap between these issues and what is presented in museums as an ethical issue, and begin to reassess what should be fundamental topics for museums, and for ethnographic museums or museums of world cultures in particular?

Decolonising curatorial practices do not exist in an organisational vacuum. Curators can rarely, in the long run, be more critical in their practices than the intellectual capacity and the political allegiances or courage of the director will allow. Correspondingly, in the interdependent relationship between curating and directing, a museum director cannot, in the long run, realise more radical visions or critical positions than the curators' knowledge, scientific scope and fearlessness towards professional ostracisation will allow and deliver. But in the current intellectual and political climate, anticipatory obedience, at any level of museum practice, will equal collusion and complicity.

Notes

1 All quotationss from Erland Nordenskiöld are from C. Lindberg, *Erland Nordenskiöld – ett indianlif* (Stockholm: Natur och Kultur, 1996), pp. 84, 161, 163, 176, 123, 182. My translations from Swedish to English.

2 I am sticking closely to the process of collecting, and am leaving out his ambiguous feelings for the people whose objects he appropriated and how this appropriation should serve as a vehicle for his own career.

3 J. Baldwin, *On Being White … and Other Lies*, reproduced from 'Essence', 1984, www.cwsworkshop.org/pdfs/CARC/Family_Herstories/2_On_Being_White. PDF. Accessed 1 March 2017. See also The Cross of Redemption, http://faculty. gordonstate.edu/lsanders-senu/On%20Being%20White%20and%20Other%20 Lies.pdf. Accessed 1 March 2017.

4 Whiteness in the meaning of skin colour inscribed into the symbolic universe of power.

5 Reproduced for instance by ICOM: Declaration on the Importance and Value of Universal Museums, http://icom.museum/fileadmin/user_upload/pdf/ICOM_ News/2004–1/ENG/p4_2004–1.pdf. Accessed 1 March 2017.

6 See for instance the discussions by Georg Abungu, 'The Declaration: A Contested Issue', *ICOM News*, 2004, http://icom.museum/fileadmin/user_ upload/pdf/ICOM_News/2004–1/ENG/p4_2004–1.pdf. Accessed 1 March 2017. See also Kwame Opuku, 'Declaration on the Importance and Value of Universal Museums: Singular Failure of an Arrogant Imperialist Project', www.africavenir.org/fileadmin/downloads/Opoku_UniversalMuseum. pdf. Accessed 25 January 2013. See also Geoffrey Lewis, 'The Universal Museum: A Special Case?', *ICOM News*, 2004, http://icom.museum/fileadmin/user_ upload/pdf/ICOM_News/2004–1/ENG/p3_2004–1.pdf. Accessed 1 March 2017.

7 W.R. West Jr, 'Native America in the Twenty-first Century', in B.L. Murphy (ed.), *Museums, Ethics and Cultural Heritage* (London: Routledge, 2016), pp. 281, 287.

8 Lindberg. *Erland Nordenskiöld – ett indianlif*, 108.

9 Kwame Opuku, 'Declaration on the Importance and Value of Universal Museums: Singular Failure of an Arrogant Imperialist Project'.

10 Information on NAGPRA at National Park Service, www.nps.gov/nagpra/. Accessed 1 March 2017.

11 The NMAI Act, http://nmai.si.edu/sites/1/files/pdf/about/NMAIAct.pdf. Accessed 1 March 2017.

12 West Jr, 'Native America in the Twenty-First Century', pp. 281, 287.

13 Museum of New Zealand Te Papa Tongarewa Act 1992, www.legislation.govt. nz/act/public/1992/0019/latest/DLM260229.html. Accessed 1 March 2017.

14 The term 'Dwelling of Demons' is a reference to the title *Dwelling of the Demons* of the artist Fred Wilson's installation at the Museum of World Culture.

15 See for instance A. Munoz, *From Curiosa to World Culture: The History of the Latin American Collections at the Museum of World Culture in Sweden* (Gothenburg: Museum of World Culture, 2011), https://gupea.ub.gu.se/bit stream/2077/25554/4/gupea_2077_25554_4.pdf. Accessed 1 March 2017. See also A. Munoz, *The Power of Labelling* (Gothenburg: Museum of World Culture, 2009), www.varldskulturmuseerna.se/files/varldskultur/vkm-forskningsamlin gar/e21bc935b861.pdf. Accessed 1 March 2017.

16 For a longer version of the creation of the Museum of World Culture see, for instance, J. Sandahl, 'The Included Other – the Oxymoron of Contemporary Ethnographic Collections?', *Forum for Anthropology and Culture*, 4 (2007), 208–17.

17 The term is often attributed to D. Haraway, 'Situated Knowledges: The Science Question in Feminism and the Privilege of Partial Perspective', *Feminist* Studies, 14:3 (1988), 575–99.

18 At the time when we were shaping the Museum of World Culture we learned from and were supported by not least the National Museum of the American Indian and the National Museum of Australia as well as the Museum of New Zealand Te Papa Tongarewa. See for instance J. Sandahl, 'Living Entities', in *The Native Universe and Museums in the Twenty-First Century* (Washington, DC: NMAI, 2005), written for the opening symposium of the NMAI.

19 J. Baldwin, *On Being White … and Other Lies*.

20 H. Smith, *E Tu Ake: Māori Standing Strong* (Wellington: Te Papa Press, 2011). See this publication also for an understanding of the multidimensionality of Māori terms.

21 E. Rothstein, 'French Museums Atone for a Colonial History', *New York Times* (25 November 2011), www.nytimes.com/2011/11/26/arts/design/quai-branly-museum-in-paris-glorifies-the-other.html?_r=0. Accessed 1 March 2017.

22 The NMAI, Te Papa and National Museum of Australia are obviously not infallible, nor should the tragic history behind them or their current political importance place them beyond critique or reproach. Numerous dissertations have been written about these institutions. Personally, I think all three of these museums suffered from terribly bad exhibition design – conventional, formulaic, stereotypical – which in no way supported or facilitated, released or expressed innovative curatorial methods or alternative worldviews, but rather exacerbated all potential weaknesses. What interests me here, however, is the barely contained anger informing much of the writing or the conversations about these three museums.

23 'They have forgotten the scale of the theft that enriched them in slavery' is actually the full sentence by Ta Nahesi Coates, *Between the World and Me* (New York: Spiegel and Grau, 2015).

24 Joe Horse Capture, 'Native People Have a Story to Tell – Their Own', http://indiancountrytodaymedianetwork.com/2015/04/25/horse-capture-native-people-have-story-tell-their-own-160144. Accessed 26 April 2015. Both George Horse Capture and Joe Horse Capture have been curators at the NMAI as well as at other US museums.

25 I served as a member of the evaluation committee for the exhibition design tender process for the Humboldt Forum, as a member of the advisory boards for the Humboldt Forum agora and for the Dahlem Lab, and as a member of the international advisory board.

26 H. Parzinger, 'Remodelling Shared Heritage and Collections Access', in B.L. Murphy (ed.), *Museums, Ethics and Cultural Heritage* (London: Routledge, 2016), pp. 149, 150, 152, 152, 149, 149, 149.

27 T.N. Coates, *Between the World and Me* (New York: Spiegel and Grau, 2015).

28 'After Ferguson' became a code phrase for the mounting protests, beginning in 2014, against official, racialised violence, named after the protests that followed the killing of Michael Brown in the US city of Ferguson, one among too many unarmed black people shot by police officers, who are too often not charged and too often acquitted.

29 Leith Mullings, 'Trayvon Martin: Race and Anthropology', City University of New York: Graduate Centre, Student Research Commons, http://arc.commons. gc.cuny.edu/2013/07/30/trayvon-martin-race-and-anthropology/. Accessed 1 March 2017. Leith Mullings was president of the AAA at the time.

30 Ryan Anderson, 'Anthropology: It's Still White Public Space – an Interview with Karen Brodnik', Savageminds.org: http://savageminds.org/2014/11/15/anthro pology-still-white-public-space-brodkin/. Accessed 1 November 2014.

31 Art Museum Staff Demographic Survey, The Andrew W. Mellon Foundation, https://mellon.org/programs/arts-and-cultural-heritage/art-history-conserva tion-museums/demographic-survey/. Accessed 1 March 2017, and The Museum Diversity Report, The Andrew W. Mellon Foundation, https://mellon.org/ media/filer_public/ba/99/ba99e53a-48d5–4038–80e1–66f9ba1c020e/awmf_ museum_diversity_report_aamd_7-28-15.pdf. Accessed 1 July 2015. See also: Clair Voon, 'The Diversity Problem at American Museums Gets a Report', Hyperallergic.com, http://hyperallergic.com/226959/the-diversity-problem-at-american-museums-gets-a-report/. Accessed 1 August 2015. It is of course remarkable and significant that museums seem to see no intrinsic value in a diverse staff, but require encouragement in terms of special funding to realise this need.

32 Museums and Race: Transformations and Justice, blog, https://museumsan drace.org/. Accessed 1 March 2017.

33 Seph Rodney, 'The Conflict around Diversity at the American Alliance of Museums', Hyperallergic.com, http://hyperallergic.com/302752/the-conflict-around-diversity-at-the-american-alliance-of-museums/. Accessed 1 June 2016.

34 This chapter was written before the opening of the National Museum of African American History and Culture (NMAAHC). Specialist museums, like the NMAAHC and the NMAI, are – as are also, for example, women's museums and museums of slavery and the slave trade – institutional and institutionalised versions of this gruelling work of decoding oppression. Much can be said, and much has been said, of the strengths and weaknesses of specialist museums in addressing these issues relative to embedding them within mainstream museums, like the NMA and Te Papa. While mainstream museums should be in a good position to document and explore the interstices and entanglements between different and, in this context, opposing people, they can easily, in shifting political environments, be made to lose sight of the importance of the conflicting cultures. Specialist museums have their strength in showcasing the uniqueness and specific qualities of the cultures of their subject matter, and, once established, they lend a significant and stable authority to the issues, which is less sensitive to, for instance, changes in governments or board composition. Some museums in the Caribbean, for example Puerto Rico, and Latin America, for example Brazil, have a very different methodological and museological approach to the colonial divides, in which a bold point of departure in the genocidal violence exerted by the European colonisers towards both the original populations and African people enslaved through the transatlantic slave trade create a consistent interpretative background for the subsequent entanglements and unique cultural *métissage* between these three groups.

35 The surveys of discrimination in the sector carried out by the UK Museums Association are an important exception.

36 Museums, their supporting disciplines and their professions have tended to ignore or dismiss psychoanalytically based theories of the function of

the racialised other, such as C. Brickman, *The Aboriginal Population in the Mind: Race and Primitivity in Psychoanalysis* (New York: Columbia University Press, 2003).

37 Quoted from Zeba Blay, 'Watch Toni Morrison Break Down Why Racism Is a White Problem', *Huffington Post*, www.huffingtonpost.com/entry/watch-toni-morrison-break-down-why-racism-is-a-white-problem_us_56422f72e4b0411d3072b187/. Accessed 1 November 2015.

38 F. Fanon, *Black Skin, White Masks*, 1952, quoted from http://abahlali.org/files/__Black_Skin__White_Masks__Pluto_Classics_.pdf. Accessed 1 March 2017.

39 S. Sullivan, *Race and Epistemologies of Ignorance* (Albany: SYNU Press, 2007), pp. 24, 28, 33, 39, 41, 47, 60.

40 *The Autobiography of Malcolm X,* pp. 383–4, quoted from Robert Weisberg, 'What We in Museums Talk about When We Talk about Diversity', www.robertjweisberg.com/what-we-in-museums-talk-about-when-we-talk-about-diversity/. Accessed 1 August 2016.

41 J. Sandahl, 'A Continuous Process of Re-Conciliation', in Humboldt Forum Berlin, *Das Projekt*, ed. T. Flieri and H. Parzinger (Berlin: Theater der Zeit, 2009).

42 Learning to decipher or decode the real priorities of a given institution from the ratios between the different functions and budget streams was one of the most basic, but no less profound, lessons I got from the J. Paul Getty Trust's Museum Management Institute training.

43 Hanno Rauterberg, 'Palast der Verlogenheit', www.zeit.de/2015/24/humboldt-forum-berlin-richtfest. Accessed 1 June 2015.

44 Fanon's term.

6

Thinking and working through difference: remaking the ethnographic museum in the global contemporary

Viv Golding and Wayne Modest

Introduction: anxiety politics and museums

In this chapter, we reflect on ways that museums might, as Audre Lorde put it, take our differences and work through them as our strengths.[1] This has been a long-term project for both of us, starting from our individual positioning and alliances and situated knowledge(s) shifting over time and place, as we work in shifting institutional frameworks and with diverse collaborators globally. Overall, we reconsider our 2013 volume, *Museum and Communities: Curators, Collections, Collaboration*, with its geographical absences and silences, while addressing the complexity of identities and global entanglements within wider networks of power and control.[2] We ponder activist practice since the 1970s, from the murder by arson of black teenagers in New Cross, London, where one of us has roots, to Black Lives Matter in the USA today. In our current work with fellow museum professionals in Europe and internationally, including ICOM-ICME (the International Council of Museums of Ethnography), we consider translation across cultures and disciplines. We also note university work on prison museums and human rights, artist collaborations and the development of feminist pedagogy. Theoretically, the chapter unpacks the notion of the 'human', the 'cosmopolitan' and the inextricable relations between theory and practice, informed by collaborative work by one of the authors at the National Museum of World Cultures, Netherlands.

Groundings

2017. Just four years ago, during our editorial work on *Museum and Communities*, a volume that brought together the work of fifteen scholars and practitioners from across the world to explore the work of museum curation in fashioning more inclusive societies, we would not have imagined the rise in unmasked acts of racist and sexist violence and exclusion that now marks Euro-American political and popular landscapes. Indeed, the end of 2016, with the election of Donald Trump as the forty-fifth president of the United States, signals a new high point in racism and sexism in the USA. Trump's anti-Islam, anti-Mexican, anti-black taglines throughout his campaign gave justification to, and unleashed, unhinged acts of racism against people of colour and women in the wake of his win. White America, it has been said, came out fighting to 'make America great again', to make America white (again).

The election of Donald Trump followed on the heels of the Brexit referendum in the UK. Fuelled by the toxic tabloid press and winning with only a small margin (not even 52 per cent), millions of Britons voted to give up their membership to the European Union. This vote, on the face of it, may have been about questions of sovereign power in the face of a troubled EU government. However, it too had similar anti-immigrant and anti-Muslim undertones, and gave rise to everyday, unabated white hate-speech against non-white British citizens, and to the questioning of people's rights in Britain based on their visible difference.

Meanwhile in Europe, far- (and not so far-) right, anti-immigrant political parties – including Geert Wilder's Freedom Party (PVV) in the Netherlands and Marine le Pen's National Front in France – made gains through campaigns against what was perceived as uncontrolled migration and multiculturalism. The 'people' wanted their countries back. At the time of writing, several countries across Europe were preparing for national elections, with right-wing parties gaining in polls, although in the case of le Pen finally failing to achieve government power. In the UK a welcome and unexpected rise in the left vote, thanks to a surge of young voters, similarly failed to move the government, who continue to work on a Brexit agenda, which is an aspect of right-wing popularism. We concur with other commentators who have argued that the failure of these far-right parties in national elections should not be heralded as a victory for the left. Rather it should be seen as centre-right parties co-opting the right-wing ideologies of anxiety and exclusion to gain votes.

While it may be too soon to proffer any deep and empirically driven analysis of what these new political shifts across Euro-America may mean, for our purposes in museum work, we concur with Anouk de Koning and Wayne Modest, who have described our current moment as one marked by an anxious politics.[3] In their recent special issue of *Patterns of Prejudice*, they argue that increasing anxieties about the future of the nation state across Europe are based on the presumed vulnerabilities of an imagined *autochthonous* population, as the welfare state is dismantled. The feared loss of employment or housing, for example, is blamed on an often racialised 'Other' who is believed to be 'swamping' European cities.

Achille Mbembe has described the moment as the death of humanism (see Sandahl, Chapter 5 above). This death, he suggests, is characterised by an anti-humanist stance that is threatening democracy. At this moment, in Mbembe's account, there is a seeming normalisation of warfare: war against minorities, women, Muslims, disabled people and the working classes.[4] The effect not only blurs 'the supposed relationship between citizenship and democracy' but serves to '*incapacitate* whole sections of the population politically'.[5] Mbembe's critical thinking on recent events in South Africa resonates with our anti/decolonial stance in Western museums, and we highlight him here in solidarity with freedom movements globally.

These scenarios above mark out the conjuncture in which we are invited to reflect on our 2013 edited volume. What do these changes mean for museums and for curatorial practice? What kind of collaborative work with communities can we, or should we, expect in this new political moment? Over the last decade many museums, especially ethnographic museums, have been trying to rethink their practices under rubrics such as inclusivity or spaces of recognition, or have been working within the framework of 'source communities'. But the growing anxiety around those whom museums sought to include, namely (post)colonial or labour migrants from the formerly colonised regions of the world, create challenges for how museums and curators work.

In contrast to our work four years ago, today we have to address the present and future of collaborative curatorial work in which anxiety politics, or Mbembe's proclaimed death of humanism, dominates our popular and political imaginary. Put directly, we might ask: what is the future of curatorial collaborations, done so generously (even if naively) in the past under governments supportive of the multicultural project, within a new framework of right-wing and exclusionary politics marked by growing xenophobia? Concomitantly, how do new modes of refusal and acts of global 'decolonial' solidarity practices, from Rhodes Must Fall to Black Lives Matter, provide opportunity for the emergence of other curatorial possibilities?

Museum and communities of the global now: paradoxical cosmopolitanism

Kwame Anthony Appiah observes in *Cosmopolitanism: Ethics in a World of Strangers* that 'Our ancestors have been *human* for a very long time' (our emphasis).[6] Appiah consistently points to similarity across and within difference, which was a major theme in the 2013 publication *Museum and Communities*. Our book emerged out of a conference that we jointly organised at the Horniman Museum and Gardens, UK, in 2009. At that time, Modest worked as Keeper of Anthropology at the museum. Viv Golding, then lecturer in Museum Studies at the University of Leicester, had worked at the Horniman previously, leading the learning initiatives. Both of us were committed to museum work, not as a facile site for educative entertainment, but as an active site of politics – where differently constituted citizen-subjects, whether raced, classed or gendered, are governed, included or excluded.[7] Our work was informed by the robust scholarly work in the humanities and social sciences, and in postcolonial and critical theory that located the museum within a broader political landscape where definitions of cultural heritage formed part of contestations about how to define and who to include within the category of the citizen.

In 2013, when we pointed to what Rajagopalen Rhadakrishnan terms the economically 'uneven' world,[8] and how this inequity remains a blight on humanity, it was to underscore this commitment to activist museological practices. As we pulled the different contributions together, we were aware that each author not only explored local museum activities but located them within broader contexts of critique and practice. By 2013, museological practices worldwide had developed shared discourses about questions of inclusion or exclusion and politics of recognition. Our aim was to locate curatorial work at the centre of such activities that were generally relegated to the margins in education or learning departments.

Having both worked with ethnographic collections in London, we were deeply aware of the critical histories of those kinds of institutions that Tony Bennett describes as machines, differencing through exhibitionary apparatuses.[9] We were and are also committed, however, to the more hopeful anthropological commitment of which those collections were part, that is, to the study and understanding of the global diversity of humanity. London, our local home, had long provided a backdrop for our thinking: a global city that was hopeful and emancipatory in its possibilities of living with difference and at the same time marked by histories and presents of racialised violence and exclusion. Such was the complex, even paradoxical, cosmopolitan commitment to difference as not fixed or reductive but fluid which animated our work. It was not something to be feared but constitutive of the world in which we live, work and raise our children.

The political conjuncture we sketched above is one that resists the cosmopolitan for more parochial politics predicated on the nostalgic idea of a return to sameness. This sameness is mythical yet seen as a necessary, if not urgent, return to provide more prosperous futures for a population under threat. However, a large body of academic and policy work developed since the 1990s, and increasingly from 2000, has been dedicated to thinking about what it means to constitute a society *through* difference. We argue that these contemporary retreats to restrictive nation-state thinking, determinedly local in focus and articulation, fail to comprehend the historically contingent present in which we live. Moreover, they are based in a denial of our globally interconnected world, as well as the necessary work needed to fashion more just, equitable and fairer futures.

These historical and transnational contingencies are seen in Appiah's cosmopolitanism as part of an ethical life, in which our responsibilities to each other are central to the notion of morality in the present. Such a cosmopolitan morality conscripts those living in the financially affluent, or overdeveloped West into thinking about how they can positively or negatively affect 'the lives of others across the globe'.[10] We would argue that a key role for cultural institutions such as museums within this economically uneven world is to be concerned for individual human lives not only in our homelands but also around the world.[11] Appiah proposes two interrelated ideas, and these thread through our thinking on museums. First, we have obligations to 'others', and these extend beyond our family and fellow citizens in our nation states. Secondly, we need to take seriously the value of *particular* human lives, and in ethnographic museums this means taking an interest not only in objects as things but also in the people, changing practices and belief systems that lend them meaning.

We are also mindful that these thoughts have long been of significance to many anthropologists for whom diversity and a commitment to understanding the plurality of human existence are their core business, while recognising possible clashes between ideals that challenge cosmopolitan citizenship. Universal concern for human rights may clash with local beliefs and practices, for example when LBGTQ people may be incarcerated or condemned to death in countries where their sexual orientation is illegal. For example, it would be legally impossible for Ugandan museums to exhibit *Hello Sailor!* (Liverpool, UK, 2012) on the hidden history of gay lives at sea or the collaborative project that resulted in a display *LGBTQ Stories by Allsorts Youth Project* (Brighton Pavilion, UK, 2015–2016). Still, we hold firm to the notion of cosmopolitanism and its value to museums. With deep rhizome roots and wide-ranging responsibilities, we contend that local and global citizens *can* forge alliances to progress inclusion and engagement in civil society. The good work on cosmopolitanism shows how museums can become a springboard to the future, a cosmopolitan (and curatopian) future where we stand together for human rights.[12]

'Get Up Stand Up': history, rebellion and reconciliation

Bob Marley and the Wailers released 'Get Up Stand Up, Stand Up For Your Rights' in 1973, but it took thirty years, until 2005, for the curator Paul Gilroy to raise Marley's voice in the Museum of World Culture in Sweden. Arguably belated in its embrace of Marley's beckoning for the political, this was a welcomed shift within a museum landscape, which rarely narrates a resistance to politics, even if scholars such as Richard Sandell have tried to push a more political approach to museum practice over the years.[13] As we write in early 2017, the Smithsonian National Museum of African American History and Culture (NMAAHC, Washington, DC) has opened its doors, and we look forward to experiencing the fruits of the director Lonnie Bunch's collaborative curatorship. This opening is almost 150 years after the founding of the Smithsonian's National Museum of American History in 1858. It has taken a long time for the stories of African American people to take their rightful place on the National Mall.

On 24 April 2015, eighteen months before opening, the NMAAHC presented a symposium examining race, justice and community activism. The event, generously hosted by director Kevin Gover at the National Museum of the American Indian (NMAI, Washington, DC), was entitled *History,*

Rebellion and Reconciliation: Communities Mobilized for Social Change. In the video recording the day, available from the NMAAHC website, we can hear a myriad of voices, young and more experienced, from the museum world and the related fields of the arts and media, as well as activist and faith groups.[14] At the outset, the deputy director Kinshasha Holan Connell and founding director Lonnie Bunch highlighted the design of NMAAHC as a place of laughter, hope, meaning, memory and reflection on contemporary issues, alongside the traditional role of the museum as a space for beautiful objects and histories. Overall, this symposium demonstrated the power of the museum as a forum for productive dialogue, a sharing space to consider questions of racial subjectivities and fairness, difficult histories of injustice, struggles for freedom and reconciliation following moments of unrest.

It was one such moment on 9 August 2014 in Fergusson, Missouri, which prompted *History, Rebellion and Reconciliation*. This was when the eighteen-year-old black teenager Michael Brown was shot by a white police officer, Darren Wilson, twenty-eight years old, who was later exonerated. The excessive force used against this young man for the crime of stealing a few packets of cigarillos led to another moment, when the subsequent Black Lives Matter movement was born. At the symposium, director Bunch acknowledged the profound pain that present-day communities suffer under this shadow of injustice. In conversation with the Pastor of Wellspring Church, Fergusson, F. Willis Johnson, he asked how we might deal with this anger and show other ways than violence to deal with pain; how we, in the church and the museum, might use the moment and not let it break us. Willis Johnson highlighted the need to recall the elders who have been working for a long time and the many millions over the centuries before, born in the hulls of slave ships. As a follow-up Bunch stressed the contemporary museum's vital role in thinking and working through differ-ence. He urges us to consider the educational *use* of history and culture, to look back *and* ease present pain by shining a light on the future, to what we can become. We align ourselves with Bunch and Willis Johnson's conclu-sion that care and hope are key to museum and religious practices today.

Opal Tometi, founder of Black Lives Matter, emphasised this caring and responsible role at the symposium. Tometi spoke of the movement coming out of the 1960s Black and Proud work that was grounded in radical black love, inclusive not indifferent to black lives. Black Lives Matter promotes a more nuanced understanding of the black community today and of those on whose shoulders they stand. Fellow panellists, the law professor Lisa Crooms and writer for the *Nation* Mychal Denzel Smith, reinforced the observations that care and love for all means standing up for inherent human dignity. Most importantly, they challenged the narrative of black danger that criminalises black people and demanded the body politic to deal with the social ills and poverty that lie behind crime.

This discussion marks out a different terrain within which museums now work. Black lives Matter, like other similar social movements groups, made even more global through social media and that emerged to secure the rights of those most vulnerable, presents museums with new challenges. The NMAAHC actively creates safe spaces where all human beings are respected, valued and cared for. The museum holds itself accountable in communicating a message of hope that has shaped black communities for generations. It is difficult to express in words the multisensory museum space we are referring to, and we direct our readers to the NMAAHC video in which Kinshasha Holan Connell and Rex Ellis raise their voices in song, bringing the words of Ella Baker, 'shero' of the civil rights freedom movement, to life.[15] Baker's message is vital to the museum. She calls us to learn to stand and fight together:

> We who believe in freedom cannot rest.
> We who believe in freedom cannot rest until it comes.
> Until the killing of Black men, Black mothers' sons
> Is as important as the killing of White men, White mothers' sons.
> We who believe in freedom cannot rest.
> We who believe in freedom cannot rest until it comes.

Closer to our home, 13 August 2017 was the fortieth anniversary of a major anti-racism march. In 1977, thousands of local people in South-East London and anti-racists from further afield mobilised in opposition to the far-right National Front's (NF) attempt to march from the boroughs of New Cross, where we lived, studied and worked, to Lewisham. Collective action on 13 August ensured that the NF march through our multicultural community failed. The community stood firm in opposing the NF hatred of difference that Prime Minister Margaret Thatcher's conservative government and her call for police protection of these NF marches would seem to condone. While most of the protest took the form of peaceful resistance there were violent clashes between the NF, anti-fascists and the police. The day became known as the Battle of Lewisham.

Throughout the 1970s, there was a significant far-right presence in South-East London, and it must be admitted that there was widespread support for these racist groups. In a Deptford council by-election in 1976, the NF and the National Party achieved a combined vote of 44.5 per cent. Racist and fascist attacks against black and Asian people, their homes, shops and clubs, were proliferating. One of the most horrific incidents took place at 439 New Cross Road in the early hours of 18 January 1981, when a devastating fire ended the teenage birthday celebrations of Yvonne Ruddock and Angela Jackson. The lives of thirteen young black people between the ages of fourteen and twenty-two were cut short from burns and suffocation, and twenty-six others suffered serious injury. Two years later, another victim, haunted by the memory, committed suicide.

The white establishment, including museums, offered no condolences, sending another message that black lives were insignificant. But communities mourned and marched together in ways that foreshadowed the Black Lives Matter protests in the USA today. Importantly, some museums, such as the Horniman where we worked, began to learn from poets, musicians and artists that taking creative action against prejudice and injustice can be effective in demonstrating to staff and diverse audiences that curatorial work and object biographies extend beyond the historical record. These events and more collaborative work that continues are discussed in detail elsewhere but a brief précis may be useful here.[16]

In the 1990s, Golding began working closely with Joan Anim-Addo, director of the Caribbean Centre at Goldsmiths College, on the 'difficult' histories of transatlantic enslavement that were entangled with some of the Horniman Collections. Together they worked with teachers in service, holding after-school events on creative ways of connecting the Horniman with a multicultural curriculum focused on challenging racism and sexism. They also held regular sessions for communities. One project worked to engage audiences in creative writing activity inspired by Horniman objects and histories over a two-year period, which culminated in Anim-Addo's *Another Doorway Visible in the Museum* (London: Mango, 1999). Annually on 1 August, they celebrated the passing of the British Emancipation Bill through Parliament, with storytellers, musicians, and poets making the museum a 'homeplace' for the whole community.

The wide range of Modest's projects at Horniman include the *Stories of the World* youth curatorial project, which he discusses in *Museums and Communities*. This project adopts 'peer ethnography', where teenagers explore the complexity of their identities through material culture close to home, such as in their wardrobes, and what made it special. Over time and in conversation with experts, including photographers, curators, friends and members of the public whom they recorded about their clothing and style choices, as well as the museum staff, the youth came to see the familiar as enchanting, 'strange' and worthy of a second look. They recognised complex ways in which they or we contribute to the fashioning of ourselves, even within already existing structures. They also came to see the politics of difference and identification that marked the (global) city in which they lived (and even took for granted).[17]

We have been discussing our locally based museum projects, rooted in the concept of cosmopolitanism, with links to the wider world and spanning our lifetimes. Now we want to ask how, if at all, these ideas of thinking and working through difference translate to the global field. In what ways has collaborative museum action benefited international communities? Are the voices and lives of economically disadvantaged people raised, or are they condemned to simply listen? We turn to one global organisation, ICOM (The International Council of Museums), and to ICME (The International Committee for Museums of Ethnography), which tackles these questions.

The International Council of Museums

Translating across disciplinary boundaries and working across national borders is a feature of ICOM. ICOM has a consultative status with

UNESCO, the United Nations Economic and Social Council. The ICOM website celebrates being a 'diplomatic forum of experts from 136 countries and territories' who are 'a leading force in ethical matters'. ICOM, formed in 1946, is a 'unique network of more than 35,000 members and museum professionals who represent the global museum community' and 'respond to the challenges museums face worldwide'.[18] Today, there are 119 National Committees and thirty International Committees dedicated to various museum specialties.

We are involved with ICME (the International Council for Museums of Ethnography).[19] Golding has served on the Board since 2004 as newsletter editor and secretary. She was elected president (2013–2016; 2016–2019) and, in this current role, issues of translation between and within cultures, as well as hierarchies of power and control, are spotlighted. For example, the charge of linguistic imperialism rings true as ICOM has three official languages: English, French and Spanish. Nevertheless, there are sincere and practical efforts to tackle global inequality. ICOM funds are set aside for individual committees to fully sponsor fellows from 'category 3 and 4 countries' or economically challenged nations and youth 'under 35' members to attend the annual conferences. These funds are competitive and ICME has been successful in sponsoring three conference fellows every year. ICME has been developing productive discussions in recent years about the future role of ethnographic collections, notably since our annual conferences in Windhoek, Namibia, in 2012; Zagreb, Croatia, in 2014; Hanoi, Vietnam, in 2015; and Milan, Italy, in 2016.

ICME also secured special project funding to engage in *Africa Accessioned* (2014–16). Dr Jeremy Silvester of ICOM Namibia worked with us to launch a pilot project in 2014 in response to ICOM's theme for International Museum Day – *Museum Collections Make Connections*. A small working group began to establish a database that lists African ethnographic collections held in European museums. Four African countries provided the initial focus for the project: Botswana, Namibia, Zambia and Zimbabwe. The project has begun to 'map' relevant collections held in museums in Finland, Germany, Sweden and the UK. A firm knowledge network was established and an extensive number of goodwill partnerships were formed. In 2015, with bilateral assistance from Finland, a Namibian delegation visited the major collections from Namibia held in Finnish museums and produced a country report indicating the type of collaborative projects that might be developed as a result. The report indicates the ways in which the *Africa Accessioned* project can have a 'multiplier' effect in generating increased co-operation between museums internationally, using collections as a springboard.

Africa Accessioned is now developing a user-friendly web platform to facilitate extended dialogue and communication between those museums and sister museums linked to communities in the regions where artefacts were originally obtained. We aim to work productively with the transcultural aspect of the museum world, where many African museum displays feature objects of daily life (e.g. furniture and costumes) made in Europe, while many European museums contain displays of ethnographic collections from Africa, to show the ways in which centuries of exchange have shaped cultural landscapes and how histories are connected. *Africa Accessioned* on the web will provide a forum for the exchange of ideas and raise themes of importance to ICOM, pointing to the dynamic nature of cultures and societies and the complexity of object biographies. It will challenge the stereotypes and prejudice that linger on from the colonial periods, by stimulating collaborative global research. Most notably, it will provide a platform for African voices to engage more effectively with the material culture and intangible heritage housed in museums within and beyond Africa.

The global conversation will enable heritage communities to provide greater historical depth regarding the intangible cultural heritage and geographical places which can provide a more complete biography of an object in a collection. We argue here that ethnographic objects in particular need to be linked, somehow, with the place, practices and stories that gave them meaning – a triangular perspective – while recognising that they subsequently acquire new layers of meanings in the sense of object biographies. The use of collections to forge contemporary links between different places can also provide the basis for additional forms of cultural exchange. As many ethnographic collections were formed during the colonial period, such international exchanges can stimulate and inform debates about contemporary issues and emphasise the conditions under which some traditions might endure, while others have faded or evolved.

The willingness to revise displays and review collections so as to address the past will enable increased cultural dialogue and positive co-operation in the present and future. Africa has been accessioned, but we can use the connections that these collections create to build bridges across our cultural landscapes, rather than barriers. The ICME project adds value to ICOM, significantly supporting the aim of increasing its membership within Africa. African ICOM members do not gain a great deal of benefit from the free entry into museums provided by the ICOM card. However, direct involvement in an ICOM-funded pilot project of direct benefit to African museums significantly increases ICOM's profile on the continent. Additionally, ICME aims to raise the global dialogue on what a museum is, and can be, through a series of collaborative workshops, which employ material culture and intangible heritage as vehicles for addressing contemporary concerns for human rights and social justice.

Developing pedagogies of human rights and social justice

A key strand of our recent academic work concerns pedagogy. For example, we have been exploring the development of feminist pedagogies and pedagogy in prison museums.[20] Prisons around the world today incarcerate overwhelming numbers of economically disadvantaged people, too often black people, and our focus is on the prison museum as a learning space.

Today, at prison museum sites of 'difficult histories', we remember the lives of the famous heroes who resisted oppression, and also the ordinary men, women and children who suffered for attempting to obtain their basic human rights. A wide range of pedagogic work is undertaken at prison museums. For example, contemporary collaboration with artists and psychologists can help engage audiences' minds, bodies and emotions with the 'terrible gift' of the past, to employ Roger Simon's term.[21] When we as curators or as audiences accept this terrible gift, we are impelled to take responsibility for the future and act at local and global levels.

Pedagogy in the prison museum is informed by feminism and philosophical thought that addresses power hierarchies. It promotes the museum as a site of what Éduoard Glissant terms affective relation.[22] This pedagogic praxis understands the museum as a creolised and affective multilingual space where respectful conversations raise the diverse voices of those who were previously marginalised or silenced within the institutional walls.[23] Pedagogy is marked by a productive both/and stance, rather than the negative either/or binaries, to enrich intercultural understandings and cosmopolitan identifications that we alluded to above.

Since the publication of *Museums and Communities*, Modest has moved on to work in the Netherlands at the National Museum of World Culture, where he heads the Research Center for Material Culture.[24] This new national museum was created in 2014 out of the merger of the Tropenmuseum in Amsterdam, the Museum Volkenkunde in Leiden and the Africa Museum in Berg en Dal. Taking on a new and distinctly societal mission focused on the correlated concerns of what it means to share a world with others and the plural possibilities of being human, the museum reorganised its programming from outside in, with an emphasis on its social relevance for a changing Dutch (but also global) society. The museums adopted two interrelated frameworks that govern their practice. On the one hand, it describes itself as a museum about and for people. This was intended to move away from the focus on the more ICOM-oriented definition of collecting, preserving and displaying objects towards a practice where the lives of the people for whom these objects have and make meaning became central. Secondly, the museum's mission became focused on contributing to the development of world citizens. This is intended to emphasise notions of empathy and understanding for others while also suggesting the need to live responsibly in the world we share with others.

Modest contributes to this new mission by leading a research and public programmes agenda that helps to articulate these 'missionary' concerns. In research work, the museum has been committed to rethinking the collections to articulate more contemporary political concerns from questions around planetary histories and gender, to thinking through the museum as a site for redressing historical wrongs.[25] The programming of the centre becomes an extension of these concerns, addressing questions of slavery's afterlife in the present, decolonial practices for museums and questions of citizenship and belonging. For Modest, these projects have coincided with an ongoing project of trying to think critically about Europe in the postcolonial moment, and the role of museums and other heritage institutions in shaping Europe today.

This has meant thinking through a politics of community, about how a new politics surrounding racialised belonging might be impacting on museums differently now. One project that emerged out of this thinking was a collaboration with the young activist group Decolonise The Museum (DTM). Established together with the Tropenmuseum, this group of young people created a platform for criticism that was invested in pushing museums towards representational practices that did not hide from their colonial genealogies but rather used them towards more ethical or redressive practices for a more equal world. DTM organised a series of workshops and a seminar at the Tropenmuseum, inviting a diverse network (chosen intersectionally) of young people to critique the Tropenmuseum to highlight blind spots and exclusionary language in the narratives the galleries presented. In addition to the live workshops, the conversations were expanded through Twitter, through #decolonisethemuseum.[26]

The outcome was a robust critique of the museum, which eventually resulted in new improvisational text panels as prototypes for future texts and a conference organised to share the group's findings. In addition to highlighting the museum's 'complicity' in underplaying the role of the colonial in shaping the museum, and indeed our contemporary world, they also pointed out the need to be committed not just to objects but to the humanity of the people whose lifeworlds these objects represent. Since the beginning of the collaboration, DTM has continued to work with different sections of the museum to identify representational blind spots. This process will impact the new permanent exhibitions that will open in the coming years.

This review of our recent work shows how our thinking has developed over the last few years. The contributors to our book back in 2013 celebrated humanity together with us in that project, and we continue to carry this work on with a range of human projects. For our part, we have become more attuned to the anxiety politics that now ensnares the UK, Europe and more globally. Similarly, we have had to ponder the ways in which (global) solidarity around questions of decolonising institutions (beyond diversity for some), which includes museums and universities and curricula or programming, has taken new forms aided by new media.

Concluding thoughts: the responsible relational museum

In 'Geographies of Responsibility', Doreen Massey considers notions of space and place within political positions in ways that resonate with our understanding of curatorial cosmopolitanism in the museum context.[27] Like Massey, we object to the opposition of space as abstract and place as real, grounded or local, and we also want to work through an active politics of local place in wider global ways of thinking and doing. We draw once again on Éduoard Glissant's ideas of relation and creolisation to reinforce Massey's view of relational space, that the world is constituted relationally and there is no space outside of lived place.[28] Furthermore, we agree that 'forms of emplacedness and embodiedness' can entail meaningfulness and the creation of new identities.[29] In other words, cultural practices are emplaced and embodied. Bodies are not frozen; they move and carry culture into place over time and space. This thinking opens up a politics of place that recognises networks and connections, relations and practices, while, at the same time, it moves beyond the parochial.

We appreciate Massey's highlighting of feminist philosophy, the collective and the imagination as aspects of a responsibility entangled in the relational present and, most importantly, extended back in time to emphasise present-day responsibility for historical events.[30] Acknowledging that we are *responsible* in the here and now gives impetus and greater force to our contemporary action, because responsibility is not relegated to an abstract temporal space when embodied relations are extended geographically as well as historically. In the museum, we also see our research and practice applying a 'politics of connectivity' and a series of 'imaginative leap[s]' to progress thinking and acting relationally.[31] Relational practice observes identities as constituted in and through engagements, 'which include non-relations, absences and hiatus' that are emotionally fraught.[32]

How can this thinking be translated into museum practice? We want to illustrate this through the Australian Aboriginal artist Christian Thompson's ongoing collaboration with the Pitt Rivers Museum, Oxford, UK. Thompson was born in 1978 to a father of the Bidjara Indigenous people of central South West Queensland, Australia, and a mother of British heritage. He was educated in the Netherlands and in England, winning a Charlie Perkins Scholarship to the University of Oxford in 2010, making him one of the first two Australian Aboriginal students to study at this prestigious institution. In later years, his concern for the Bidjara traditional language, which is endangered, led to a creative engagement introducing Bidjara back into popular culture through music.

Thompson's collaboration with Pitt Rivers was initiated in 2011, when curator Dr Christopher Morton invited Thompson to engage with the photographic archive of Australian Aboriginal people. This dated from the birth of the museum in 1884 and resulted from the relationship between Pitt Rivers' first curator Henry Balfour and his Australian friend Stanley Baldwin. A photographic performance work, *We Bury Our Own* (2012), was the fruit of the first collaboration, and his latest piece was created five years on in 2017.[33]

Thompson wanted to work directly – physically and emotionally – rather than digitally with the photographic collection. He was moved by the 'ethnographic' portrait images of men staring straight at the colonial lens of the camera, and the head and shoulder framing showing traditional scarification and body painting, as well as Western hair combing. His ancestors touched

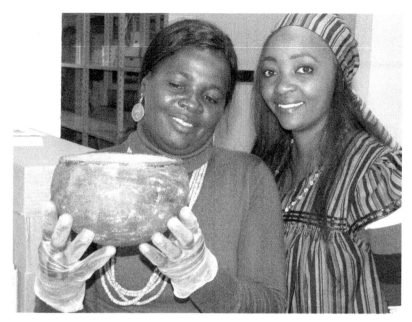

6.1 Magdalena Kaanante of Nakambale Museum and Charmaine Tjizezenga from the Museums Association of Namibia inspecting artefacts at the National Museum of Finland in Helsinki. Africa Accessioned project, ICME.

him. Their images remain in the archive stores after digital repatriation and they seem to speak to him from this ancestral resting place. He describes his own living experience with the ancestors as one of 'spiritual repatriation', which he draws equally on his own 'fluid and evolving transcultural identity' including the recent biographical markers as an Oxford scholar.

Thompson's *We Bury Our Own* is, in our view, relational and cosmopolitan. It can also be seen as part of the creolising museum discussed above, in addressing historical wrongs and creating something new. Most importantly, Thompson appropriates and plays with the means of colonial representation – photography – inverting key markers of identity along the way. We are not given the easy access to Thompson's eyes and hair that the ancestral images, probably coerced, give. Thompson covers his eyes with flowers in *Lamenting the Flowers*, and a mapping dot pattern of Aboriginal cloth covers his hair in *Forgiveness of Land*. In collaborating with the museum, Thompson could be said to appropriate the curatorial role himself in selecting, rearranging and re-representing the collection.

Thompson's relation with the creolising museum, we wish to suggest, invites further creative conversations and repatriations in the open spirit of the cosmopolitan. In the online catalogue essay, Christopher Morton quotes the Aboriginal writer and curator Michael Aird who argues:

> One of the biggest responsibilities of museums and archives today … is to make collections available to Aboriginal communities, despite the anxieties

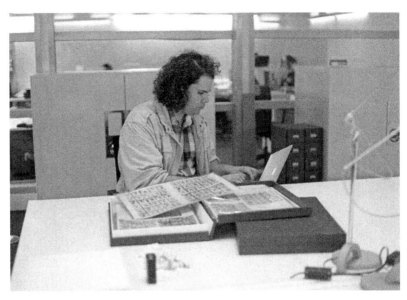

6.2 Aboriginal artist Christian Thompson working at the Pitt Rivers Museum, Oxford University, UK.

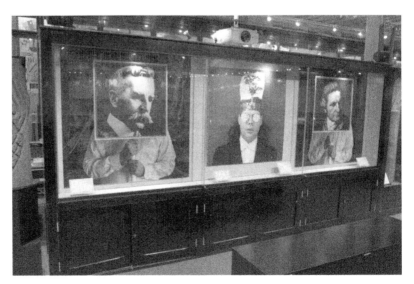

6.3 Christian Thompson works in situ at the Pitt Rivers Museum, Oxford University, UK.

of curators about the best ways to go about this. As Christian Thompson's new work shows us, Aboriginal artists and curators are moving into an exciting new phase of creative engagement with their visual history, one that moves the debate on from the politics of race and injustice, towards multiple, complex, and hybrid identities in the present, and into the future.[34]

It is fitting that we end our collaborative chapter with Christian Thompson's intervention, as a cosmopolitan artist-curator, in the Pitt Rivers Museum. This culture-jamming and mixing-things-up, evident in Thompson's photographic performance work, exemplifies the responsible and relational museum with creolised relational roots, inspiring and impelling us to stand together across divides. We salute him.

Notes

1 A. Lorde. *The Audre Lorde Compendium: Essays, Speeches and Journals. The Cancer Journals. Sister Outsider* (London: A Burst of Light Pandora, 1996).

2 V. Golding and W. Modest (eds), *Museums and Communities: Curators, Collections and Collaboration* (London and New York: Bloomsbury, 2013).

3 W. Modest and A. de Koning, 'Anxious Politics in the European City: An Introduction', in *Patterns of Prejudice*, 50:2 (2016), 97–108.

4 A. Mbembe, 'The Age of Humanism is Ending', *Mail & Guardian*, 22 December 2016. See https://mg.co.za/article/2016-12-22-00-the-age-of-humanism-is-ending. Accessed 11 January 2017.

5 A. Mbembe, *On the Postcolony* (Berkeley, CA: University of California Press, 2001), p. 88 [original emphasis].

6 K.A. Appiah, *Cosmopolitanism: Ethics in a World of Strangers* (New York: W.W. Norton and Company, Inc., 2006), p. xi.

7 V. Golding and W. Modest, 'Introduction', in Golding and Modest (eds), *Museums and Communities*, pp. 1–12; V. Golding, 'Collaborative Museums: Curators, Communities, Collections', in Golding and Modest (eds), *Museums and Communities*, 13–31; V. Golding, 'Creolizing the Museum: Art, Humour, Young Audiences', in Golding and Modest (eds), *Museums and Communities*, 195–216; W. Modest, 'Co-curating with Teenagers at the Horniman Museum', in Golding and Modest (eds), *Museums and Communities*, 98–109.

8 R. Rhadakrishnan, *Theory in an Uneven World* (Oxford: Blackwell, 2003).

9 T. Bennett, 'The Exhibitionary Complex', in D. Preziosi and C. Farago (eds), *Grasping the World: The Idea of the Museum* (Aldershot: Ashgate, 2004), pp. 413–41.

10 Appiah, *Cosmopolitan*, xii–xiii.

11 These ideas are not new. Appiah traces cosmopolitanism to the cynics in Greece in the fourth century BCE, and, more recently, to the Declaration of the Rights of Man and the League of Nations.

12 R. Mason, 'National Museums, Globalization, and Postnationalism: Imagining a Cosmopolitan Museology', *Museum Worlds: Advances in Research*, 1 (2013), 40–64. P. Schorch, 'The Cosmohermeneutics of Migration Encounters at the Immigration Museum, Melbourne', *Museum Worlds: Advances in Research*, 2 (2014), 81–98. P. Schorch, E. Waterton and S. Watson, 'Museum Canopies and Affective Cosmopolitanism. Cultivating Cross-Cultural Landscapes for Ethical Embodied Responses', in D.P. Tolia-Kelly, E. Waterton and S. Watson. *Heritage, Affect and Emotion* (Oxford: Taylor and Francis, 2016), pp. 93–113.

13 See R. Sandell and E. Nightingale, *Museums, Equality and Social Justice* (London and New York: Routledge, 2012).

14 See National Museum of African American History and Culture website, https://nmaahc.si.edu/explore/initiatives/history-rebellion-and-reconciliation. Accessed 1 April 2017.

15 *Ibid.*

16 V. Golding. 'Museums, Poetics, Affect', *Feminist Review*, 104:1 (July 2013), 80–99; V. Golding, *Learning at the Museum Frontiers: Identity Race and Power* (London: Routledge, 2016 [2009]).

17 Modest, 'Co-curating with Teenagers at the Horniman Museum'.

18 See ICOM website, http://icom.museum/. Accessed 1 April 2017.

19 ICME website, http://icom.museum/the-committees/international-committees/international-committee/international-committee-for-museums-and-collections-of-ethnography/. Accessed 1 April 2017.

20 V. Golding, 'Exploring Identities through Feminist Pedagogy', in R. Wilson and W. Grahn (eds), *Museums and Heritage* (London: Routledge, 2017); V. Golding, 'Developing Pedagogies of Human Rights and Social Justice in the Prison Museum', in J.Wilson, S. Hodgkinson, J. Piché and K. Walby (eds), *The Palgrave Handbook of Prison Tourism* (London: Palgrave Macmillan, 2017), pp. 987–1008.

21 R. Simon, 'The Terrible Gift: Museums and the Possibility of Hope without Consolation', *Museum Management and Curatorship*, 21 (2006), 187–204.

22 É. Glissant, *Poetics of Relation*, trans. by B. Wing (Ann Arbor: University of Michigan Press, 1997 [1990]).

23 V. Golding, 'Creolizing the Museum: Art, Humour, Young Audiences'; V. Golding, 'Museums, Poetics, Affect', *Feminist Review*, 104:1 (2013), 80–99, https://link.springer.com/article/10.1057/fr.2013.2. Accessed 1 April 2017.

24 See the website, www.materialculture.nl/?gclid=CM3X5fScsNMCFYGavAodhX IEEA. Accessed 15 April 2017.

25 See Research Center for Material Culture website, www.materialculture.nl/. Accessed 1 April 2017.

26 See 'On the Poetics and Politics of Redress', #Decolonise The Museum, 13–15 November 2015, https://vimeo.com/164082870. Accessed 15 April 2017.

27 D. Massey, 'Geographies of Responsibility', *Geograrafiska Annaler*: Series B. Human Geography, 86:1 (2004), 5–18 [1–29]. Available at Open Research Online, http://oro.open.ac.uk/7224/. Accessed 15 April 2017.

28 Golding. 'Museums, Poetics, Affect', *Feminist Review*.

29 Massey 'Geographies of Responsibility', 5.

30 *Ibid.*, 10.

31 *Ibid.*, 4.

32 *Ibid.*

33 C. Morton, 'Christian Thompson at the Pitt Rivers Museum', Returning Photos: Australian Aboriginal Photographs from European Collections: Pitt Rivers Museum website 2015, https://ipp.arts.uwa.edu.au/christian-thompson-at-the-pitt-rivers-museum/ and www.prm.ox.ac.uk/christianthompson.html. Accessed 23 March 2017. See also C. Thompson, Interview with Janet Mckenzie: Christian Thompson.net, www.christianthompson.net/single-post/2014/11/13/Christian-Thompson-interview-'My-work-does-not-need-to-be-read-through-the-optical-lens-of-my-race'. Accessed 22 March 2017.

34 Available at www.prm.ox.ac.uk/christianthompson.html. Accessed 29 April 2017.

NORTH AMERICA

 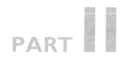

The times of the curator

James Clifford

7

My title tropes the title of a conference where this chapter began its life: 'The Task of the Curator'.[1] In what follows I evoke two senses of temporality: first 'The Times': as in the historical moment or context, 'the life and times of x', and second 'Times' plural: a sense of the curator's task as enmeshed in multiple, overlapping, sometimes conflicting times.

My primary concern is the discrepant temporalities (sometimes I want to say 'histories', or even 'futures') that are integral to the task of the curator today. I liked the conference title because of its invocation of Walter Benjamin and the problematic of translation, which in his famous essay 'The Task of the Translator' is fundamentally a temporal and open-ended process. For Benjamin, of course, the discordant times of the past would be activated and 'made new' by a critical-materialist form of historicising that could challenge and open up closed narratives, the inevitable realisms of the victors.[2]

I believe that what is going on currently in museums has the potential to make this kind of critical intervention. For the museum is an inventive, globally and locally *translated* form, no longer anchored to its modern origins in Europe. Contemporary curatorial work, in the excessive times of decolonisation and globalisation, by *engaging with* discrepant temporalities – not resisting, or homogenising, their inescapable friction – has the potential to open up commonsense, 'given' histories. It does so under serious constraints – a push and pull of material forces and ideological legacies it cannot evade.

Museum curating in nineteenth-century Europe was inseparable from the gathering, valuing and preservation of heritage – art and culture – in the context of bourgeois, national projects. Museums, as they became established, were purveyors of normative models of citizenship, taste, education and progress, as is detailed in the well-known work of scholars like Carol Duncan, Tony Bennett and others.[3] In the nineteenth century, the times of the curator were normatively lined up in a singular, developmental History. But it is important to recognise that this history was less and less anchored by the teleologies of either Christian salvation or Enlightenment reason. What might be called Darwinian time – developmental, materially adaptive and without any guaranteed destination – interjected a new, and troubling, ontological 'ground', or lack of ground. This unmanageable seriality may account for the anxiety, as well as the desire, associated with the collecting and preserving in museums around 1900. And it may have something to do with the remarkable productivity and dissemination of the museum form in the present moment of historical uncertainty.

Since the eighteenth century, Western curating has been associated with the creation and management of *colonial* collections. These collections were built on conquest (the Napoleonic expeditions, the Benin Bronzes ...) and on assumptions of 'salvage', the necessity and the right (guaranteed by a linear, progressive History) to collect vanishing or endangered artefacts, as well as written and oral records.[4] Colonial collecting, which reached something like a fever pitch in the late nineteenth century, conceived of museums and archives as ultimate resting places, repositories for a precious legacy, kept in trust for science, for the nation, for Civilisation or for Humanity. Museums were treasure houses, and curators were their knowledgeable and loving guardians. The times of the curator were aligned in evolutionary sequences that (unlike Darwin's time) assumed a vantage point at the end or cutting edge of development, and a place at the centre of a world system, a stable hierarchy of places and times.[5]

I do not need to dwell on this map or history, this 'worlding'. The fact that we see it clearly now, as if from a distance, suggests that a shift has occurred, or, better, is occurring. Call it a 'decentring of the West', perhaps the principal achievement of the last half of the twentieth century. Two driving forces of this shift can be named, in shorthand: decolonisation and globalisation. Proceeding at economic, social, political and cultural levels, these processes are uneven and sometimes contradictory. Decolonisation and globalisation are linked, but distinct, historical dynamics.

This is, naturally, a crude generalisation, painting with a broom. But it will have to suffice, for now, to characterise the changing times of the curator in a new millennium. Times of confusion, of intersecting, crossing historical vectors, of alternative pasts and futures. I hasten to add that displacing the West (a dominant but always permeable and negotiated cultural location and economic power) does not mean leaving behind, getting free of, the legacies of colonisation or the capitalist world system. Far from it. It does mean that other big, or big enough, historical stories now need to be taken seriously alongside the former 'realistic' narratives of Westernisation, Modernisation, Progress, Development and the like.

There are many examples of this decentring. There is the opening of what seems to be a new Crystal Palace Exhibition, not in London, but the Shanghai World Expo in China. It has been a while since London was the centre of the world. Another example can be found in Bolivia, where Evo Morales has hosted an alternative global climate change convention, in counterpoint to the failed Copenhagen summit. Or there is Emmanuel Wallerstein, who has been writing about what he sees as the end of the five-hundred-year Modern World System that he himself put on the historical map. That system is over, Wallerstein now believes: we are in a period of 'transition' and radical indeterminacy about what will come next.[6]

These are just a few signs of the decentring of the West, the branching and crossing of its historical teleologies in emergent, translational practices. My own awareness of these shifts has been deepened, over the past several decades, by the emergence of 'Indigenous' politics, social movements and cultural renewals in new public, performative contexts (peoples once thought to be destined for extinction reappearing rather suddenly, as Marx might have put it, 'on the world stage').[7]

I write here largely from the perspective of this Indigenous emergence, the focus of my recent research. Of course, curatorial practices, as conceived in this book, embrace a very wide variety of social contexts, historical constraints and sites of intervention. I am certainly not privileging the experiences of 'Indigenous curating' I will be evoking. But I do think they shed important, cross-cutting light on some persistent assumptions about time and history that have organised the Western institution of the museum, a cultural form that (as I have already suggested) is being translated throughout the world, in novel and unexpected ways.

My wake-up call was the Mashpee tribal recognition trial of 1977, which I attended in Boston as a graduate student and wrote about later in *The Predicament of Culture*.[8] A living Indian tribe on Cape Cod simply was not on my map of historical reality. All of my categories of cultural form and social and temporal continuity were shaken up. And in a way, I have been grappling with the questions posed by the Mashpee ever since. They led me to an interest in the ways tribal people were remembering, telling, performing their histories – deep pasts inseparable from specific places, and violent colonial histories of rupture, loss and inventive survival. Tribal museums and cultural centres would become a research focus for me, places where I could see in action the gathering and transmission – the curating – of heritage, processes of preservation and valuing, but not in a classic 'museological' sense. Instead I had to recognise old and ongoing social processes of articulation, performance and translation, across generations, and across fraught borders of culture and place.

It was a time when we were coming to see the borders of identity as dynamic, continually transgressed and remade, in specific historical relations of power, often unequal, but never static or unidirectional. Mary Pratt's concept of the 'contact zone', drawn from colonial situations of dominance and transculturation, gave me a way of reconceiving the hierarchical, authoritative spaces of the Western museum. Readers may recall that the essay 'Museums as Contact Zones', which appeared in my book *Routes*, begins with Tlingit elders in the basement of an art museum in Portland, telling (singing) unexpected stories inspired by objects of their heritage, reopening (re-membering) histories and powers associated with museum artefacts no longer collected 'once and for all'.[9]

For me, the contact zone idea was a way to think about constitutive translations, opening up closed spaces (like museum basements, more crowded places now …). At that time, I saw the work of the curator – whether aesthetic, ethnographic or historical – as essentially conservative. In French, it is unambiguous: *conservateur*. Museums were collections of valuable things, and the job of the curator was to keep them safe, carefully displayed for public edification, or preserved in storage for research purposes.

I always felt uncomfortable in museum basements: all those undisplayed objects, silenced drums, powerful presences wrapped in plastic. The sheer, historical injustice of massive collections held in Western capitals while few old examples of African, Torres Straits or Alaskan art and culture could be seen in their places of origin. This made me want to open everything up, disperse the collections and bring outsiders into the museums to make new meanings, like Fred Wilson with his artist interventions.[10]

There were movements in the air that pointed in this direction. A leading influence for me, and many others, was the University of British Columbia (UBC) Museum of Anthropology in Vancouver, Canada, moving decisively towards collaboration under the directorship of Michael Ames, and under the *pressure* of North-West Coast Indian artists and tribes.[11] And we might recall the subversive work of Mary Nooter Roberts and Susan Vogel at the Museum for African Art in New York City, USA. shaking up what a museum could be.[12] They sponsored, for example, William Farris Thompson's pioneering exhibit of 'living' altars from African-descended religions in the Americas – altars that needed to be fed, that attracted offerings, dancing, drumming in spaces like the Berkeley University Art Museum, USA, where I saw it during its travelling phase. It was at this time, too, that the Oakland Museum began to open up its galleries to amazing and moving constructions by community-based *altaristas* during the autumn weeks of *Dia de los Muertos*. It seemed the work of the curator was getting more interesting.

If you consult 'curator' and 'curate' in a dictionary you find that they come from *curare*, which means to care for something. In the recent work of Donna Haraway on inter-species relations, the idea of *caring* ceases to be a practice of protecting by enclosing and becomes a profoundly relational activity of crossing and translating.[13] The 'care' of curating, in this perspective, is about preservation (in the sense of thriving) through active relations of reciprocity and dialogue – not administration or tutelage.

In the activities of Indigenous museums and cultural centres, curatorial practices were being translated and remade. 'Salvage' collecting and preservation would take on new meanings, no longer about gathering up what is doomed but rather supporting continuity and renovation. The Tlinglit elders in the Portland museum basement *cared* deeply for the material objects there, but did not need them back. Material possession was not their first priority. They wanted the *stories* embodied in old masks and carved headpieces to be *renewed*, and they also wanted to forge relations of alliance and responsibility with the museum, in the midst of ongoing struggles to thrive as a people in a complex, dangerous postmodernity. Indigenous curating has made me think again about the difficult, essential work of cultural politics: the relational, power-charged, processes of sustaining *difference through relationships*: keeping while sharing.

Around the world we see examples of current experiments and signs of the changing times I have been describing. First, the 'Multiversity Gallery' at the Museum of Anthropology UBC, Canada, which was designed in collaboration with First Nations, and its digital Reciprocal Research Network linking British Columbia tribal museums with collections in Ottawa, Washington, Oxford, Cambridge and more. Second, the Arctic Studies Center in Anchorage Alaska, USA, purpose-built for circulating collections from the Smithsonian, and for facilitating Native, hands-on access to their heritage. Third, the growth of digital archives which are collaborative in design and sensitive to Native protocols, such as Ruth Phillips's project in the Great Lakes area, and an experimental alliance between the Zuni tribe and the Cambridge Museum of Archaeology and Anthropology, UK. Fourth are tribal museums, for example the Native-run Alutiiq Museum on Kodiak Island, Alaska, USA, and the Chateau Musée, in provincial France, working closely together to return on-loan iconic masks from Alutiiq heritage, not seen since the 1870s. These two 'marginal' museums are bypassing the national cultural institutions (Smithsonian, Quai Branly) to create their own reciprocal network, an alter-globalisation from below.[14]

And lest we think that the insides and outsides of identity are clear, that everyone agrees on just who they are, or that collaborative curating is somehow simply a matter of respect and reciprocity, we will always have Paul Chaat-Smith, Comanche curator and writer at the National Museum of the American Indian in Washington, DC, USA, to keep us honest, reminding us (with humorous and mordant irony, never cynicism) of the pitfalls, the mistakes and misunderstandings, the ways that cultural authority is shored up and contested in the non-innocent contact zones of inter-tribal life today.[15]

'Curating', as cultural performance and heritage management, emerges as a newly complicated and relational task. What do we value and hold on to, what do we let go? What stories can be told? To whom? When? Which relations do we nourish? Curating involves complex negotiations, performances and translations in given *fields of force*: historical, economic, political.

I will not try to provide anything like a map or overview of these terrains of struggle and synergy. Things are too volatile and diverse for that. Rather I would like to offer a few specific examples of 'Indigenous curating' which bring the temporalities of curating back into view – now that the nineteenth-century museum chronotope of finality and centrality is up for grabs.

Let me offer three examples of what I have come to think of as 'Indigenous curating', working with things and relations in transforming times. I hope it will be clear that the temporal predicaments and strategies I am highlighting are not limited to tribal or Native heritage work, or to museums with collections. Even in the so-called new museums or in local cultural centres, the task of the curator always involves deciding what to save and what to lose, what to remember and what to tell, what gets performed and what stays off-stage, what is translated (made new) and what is consigned to oblivion. Moreover, to speak of 'deciding' these questions is misleading. Time does not wait for us to make up our minds.

My first example is provided by the anthropologist Nelson Graburn in an article for a special section on 'Indigenous curating' in the journal *Museum Anthropology* in 1998.[16] Graburn is well known for his long ethnographic experience with the Inuit of North-East Canada. The region has been named and renamed, reflecting altered relations of power: from the Hudson's Bay Area to Nouveau Quebec to Nunavut. There are also, of course, a great many local names. The protagonist of Graburn's article, Tamusi Qumak Nuvalinga, who died in 1993, was raised in igloos and tents. Monolingual in Inuttitut, he devoted many years to constructing a dictionary, which he hoped would preserve the language and support its use in schools. He also created a 'museum', which he called *Saputik* or 'Weir'. It opened in 1978. As an aside, it is fascinating to consider the various names of non-Western museums or cultural centres: 'Box of Treasures', 'Fortunate Return', 'Common Bowl', 'Winter storage', 'Attic', to list a few in English translation.

A weir is not exactly a 'dam', which *blocks* a stream, it is rather more like a strainer; a weir as Tamusi knew it, was a barrier of stones and wood, used to catch fish without stopping the river's flow. This means of *selective* capture provided an image of collecting and remembering. The contents of Tamusi's 'weir' (a two-storey wooden faux 'igloo') included: clothes and possessions of loved ones; dog sleds (but not snowmobiles); soapstone carvings (a relatively new art form that has become a source of Inuit pride); 1950s and 1960s photographs of Inuit people; upstairs, a re-created igloo interior, with old and newly commissioned furnishings. A 'traditional' world is gathered here in a retrospective project that is not, however, a re-creation of the 'pre-contact' past. Rather it gathers up things that need to be saved from the immediate, familiar, mixed and usable past.

According to Graburn, The Weir reflected a new historical awareness: 'Tamusi envisaged time as a river carrying everything irrevocably out to sea to be lost forever.'[17] Things swept down Tamusi's river cannot be expected to come around again. And this feeling of non-return evokes something like Western historical time. *Something like*: for the transition experienced by Inuit in the later twentieth century is also a translation. What emerges with The Weir is surely different from other Inuit senses of time, whether these are conceived of as prior to or coexisting with Tamusi's river metaphor. But is the difference necessarily one of replacement or epochal succession?

Inuit, like other circumpolar Indigenous people, have conceived the material present as cycles of animistic or spiritual renewal: natural patterns of death and rebirth, the life cycles of humans and animals, the killing and return of hunted animals. They have organised the succession of social time in a recirculation of 'name-souls': the same person renewed in new circumstances from generation to generation. This ontology of cycles and renewals was certainly more prominent in the past. But it is still active in a temporal reality experienced as process rather than sequence.

Tamusi's sense of temporal *linearity* confronts apparently irretrievable loss, a one-way river of time, and the need for 'Weirs' – for technologies of collecting and heritage. No doubt, as Graburn asserts, this is a new historical vision. But how is newness articulated in practice? Is it adequate to say that *this* sense of time is emergent, the *others* residual? I do not think we can be sure. There may indeed be some sort of overall development, but with many overlays, loops and intersecting temporal paths.

Tamusi's 'Weir' project is not simply elegiac, or museological in the usual senses, but linked, as Graburn details, to local co-operative movements, ongoing land and language reclamation projects, art and tourist markets, national- and international-scale 'sovereignty' politics – the bundle of 'Indigenous' actions that have made space in global discourses for names like 'Inuit' (no longer 'Eskimo'). In North-East Canada, these politics have led to the creation of the large, semi-autonomous region, Nunavut, along with a proliferation of neo-traditional institutions, discourses, arts and social movements. This is no longer the 'middle ground' world of the early and mid-twentieth century – igloos, tents, dogsleds, hunting rifles, a thriving fur trade and Inuttitut monolingualism that Tamusi's generation grew up in. But it is not an undifferentiated 'modernity' either– all of us 'flowing' the same way, down the same river.

The specificity of Inuit social survival, political struggle and cultural change is a crucial context for Tamusi's 'museum'. It is not a figure of ending, or even of loss. The Weir, which unlike the dam does not try to hold back the river, is a *pragmatic selection* of cultural resources and models, a technology of transformation. In any event, we cannot assume that Tamusi's river is the 'arrow of time' familiar to Western meta-historians, at least not inasmuch as an arrow points somewhere. The ocean into which this river of time empties may not be any specific future, but simply a figure for non-recurrence in the flow of existence. In the book from which this example is excerpted, I argue that we should not see this one-way flow, this 'linearity', as something immediately and fully recognisable – as history in its Western, modernising form.[18]

Recent ethnographic research on the historical knowledge and mnemonic practices of the peoples once assumed to be 'without history' has opened up a complex zone of translations, such as the work of Renato Rosaldo, Marshall Sahlins and particularly David Delgado Shorter, whose thesis on Yoeme (formerly Yaqui) historicising has been published as a compelling book.[19] It has become evident that non-repeating time (and the 'historical' ontology it guarantees) can find expression in a variety of shapes, scales, uses and idioms. Recognising this diversity can help us be alive to historical practices and discourses in the contact histories of the past as well as in the current encounters of globalisation, neocolonialism, postmodernity (or whatever periodising term for the present we adopt).

I offer two more short case studies. The Hawaiian historian Lilikala Kameʻeleihiwā, in her book *Native Land and Foreign Desires*, writes that

> It is interesting to note that in Hawaiian, the past is referred to as Ka wa mamua, or 'the time in front or before.' Whereas the future, when thought of at all, is Ka wa mahope, or 'the time which comes after or behind.' It is as if the Hawaiian stands firmly in the present, with his back to the future, and his eyes fixed upon the past, seeking historical answers for present-day dilemmas. Such an orientation is to the Hawaiian an eminently practical one, for the future is always unknown, whereas the past is rich in glory and knowledge.[20]

This image of going backwards into the future may remind many of Benjamin's famous 'Angel of History', from his 'Theses on the Philosophy of History'. Benjamin's angel is blown into the future, while facing the past. But the differences are telling. Kameʻeleihiwā's Hawaiian does not, like Benjamin's angel, confront the past as a ruin, a heap of broken scraps. Rather, she engages a generative, socio-mythic *tradition*, 'rich in glory and knowledge'. Most significantly, perhaps, there is no relentless 'wind' of 'Progress' blowing the Indigenous Hawaiian backwards into the future. Time has no single, violent direction, but tacks resourcefully between present dilemmas and remembered answers: a pragmatic, not a teleological or a messianic orientation.

Let us hesitate, again, before we view this temporality as the opposite of a linear, progressive Western historical vision. For Kameʻeleihiwā is not invoking repetition or cycles of recurrence. It might be better, instead, to think of looping lines of recollection, and specific paths spiralling forward. There is no either/or, tradition or modernity, here. And Kameʻeleihiwā's tradition is about generativity, not recurrence.

In this she is engaged in an activity comparable to – but not the same as – Benjamin's materialist historian, for whom the junk heap of the past contains possible other histories, prefigurations of outcomes different from the apparently inevitable reality of 'what actually happened.' Both look to the past to find a way, a new path, in time: one historical process is pragmatic and genealogical, the other critical and messianic. Neither is about lining up past, present and future in a linear series. The future is open.

Hawaiian tradition is not, of course, a wholesale revival of past ways, but a practical selection and critical reweaving of roots. Gender roles show this clearly (where women's status has irreversibly changed), as do engagements with Christianity, with national politics, with transnational Indigenous coalitions. These and many other strategies are connected through appeals to genealogy and grounded by attachments to a common homeland. In today's Indigenous movements, as in any living tradition, some past elements are actively remembered, others are forgotten and some are appropriated and translated from histories originating elsewhere. Kameʻeleihiwā concludes: the Hawaiian way of looking back to the future is an 'eminently practical one, for the future is always unknown, whereas the past is rich in glory and knowledge'. And we might add, with a nod to Benjamin, that the past is also rich in ambiguity and power.[21]

Finally, another example of an Indigenous vision of 'historical' survival and transformation. I have been thinking for some time now about the following quotation, from an exhibition catalogue on the Native people of Alaska and Eastern Siberia. Barbara Shangin – an Alutiiq elder – is speaking some time in the 1970s, on the Alaska Peninsula, near Kodiak Island:

> Our people have made it through lots of storms and disasters for thousands of years. All the troubles since the Russians are like one long stretch of bad weather. Like everything else, this storm will pass over some day.[22]

One can, without too much difficulty, read this as narrating a recognisable history, of non-repeatable events in time: she refers to quite specific 'troubles': the colonisation of Alaska and its consequences. Shangin is not saying that Alutiiq people will eventually go back to what they were before the Modern World System arrived with the violent, extractive Russian fur trade in the late eighteenth century. At least as I interpret her, she knows that the bad weather brings irreversible changes – some, like the Russian Orthodoxy that has taken root as a genuine Native religion, of real value. I conclude that the weather cycles she evokes are not unhistorical, mythic returns, but *structuring patterns* for transformation, for an ongoing history. Temporally deep stories, an Indigenous *longue durée* reaching before and after colonisation, are fundamental to contemporary Native ways of narrating history. So, I can listen to Barbara Shagnin's words as something more than wishful thinking, and rather as a distinct 'historical idiom', making realist claims about the linking of past and future.

Perhaps it would be better to think of this historical idiom as a kind of 'temporal ecology', composed of 'material/semiotic practices' (as Haraway might say).[23] The changing weather – discursive *and* embodied, human *and* non-human – here translates a developing, shared experience of transformation. For 'weather' is always different and the same, always returning. The visionary Tongan writer Epeli Hau'ofa has proposed the 'spiral' as a genealogical figure for Indigenous persistence – transformations and returns in developing time.[24] No longer the 'arrow of time' but a swirl of contemporary times, histories, going somewhere, separately and together, in ways that cannot be mapped. This, in 2016, seems a realist observation. Curating in these times, then, is a work of caring and connecting, protecting and letting go, speaking and remaining silent, building weirs and then, in another season, letting them wash away.

Postscript

Curatopia's editors have suggested that I provide an update – for a chapter that is already an unfinished collage. So, I offer a few pages that reflect my recent research – visits and conversations – in Western European museums, sites that can be called, with appropriate hesitation, 'post-ethnological'. Of course, comparable institutions in places like Canada, the USA, Aotearoa New Zealand, Australia, or Alaska are more closely engaged with source communities and Indigenous curating. But, somewhat to my surprise, I found many European museums, while differently positioned and constrained, responding to similar pressures and possibilities.

Post-ethnological museums today find themselves challenged to do something new with the vast collections that complex and sometimes violent histories have deposited in their storage areas. While sustaining an essential work of conservation and stewardship, how can they address the postcolonial realisation that the cultural traditions and travel stories gathered in these collections are unfinished? How will they think about practices of heritage preservation and public communication that engage multiple, often discrepant audiences?

'Ethnological' denotes a cluster of institutions sometimes called 'anthropological' or 'ethnographic' – museums of *Völkerkunde*, of Man, of the Colonies – what Benôit de l'Estoile simply names '*musées des autres*'.[25] I settled on the term 'ethnological' for its fusion of ethnos and logos. The name evokes a crucial vocation: the work of serious cross-cultural research and interpretation, inextricably ethnographic and historical. Like Nicholas Thomas, in his important new book *The Return of Curiosity*,[26] I think that ethnology museums, or their successor institutions, have a critical role to play in the present moment – a contradictory time of unprecedented mobility and openness but also of renewed ethnocentrism and aggressive ignorance.

'Post-ethnological museum' is a phrase one hears more frequently. I am ready to adopt the prefix, as long as 'post' does not mean, simply, 'after'. 'Post' evokes something new that we cannot name yet. 'Post' suggests following-from, with a difference – still very much entangled in what is being displaced. So, we are not talking about an epochal shift, a whole new kind of museum ... 'Post' thus denotes a predicament: working in a time of transition, without a trustworthy sense of direction, a time of possibility and constraint, invention and contradiction.

Several years ago, I gave an address to a conference at the Pitt Rivers Museum at Oxford, UK, the culmination of a three-year European research project on 'The Future of Ethnographic Museums'. I was worried about what seemed to me a pervasive move towards 'art', away from 'culture'. For many (post-)ethnological museums were rebranding themselves as, for example, 'Museums of World Arts and Cultures'. After further research – most recently at the Volkenkunde Museum in Leiden – I now think the trend is more complex and less one-sided.

In a changing 'art-culture system',[27] 'art' is certainly the more fundable (and commodifiable) partner. But ethnology museums, while adopting aesthetic strategies and making space for contemporary art and artists, are not just turning themselves into art galleries of the non-West. They are experimenting with strategies that are more hybrid, contradictory and potentially more significant. These transformed institutions are, perhaps, uniquely well placed to offer non-reductive visions of human possibility. Drawing critically on ethnological traditions, they no longer promise an authoritative tour of the world's cultures – ways of life circumscribed in time and space, or arranged in evolutionary sequences. Post-ethnological museums explore plural histories that connect, converse with and interrupt each other.

This is my optimistic vision, on days when the glass seems half-full. But it is far from guaranteed. Post-ethnological museums face serious obstacles. They struggle to resist powerful pressures for purification, for uncomplicated messages, for a return to simpler times. Post-ethnological museums, in Europe and North America, aspire, in their different national contexts, to transcend colonial pasts. But they have limited room to manoeuvre, constrained as they are by funding cuts, neo-liberal governments and marketing, all structural features of contemporary capitalism. There is also a growing ideological climate of hostility to multiculturalism (so-called 'political correctness'). As renewed forms of nationalism, ethnocentrism and racism gain ground – not only on the extreme Right – cultural diversity of any kind comes under suspicion. Yet what can ethnology museums be about, if not cultural diversity?

Ethnology's post-Boasian brief for cultural relativity – while it has sometimes been expressed in Eurocentric ways– is a legacy that urgently needs to be preserved and reinvented. Yet the authority and public reputation of ethnology – some might say its marketability – is much diminished these days. The deeper reasons for this state of affairs are beyond my present scope. But a tendency to abandon anthropology, ethnology or *Völkerkunde* as museums rename themselves is worth noting. The UBC Museum of Anthropology is now called 'MOA: A place for world arts and cultures'. An important factor in its rebranding exercise was the reluctance of wealthy Asian populations in Vancouver to fund a new extension devoted to Asian art. The great civilisations of Asia did not belong, they thought, in an anthropology museum! Now the word anthropology is largely suppressed, hidden underneath the acronym MOA: 'World Arts and Cultures'.

I do not want to exaggerate the significance of the rebranding exercise. The Vancouver museum continues its pioneering work with North-West Coast societies, collaborations that have made it famous, even as it opens out to Asian, Latin American and Afro-Caribbean projects.[28] But name changes are not superficial. Not when understood as part of a pervasive shift. Musée de l'Homme becomes Musée du Quai Branly; Berlin's Ethnologisches Museum is absorbed by the Humboldt Forum; in Vienna the Museum of Ethnology turns into a World Museum (Weltmuseum); Bern's Museum für Völkerkunde is renamed Museum der Kulturen; in Frankfurt, 'Ethnology' changes to 'World Cultures'; in Cologne's rebuilt Rautenstrauch-Joest Museum, anthropology is now 'Cultures of the World'; and a troika of museums in the Netherlands (Volkenkunde, Tropen and Afrika) is rebaptised a 'Museum of World Cultures'.

The word 'world', in many of these new names, resonates with 'globalisation'. (In French, '*monde*', '*mondialisation*'.) And it is not hard to recognise the neo-liberal force fields within, and against, which museums now operate. Brand recognition and marketing are increasingly the name of the game, as Julien Stallebrass has persuasively shown for contemporary art museums.[29] Survival depends on projecting an intelligible and attractive profile to maintain and increase the number of visitors. Museum managers, government bureaucrats and donors are paying attention. Names, logos, slogans, iconic objects and blockbuster exhibitions risk becoming more important than scholarly integrity and curatorial risk-taking. The threat of defunding, downsizing and consolidation is ever present.

The landscape, or 'museumscape' as Sharon Macdonald calls it,[30] is not unified. We need to consider a wide range of different local situations, political contexts and funding sources. In the United States, not surprisingly, the withdrawal of public funding and the pressure to find private sources is extreme. Sink or swim. In France and elsewhere in Europe, the participation of the state seems more assured, at least for now. In the United States, as the sadly outdated 'culture galleries' of the American Museum of Natural History attest, locating ethnology collections in natural history museums has not turned out well.[31] 'Culture' tends to disappear between the better-funded institutions of 'science' and 'art'.

Pressures from the market, from funding sources, from diverse regimes of accountability and recognition, are not, however the whole story. Many of the changes currently under way, small and large initiatives, reconnect historical pasts with future possibilities in ways that potentially exceed the current neo-liberal hegemony. Hegemony, as I understand it, in the Gramscian tradition, is never permanent, always contested. Moreover, if post-ethnological museums are now forced to justify their existence, this is a challenge worth engaging. The old anthropology museums – rooted in 'salvage' collecting, devoted to conservation in the name of a universal human patrimony – had to change. The naturalised oppositions that guaranteed their existence are everywhere in question: art v. artefact, authenticity v. commodity, preservation v. invention, evolutionism v. creolisation.

Curators in virtually every post-ethnological museum I have visited in Europe are struggling to reinvent their institution in new, often post-Western, ways. Of many possible examples, I will mention just one: an update on the partnership I have already cited that links the Chateau Musée in Boulogne sur Mer with the Native-administered Alutiiq Museum in Kodiak, Alaska. The relationship reconceives the precious Pinart Collection of nineteenth-century Kodiak materials as an unfinished, 'shared heritage'.[32] In the process both partners are transcending absolute concepts of ownership and repatriation. They have discovered how collections made under 'salvage' assumptions can inspire new arts and rituals, finding a second life in living culture. In the exhibition, at the Chateau

Musée, *Alaska passé/present* (2016–2017), contemporary art from Native Alaska is on display. New creations, both traditional and experimental in style, are juxtaposed with nineteenth-century masks from the museum's collection.[33]

The project, curated by the Kodiak Sugpiaq carver Perry Eaton and museum director Céline Ramio, has been co-operative at every level. And perhaps most significantly the Chateau Musée is actively developing an acquisitions programme for contemporary Alaskan art. Indeed, an increasing number of curators now think of their task not simply as conserving and interpreting artefacts from the past but also as stimulating cultural renewal. At Minpaku, the National Museum of Ethnology in Osaka, Japan, this is established policy. Elsewhere it requires a struggle against established ideas of conservation to open up ethnology's deep commitment to collecting pasts, rather than pasts-becoming-futures.[34]

Little by little, against resistance, a lot is changing. Do I need to add that consensus is not always smooth in the emerging contact zones? Suspicion and unequal power subvert reciprocity. Of course, demands for physical repatriation, whether made by tribes or nation-states, can be intransigent, non-negotiable. We are not in an age of postcolonial innocence. But through the development of specific relationships, historical legacies of mistrust (both within and outside museums) can be overcome. Post-ethnological museums are becoming places for the co-creation of new knowledge, sites of – if the phrase be permitted – 'collaborative conservation'. The times of the curator, contested and uncontrolled, have become more interesting.

Notes

1 The opening sections of this chapter were originally presented as the keynote address at 'The Task of the Curator' Conference, UC Santa Cruz, 14 May 2010, and published in *Collections*, 7:4 (2011), 399–405. The sections on Indigenous curating were added later and appear in my 2013 book *Returns: Becoming Indigenous in the Twenty-First Century* (Cambridge, MA: Harvard University Press). The 'Postscript' was written for the present occasion.
2 W. Benjamin, 'The Task of the Translator', in M. Bullock and M. Jennings (eds), *Walter Benjamin: Selected Writings Vol. 1 1913–26* (Cambridge MA: Belknap Press of Harvard University Press, 2002), pp. 253–62.
3 T. Bennett, *The Birth of the Museum: History, Theory, Politics* (London: Routledge, 1995). C. Duncan, *Civilizing Rituals: Inside Public Art Museums* (New York: Routledge, 1995).
4 A.A. Shelton, 'The Collector's Zeal: Towards an Anthropology of Intentionality, Instrumentality and Desire', in P. Ter Keurs (ed.), *Colonial Collections Revisited* (Leiden: CNWS Publications, 2007). See also J. Clifford, *The Predicament of Culture: Twentieth-Century Ethnography, Literature, and Art* (Cambridge, MA: Harvard University Press, 1988).
5 C. Gosden and C. Knowles. *Collecting Colonialism: Material Culture and Colonial Change* (London and New York: Berg, 2001).

6 E. Wallerstein, 'Structural Crises', *New Left Review*, 62 (2010), 133–42. See also E. Wallerstein, 'Reading Fanon in the 21st Century', *New Left Review*, 57 (2009), 117–25.

7 Clifford, *Returns*. J. Clifford, 'Indigenous Articulations', *The Contemporary Pacific*, 13:2 (2001), 468–90.

8 J. Clifford. *The Predicament of Culture*.

9 J. Clifford, *Routes: Travel and Translation in the Late Twentieth Century* (Cambridge, MA: Harvard University Press, 1997).

10 I. Karp and F. Wilson, 'Constructing the Spectacle of Culture in Museums', in B. Ferguson, S. Nairne and R. Greenburg (eds), *Thinking about Exhibitions* (London: Routledge, 1996).

11 M. Ames, *Cannibal Tours and Glass Boxes: The Anthropology of Museums*, 2nd edition (Vancouver: University of British Columbia Press, 1992).

12 S. Vogel, 'Always True to the Object, in Our Fashion', in I. Karp and S.D. Lavine (eds), *Exhibiting Cultures: The Poetics and Politics of Museum Display* (Washington, DC: Smithsonian Institution Press, 1991).

13 D. Haraway, *When Species Meet* (Minneapolis: University of Minnesota Press, 2008).

14 Clifford, *Returns*, 261–314. See Museum of Anthropology (MOA), http://moa.ubc.ca/, Arctic Studies Center, https://naturalhistory.si.edu/Arctic/html/alaska.htm, Great Lakes Research Alliance for the Study of Aboriginal Arts and Cultures (GRASAC), https://grasac.org/gks/gks_about.php, Alutiiq Museum, https://alutiiqmuseum.org/, Chateau Musée, www. musee.ville-boulogne-sur-mer.fr/.

15 P. Chaat-Smith, *Everything You Know About Indians Is Wrong* (Minneapolis: University of Minnesota Press, 2009).

16 N. Graburn, 'Weirs in the River of Time: The Development of Historical Consciousness among Canadian Inuit', *Museum Anthropology*, 22:1 (1998), 18–32.

17 *Ibid.*, 26.

18 Clifford, *Returns*, 35.

19 D. Shorter, *We Will Dance Our Truth: Yaqui History in Yoeme Performance* (Lincoln: University of Nebraska Press, 2009).

20 L. Kame'eleihiwa, *Native Land and Foreign Desires: Pehea La E Pono Ai? How Shall We Live in Harmony?* (Honolulu: Bishop Museum, 1992), pp. 22–3.

21 *Ibid.*, 23.

22 B. Shangin. 'Epigraph'; G. Pullar and R. Knecht, 'Alutiiq', in V. Chaussonnet (ed.), *Crossroads Alaska: Native Cultures in Alaska and Siberia* (Washington, DC: Arctic Studies Center, National Museum of Natural History, Smithsonian Institution Press, 1995), pp. 14–15.

23 D. Haraway, *When Species Meet*, *passim*.

24 E. Hauofa, *We Are the Ocean* (Honolulu: University of Hawaii Press, 2008), p. 69.

25 B. De L'Estoile, *Le Goût des autres: de l'exposition colonial aux arts premiers* (Paris: Flammarion, 2007).

26 N. Thomas, *The Return of Curiosity: What Museums Are Good For in the Twenty-First Century* (London: Reaktion Books, 2016).

27 Clifford, *The Predicament of Culture*, 224.

28 See Shelton, Chapter 8 below.

29 J. Stallabrass, 'The Branding of the Museum', *Art History*, 37:1 (2014), 148–65.

30 S. Macdonald, 'New Constellations of Difference in Europe's Twenty-First Century', *Museum Anthropology*, 39:1 (2016), 4–19.

31 S. Harding and E. Martin. 'Anthropology Now and Then in the American Museum of Natural History', *Anthropology Now*, 8:3 (2016), 1–13.

32 In the case of the Humboldt Forum in Berlin this claim of 'shared heritage' is heavily contested within Germany and beyond. See Sandahl's critique (Chapter 5 above), and Förster and von Bose (Chapter 3 above) on 'strategic reflexivity'.

33 Musée Boulogne sur Mer, *Alaska: Passé/Présent*, Exhibition Catalogue, 2016.

34 See McCarthy, Hakiwai and Schorch, Chapter 13 below.

8

Baroque modernity, critique and Indigenous epistemologies in museum representations of the Andes and Amazonia

Anthony Alan Shelton

The Andes and Amazonia have long undergone profound mythologisation in European and American literature, art, and, more recently, in widely circulated and proliferative museum exhibitions. This chapter sets out to identify and describe five specific genres and characteristics of exhibitions from 1980 to the present, and, by focusing on two uniquely important examples, *The Potosí Principle* (2010–2011) and *Amazonie: Le chamane et la pensée de la forêt* (2016–2017), to examine the strengths and shortfalls of exhibition curators adopting critical and collaborative methodologies. It is argued that the use of heterodoxy, adopted in *Amazonie*, can resolve the contradictions that inevitably arise when multiple epistemologies and different interpretive models are incorporated into exhibitions. Moreover, it is suggested that the embrace of heterodoxy may help blunt the worst effects of Western institutional hierarchies that in many cases still work against effective curatorial partnerships and Indigenous empowerment.[1]

Treasures, spectacles and exoticism

During the period 1980–2016, the most widespread exhibition genres re-presented pre-Columbian Andean cultures through the constructed category of 'treasures' and depicted Amazonia through the lens of salvage ethnography and the idealisation of a pristine nature. *Arte plumária do Brazil* (1980, Museu de Arte Moderna, São Paulo, Brazil) exemplifies this romantic genre. In Brazil, *Arte Plumária* was awarded a national prize, before it travelled to the Smithsonian Institution, Washington, DC, USA; the Museo Nacional de Antropología y Historia, Mexico City; and the Museo Nacional de Colombia, Bogotá. After being expanded, the exhibition was re-presented in 1983 at the Seventeenth São Paulo Biennial, Brazil. Despite the different cultural contexts of its various venues, interpretation remained the same: featherwork was arranged by tribal provenance and the interpretation focused on techniques of production and social function, which emphasised its exotic value and status as 'primitive art'.

While neither solely confined to nor determined by Western aesthetic principles, in London, UK, the *Hidden Peoples of the Amazon* exhibition (1985), at the Museum of Mankind[2] mobilised different exoticising practices. The exhibition, curated by Elizabeth Carmichael, represented the tropical lowlands as insular regions, displayed through survey-like presentations, which emphasised anachronistic cultural survivals and continuities between linguistic communities over space and time.[3] It largely ignored trade and the interconnections between communities, economic and political relations with the Highlands, and only grudgingly acknowledged the impingements of Western colonisation and the import of foreign goods and technologies.[4] The history of the British Museum's own collection, and the encompassing world system of which Amazonia has long been part, were notably ignored.[5]

Large-scale survey exhibitions peaked in the decade leading up to the 1992 celebration of the quincentennial of what was variously described as the European 'encounter' or 'discovery' of the Americas. Deconstructivist approaches to European images of the New World were earlier explored in the 1982 exhibition, *Mythen der Neuen Welt: Zur Entdeckungsgeschichte Lateinamerikas* at the Martin-Gropius-Bau, Berlin, Germany. Using an older established narrative approach, the US National Gallery of Art in Washington, DC, presented *Circa 1492: Art in the Age of Exploration* (1991–1992), and enlarged the geographical framework of regional exhibitions by placing the events of the 'discoveries' in the context of fifteenth-century world history. Other ambitious ventures focused not only on South America but, as in the case of *Amerika 1492–1992. Neue Welten – Neue Wirklichkeiten* (1992–1993) – also hosted at the Martin-Gropius-Bau – sought to provide a comprehensive panorama of America's Indigenous population. As in the case of these three exhibitions, museums widely adopted the survey model to encompass and display their extensive historical collections. The 1992 Belgian exhibition, *America: Bruid van de zon*, Koninklijk Museum voor Shone Kunsten, Antwerp, further strengthened this revisionist history by relinquishing the focus on military deeds and personalities in favour of the historical and cultural encounter between the two continents. Similar deconstructivist approaches also guided smaller quincentennial exhibitions like *New World of Wonders: European Images of the Americas 1492–1700* (1992),[6] and *Mapping the Americas* (1992).[7]

More ambitious, and larger still, were the exhibitions mounted by Spain's Comisión Nacional Quinto Centenario and Sociedad Estatal Quinto Centenario, under Luis Yáñez-Barnuevo and Almudena Cavestany. Exhibitions like *Los Indios amazónicos* (1986–1987) and *Los Incas y el antigua Perú. 3,000 años de historia* (1991)[8] provided a panorama of the continent's heterogeneous cultures. Though adopting the well-orchestrated survey methodology and collaborating with South American partners, the Spanish exhibitions were nevertheless widely criticised for celebrating 'discovery' from a European perspective while omitting the political, military and economic implications of Spanish colonisation. Eduardo Subirats[9] positioned Spain's Quinto Centenario within the politics of Hispanidad, the ideas of a shared Hispanic and mestizo heritage and Spain's reassertion of a sphere of economic and cultural influence, an observation that might equally be applied to the country's later exhibitions marking the two hundred years of Spanish American independence.[10] A similarly extensive exhibition programme was mounted by Portugal between 1988 and 2002 but, instead of focusing on the 'discoveries' of land and peoples as Spain did, it concentrated on the 'discovery' of sea routes, the cultural encounters they engendered and their mutual implications in shaping a new historical period.[11] While critical discourse focused on the ideological underpinnings of images of the New World from a European perspective and seldom acknowledged Indigenous agency or counter-hegemonic practices, the Portuguese exhibitions avoided much of the criticism levelled at their Spanish counterparts.

Over the last three decades, major exhibitions focused on Andean civilisations including *Inca-Perú: 3000 ans d'histoire* (1990);[12] *De erfenis van de Inca's: Zonen van de Zon & Dochters van de Maan* (1992);[13] *Ancestors of the Incas: The Lost Civilizations of Peru* (1998);[14] and *Art from the Chavín to the Incas* (2006)[15] have largely subordinated less known pre-Columbian societies to that of the Incas. Other Andean exhibitions prefaced their descriptive subtitles with appellations of treasure or gold, exemplified in *Sweat of the Sun: Gold of Peru* (1990);[16] *Rain of the Moon: Silver in Ancient Peru* (2000);[17] *Gold of the Incas: Treasures of an Empire* (2013);[18] and *Peruvian Gold: Ancient Treasures Unearthed* (2014).[19] Not until recently, after the media had familiarised the public with a series of spectacular pre-Inca archaeological discoveries, have mainstream institutions like the Lima Museum of Art in its exhibition *Moche and Its Neighbors: Reconstructing Identities* (2016) introduced unfamiliar names of civilisations into their marketing campaigns. The genre of exhibition oriented to treasure and gold has recently been broadened by allusions to lost empires and royalty – *The Royal Tombs of Sipan* (2015),[20] and *Peru: Kingdoms of the Sun and Moon* (2013–2014).[21]

This latter treasures genre was foreshadowed by earlier survey exhibitions, many of which were curated and circulated by the Oro del Perú Museum, Lima, and the Museo del Oro, Bogotá, Colombia.[22] Their exhibitions, like *El oro de Colombia* (1983),[23] toured throughout Latin America, and, as in the case of *The Power of the Sun: The Gold of Colombia*, were circulated outside of the region, in this case in Belgium and the Netherlands (1993–1994).[24] These tours were sponsored by the Peruvian or Colombian governments and coincided with major cultural initiatives,[25] which acted as 'intricate, multilayered engines of global diplomacy'.[26] These spectacular blockbuster exhibitions, from their lenders' points of view, attempted to garner national prestige, project a glorious past, reassert culture as the cornerstone of national identity and promote commercial interest, thereby making them an integral part of soft diplomacy. Conversely, for their North

American or European hosts, exhibitions like these, by bringing culture and trade together, although implicitly recalling colonial history, also re-expressed the supposed cultural rewards of neo-liberal political and economic co-operation.

State-sponsored exhibitions redefine and dramatise national images and amplify cultural differences while supressing or excluding other images and relationships.[27] Early treasure and exotic exhibition genres, which converted archaeological objects into national icons, often emphasised technology, metallurgy and feather-working techniques over political, religious or cultural interpretations. These foci limit serious consideration of pre-Columbian history and deflected issues of European colonisation to provide sanitised platforms to celebrate and reproduce the economic and political ties that bound international elites together. Members of this privileged class, as well as the economic and political alignments they express, are obtusely rendered visible in the lists of named patrons, members of honorary committees and the financial credits acknowledged in exhibition texts and catalogues.

Although Andean exhibitions continued to use the treasure genre alluding to gold, riches and wherever possible royalty, beginning in the late twentieth century, museums began to re-embed their narratives in more nuanced, historically and geographically specific, cultural interpretations. The growth of Andean archaeological and anthropological studies and the expansion of national schools in Latin America in the 1970s, increased focus on iconographic analysis, linguistics, ethnographic models and the excavation of burial sites which considerably expanded knowledge of pre-Columbian religions, state formation, economies and government. At the same time, ethnographic and art historical interests in Bolivia and Peru shifted to a new focus on Indigenous interpretations of land, mining, the body and sickness, which led to new political readings of colonial paintings, and Indigenous exegeses of local political and economic conditions. These new conditions contributed to the development of emerging methodologies and knowledges that disrupted old paradigms, and introduced previously ignored foci on marginalisation and exploitation. These studies in turn prompted widespread revision of Andean history, culture and art that inevitably impacted on museum exhibitions.[28] The treasure genre remained effective in promoting national economic and cultural interests, but, instead of technology and the glitter of gold providing the public stimuli, this was provided by the exotic, the reconstruction of ancient lost civilisations, sometimes with subtle allusions to the neo-romantic cinematographic world of Indiana Jones.

Christopher Donnan's *Moche Art of Peru: Pre-Columbian Symbolic Communication* (1978–1979)[29] was one of the first examples of this new exhibition genre. Based on intensive iconographic analysis, reinforced by archaeological, historical and ethnographic studies, this impressive exhibition presented Moche cosmology through the pictures and anthropomorphic and zoomorphic forms of ancient burial vessels. Similarly, *Amazonie*

Précolombienne (2002)[30] assembled a remarkable collection of historical Marajó ceramics from the mouth of the Amazon. Through comparing ancient and contemporary painted motifs, the exhibition opened new exotic frontiers to public view, without, unfortunately, providing convincing historical or Indigenous exegesis of their significance.

Less scholarly than Donnan's Moche exhibition, but likewise based on new archaeological discoveries, was a later series of exhibitions curated and toured by Peruvian governmental agencies. Notably, these were circulated after the defeat of the Maoist Sendero Luminosa movement (1980–2000), a struggle that had threatened Peru's nation state and brought widespread terror and economic hardship. Exhibitions, particularly after the millennium, attempted to recalibrate the public image of Peru and, like those before them, through soft diplomacy, they functioned as a vehicle to encourage renewed foreign investment and tourism. Exhibitions and cultural festivals presented the nation as a work of art,[31] spectacularising national myths, cementing relations between different international power elites and attempting to control the global cultural and aesthetic deployment of heritage and the system of identity formation. Despite this encroaching hegemony, and the frequent oscillation between different versions of the romantic genre discussed in this section, curators and museums surprisingly have embraced counter-hegemonic projects as exemplified by the *Potosí Principle* and *Amazonie* discussed at length below.

Baroque modernities: The Potosí Principle

Looking back on the 1980s, when I began my curatorial career at the Museum of Mankind in London at the height of the controversy over *Hidden Peoples of the Amazon*, I find it hard to reconcile the then undeveloped level of theoretical and critical perspectives on museum exhibitions with the postcolonial and critical theory that had at the time so completely penetrated British anthropology. Despite early conferences on the politics and poetics of exhibitions sponsored by major museums in London, Berlin and Washington, which drew attention to the problems of public representation, ethnographic curatorship remained largely insulated from self-reflexivity, until the angry responses provoked by the American quincentenary exhibitions challenged the museum's avowed political neutrality.[32] Supposedly apolitical scholarship also dominated art historical curatorship.[33] This could be seen in exhibitions like *Peruvian Colonial Painting* (1971–1972)[34] and *The Cuzco Circle* (1976),[35] which avoided political issues by focusing on technique and connoisseurship. Before the exhibition *Cambios: The Spirit of Transformation in Spanish Colonial Art* (1992),[36] George Kubler's influential view that Latin American colonial art only reflected European influence was seldom challenged. *Converging Cultures: Art and Identity in Spanish America* (1996–1997)[37] broke with Kubler's view and continued the revisionist trajectory by presenting colonial art and material culture as the products of deep cultural entanglements between Spanish and Indigenous sensibilities.

In contrast to the revisionist narrative-based exhibitions in the USA, *The Potosí Principle: Colonial Image Production in the Global Economy* (2010–2011)[38] used installation-based techniques to question the fundamental structure and format of exhibitions, and the categories and art historical assumptions on which they were based. Instead of subordinating images to narrative interpretations, *The Potosí Principle* juxtaposed them to generate new forms of relational knowledge intending to escape established deterministic narratives.

The Potosí Principle, a collaborative project begun in 2008 between three museums in Berlin, Madrid and La Paz, sought to develop a framework to compare the relationship between two periods and distinct modes of art production: sixteenth- and seventeenth-century Andean painting and European art of the same period, with two coeval stages of capitalist development: early capitalist accumulation, from which the world system that locked Latin America into the European economy emerged, and the current period of capitalist consolidation. The curators linked the two periods together by comparing current conditions of environmental destruction, pestilence and the exploitation of Asian migrant workers with earlier patterns of abuse meted out to Andean forebears. The exhibition consisted of colonial paintings, prints and books juxtaposed with film, photographs, new media, installations, Xerox copies and recorded performances by artists including Ines Doujak, Matthijs de Bruijne, Sonia Abián, Elvira Espejo, Maria Galindo, Konstanze Schmitt and Zhao Liang. The works

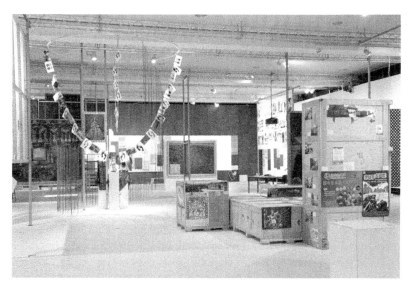

8.1 A section of the exhibition *The Potosí Principle: Colonial Image Production in the Global Economy*, 'How can we sing the song of the Lord in and alien land?' Museo Nacional Centro de Arte Reina Sofia, Madrid, Spain, August 2010 – January 2011.

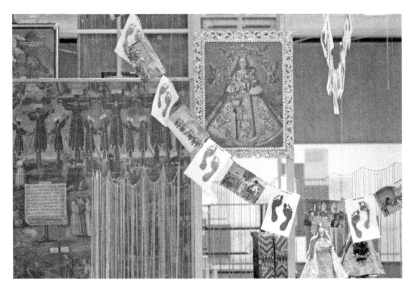

8.2 A section of the exhibition *The Potosí Principle*, 'How can we sing the song of the Lord in an alien land?'. Museo Nacional Centro de Arte Reina Sofía, Madrid, Spain, August 2010 – January 2011.

were arranged in the gallery at different levels and multiple angles in a space structured out of scaffolding, stairs and platforms. The exhibition was designed along three critical pathways that offered alternative journeys to specific junctions where subsets of the two series of images were juxtaposed.

The exhibition design was intended to subvert the linear concept of history with its implicit temporal or geographic and stylistic correlations which served to undermine basic categorisations fundamental to modernism's instrumental vision of the world. It thereby attempted to transform the perception of 'the colonial past, together with its mechanisms of power and legitimization [to] become part of our conscious world'.[39] Alice Creischer, Max Jorge Hinderer and Andreas Siekmann, the European curators of the project, rejected historiography predicated on the nation state in favour of a global purview. The resulting space/time compression with its proliferation of images was intended to reconstitute a radical *Gesamtkunstwerk*, a total art work. Like the arbitrary premodernist spaces, predicated on baroque aesthetics, that these curators equated with early curiosity cabinets, the exhibition and its catalogues sought to reject the rules of classical composition, aesthetics, serial classification and writing, and the knowledges that flow from such preconceptions, in order to generate new understandings of the 'global world from the perspective of Potosí'.[40] The interpretation of art was reduced to its educational and political function where portraiture reinforced personal prestige and the authority of the Spanish grandees, while fearful counter-Reformation images of hell and mortal torment expressed an Indigenous destiny which the Spanish claimed was inevitable without the redemptive power of work.

Despite concerted proselytisation, the pre-Hispanic world of Potosí did not vanish. Regardless of systematic slavery, torture and the resulting trauma, this world continued to subsist particularly among women to become recast into a specifically Andean counter-reading of Christianity. Although politically manipulated, the baroque's allegorical quality and excess limited its controlled mobilisation. For Manuel Borja-Villel, the director of the Reina Sofía in Madrid, the exhibition's radical intention would emerge from his museum creating a similar transgressive effect. 'By creating tensions between the colonial works and surroundings that are alien to them,' he announced, 'the museum *becomes Baroque* and behaves like the forms of Indigenous resistance to the colonial project'.[41] Berndt Scherer, his German counterpart, agreed with this interpretation, describing the project as an 'interesting experiment' which brought out new insights and ultimately helps us to 'learn to see the world anew from a fresh perspective'.[42] *The Potosí Principle* rejected not only art's avowed neutrality but all essentialised correlations between it and cultural identity. For the exhibition's sponsors, therefore, art acted not only as a political representation but as power itself; 'culture is not the independent and privileged site of ideas; it not only reflects a power structure but is the very power that is fought over'.[43]

Despite the interpretative audacity of the exhibition, disagreement emerged between the German and Bolivian curatorial teams. The German curators' Marxist deterministic perspective was rejected by their Bolivian counterparts who, organised under the banner El Colectivo, fractured the attempt at a unitary interpretation of colonial history. The first problems emerged early on in the project over the Reina Sofía's loan negotiations with communities and its complaints of excessive transportation and insurance costs associated with loans from Bolivian museums.[44] However, some members of El Colectivo had already been offended by Berlin's Ethnologisches Museum's refusal to extend loans from its collections to the Bolivian venue. Distrust and accusations of coercion from communities reluctant to lend their paintings led to complaints about the revival of old asymmetrical power relations that had historically divided the two countries;[45] claims confirmed by the anecdotal stories reported in the exhibition catalogues. Mistrust may have been exacerbated by the confusion caused by the curatorial methodology which disavowed established strategies in favour of an experimental methodology that called for the suspension of the usual division of labour between museum professionals and a prolongation of research time. Loan negotiations became so difficult that Borja-Villel appealed directly to many of the communities and museums. Subsequently, he recorded his surprise at the open democratic process through which community members engaged in loan discussions, a process far removed from the top-down exercise of authority in Spain. If the process of decision-making caused consternation among its European organisers, local concerns in Bolivia about the loss of paintings from the community, fear of their removal causing disequilibrium of spiritual forces which might provoke catastrophic consequences for example,[46] must have seemed equally inexplicable to the representatives of these Western bureaucratic rationalist institutions. When the loans of certain works from Bolivia were declined, the exhibition at the Reina Sofía substituted print copies with accompanying explanations attributing difficulties to the persistence of unequal power relations that still undermined trust between the two continents.

The most serious rupture between the German and Bolivian curators resulted from Creischer's, Hinderer's and Siekmann's rejection of Indigenous interpretations of history, which they dismissed as the product of cultural essentialism that privileged Native exegesis above others. For the German curatorial team, equating culture with ethnic identity obscured the global interdependence of politics and economics and, among other negative consequences, obfuscated alliances between local and foreign classes that cut across culture. In opposition, El Colectivo argued for the incorporation of video presentations and first voices to express the Indigenous historical perspectives of how Andean communities had appropriated Spanish colonial imagery which they had ritually rearticulated and transmuted into an efficacious source of power to fortify resistance against external aggressors and to strengthen local values and network villages. El Colectivo further questioned the relevance of the comparison between Andean peoples and the position of contemporary Chinese and Indian migrant workers who, unlike themselves, had not resisted domination through their appropriation and redeployment of the images and ideologies pitted against them. Their German counterparts were accused of monopolising control over interpretation, unilaterally defining the exhibition's core themes, choosing most of the invited artists and also deciding upon its design, and in so doing relegating their Bolivian colleagues to the role of advisers or informants.[47]

By late 2009, divergencies of interpretation between El Colectivo and their German colleagues had become so acute that they declared their intention to publish a dissident catalogue.[48] At the centre of the Indigenous view was the land that they conceptualised as animate, divided into communities, each protected by divine powers, but woven together through ritual and commercial networks. Despite reorganisation under Spanish rule, Indigenous peoples had conserved their worldview by having endowed the saints, Christs, and Virgins of their conquerors, now zealously guarded in their parish churches, with older pre-Hispanic significances and powers, linked together through rituals and pilgrimages in a similar fluid order to that of their forebears.[49]

These differences between two worldviews and interpretations were starkly reflected in their respective publications. The European catalogue was arranged into three standard sections; the first described and mapped the routes through the exhibition and was interleaved with interviews, essays and descriptions of the significance of each of its junctures. The second presented coloured photographs of the exhibition; and the third reproduced full interviews and documents in their original language to corroborate the interpretative view given in section one. The catalogue produced for the exhibition's European venues appeared in Spanish and English editions, while the circulation of its dissident Bolivian counterpart, printed only in Spanish, was much more limited. The Bolivian catalogue, entitled *El Principio Potosí reverso*, edited by Silvia Rivera Cusicanqui and El Colectivo, is organised according to an Indigenous literary structure designed to be read from the centre page to the back, followed by reading backwards from the centre to the book's front. The first half of the book, printed in black ink on white paper, represents the book's white masculine face, contains critical essays on the process and differences between the German and Andean views of the interpretation of the images and the history of looting and art theft from communities. The pages in the second half, which for the most part have white print on black paper, constitute the book's feminine lived face and focus on historical studies of specific images, ritual prescriptions, the relationships between images and ceremonies, and the histories of the communities in which paintings are located.[50] Despite good intentions, the politics of *The Potosí Principle* aptly confirms Ziauddin Sardar's assertion that 'Columbus did not "discover" America: he globalized a world view', moving the focus of visual interpretation from the factual to the hermeneutic.[51] *The Potosí Principle* presented a Marxist worldview in place of commonplace narrative descriptions and subsumed Indigenous exegesis and local knowledge under its interpretative embrace.

The exhibition, its two accompanying catalogues and its reviews provide fascinating documentation of an attempt at a thoroughly reflexive museum project, focused on the difficulties of intercultural collaborations and the challenges of negotiating distinct epistemological positions. For these reasons the project marks a watershed in exhibition history and curatorial practice, which warrants wider discussion.

Nature and agency – Amazonie: Le chamane et la pensée de la forêt

Seven recent exhibitions illustrate the current diversity of exhibitions on Amazonia. The British Museum's *Unknown Amazon* (2001), curated by Colin McEwan, dissolved the fallacy of the insularity and pristine nature of the region, reversing the vision the museum had promoted sixteen years earlier in its *Hidden Peoples* exhibition. *Unknown Amazon* presented new archaeological data to demonstrate the existence of large pre-Hispanic settlements and trade networks that once integrated the area. *Os Índios Nos* (2000, Museu Nacional de Etnologia, Lisbon, Portugal), curated by Joaquim Pais de Brito, adopted a postcolonial reflexive approach that focused on the process of frontier construction and the represention of Amazonian peoples by Portuguese colonisers. The exhibition incorporated Indigenous perspectives and described the dissemination of Western scientific views of the area through the collections the Portuguese amassed.[52] This protracted project included field research and systematic collecting among the Wauja, under-taken by Aristóteles Barcelo Neto, which resulted in a second exhibition and publication that contrasted the 'double world' of artefacts embedded in their culture of origin and their multiple networks including those which connect them to museums.[53] Less critical exhibitions have approached the Amazon through historical expeditions and their collected materials.[54] Two large-scale Amazonian exhibitions, *Brèzil Indien: Les arts des Amérindiens du Brèsil* (2005),[55] a homage to Claude Lévi-Strauss, and *Orinoco – Parima: Indian Societies in Venezuela – The Cisneros Collection* (1999–2000),[56] both mobilised considerable academic expertise in conveying increased under-standing of different ecological and cultural subjects, including aesthetic categories, epistemologies and pre-Columbian settlement and economic integration. Although these exhibitions reflected greater sensibility towards Amazonian history and better appreciation of the cultural uniqueness of the region, they gave little consideration to Indigenous perspectives.

Not until the late twentieth century were Indigenous community museums established like the Museu dos Povos Indígenas do Oiapoque, Brazil. In Peru, the Inter-Ethnic Association for the Peruvian Amazon Region (AIDESEP), an Indigenous association of activists, curated *Serpiente de agua: la vida indígena en la Amazonía* (2003),[57] which marked the begin-ning of Indigenous exhibition curation. Concepts of an animate nature, which Native Amazonians acknowledge has intrinsic rights of its own, were imported into art history through T.J. Demos's writings and exhibition *The Rights of Nature: Art and Ecology in the Americas* (2015),[58] and later reiter-ated in Nuno Porto's *Amazonia: The Rights of Nature* (2017).[59]

Amazonie: Le chamane et la pensée de la forêt (2016–2017, Musée d'Ethnographie de Genève (MEG)) aimed to provide another broad purview of a museum collection, but also positioned Amazonian history as intrinsi-cally bound up with colonialism and its violent, conflicted legacy, entangled with foreign and domestic governments, multinational corporations, land conflicts and its disjunctured epistemological mediations. The introduc-tion to the exhibition is uncompromising: the text panel reads: 'Since the European conquest in the 16th century, the Indigenous people of Amazonia have seen their culture attacked from all sides, their territory invaded and their environment destroyed in the names of kings, Christianity, civilization and economic progress.' Instead of reiterating simplistic interpretations like 'tradition' versus 'modernity', Boris Wastiau, the museum's director and exhibition curator, emphasises in the same text the Indigenous perspective on the importance of mediation between species in which 'All living beings and forest spirits share with humans the power to reason and interact with the environment' to safeguard and reiterate their essential symbiotic rela-tionships. The introductory text panel is followed by another political text on the conquest, to the side of which three large photographs of Amazonian leaders, with whom the museum worked, carry their own messages.

A second text on the power of shamans by Davi Kopenawa is opened by informing visitors that a bounty of US$100,000 had been placed on his

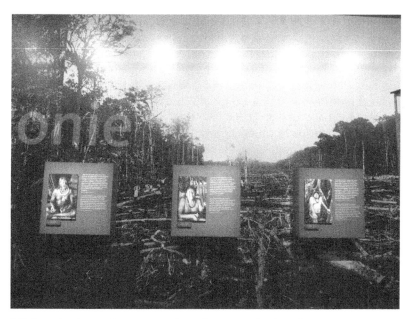

8.3 Introduction, with statements from Amazonian leaders. *Amazonie: Le chamane et la pensée de la forêt*, Musée d'Ethnographie de Genève, Switzerland, 2016–2017.

life by gold diggers. Another leader, Raoni Metuktire, gives a provocative explanation of the symbolism that links lip plugs to a person's commitment to defend the land. The remainder of this first section of the exhibition switches to European engagements which particularly focus on Geneva's relationship with the Amazon. This section exhibits early maps of the Amazon and the travelogue journals and maps of the churchman sent to Brazil by John Calvin, Jean de Léeiry (1536–1613), including a video of Claude Lévi-Strauss talking of his intellectual debt to Léeiry, and the works of the collectors who donated their holdings to the museum between the eighteenth and nineteenth centuries,[60] as well as the twentieth-century scientists and curators,[61] who continued their work through systematic field collecting. A section on 'Rubber and the Crucifix' brings together European commercial and religious interests in the Amazon with plant specimens, boots and machetes carried by rubber planters, photo albums, photographs, boxes of glass negatives, manuscripts of travel from 1903 and expedition equipment. The first part of the exhibition ends with a large format-film projection of the forest on the far wall.

Section two of *Amazonie* refocuses attention on shamanism and Indigenous epistemology. Cases exhibit the shaman's instruments and psychotropic plants, while text panels discuss trance, the practices and powers of shamans, 'perspectivism' (the ability of Indians to project themselves into animal beings to see the forest from multiple perspectives) and the sensory dominance of sound above sight. A text panel explains: 'All the creatures of the forest think and interact in a complex system. The forest is alive, it has a soul, it thinks, and acts on every being that dwells in it.' The link between material culture and text is made through three large photos by the photojournalist Claudia Andujar, '*Rêves Yanomami*', evoking different dream states. The material culture and text are further spliced together by another large AV installation, *Amoahiki* (2008) by Gisela Motta and Leandro Lima. The work is projected on to a black wall covered with strips of white cloth which enhance the images of luscious green leaves gently moving in the breeze. Across this shimmering verdant forest curtain, faint images of spirits take momentary form before fading into the canopy.

The exhibition's third section displays the collections divided into fifteen cultural areas, with objects contained in cases arranged along dark labyrinthine paths with a green forest-like canopy made of gauze and green and brown fabrics resembling leaves and fronds streaming down from the ceiling that cast shadows throughout the area. This is the ubiquitous collection survey, but a survey dividing up groups according to distinctive language families, with text panels that not only describe the objects but compare the decline of each population over time and give information on current economic activities and conditions, and their histories of resistance. The juxtaposition of these grim statistics with the exotic splendour of feather and barkcloth masks, costumes and personal decoration powerfully evokes human and cultural loss, which parallels the Native inhabitants'

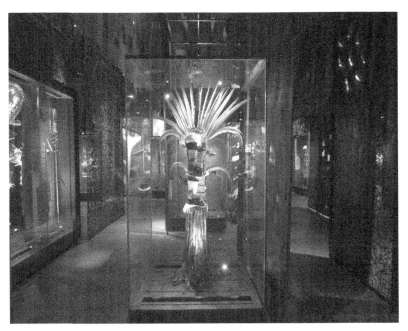

8.4 Section three: divided by Amazonian cultural groups. *Amazonie*, Musée d'Ethnographie de Genève, Switzerland, 2016–2017.

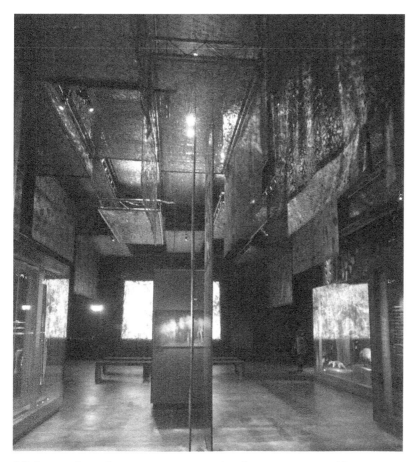

8.5 Section three: divided by Amazonian cultural groups. *Amazonie*, Musée d'Ethnographie de Genève, Switzerland, 2016–2017.

persistent adherence to practices and actions endemic to their epistemologies and values. This section is overlaid by sixteen diverse 'sound stories', soft and loud recordings drawn from hunting and fishing expeditions, birdsong, the scuttling of animals, rain, thunder, chain saws and the loud crash of felled trees.

The exhibition's final section, entitled 'The People of Amazonia in the 21st Century' – while acknowledging that the dispossession of land and the loss of traditional knowledge lead everywhere to poverty and marginalisation – focuses on how technologies are being used, in accordance with traditional values, to organise, record and disseminate actions aimed to preserve the natural environment and gain governmental recognition of territorial rights. These stories are told through small video presentations by Amazonian peoples on screens scattered throughout the section, but the strongest message is presented in the final installation, a large circular maloca, a wooden structure divided into two halves; the first displaying a set of photographs by Auréliean Fontanet, *The Future of Forest Peoples* (2016), and the second housing a concentric bench with three touch screens through which visitors can access twenty-three statements recorded on film by Amazonians who wanted to address visitors 'personally and directly'. To accomplish this, the MEG collaborated with two activists, Délio Firmo Alves and Jaelson Felix, who, equipped with just two smartphones, recorded these messages and brought them to Geneva. The MEG also worked with the Federation of the Indigenous Communities of the Upper

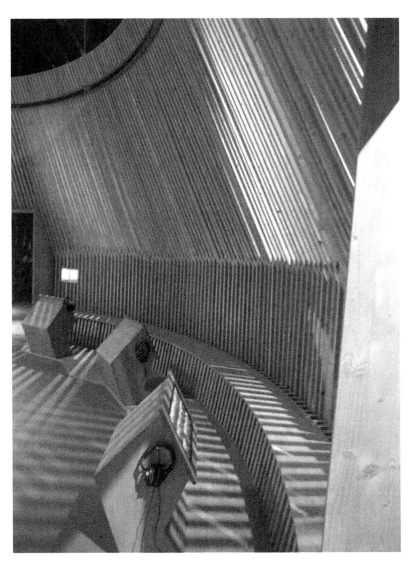

8.6 Section four: reproduction of a malaca with screens running 23 presentations from the peoples of the Amazon to the citizens of Geneva and the world. *Amazonie*, Musée d'Ethnographie de Genève, Switzerland, 2016–2017.

Tigre (FECONAT), an organisation of ten Indigenous observers who 'keep track of contaminated sites. Equipped with smartphones, the observers take geo-referenced photographs, which they up-load to online data bases. This material is used for anti-pollution campaigns aimed at the State, the mining and oil companies involved and public opinion' (exhibition text). Having been successful, the watchers' programme has been implemented in other parts of the Peruvian Amazon. The terminal in the gallery accesses photographs of polluted landscapes, evidence of companies transgressing the law and the mobilisation of people to expel illegal miners from their territories. The final AV presentation at the end of the gallery consists of four projections, each in shades of red and orange that attempt to capture the trance images of the Yanomami shaman Davi Kopenawa. The work, *Xapiri* (2013) by Gisela Motta and Leandro Lima, leaves visitors to experience the final image of the exhibition as one coming from the deepest world of Amazonian peoples.

Final remarks

Late twentieth- and early twenty-first-century curatorial practices disclose five distinct exhibition genres through which Amazonian and Andean peoples have commonly been presented in majority museums. The widespread romantic genre has been variously instantiated through the tropes of treasure, relics and the exotic exquisite. A second genre adopted a more historical but Inca-centric interpretation, while the third is characterised by more specific and scholarly approaches. These three genres, distributed across a broad spectrum stretching from aesthetic to empirical presentations, all adopted survey methodologies as a way of dealing with large collections in Western repositories and, politically, have often been mobilised in support of soft diplomacy. What is unusual in the case of Amazonia is the number of counter-hegemonic, experimental and alternative methodologies that the encounters between Western and non-Western intellectual cultures have stimulated. This fourth genre includes reflexive and deconstructivist exhibitions, while a fifth genre is made-up of Indigenous approaches.

Amazonie is itself a multimedia, multisensory immersive experience that switches between different knowledge paradigms and different professional and cultural communities to provide a deep, complex and politically relevant picture of the history and contemporary conditions and issues facing Amazonian peoples today. The exhibition clearly acknowledges critical theory but ingests it as a method that guides the exhibit's production, instead of reiterating methodological polemics. Rather than constructing an opposition between epistemologies or privilege one over the other, the exhibition's curator Boris Wastiau shifts back and forth using multiple perspectives to provide different lenses on a complex situation.[62] *Amazonie* demonstrates the advantages of applying different knowledges rather than dispensing one in preference for another.

Critical museology needs to develop a genre theory of exhibition history to better understand the limitations and politics of established practice and guide new and innovative responses such as those discussed in this chapter.[63] *Amazonie* may not constitute an Indigenisation of the museum, which is sometimes too quickly celebrated without examining the socio-political organisation or the ethnic composition of curatorial departments, but it does represent one of the most accomplished visions of the museum as a globalised multicultural, dialogical meeting place, a space that is needed even more in the age of resurgent English and US American nationalism.

Notes

1 On the notions of utopia and heterotopia in relation to museums, see the Introduction, above.

2 The Ethnography Department of the British Museum, London, UK.

3 E. Carmichael, *Hidden Peoples of the Amazon* (London, British Museum Press, 1985).

4 O. Harris and P. Gow, 'The British Museum's Representation of Amazonian Indians', *Anthropology Today*, 1:5 1985, 2.

5 The public demonstrations and radio, and television coverage of the controversy surrounding the exhibition were discussed in G. Houtman, 'Survival International: Going Public on Amazonian Indians', *Anthropology Today*, 1:5 (1985), 2–4. And the museum director's response in G. Houtman, 'Interview with Malcom McLeod', *Anthropology Today*, 3:3 (1987), 4–8.

6 The Folger Shakespeare Library, Washington, DC, USA.

7 University of Essex Gallery, Colchester, UK.

8 Centro Cultural de la Villa, Madrid, Spain.

9 E. Subirats, 'The Vacuous Quincentenary', *Third Text*, 21 (1992), 58.

10 *Ibid.*, 57–66, 58.

11 A.A. Shelton, *Heaven, Hell and Somewhere in Between: Portuguese Popular Art* (Vancouver and Berkeley: Museum of Anthropology and Figure 1 Publishing, 2015), p. 228.

12 Musées royaux d'Art et d'Histoire, Brussels, Belgium.

13 Museum voor Volkenkunde, Rotterdam, Netherlands.

14 The Pyramid, Memphis, Egypt, and Florida International Museum, Saint Petersburg, USA.

15 Petit Palais, Paris, France.

16 City Art Centre, Edinburgh, UK.

17 Metropolitan Museum, New York, USA.

18 National Gallery of Australia, Canberra.

19 National Geographic Museum, Washington DC, and the Irving Arts Centre. USA.

20 Museum of Natural History, Smithsonian Institution, Washington DC, USA.

21 Musée des Beaux Arts, Montreal, Glenbow Museum, Calgary, Canada, and the Seattle Art Museum, USA.

22 These included the *Gold of Ancient America* (1968–1969, Museum of Fine Arts, Boston, The Art Institute of Chicago, Virginia Museum, USA), followed ten years later by *El Dorado Colombian Gold* (1978, The Art Gallery of South

Australia and other Australian venues). The exhibition was later hosted by the Royal Academy, London, UK (1978–1979), under the title *The Gold of El Dorado*.

23 Museo Nacional de Antropología y Historia, Mexico City, and the Museo Regional Michoacano, Morelia, Mexico.

24 Ethnographic Museum, Antwerp, Belgium, and Museum Paleis Lange Voorhout, The Hague, Netherlands.

25 The celebration of the European 'discovery' or 'encounter'; Latin American Independence, the commemoration of historical relationships as part of municipal festivals or the celebration of European cultural capitals.

26 B. Wallis, 'Selling Nations: International Exhibitions and Cultural Diplomacy', in D. Sherman and I. Rogoff (eds), *Museum Culture: Histories, Discourses, Spectacles* (Minneapolis: University of Minnesota Press, 1994), p. 267.

27 *Ibid.*, 271.

28 J. Nash, *We Eat the Mines and the Mines Eat Us: Dependency and Exploitation in Bolivian Tin Mines* (New York: Columbia University Press, 1993), and M. Taussig, *The Devil and Commodity Fitishism in South America* (Chapel Hill: University of North Carolina Press, 1987) were highly influential in incorporating an economic interpretation into my 1987 exhibition *Bolivian Worlds* (Museum of Mankind, London, UK). See A.A. Shelton, 'Bolivian Carnival', *British Museum Society Bulletin*, 55:18 (1987). In a subsequent exhibition, *Luminescence. The Silver of Peru* (2012, Museum of Anthropology, Vancouver, Canada), Nash and Taussig's discussions of religious ideology provided the interpretative framework for the exhibition: see A.A. Shelton (ed.), *Luminescence: The Silver of Peru* (Lima and Vancouver: Patronato Plato del Perú, 2012).

29 Frederick S. Wright Gallery, Los Angeles, the Heard Museum, Phoenix and the Denver Art Museum, USA.

30 Museo Barbier-Muller de Arte Precolombino, Barcelona, Spain.

31 Wallis, 'Selling Nations', 265.

32 See for example: T. Platt, 'What Are Museums For? Museums, Objects and Representation', *Anthropology Today*, 3:4 (1987), 13–16; I. Karp and S.D. Lavine (eds), *Exhibiting Cultures: The Poetics and Politics of Museum Display* (Washington, DC: Smithsonian Institution Press, 1991); H. Lidchi, 'The Politics and Poetics of Exhibiting Other Cultures', in S. Hall (ed.), *Representation: Cultural Representations and Signifying Practices* (London: Sage / Open University, 1997), pp. 153–208. On the reaction to the quincentennery exhibitions, see A.A. Shelton, 'The Future of Museum Ethnography', *Journal of Museum Ethnography*, 9 (2009), 33–48, 38–9.

33 See for example: B. Ferguson, S. Nairne and R. Greenburg (eds), *Thinking about Exhibitions* (London: Routledge, 1996).

34 Brooklyn Museum, USA.

35 Centre for Inter-American Relations, New York, USA.

36 Santa Barbara Museum of Art, USA.

37 Brooklyn Museum, Phoenix Art Museum, Los Angeles County Museum of Art, USA.

38 Museo Nacional Centro del Arte Reina Sofía, Madrid, Spain, Haus der Kulturen der Welt, Berlin, Germany, Museo Nacional de Arte and Museo Nacional de Etnografía y Folklore, La Paz, Bolivia. Because of copyright, the Museo Nacional Centro del Arte Reina Sofía is unable to release photographs of the exhibition for publication.

39 B. Scherer, 'Words of Welcome', in A. Creischer, M.J. Hinderer and A. Siekmann (eds), *The Potosí Principle: Colonial Image Production in the Global Economy* (Cologne: Verlag der Buchhandlung Walther Konig, 2010), p. 4.

40 *Ibid.*

41 M. Borja-Villel, 'Words of Welcome', in Creischer, Hinderer and Siekmann (eds), *The Potosi Principle*, p. 3.

42 Scherer, 'Words of Welcome', 5.

43 Borja-Villel, 'Words of Welcome', 2.

44 Creischer, Hindere and Siekmann (eds), *The Potosí Principle*, p. 18.

45 E. Schwartzberg Arteaga, 'Principio Postosi Reverso', in S. Rivera Cusicanque and El Colectivo (eds), *Principio Potosí Reverso* (Madrid: Museo Nacional Centro de Arte Reina Sofia, 2010), p. 49.

46 Arteaga, 'Principio Postosi Reverso', 50–2.

47 M. Geidel, 'Una Mirada desde Afuera: Explicando el Fracaso de una Colaboracion con Principio Potosi', in Rivera Cusicanqui and El Colectivo (eds), *Principio Potosí Reverso*, p. 56.

48 Arteaga, 'Principio Postosi Reverso', 52.

49 Rivera Cusicanqui and El Colectivo (eds), *Principio Potosí Reverso*, p. 6.

50 *Ibid.*, 2.

51 S. Ziauddin, 'Lies, Damn Lies and Columbus: The Dynamics of Constructed Ignorance', *Third Text*, 21 (1992), 47.

52 Shelton, *Heaven, Hell and Somewhere in Between*, 231–2.

53 After the exhibition's close, the museum opened its stored Amazonian collections to the public in an impressive new visible storage gallery.

54 1991, Memória da Amazónia: Alexandre Rodrigues Ferreira e a Viagem Philosophica, Lisbon, Portugal, and 2012, Plumes Amérindiennes Guyane. Don Dr Marcel Heckenroth, Musée d'Arts Africains, Océaniens et Amérindiens, Marseille, France.

55 Grand Palais, Paris, France.

56 Kunst- und Ausstellungshalle der Bundesrepublic Deutschland, Bonn, Germany.

57 Desamparados Centro Cultural, Lima, Peru.

58 Nottingham Contemporary, UK.

59 UBC Museum of Anthropology, Vancouver, Canada.

60 Césaer Hippolyte Bacle, Ami Butini and Oscar Dusendschön.

61 Jean-Luis Christinat, René Fuerst, Gustaaf Verswiyer and Daniel Schoepf.

62 B. Wastiau, *Amazonie: Le Chamane et la pensée de la forêt*, Paris, Somogy éditions d'art (Geneva, Musée d'ethnographie, 2016).

63 On critical museology, see A.A. Shelton, 'Critical Museology: A Manifesto', *Museum Worlds*, 1 (2013), 7–23.

Swings and roundabouts: pluralism and the politics of change in Canada's national museums

Ruth B. Phillips

What's lost upon the roundabouts we pulls up on the swings.[1]

A trio of national museums surrounds the neo-Gothic buildings of the Canadian Parliament. They are destinations along the 'ceremonial route' linking major federal buildings on the Ontario and Quebec sides of the Ottawa River that runs through Canada's National Capital Region. To the east, the modern glass dome designed by Moshe Safdie for the National Gallery of Canada (NGC) echoes the distinctive contours of the Senate Library, while to the west the long, low-slung contours of Moriyama and Teshima's Canadian War Museum emerge from a grassy embankment. On the Quebec side of the river, the curving organic forms created by Douglas Cardinal for the Canadian Museum of History face across to the high bluff crowned by the Parliament buildings. The commissioning of Israeli-Canadian, Japanese-Canadian and Blackfoot architects to design new homes for these three museums was as emblematic of the multicultural construct of Canadian identity promoted by late twentieth-century Liberal governments as was the mid-nineteenth-century decision to situate Canada's capital on the border between Ontario and Quebec. Although the Anglo-French tensions that dominated Canada's first century of confederation have not disappeared, the latter half of the twentieth century was marked by the challenge to enlarge a bicultural French/English construct of Canadian identity to accommodate powerful movements of Indigenous decolonisation and global immigration.

Even as the new buildings were rising from the ground, the curatorial processes that determine the historical and cultural representations inside were being transformed by curators and other museum professionals seeking new ways to respond to the politics of decolonisation and democratisation. A series of much-analysed controversies sparked by major exhibitions held during the 1980s and 1990s from New York, Toronto and Washington, DC, to Calgary, Alberta and Gainesville, Florida, had lent urgency to these reforms.[2] Ethnographic museums were at the epicentre of the debates, but the new models of collaboration and multivocality were soon picked up by museums of art, history and other heritage institutions.

By the beginning of the new millennium, most museum professionals would have said that the new priorities and practices had been broadly accepted and that the government programmes that supported them were securely established.[3] It was thus all the more shocking to witness the shutting down of many decolonising and democratising initiatives under the three Conservative governments headed by Prime Minister Steven Harper between 2006 and 2015. The changes, unprecedented in scope and degree, were imposed through budgetary cutbacks, restructurings, appointments to boards of trustees and tighter ministerial scrutiny. The Canadian Museum of Civilization, Canada's national museum of anthropology and history, was renamed the Canadian Museum of History (CMH) and given a new, more nationalist mandate which effectively moved it away from its historical focus on Indigenous peoples, diasporic and minority communities, and world cultures. A critical contingent of ethnology curators and senior staff who had pioneered new models of collaboration left their jobs, taking with them decades of corporate memory and rupturing carefully nurtured relationships with Indigenous communities. Even more devastating cuts were imposed on the archaeological work of Parks Canada and the Indigenous initiatives under way at Library and Archives Canada and the Department of Canadian Heritage. At the National Gallery, financial constraints led to the loss of curatorial positions and effectively stalled the ground-breaking integration of Indigenous arts into the Canadian galleries begun in 2003.[4]

In Canada, as elsewhere, the global financial crisis of 2008 was invoked as a justification for such belt-tightening exercises, but financial considerations alone cannot account for the changes of direction the Harper government imposed on the national museums and heritage organisations. Not only did Canada weather the recession better than most countries, but the most devastating cuts were announced as the recession was ending, after the Conservative Party gained a majority in the federal election of 2011. Rather, financial stringency was used to trigger ideologically motivated shifts in the priorities of cultural institutions aimed at realising Conservative commitments to small government, the restoration of British imperialist interpretations of Canada's past and more narrowly nationalist representations of its present.

With the election of a Liberal government led by Justin Trudeau in autumn 2015, the political pendulum began to swing back once again, restoring the earlier focus on pluralism and issues of social justice. The government's promise to implement the recommendations of the 2015 report of the Truth and Reconciliation Commission on Indian Residential Schools and to comply fully with the United Nations Declaration of the Rights of Indigenous Peoples, as well as its stated determination to address long-standing inequalities between settler and Indigenous populations are encouraging cultural institutions to resume or initiate Indigenous programmes. Many of the historical narratives presented in the raft of special exhibitions planned for the 2017 sesquicentennial of Canadian confederation that were initiated by the Conservative government have been realised under the watch of a Liberal minister of Canadian Heritage. It will perhaps be impossible to define fully the impact of the political shifts that occurred mid-way in these processes – how, in other words, they would have been different if carried out without the change in government. For example, although the narrative of Canadian history presented in the largest and most ambitious of these projects, the new 50,000 square foot Canada History Hall at the Canadian Museum of History, took final shape in the months following the Trudeau electoral victory, the extensive public consultations and appointment to advisory committees were in place earlier. The national consultations had revealed a broad interest in Indigenous histories and issues, which was already guiding the conceptualisation of the new hall. The dizzying pattern of advance, retreat and restore at the CMH and other institutions recalls, rather, the old saying that what is lost in the swings is made up at the roundabouts.

In this chapter, I examine the relationship between representations at national museums and the political rhythms that operate at a deeper level. I argue that a review of the activities of national museums in Canada under successive Conservative and Liberal governments suggests that museums do *not* march in lock-step with their governmental masters, but respond, rather, to slower-moving shifts in national historical consciousness. As arms-length institutions operating under ministerial aegis, the tendency of national museums is to avoid extremes of radical innovation or reaction. They are, instead, sensitive barometers of the nation's consensual politics over a longer durée. Three exhibitionary events that unfolded in the national museums that ring Parliament Hill demonstrate this kind of museological arrhythmia because they unfolded *during* the Harper years yet did *not* reflect that government's ideological positions. Rather, they manifest the currents of pluralism, decolonisation and globalisation that have been gaining in strength throughout the past half century.

The Canadian War Museum: four stories of 1812

The first of my three episodes concerns an exhibition commemorating a rather obscure war that became the centrepiece of a federal government-funded celebration which redefined it as an originating moment of Canada's national identity. The War of 1812 pitched Britain against the newly independent United States and has been taught to generations of students as a kind of addendum to the American Revolution. It had no clear winners; the British failed to win back their American colonies and the Americans failed to conquer the British colonies in Canada. It did, however, have clear losers, for the First Nations allies who fought on both sides lost their last chance to preserve their political sovereignty and their lands. To general surprise, the Harper government decided to position the War of 1812 as the first of a series of 'milestone' commemorations that would culminate in the 2017 celebration of Canada's 150th birthday as a federated nation. Harper's interpretation of the War of 1812 on the official government website also seemed riddled with anachronisms; although there was no 'Canada' in the early nineteenth century, but only a cluster of separate colonies,[5] he affirmed that 'the War was instrumental in creating Canada's armed forces ... laid the foundation for Confederation and established the cornerstones of many of our political institutions', and he also positioned it as a founding moment of multicultural co-operation in which Indigenous, British and French peoples joined forces to defend 'Canada' from 'American invasion'.[6] The milestone announcement thus gave rise to fears among many historians that a Conservative historical agenda focused on the monarchy, military sacrifice and glory, white male prime ministers and settler history would also shape the new exhibits at the Canadian Museum of History.

Amidst this remythologisation of Canadian history, it seemed a small miracle that *1812: One War, Four Perspectives* turned out to be a model of multiperspectivalism which realised with exceptional economy and clarity of design the multivocal approaches to historical narrative that had come to dominate academic historiography during the last four decades of the twentieth century.[7] Instead of trying to fold British, Canadian settler, American and Indigenous narratives into an integrated story line, the curator, Peter MacLeod, decided to recount the war's history and rationale four times from the perspectives of British, American, Canadian (settler and Indigenous) and Native American participants, giving each equal weight.[8] It is striking that the exhibition team received approval for an approach whose central message was the multiplicity of 'truth' from a museum executive which, in its efforts to represent Canada's military history, has had to negotiate highly charged disputes among veterans' groups, academics, partisan government officials and the public over facts and interpretations.[9]

Glenn Ogden's exhibition design successfully realised the multiperspectival theme through its handling of space, text and imagery. The visitor entered the exhibition through an introductory room featuring a multi-screen montage of changing images, interview quotes and short texts, and a main text panel which read:

> This exhibition is about the War of 1812. But it is also about perspectives, and how people can each have their own view of events. This applies to any event, great or small, contemporary or historical, public or private.
>
> The key participants in the War of 1812 – Americans, the British, Canadians, including Canadian First Peoples, and Native Americans – all experienced and perceived it differently.
>
> So this exhibition tells the story of the war four times, from each of these perspectives. Each story highlights those aspects of the war that mattered most to one participant.

By destabilising the idea of a single historical 'truth', the introduction prepared the visitor to expect four different narratives of the war that would not agree with each other – in my experience a difficult proposition to sell to museologists with less faith in the public than the team at the Canadian War

Museum (CWM). Rather than previous exhibits commemorating wars, it recalls the classic Japanese film *Rashomon*, with its impartial and inconclusive retelling of the story of a rape and a murder from the perspectives of the woman, her husband, a bandit and an onlooker.[10]

The visitor then entered 'the hub', a circular space which provided a floor plan of the four roughly equal wedge-shaped galleries that led out of it, each recounting the war from a different perspective (Figure 9.1). Within each, a further diversity of perspectives was also provided. For example, the American story included an account of the motivations of the Muskogee 'Red Sticks' who fought for the Americans in Alabama, while the Canadian narrative includes an account of the arrival of freed African American slaves in Nova Scotia and the subsequent participation of soldiers of African descent in the Canadian army, as well as a module on Indigenous participation which explained the motivations of individual leaders allied to the British.[11]

The CWM tracked visitors' responses closely and learned that they spent much more than the normal time in the exhibition.[12] This success was unexpected, even by the project team; 'I was surprised', project manager Miriam Proulx said, 'by how many people were reading everything. This was a different kind of exhibit.'[13] When asked how he had initially arrived at the four-story structure, curator MacLeod responded that this is 'how I do history', and cited the changes in his discipline that began in the 1960s, as theorists like Hayden White and Michel Foucault exposed the importance of attending to narrative tropes and epistemic changes. Indeed, MacLeod's doctoral thesis and first book dealt with First Nations participation in colonial conflicts in North America during the eighteenth century.[14] The ready embrace of the exhibition by federal government representatives was more

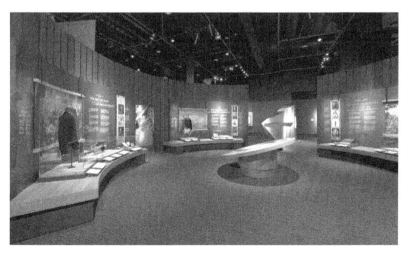

9.1 'The Hub', the circular visitor orientation area of the exhibition *1812*, Canadian War Museum, Ottawa, showing one of the four doorways leading into the exhibition's four parallel narratives.

surprising. Proulx noted that, when the Minister of Canadian Heritage James Moore met the press after visiting *1812*, he affirmed the value of the exhibition's focus on multiple perspectives. Despite the more monological narratives featured on his government's website, Moore's response appears to demonstrate a political sensitivity to Canada's diversity or a parallel formation to MacLeod's – or both.

The Canadian Museum of History: two stories of the Nishga Girl

My second museum episode concerns not the creation of an exhibition but the dismantling of one in preparation for the creation of the new Canadian History Hall commissioned by the Harper government in October 2012. It would replace the Canada Hall, first installed in 1989 as one of the opening installations of the Douglas Cardinal building. The earlier exhibit was designed as a 'Milwaukee-style' streetscape exhibition whose more immediate models were to be found at the Royal British Columbia Museum and the Epcot Center at Disneyworld.[15] Its visitor path traced the temporal and spatial expansion of Canada as a settler nation by taking visitors through a sequence of recreated three-dimensional historical environments. Each featured a representative vignette of social history and was intended to provide an immersive, experiential understanding of what life was like for common citizens in a particular time and place. Visitors moved from a sixteenth-century Basque fishing fleet off the Atlantic coast to a seventeenth-century tavern in New France, to a street of shops in a nineteenth-century Ontario town, an early twentieth-century union hall in Winnipeg, Manitoba, a Ukrainian church and grain elevator on the prairies, until finally arriving in the present-day North-West Territories and the Arctic.

British Columbia was represented by the coastal commercial salmon fishery. Its centrepiece was the *Nishga Girl*, a large wooden gill net boat used for thirty years by Nisga'a Chief Harry Nyce and his family (Figure 9.2). Chief Nyce and his wife Deanna had presented it to the museum for display in the Canada Hall in 1997, following the landmark Nisga'a Agreement, which settled a century-old land claim against the Canadian government. For Canadian First Nations, as CMH curators pointed out to the museum's administrators, a presentation made in such a context constitutes a nation-to-nation diplomatic gift which, when accepted, symbolically validates the formal agreements and good relations that have been negotiated.

The *Nishga Girl* was built for the Nyce family in 1967 by master boat builder Judo 'Jack' Tasaka. During the Second World War, Tasaka, like other Japanese-Canadians, had suffered internment and the confiscation of his property. (The Canadian government destroyed a thousand Japanese fishing boats similar to the *Nishga Girl* at that time.) The display thus represented two stories, one highlighting the modern entrepreneurial energies of British Columbia First Nations and the other the skills of Japanese-Canadians and their resilience in the face of racist and discriminatory

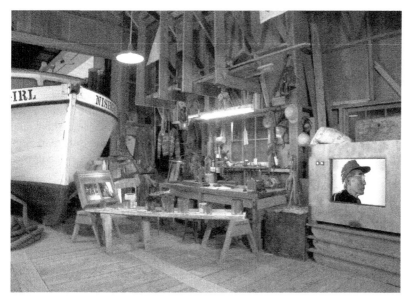

9.2 The *Nishga Girl*, installation photographed by the author in 2011 in the Canada Hall, Canadian Museum of Civilization (Now Canadian Museum of History, Ottawa), showing re-creation of the workshop of the builder, Jack Tasaka (far right).

policies, as well as the entwined histories of the peoples of the coast. Because of its significance to them, Japanese-Canadians had raised funds to send the boat across the country to its new home in the national capital.

Soon after the announcement that the Canada Hall was to be replaced, the museum set out to review what should be kept or removed. The *Nishga Girl*, it was felt, would not fit into the new installations, and the decision was taken to deaccession it and send it to a new home at the North Pacific Cannery National Historic Site near Prince Rupert, British Columbia. The boat was removed from display in May 2013 and the decision became public in June, when the *Ottawa Citizen* reporter Don Butler picked up the story. He interviewed Chief Nyce, who stated 'We thought it was a gift from us to the nation', and recalled that when the museum's curator telephoned him, 'All I could say was, "OK".' Butler reported that Chief Nice 'felt "a little bit" betrayed by the museum's decision'.[16]

Ken Noma, president of the Japanese Canadian National Association, expressed his sense of offence more strongly, stating that the decision was 'a tremendous insult'. He explained the great symbolic importance of the *Nishga Girl* to Japanese-Canadians, for whom it represented both the gill net boats seized from them during the Second World War and the arrival in Canada by boat of the first Japanese immigrants.[17] 'If this isn't Canadian history', he said, 'I don't know what else is'.[18] Noma then sent a formal complaint to the Minister of Citizenship, Immigration and Multiculturalism, Jason Kenney, who in turn wrote to the museum's director, urging him to reconsider the decision: 'This is a significant part of Canada's history which suits the new display that will offer a narrative of our country's history. It is regrettable that this gift is now to be shipped back.' So direct and public an intervention by a government minister in the work of an arm's-length crown corporation is unusual and improper, but within days the museum's director announced that he would meet with Noma and Chief Nyce.[19] The meeting took place on 8 July 2013 and resulted in the announcement two days later that the *Nishga Girl* would be returning to the museum and would be included in the new exhibition. 'The museum', a spokeswoman said, 'quickly recognized that it did not consult adequately with the two communities prior to making the decision to remove the boat'.[20]

What happened here? On one level, clearly, there was a failure to understand the principle established during the years of reform that originating communities have a right to be consulted when representations of their cultures are being mounted by a museum.[21] It appears that the senior staff who made the deaccessioning decision were unused to these protocols and failed to heed the warnings of the museum's own curators to whom the original context of the gift and its significance were well known. In a letter written to the director of the CMH in July 2013, Dr Andrea Laforet, the museum's former head of ethnography and a North-West Coast specialist, explained the broader historical significance of the *Nishga Girl*. She noted the important connections of the Indigenous commercial fishery in British Columbia to political agency and activism and the significance of boat building to Japanese-Canadians in the region, as well as to Tasaka specifically: 'As one of the last boats he built, it represents his successful reclamation of his profession after his return from internment.'[22]

On the level of *realpolitik*, the Minister of Immigration, Citizenship and Multiculturalism was doing his job by supporting the interests of minorities and 'new Canadians' and running political interference for the Prime Minister, who was scheduled to speak to Japanese-Canadians the following September on the occasion of the twenty-fifth anniversary of the Canadian government's formal apology for their internment during the Second World War. In early twenty-first-century Canada, maintaining good relationships with diasporic and minority communities is not just a matter of compliance with official multicultural policy but a political necessity for those who wish to remain in power. In many key ridings, federal elections cannot be won these days without the support of minorities and recent immigrants who in the 2011 census made up 20.6 per cent of the population and comprised half of the population of Toronto, Canada's largest city.[23]

It is Louis Althusser, however, who can help us to parse this story on a deeper level, for it is a textbook example of the interaction of the (Repressive) State Apparatus of government – represented by Minister Kenney – with the Ideological State Apparatuses – here, the museum – which ensures a society's ability to reproduce its characteristic relations of production.[24] As Althusser explains, the action of the two levels is conceptually separate, yet:

Very subtle explicit or tacit combinations may be woven from the interplay of the two bodies ... Whereas the (Repressive) State Apparatus constitutes an organized whole whose different parts are centralized beneath a commanding unity ... the Ideological State Apparatuses are multiple, distinct, 'relatively autonomous' and capable of providing an objective field to contradictions which express, in forms which may be limited or extreme, the effects of the clashes between the capitalist class struggle, as well as their subordinate forms.[25]

These contradictions and clashes surfaced in the affair of the *Nishga Girl*, revealing the Canadian Museum of History as a site of struggle in which the State's commitment to multiculturalism triumphed over its desire to impose a more narrowly based, ideologically infused narrative.

When the new Canada History Hall opened in 2017, the *Nishga Girl*, which, it has been determined, is too big to be accommodated within the hall itself, was displayed just outside it, having been moved from an open area near the First Peoples Hall. A carefully worded text panel finesses its recent vicissitudes:

In 1998, the Museum acquired the boat for the Canada Hall, where it helped tell the story of west coast fishing communities. It was later removed from display in preparation for the development of the new Canadian History Hall, opening in 2017. The Nisga'a First Nation and the National Association of Japanese Canadians met with the Museum in 2013 to request that the boat remain on display.

The Museum is proud to present *Nishga Girl* and its story to all Canadians.

The National Gallery of Canada: the many stories of world Indigenous art

Another kind of struggle has worked itself out over the past three decades at the National Gallery of Canada, as Indigenous artists have sought recognition as contemporary fine artists rather than producers of ethnographic artefacts. Despite the NGC's open-ended mandate to 'develop, maintain, and make known, throughout Canada and internationally, a collection of works of art, both historic and contemporary, with special, but not exclusive, reference to Canada',[26] it did not begin to collect Canadian Indigenous art until 2003, and exhibited historical works only occasionally in special exhibitions.[27] In 1985, however, the Gallery's policies regarding contemporary art began to change as a result of pressures that had been building both within and without. Once the move to the NGC's first purpose-built building was completed in 1988, the way was open to initiate an exhibition which would, in the words of the curator Diana Nemiroff, 'recognize a new generation of First Nations artists whose work was individual and personal, yet reflected a distinct cultural experience within mainstream North American art'.[28] She spearheaded the exhibition *Land Spirit Power: First Nations at the*

National Gallery of Canada, and co-curated it with the Anishinaabe artist and curator Robert Houle and art historian Charlotte Townsend-Gault. The showing of work by eighteen contemporary Indigenous artists from Canada and the United States made a permanent breach in the wall that had segregated settler and Indigenous arts into different museological spaces. In the two decades that followed, the museum – which already held and exhibited a major collection of Inuit art – organised authoritative retrospectives of several First Nations artists and integrated loans of historic art into its Canadian galleries. With the establishment of a new Indigenous department in 2003, it also began to collect world Indigenous art and announced that it would hold a major exhibition of contemporary world Indigenous arts every five years. The first of these quinquennials, *Sakahàn: International Indigenous Art*, took place during the summer of 2013.

Perhaps the first thing that struck visitors who had also seen *Land Spirit Power* was the sheer size of *Sakahàn*. Twenty years earlier, Nemiroff, Houle and Townsend-Gault had mounted a disciplined, tightly curated show that was decorously – if also exuberantly – contained within the NGC's suite of temporary exhibition galleries. *Sakahàn*, in contrast, was a huge and sprawling project that spilled out of the temporary exhibition space to occupy part of the contemporary art section, the whole of the print and photography section and seven sites outside the building. The project included an ambitious series of video presentations, a billboard piece in the old market area nearby, and satellite exhibits in nine other art galleries and exhibition spaces in the city. The NGC curators Greg Hill and Christine Lalonde, and guest curator Candice Hopkins, are specialists in North American Aboriginal art. Working with an international advisory committee scattered around the globe, they selected seventy-seven artists from Canada, the USA, Greenland, Australia, Aotearoa New Zealand, Samoa, Hawai'i, Mexico, Columbia, Brazil, Japan, Taiwan, India and Scandinavia.[29]

Other messages were more slippery. A number of artists identified themselves as Mestizo or Metis, and Lalonde explained in the catalogue that 'the potential of multiple meanings of Indigenous identity ... is ... at the core of the exhibition'.[30] She also wrote that the themes and conceptual framework evolved organically as the curators presented to each other artists whose work interested them:

> Visual and conceptual connections among them emerged, not so much as neat themes as instances of overlay and resonance. The curatorial framework evolved from the number of artworks that touched upon self-representation, histories and encounters, the value of the handmade, transmigration between the spiritual, the uncanny and the everyday, homelands and exile, and personal expressions of the impact of physical violence and societal trauma.[31]

For Hopkins, a unifying concern was resistance to 'historical amnesia, an active forgetting that forms the basis of the national narratives of countries such as Canada, the United States, Australia, New Zealand and Brazil'.[32]

She also noted the artists' reflexivity with regard to their shared heritage of artistic modernity. They 'look at the way in which images emerged within modernity and how they circulate now, how these images relate back to history, and the complicated ways in which other cultures were represented under imperialism'.[33] Such a theme was announced by the positioning of Michael Parekowhai's *My Sister, Myself*, with its commentary on Duchamp and the late eighteenth- and early nineteenth-century Māori involvement with commercial seal hunting, at the entrance to the exhibition.

It would be necessary to devote the whole of this chapter to *Sakahàn* even to sample its diversity. Let me, rather, focus on one work which, in its mixture of ethnographic and contemporary art strategies, exemplified the argument I want to make about the blurring of mandates that have distinguished museums of art, history and ethnography, and the concerns with decolonisation, histories of racism and issues of social justice and marginalisation they share today. The Australian Aboriginal artist Vernon Ah Kee's *cantchant* occupied two rooms at the core of the temporary exhibition galleries. (Figure 9.3). Around the walls of the first room the artist placed a suite of word pieces lettered – à la Barbara Kruger or Edgar Heap of Birds – with the cant of racial slur and the manifestos of Indigenous resistance. In the central space he hung a set of surfboards, displaying on one side north Queensland rainforest shield designs and on the other cropped portions of the artist's finely drawn pencil portraits of Aboriginal people. A three-screen video presentation in the second room centred on the iconic Australian realm of the beach, which Ah Kee has explained to be

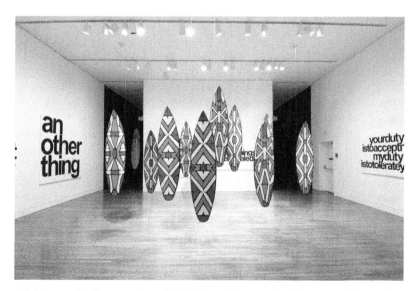

9.3 Vernon Ah Kee, *cantchant*, 2009. Video, 12 painted surfboards, and 9 acrylic paintings on canvas, installation dimensions variable. Installation shot *Sakahàn: International Indigenous Art*, 2013. Purchased 2010. National Gallery of Canada, Ottawa.

'a contested space territorial, a place of exclusion'.[34] In scenes of Aboriginal youths surfing and walking on an otherwise empty beach, Ah Kee portrayed both the invisibility of Aboriginal people in the environments claimed by settlers and their oneness with these environments. The violence and racism of colonial and neocolonial Aboriginal life is conveyed by scenes in which the shields, representing Aboriginal bodies, hang from trees and are subjected to violent attack by gunfire.

In their selection and positioning of *cantchant* and many other works in *Sakahàn*, the curators brought into high relief the technical virtuosity and complex criticality that characterise contemporary Indigenous art. These qualities had also been evident in *Land Spirit Power*, but in *Sakahàn* the curators claimed and occupied space for the display of contemporary Indigenous art with even more confidence and assurance, and engaged a much larger and global pool of artists. Success on a world stage raises earlier equations of art and criticality to a higher power. In the convergence of ethnography and art, it is the Indigenous, rather than the postmodern Western artist who has – *pace* Hal Foster – become the ethnographer.[35] *Sakahàn* left the impression that, during the summer of 2013 at least, Indigenous artists and curators committed to foregrounding those artists had taken over the National Capital Region. The sheer expansiveness of the exhibition was central, I suggest, to its message, demonstrating the power of globalisation to supersede the narrow settler nationalism that not too long ago defined the National Gallery itself, and asserting the decolonising potential of Indigenous transnationalism.

Conclusion

Taken together, my three museum stories evidence a contradictory and confusing social, political and professional field of forces, at once regressive and progressive, constrained and creative, timid and confident. It is a panorama that, I would guess, is all too familiar. Budget cuts, closures and restructurings have been depriving everyone of resources – the achievement of *Sakahàn* was all the greater because travel funding for curators and artists had been so limited. As noted, the cuts have also provided opportunities for right-wing governments and the museum managers they appoint to pull back from activities they did not want to support, from power sharing with originating communities to the traditional research mandate of museums. In Canada, the national heritage institutions became more hierarchical than in past decades and instituted frightening new forms of control over the abilities of their professional staff to speak freely about their own work. Yet the three episodes also evidence a convergence of disciplinary and representational domains informed by pluralist redefinitions of national culture and curatorial commitments – on the part of both Indigenous and settler curators – to recognising and restituting voice to Indigenous peoples. As much as the politics of reaction and reform, this convergence is transforming modernist constructs of ethnography, history and art. The Canadian national museumscape of the past decade has thus evidenced *both* what Paul Ashton and Paula Hamilton have termed the 'politics of reaction' *and* the seemingly irreversible effects of the processes of reform, demographic changes and social movements of the recent three decades.[36]

When Conservative regimes sponsor apparently reformist events, furthermore, it can be hard for the reformers to accept the positive value of the projects themselves. Is state multiculturalism *always* a ploy for managing diversity as critics such as Richard Day suggest?[37] Are linear narratives *always* reductive and hegemonic? What constitutes a sell-out and what a realistic strategy, and who is on which side? Yet at the same time, it is important to avoid the dangers of failing to recognise the ground swells of popular opinion to which contemporary museum managers pay close attention. In response, two large national museums produced exhibitions that decentred hierarchies of discourse and power in compelling ways. A third was forced to reinstate an exhibit it had decided to deaccession because of its importance to specific minority communities within Canada. We can, I think, interpret all this in two different ways. One interpretation is that *1812* and *Sakahàn*, as projects that began several years before the politics of reaction had taken hold in Ottawa, are the products of a progressive museum culture that, for a time, was fatally weakened. The interpretation I prefer, however, is that during the past three or four decades an academic culture transformed by post-structuralist and postcolonial critique, and a population transformed by demographic diversity, have, in combination, transformed museums and public consciousness so profoundly that they cannot easily be reversed. This is, I think, the lesson of the episode of the *Nishga Girl* and also of the positive popular response to the four-perspectives approach to *1812*. Both provide reasons for optimism at the same time that they highlight the need to maintain the commitment to progressive curatorial models even as the political pendulum swings in a different direction, in the faith that we will inevitably pick up again when we arrive at the roundabouts.

Notes

1 Quoted from Patrick R. Chalmers, 'Roundabouts and Swings', https://allpoetry. com/Roundabouts-and-Swings. Accessed 12 August 2016.

2 I refer to *Primitivism and Twentieth-Century Art: Affinities of the Tribal and the Modern* (1984) at the Museum of Modern Art, New York, USA; *Art / artifact: African Art in Anthropology Collections* (1988) at the Center for African Art, New York, USA; *The Spirit Sings: Arts of Canada's First Peoples* (1988) at the Glenbow Museum, Calgary, Alberta, Canada; *Into the Heart of Africa* (1989) at Toronto's Royal Ontario Museum, Canada; *Circa 1492* (1992) at the National Gallery of Art in Washington, DC, USA; *First Encounters: Spanish Explorations in Florida and the Caribbean, 1492–1570* (1992) at the Florida Museum of Natural History in Gainesville, Florida, USA; and *Mining the Museum: An Installation by Fred Wilson* (1992) at the Maryland Historical Society, Baltimore, USA. These have

stimulated a critical literature too large to list here in full, but for introductory discussions see J. Clifford, 'Histories of the Tribal and the Modern', in *The Predicament of Culture: Twentieth-Century Ethnography, Literature, and Art* (Cambridge, MA: Harvard University Press, 1988); R. Phillips, '"The Spirit Sings" as Critical Event and the Exhibition Within It', in *Museum Pieces: Toward the Indigenization of Canadian Museums* (Montreal: McGill-Queen's University Press, 2011); S.R. Butler, *Contested Representations: Revisiting Into the Heart of Africa* (Toronto: University of Toronto Press, 2007); H.K. Bhabha, 'Double Visions: Circa. 1492', *Artforum* (January 1992); and L.G. Corrin, *Mining the Museum: An Installation* (New York: New Press, 1994).

3 I have discussed the processes by which these changes occurred in my book *Museum Pieces: Toward the Indigenization of Canadian Museums* (Montreal: McGill-Queen's University Press, 2011).

4 Because the NGC had not collected Indigenous historical arts, the new installations (entitled *Art of This Land*) were heavily dependent on expensive loans from other institutions. See Anne Whitelaw's account of Canadian art museum installations in L. Young, A. Whitelaw and R. Beier de Haan, 'Museum Exhibition Practice: Recent Developments in Europe, Canada, and Australia', in C. McCarthy (ed.), *Museum Practice* (London: Wiley-Blackwell, 2015), pp. 403–29. In 2017 the NGC relaunched and expanded the initiative, under the new title *Canadian and Indigenous Art: From Time Immemorial to 1967*.

5 'The War of 1812', http://1812.gc.ca/eng/1305743548294/1305743621243. Accessed 4 July 2013. The Canadian Broadcasting Company reported the popularity of the website and reproduced its opening page, www.cbc.ca/news/politics/exit-proves-popular-on-canada-s-war-of-1812-website-1.1381430. Accessed 9 March 2017.

6 *Ibid.*

7 The exhibition was shown from June 2012 to January 2013 and a smaller version toured nationally.

8 Telephone interview with Peter MacLeod, 5 July 2013.

9 Proulx emphasises that the team 'developed this intellectual project with complete freedom'. Telephone interview with Myriam Proulx and Peter MacLeod, 5 July 2013. For a summary of debates at the Canadian War Museum over the creation of a Holocaust Gallery and bombing campaigns during the Second World War see the Historica Canada article on 'The Canadian War Museum', www.thecanadianencyclopedia.ca/en/article/the-canadian-war-museum-feature/. Accessed 14 August 2016.

10 Akira Kurowawa's 1950 film has been interpreted as an allegory of Japan's defeat in the Second World War. See J.F. Davidson, 'Memory of Defeat in Japan: A Reappraisal of "Rashomon"', *Antioch Review* (December 1954).

11 Personal communication, Alan Corbiere, historian and former director of the Ojibwe Cultural Foundation, 2013. Corbiere also spoke at a roundtable organised by the War Museum in conjunction with the exhibition.

12 Visitors stayed for an average of forty-five minutes in contrast to the twenty-minute average for other exhibitions, and 61 per cent of visitors stayed for close to an hour.

13 '1812 Virtual Exhibition', Canadian War Museum website, www.warmuseum.ca/war-of-1812/. Accessed 24 September 2016.

14 P. MacLeod, *The Canadian Iroquois and the Seven Years' War* (Toronto: Dundurn Press, 1996).

15 The Milwaukee Public Museum pioneered this style of exhibition when it opened its *Streets of Old Milwaukee* history installations in 1965. Using a reduced scale (3/4 in Milwaukee and 5/8 in the Canadian Museum of Civilization), such installations re-create historical streetscapes and other built environments to give visitors an immersive sense of living in a past period of time. Similarly, the Royal British Columbia's *Old Town* exhibition recreates historic urban environments in Victoria. MacDonald cited it and Disneyworld's Epcot Center as models for the CMC's Canada Hall and Grand Hall. (See G.F. MacDonald and S. Alsford, *A Museum for the Global Village: The Canadian Museum of Civilization* (Hull, Quebec: Canadian Museum of Civilization, 1989).)

16 D. Butler, 'Civilization Museum Sends Home: Donated Fishing Boat Removed to Make Way for New History Hall', *The Ottawa Citizen* (10 June 2013), www.ottawacitizen.com/travel/Civilization+museum+sends+Nishga+Girl+home/8505815/story.html. Accessed 5 July 2013.

17 *Ibid.*

18 D. Butler, 'Museum's Disposal of Boat a "tremendous insult," Japanese Canadians Say', *The Ottawa Citizen* (12 June 2013), www.ottawacitizen.com/travel/Canadian+Museum+Civilization+decision+dispose+Nishga+Girl/8516938/story.html. Accessed 5 July 2013.

19 P. Simpson, 'Jason Kenney Undermines Museum Changes', *Times Colonist* [Victoria, BC] (4 July 2013), www.timescolonist.com/opinion/columnists/peter-simpson-jason-kenney-undermines-museum-changes-1.341671. Accessed 5 July 2013.

20 Chantal Schryer, Vice-president of public affairs, quoted in D. Butler, 'Museum Reverses Decision to Banish', *Ottawa Citizen* (10 July 2013), www.ottawacitizen.com/travel/Museum+reverses+decision+banish+Nishga+Girl/8641970/story.html. Accessed 11 July 2013.

21 This principle is set out in the report of the Task Force on Museums and First Peoples, *Turning the Page: The Report of the Task Force on Museums and First Peoples* (Ottawa: Canadian Museums Association, 1992), funded by the federal Department of Communications (predecessor of the Ministry of Canadian Heritage) to develop new guidelines for relationships between Indigenous peoples and Canadian museums. Accepted by its co-sponsors, the Canadian Museums Association and the Assembly of First Nations, it became the basis for policy for members of both organisations.

22 Andrea Laforet, letter to Mark O'Neill, CEO, Canadian Museum of Civilization, July 2013. The text reads: 'Aboriginal commercial fishing is, itself, intertwined with the Aboriginal fishery that has a history of thousands of years on the coast. The Aboriginal commercial fishery was a significant context for the development of the Native Brotherhood, an organisation important in the history of Aboriginal political affirmation. The twentieth-century connections between Aboriginal customary fishing and commercial fishing have also been elements of two major court cases (and Supreme Court decisions) in the late twentieth-century quest to define Aboriginal rights in Canada. Nisga'a participation in the coastal fishery is protected in the Nisga'a Final Agreement. Jack Tasaka's life and work encompass a tumultuous period in Canadian history. Born in British Columbia, he apprenticed as a boat builder in the fishing and cannery centre of Steveston on the southern coast and built boats on the Skeena River until he was forced to leave the coast during the Second World War with other residents of Japanese ancestry. After several years in the interior B.C. community of Lillooet,

he returned to the coast, where he reclaimed his profession. Built ten years before his retirement in 1977, it was among the last of the wooden boats built by his company'. I am grateful to Dr. Laforet for sharing a copy of her letter with me.

23 Statistic Canada, 'Immigration and Ethnocultural Diversity in Canada', www12.statcan.gc.ca/nhs-enm/2011/as-sa/99–010-x/99–010-x2011001-eng.cfm. Accessed 7 March 2017. The figure for Toronto refers to the Greater Toronto Area. See 'Toronto Facts', 'Diversity', www1.toronto.ca/wps/portal/contentonly?vgnextoid=dbe867b42d853410VgnVCM10000071d60f89RCRD. Accessed 14 August 2016.

24 L. Althusser, 'Ideology and Ideological State Apparatuses (Notes towards an Investigation)', in *Lenin and Philosophy, and Other Essays*, trans. by Ben Brewster (New York: Monthly Review Press, 1971), p. 143.

25 *Ibid.*, 147–9.

26 See J. Hines, 'Art of this Land and the Exhibition of Aboriginal Art at the National Gallery' (Master's Thesis, Art History, Carleton University, 2004); and J. Souliere, 'The Stone that Cracked the Wall between the Institution and the First Nation Artist: The National Gallery of Canada, 1980–2008' (Master's Thesis, Concordia University, 2008).

27 Between 2003 and 2016 the NGC's biennial reinstallations of Canadian art, entitled *Art of This Land*, integrated examples of historic Indigenous arts borrowed from other institutions.

28 D. Nemiroff, R. Houle and C. Townsend Gault, 'Land, Spirit, Power', in D. Nemiroff, R. Houle and C. Townend Gault, *Land Spirit Power: First Nations at the National Gallery of Canada* (Ottawa: National Gallery of Canada, 1992), p. 11.

29 A New-York-based Kenyan artist was also in the show, but Africa and Asia were not otherwise represented.

30 C. Lalonde, 'Introduction: At the Crossroads of Indigeneity, Globalization and Contemporary Art', in G.A. Hill, C. Hopkins and C. Lalonde (eds), *Sakahàn: International Indigenous Art* (Ottawa: National Gallery of Canada, 2013), p. 15.

31 *Ibid.*, 18.

32 C. Hopkins, 'On Other Pictures: Imperialism, Historical Amnesia and Mimesis', in Hill, Hopkins and Lalonde (eds), *Sakahàn*, 22.

33 *Ibid.*, 31.

34 'Vernon Ah Kee at the Venice Biennale 2009', interview with Jane Cleary, YouTube, www.youtube.com/watch?feature=player_embedded&v=hjVJCboL4jw. Accessed 1 December 2016.

35 H. Foster, 'The Artist as Ethnographer', in G. Marcus and F. Myers (eds), *The Traffic in Culture: Refiguring Art and Anthropology* (Berkeley, CA: University of California Press, 1995).

36 P. Ashton and P. Hamilton, 'Unfinished business: Public History in a Postcolonial Nation', in D. Walkowitz and L. Knauer (eds), *Contested Histories in Public Space* (Durham, NC: Duke University Press, 2008), p. 85. They discuss representations of Aboriginal and settler history at the National Museum of Australia during the Conservative government of Prime Minister John Howard, in power from 1996 to 2007.

37 R.J.F. Day, *Multiculturalism and the History of Canadian Diversity* (Toronto: University of Toronto Press, 2000).

Community engagement, Indigenous heritage and the complex figure of the curator: foe, facilitator, friend or forsaken?

Bryony Onciul

Current critical issues, such as decolonisation, truth and reconciliation, span the interconnected networks of peoples, places, practices and artefacts which draw museums and their curators into complex and ever-changing spheres of engagement in today's globalised world. While curation is a recognised and respected profession, the proliferation of community engagement since the 1980s has brought increased awareness of the importance of source communities' expertise, knowledge and rights to influence – even control – the way their heritage is cared for and represented. This has created new opportunities, challenges and expectations, which have enriched and complicated curatorial roles, particularly for ethnographic curators working with Indigenous communities. This chapter explores these issues and the current utopias and dystopias of contemporary curatorship in Canadian and UK contexts.

Museology has shifted away from the curator as lone expert and voice of authority,[1] towards facilitating community engagement and collaboration. These shifts have been informed by pressures from within and outside the museum profession. New approaches to exhibiting Indigenous cultural material, such as the 1984 *Te Maori* exhibition at the Metropolitan Museum of Art in New York, USA, opened up museological practices to Indigenous methods for caring for the past and representing culture on a global stage.[2] Key protests such as those in Canada about *The Spirit Sings: Artistic Traditions of Canada's First Peoples* exhibition at Glenbow, Calgary, in 1988 and *Into the Heart of Africa* at the Royal Ontario Museum, Toronto, in 1989, inspired radical rethinking of museum approaches to displaying source communities formerly thought of collectively as 'Others'.[3]

Indigenous peoples' challenges to museums through protests and calls for repatriation, and via collaborative working, have reshaped museological thinking over the past decades. In Canada, *The Spirit Sings* protest inspired the Assembly of First Nations and Canadian Museums Association to create the *Turning the Page* Task Force Report, which redefined the role of museums when representing First Peoples.[4] In the USA, the 1990 Native

American Graves Protection and Repatriation Act (NAGPRA) changed the law around human remains and funerary objects in federally funded collections. Internationally, the United Nations' 2008 Declaration on the Rights of Indigenous Peoples (UNDRIP), Article 31, reinforced the rights of Indigenous communities to control the management of their heritage. Museums have informed and responded to these changes in law and policy, embraced many aspects of postcolonial thinking, and generally supported calls for decolonisation in theory and practice. These new ways of working and thinking about heritage, and the increasing need to incorporate source communities in museological work, continue to shape current curatorship.

Reimagining the role of the curator, which has been transformed from early amateur, to established expert, to current facilitator,[5] has allowed for recognition of different rights, voices and forms of expertise, particularly those of source and local communities.[6] These changes have supported a reimagining and reinvigoration of ethnographic museums, from places that were once seen as displaying 'Others' to potential locations of collaborative exchange, cultural revitalisation, community voice and even empowerment and pride. New practices have enabled new relationships such as the repatriation of material culture to source communities: with curators facilitating connections across multinational networks of human and non-human actors,[7] to enable sacred items and human remains to return home.[8]

Curators working with Indigenous collections are increasingly being required to consider and work with a changing past and future. In Canada, and other settler and colonial nations, processes of decolonisation, truth and reconciliation are revealing hidden histories and rewriting public understandings of the past, whilst creating new relations and advocating for different approaches to caring for the past in the future. These new and changing obligations to past and future ancestors inform best practice in current curatorial work.

While the shift from 'expert' to 'facilitator' has enabled museological innovation, it has, however, also oversimplified the complexities of voice, accountability and power in the representation of culture.[9] The 'temple' versus 'forum' debate (derived from a misunderstanding of the article by Duncan Cameron where he argued that both were needed[10]) has been widely embraced in museological practice, resulting in perceptions that curators are either experts in the temple or facilitators in the forum. Such binaries limit and obscure the complexities of curation. In actuality, as Robert Janes argues, 'the temple and the forum are two sides of the same coin'.[11] Following this line of thought, this chapter explores the expertise of facilitation and the role of the curator as an expert within the forum.

There is a need for a more nuanced understanding of the role of contemporary curatorship, especially in the context of increasing expectations of community engagement and decreasing resources to support museological work. The current climate of austerity in the UK threatens the future of specialist curatorship and collections. In recent years, owing in part to economic and social changes, there has been a move away from the presumed need for curators, leading to a potential 'dystopia' in which the figure of the curator is forsaken. To draw upon the terminology invoked by this book, such a dystopia would set back the strides that have been made in museology and heritage management towards a 'utopia' which values and incorporates culturally suitable approaches to caring for the past and contributes to decolonisation, truth and reconciliation. Drawing on Philipp Schorch's idea of 'the figure of the curator',[12] the chapter attempts to complicate and situate this concept by mapping out three influential guises of curatorship: foe, facilitator and friend. The chapter considers why these traits have come to the fore and how, in reality, these identities are all interwoven.

The curator as 'foe'

It is necessary to start by analysing the idea of curators as 'foes' or 'enemies'; whilst reductive,[13] this idea highlights important (mis)conceptions about the history of museums which continue to inform and influence current collaborative efforts and perceptions of ethnographic curatorial work.[14]

Museums and collections that were born from the history of exploration and colonisation house the material evidence of the impact of contact and conquest on Indigenous peoples from around the globe. They are both resources of precolonial knowledge, embodied in material culture – through art, design, stories and practice – and emblematic of the asymmetrical power relations of colonialism which fractured many Indigenous communities and cultures. As such, the biographies of these collections are intertwined with those of the colonised and colonisers, making museums potentially politically volatile spaces as these collections can be repurposed for different agendas and are inscribed with the shifting politics of the past and present.[15]

Historically, museums, and *de facto* their curators, were sometimes seen in a negative light by Indigenous communities, as museums arrived with, and were physical manifestations of, colonialism.[16] As a 'tool of empire', museums helped to publicly justify colonisation and create an 'imperial archive' of 'specimens, objects and records'.[17] The historical practice of collecting sacred cultural material, and even the bones and bodies of Indigenous people, has, for some, made museums synonymous with sites of death and loss.[18] In Canada, salvage collecting during periods of cultural persecution ties museums into the Canadian history of cultural genocide epitomised by the residential school era (1831–1996), which systematically removed Indigenous children from their families and sent them to church- and state-run residential schools.[19] The 1895 Section 114 amendment to the Indian Act banned First Nation ceremonies.[20] This, combined with the poverty on the reserves, the work of missionaries to convert First Nations to Christianity and the removal of children from the community to residential schools, disrupted traditional intergenerational knowledge and ceremonial transfer and saw material culture flow into global collections.[21]

The intertwining of collecting and colonisation continues to play out today with museums being identified as having a role to play in current-day truth and reconciliation.[22]

As authorities on the past, museums inform public history; and, as a result of extensive collecting, museums can be exceptional cultural repositories for First Nations to utilise to revive and reinvigorate precolonial cultural knowledge and practices. Consequently, curators often find themselves in the dubious position of being a gatekeeper who could be both potential foe and ally. When Indigenous communities cannot access items vital to the maintenance and renewal of their cultural practices – owing to their location in museum collections and prohibitive policies, distances, costs or logistics – then the current-day gatekeepers can be seen as part of the problem. Conversely, when sacred items are returned, or curators adapt their collection care to respect source community protocols, then gatekeepers can gain great standing within the community and develop relationships as allies that can even become friendships.

However, community engagement, collaboration and repatriation are not simple or speedy processes. Repatriation is time-consuming, often requiring the surmounting of barriers in law, policy and institutional understanding. In Canada in 1951, Bill 79 lifted the Indian Act ban on Indigenous ceremonies, but by then many sacred items were in museum collections. The Blackfoot Confederacy, like many First Nations, have sustained their efforts over decades to repatriate their sacred items to enable the renewal of ceremonies.[23] Some of these processes are ongoing,[24] and some have come under stress to the point of conflict.[25]

There has been continued effort in Canada to rethink relations between museums and Indigenous people. This has changed the perceived role of curators in relation to Indigenous collections and communities in Canada, emphasising the need for collaboration and facilitation, to promote access and support community self-representation.[26]

The curator as 'facilitator'

The refashioning of the curator as an engaged 'facilitator' – providing access, collaboration, coproduction and even repatriation – has enabled new relationships to be built between source communities and museums. This trend extends beyond Canada: in the UK there have been examples of museums working with North American source communities to share knowledge and collections over the past three decades. In 1999, the Glasgow Kelvingrove Art Gallery repatriated a Lakota Sioux Ghost Dance Shirt, thought to have been worn during the 1890 Wounded Knee massacre, to the South Dakota State Museum.[27] The University of Aberdeen Marischal Museum repatriated a sacred Kainai Headdress in 2003.[28] In 2009, the Pitt Rivers Museum, Oxford, created a project on Blackfoot shirts that enabled the 1841 collection to visit Blackfoot communities in Canada through handling sessions and exhibitions.[29] In 2013, the Royal Albert Memorial Museum (RAMM), Exeter, was part of a Leverhulme project that brought Blackfoot Elders to visit Blackfoot collections in the UK.[30] As a consequence, RAMM is discussing the potential repatriation of Chief Crowfoot's regalia to Blackfoot Crossing Historical Park (BCHP), a Siksika Blackfoot-owned and -run centre in Alberta, Canada.[31] These examples illustrate some of the ways museums and communities have been changed and enriched through engagement.

In these situations, curators act as conductors, bringing together diverse networks of human and non-human actors.[32] The recognition of source communities as valued experts and potential research partners has revolutionised museum practice by opening up different ways of knowing and caring for the past. However, what can be silenced in this new framing of curators as facilitators is the vast amount of expert knowledge of collections, culture, history and current affairs that is needed for curators to recognise opportunities, and understand why and how to work, and who to work with within communities.[33] The skills, knowledge, dedication and long-term investments required to develop meaningful relationships with individuals within source communities are often muted within the idea of curators facilitating external community experts. The penchant for binaries results in an automatic notion that there cannot be multiple kinds of expertise, there is either the curator as expert in the temple or community as expert in the forum.[34] This false dichotomy also incorrectly implies that source communities represent one homogeneous expert unit that can be called upon by the museum. Research shows that engagement involves curators selecting and bringing together diverse people, ideas, items, places and times to co-create something new.[35]

Working with and across different cultures requires curators to be open-minded, humble and willing to learn from communities about culturally sensitive approaches and protocols. While all cultures are different, Indigenous scholars, such as Linda Tuhiwai Smith, have recommended basic research principles to follow:

1. *Aroha ki te tangata* (a respect for people)
2. *Kanohi kitea* (the seen face, that is present yourself to people face to face)[36]
3. *Titiro, whakarongo … kōrero* (look, listen … speak)
4. *Manaaki ki te tangata* (share and host people, be generous)
5. *Kia tūpato* (be cautious)
6. *Kaua e takahia te mana o te tangata* (do not trample over the *mana* [authority, reputation] of people)
7. *Kia māhaki* (don't flaunt your knowledge).[37]

These principles indicate the respect, time, resources and expertise needed for successful collaborative research with Indigenous communities by both community and non-community curators. It emphasises the unique curatorial skill set: negotiating the boundaries between public and private;

museum, community and visitor; artefact, person, place, practice and policy; authority and humility; expert and apprentice. Curatorship, when done well, can bridge divides, bring meaning to fragmented networks, accommodate differing ontologies and epistemologies, and create new approaches to working with, and caring for, the past for the future.

Canada and Aotearoa New Zealand provide examples of institutions that manage to balance the respect for the expertise of source communities and curators. The Museum of New Zealand Te Papa Tongarewa and the Museum of Anthropology (MOA), UBC, Canada, both formally recognise source community ownership of the collections.[38] Yet, they also employ subject-specific curators, whose skills enable them to work with collections, communities and exhibitions, enhancing the community and visitor experiences and enriching the shared knowledge of entangled pasts.

Curators, as keepers of the past for present and future generations, are also tasked with responding to current concerns. In 'the age of apology',[39] museums are increasingly being called upon to respond to historical wrongs and facilitate new relations. In Canada, the recent adoption of the United Nations Declaration on the Rights of Indigenous Peoples (UNDRIP) on 10 May 2016, and the Truth and Reconciliation Commission (TRC) report released in August 2015, present two fundamental new challenges for museums to address.

The Canadian TRC published ninety-four Calls to Action, two of which were directed at museums, requesting the government to establish a 'national review of museum policies and best practices to determine the level of compliance' with UNDRIP, and a 'dedicated national funding program for commemoration projects on the theme of reconciliation'.[40] Addressing this period of cultural genocide in collaboration with affected communities will require experts who know the museum collections and their histories, but more importantly have the skill and experience to work sensitively and appropriately with communities that have endured decades of intergenerational trauma.

Canadian curators are already responding to the TRC's Calls to Action. For example, in the summer of 2016, the curator Beth Carter hosted a 30-metre, temporary outdoor exhibit, as part of the Bill Reid Gallery of North-West Coast Art in Vancouver: 'The chalkboard-style mural designed by local Haida artists Robi Geary and Corey Bulpitt, ... invite[d] passers-by to write or draw their responses to the phrase *My (Re)conciliation is ...*'[41] It aimed to 'encourage creative conversations around reconciliation' and 'shape an engaging public dialogue'.[42] Similiarly, museums can play leading roles in opening up difficult discussions, addressing hidden histories and shifting historiography in public settings.

Museums can also provide platforms from which those who have been previously overlooked can gain ground and be heard through 'official, authorised' capacities. Museums can publicly validate previously denied histories such as the Residential School System, and help shape future relations. The value of museums lies, at least in part, in their ability to provide space for dialogue, debate, controversy and contestation of challenging topics, but to do this they need highly skilled cultural brokers who can work across platforms, viewpoints and agendas.[43]

Fiona Cameron's research in Australia indicates that 'bringing important challenging and controversial points of view in a democratic, free-thinking society [is] seen as a key role for museums'.[44] Addressing global concerns is vital, according to Janes, for museums to remain relevant and sustainable.[45] This is particularly pertinent because, as Bernadette Lynch notes, museums are yet to convincingly justify their social worth to all.[46] Lynch argues that participation and engagement create the dialogue necessary for reflective practice, which is essential for making museums socially responsible and sustainable as it is 'centrally about decolonising our thinking in museums'.[47] Decolonising thinking is no small task, as it was in European museum collections that the first taxonomies were tested and defined, helping to create the foundations of Western knowledge.[48]

> All museums have the responsibility and the opportunity to become synthesizers, and foster an understanding of the interconnectedness of the problems we face, both environmental and social. A mindful museum can empower and honour all people in the search for a sustainable and just world – by creating a mission that focuses on the interconnectedness of our world and its challenges, and promotes the integration of disparate perspectives.[49]

The banality of the term 'facilitator' obscures the highly complex and intricate work curators do to balance competing epistemologies and utilise the past in the present to consider our collective future. It also obscures the personal relationships curators must build with communities to do engagement, which requires notable investment from curators and museums in terms of time, money, energy and emotion. Collaborative relationships can be fragile, and curators doing engagement at its best must dance a thin line between competing agendas, requirements and desires.[50]

The curator as 'friend'

In the role of 'facilitator', curators have to negotiate difficult museum histories and associations with the 'enemy' to establish genuine, meaningful relations with community members which, over years, even decades, of collaboration can naturally develop into personal friendships between individuals. Drawing on interviews with the former Glenbow Museum curator Gerry Conaty (Canadian) and two Blackfoot Elders, Frank Weasel Head (Kainai) and Jerry Potts (Piikani), who worked together in partnership, it is possible to see the role that friendship plays in building new positive relations between former 'adversaries'. Conaty described how he first began working with the Blackfoot:

> I became friends with the Weasel Moccasin family and began to understand the significance of the holy bundles to people; not to a foreign culture. They,

in turn, began to see me as an individual who was beginning to understand and respect their culture and their holy bundles. They now asked that I fulfil some obligations to their culture: I was encouraged to prepare a daily smudge for the bundle while it resided at Glenbow; I was expected at various ceremonies, and I was requested more and more often to lend religious objects. ... As I developed similar personal relationships with other Kainai and Piikani, I moved beyond being seen as the representative of a faceless institution. This, in turn, personalized Glenbow and it became regarded less as a custodian of objects and more as a steward of living things.[51]

Working relationships grew through sharing, trust and humour (never to be undervalued),[52] and became friendships. 'As I became friends with Blackfoot people,' Conaty explained, 'I began to hear their explanations of their own culture and their own history'.[53] 'Because we began returning more and more bundles on loan, and began to get into disputes with some of the provincial government people, who disagreed with our approach ...', 'I think the Blackfoot people began to see us as sort of a friend and a supporter.'[54] The Kainai Elder Frank Weasel Head recalls how the relationship with Conaty 'was built through repatriation, through our ceremonies ... in the 90s ... and it just kept going on ... we became friends and he is still my friend, lifelong friend'.[55] Weasel Head described Conaty as a 'good friend' and a 'go-between' with museums: 'he was a curator and he was a pioneer in repatriation'.[56]

Conaty demonstrated his personal commitment, and Glenbow's, to the Blackfoot community and this helped to overcome negative feelings the communities had held towards museums.

Anytime on the [Kainai] Tribe, you start talking about a museum, it is a dirty word ... because of what they have done in the past ... For a while it took a little bit to accept Gerry [Conaty] because he was from a museum, to accept Beth [Carter] and Irene [Kerr]. It took a little bit. But when they showed a genuine interest, and they helped to return those objects, our sacred material, for the tribe, then people start changing. So it ... wasn't an overnight.[57]

Building these kinds of relations requires personal and institutional investment over the long term: 'If you counted each penny you couldn't get it done,' Conaty said, 'and if you counted every minute, would really get a chip on your shoulder, because you couldn't get it done.'[58] Conaty was honoured with membership of the Kainai Chieftainship in recognition of his dedication and repatriation work.[59] As Frank Weasel Head explains, 'People whom we once might have regarded with suspicion have become close friends.'[60]

However, such relations are fragile. They are created between individuals not institutions, thus, when team members change, new relationships have to be built. As Piikani Elder Jerry Potts noted, a new member of staff would:

Have some pretty big shoes to fill there ... all the guys that know what is going on, that have developed this positive relationship with Gerry

[Conaty], none of them are going to go banging on the door to say hey, here is me, here is what I can do, here is what I can offer. None of them will do that. It is a trust friendship, like a bond.[61]

Conaty stated, 'I can't possibly teach [it], and I've talked to other curators who have long standing relationships with Native people too in other museums, and it's not something you can hand over, a list of phone numbers, and say go do it. It is something you have to earn.'[62] Nevertheless, Conaty did guide people though his publications, university and museum classes and in his daily practice; by sharing his insight into building and maintaining positive relations, he created a legacy of people who have been inspired by his work.[63] Frank Weasel Head hoped that 'if, when they do leave, that Gerry, Beth, and the Blackfoot team have created an environment that future CEOs or future staff members can carry on the work'.[64]

Sadly, both Frank Weasel Head and Gerry Conaty have now passed on and Glenbow has not yet appointed a permanent senior curator to continue the work. This is due in part to a change in institutional priorities, with Glenbow shifting to become 'a new kind of art museum', and in part to budgetary realignments that accompany such changes.[65] It is also a reflection of the time it takes for an individual to accumulate the skills and knowledge required to fulfil such a role. UNDRIP and the TRC Calls to Action will require museum staff to have considerable expertise and institutional support to respond to and engage with efforts to decolonise museums and support reconciliation.

Long-term institutionalisation of community relations, beyond the friendships built between individuals, continues to be a challenge for museums. When changes occur that are beyond a curator's control, such as a new vision, mission statement or policy, it can have unforeseen knock-on effects on the role and standing of the curator, who can readily be reassociated with the 'enemy'.[66] Efforts to institutionalise connections between museums and Indigenous communities currently take four main forms: Memorandums of Understanding; Indigenous Advisory Boards; Indigenous employees; and Indigenous-owned and -run museums or museum-like institutions. Increasing numbers of policies, reports and declarations supporting Indigenous rights to control and represent their own heritage, combined with repatriations, have helped to create a growth in Indigenous-run cultural heritage centres.[67]

In Canada, some repatriated collections have been returned on the condition that they are cared for in 'suitable' conditions, as determined by Western museum practice: for example, U'mista and Nuyumbalees Cultural Centres in British Columbia were created to house Potlatch collections that were confiscated under the Indian Act in 1921 and repatriated to the communities in 1979.[68] Other communities have built museum-like spaces in the effort to enable more returns from museums, such as Blackfoot Crossing Historical Park in Alberta.[69]

With the development of Indigenous cultural heritage centres have come new generations of Indigenous curators, or keepers of culture, who have, in turn, redefined curatorship. As Kurin argues, 'the culture broker can facilitate participatory cultural transformation and change – both between and within culture groups'.[70] These curators often blend Western museology with Indigenous practices of caring for the past, working in culturally appropriate ways that value cultural traditions and tangible and intangible heritage, such as caring for sacred artefacts as living beings and allowing culturally appropriate handling and use of items.[71] As intermediaries working within, along and across interfaces, they break down the either/or binary and are both: community and curator, friend/family and professional, expert and apprentice (as even Indigenous curators still need to work with, and learn from the wider community and facilitate access). Such fluid roles can be challenging as curators may face conflicting obligations and expectations, and have to live with the consequences within their communities.[72] Nevertheless, Indigenous curators help to move the discourse beyond 'insiders' and 'outsiders', enemies and allies, and illustrate the complexities and value of curatorship to museums and communities. Curators, defined as keepers or carers of the past for the future, play a key role in customary and contemporary society – especially with the increasing recognition of the importance of heritage to economies, identity, nationhood and addressing difficult pasts and potentially challenging futures.

The curator forsaken?

Despite the dramatic changes that have occurred over the past decades, the idea of the curator as foe or enemy has re-emerged in current discussions of museology in the UK. As the Chief Executive of the Collections Trust, Nick Poole, argues in his blog:

> In the story of the progress of museums in the past decade, it is very often the curator that has found themselves the villain of the piece. If the thrust of museum discourse is essentially progressive, the curator has come to represent everything that is retrograde about the 'old' museology. Where much of the rhetoric about museums is about openness and equality of participation, the lazy characterisation of curators is as hoarders of knowledge, using their control over ideas to exert control over their colleagues – indeed over the museum itself.[73]

Such 'lazy characterisations' can abound because there is 'little published evidence for the direct impact curators and curatorial knowledge have on museum activities and the communities they serve. There is also little direct justification for curators, nor explicit recommendations for museums to continue to resource them.'[74] Curators, who are deeply involved in collaborative work, rarely have time or resources to publish their work. Smith's advice on humility, not flaunting knowledge and giving due credit can, in practice, be interpreted as a need to co-publish with community members, which may be beyond the scope or drive of most curatorial projects.[75] As such, often the excellent curatorial work conducted in museums across the globe goes unmapped and unrecorded in academic literature.[76] With the lack of advocacy by, or on behalf of, curators, there has been a 'devaluation of the currency of curatorship'.[77] 'In the face of cuts and cost savings', John Holt argues, 'one-time specialists are increasingly expected to be multi-tasking generalists'.[78]

While the notion of curators as facilitators has been vital to building relations across former 'enemy' lines and has reformed museological practice, it has also oversimplified and obscured the complex and skilful work of curatorship. In times of austerity and cuts, such as in the UK at present, this underselling of the role of curators makes them vulnerable to being seen as expendable. As Erwin and Erwin note, 'in the last 20 years, the numbers of curators in the UK have fallen'.[79] The former director of the British Museum Neil MacGregor gave evidence as part of the Countries of Culture Inquiry:

> He told the [select] committee that the financial constraints on local authorities meant that curators were not being recruited because they 'rarely generate revenue' in a way that can be easily quantified. 'The result has understandably been a steady erosion of curatorial strength,' ... This loss of specialist knowledge is making it difficult for some museums to borrow from other institutions or use their own collections effectively.[80]

Janes argues that 'the future of museums does not lie in a preoccupation with the financial bottom line or with efforts to make museums more popular', but in embedding themselves into the communities they serve.[81] Sadly, 'many museums have quietly stopped acquiring, stopped carrying out new research'.[82] As curatorial positions diminish, there is increasing reliance upon other staff or even volunteers and crowdsourcing to fill the void.[83] Such cuts to research and collections care will damage the relationships that have been established between museums and source communities. The curator will be neither friend nor foe, but forsaken.

Crowdsourcing cannot honour the Indigenous research principles discussed above, such as being face-to-face, nor can it share and host people generously. Volunteers are not sufficiently trained, resourced or permanent enough to invest in building long-term meaningful relations with communities dealing with the trauma of cultural genocide. Even relying on the rest of the museum team to step in does not honour the decades of reports advocating for the need to take collaboration seriously, and will be detrimental to those communities who are trying to build relations to help restore cultural practices, pride and autonomy. As Sharon Heal, the director of the UK Museums Association, notes, 'it is also worth considering the human impact and the amount that people have personally invested in these institutions, and the skill and knowledge that is lost when museums close and collections are mothballed'.[84] The forsaken figure of the curator is a dystopia that will negatively impact on the decolonising work that has been started, and the vast amounts yet to begin.

For Indigenous people, the rise of interest in collaborative museum work, whilst challenging, has created opportunities to have a say in the way people and histories are represented in former colonial nations.[85] It has helped Indigenous knowledge gain international standing and provided a platform from which formerly suppressed people can be heard in the mainstream. Recent museological approaches have begun, but not completed, the returning of sacred material culture vital to the maintenance of living cultural practice. In Canada, there is increasing weight behind the need to address the truths of colonialism and the inequalities that persist into the present, with the TRC's Calls to Action and UNDRIP. Museums have a role to play, as public authorities on the past, by working with Indigenous communities to continue current decolonising efforts. Decolonisation is a necessary process for the colonised *and* the colonisers. As such, this process applies to Britain and British colonial collections as much as it does to those in former colonies. The best practice being exemplified in current global museology is important in the 'age of apology'.[86] Museums and their curators can act on our collective obligations to address colonial pasts and help shape the future, but only if their roles are recognised and adequately resourced. The figure of the curator has always been, and should always be, multilayered and complex. As an expert and apprentice, an authority with humility, a professional and an advocate, the multifaceted guise of the curator should be celebrated and continually renewed, rather than forsaken.

Acknowledgements

I would like to thank the editors, Philipp and Conal, for the reviews which have helped shape this piece. I also want to renew my unending thanks to all the museum and heritage professionals and community members who, over the years, have generously given their time and shared their thoughts and ideas with me.

Notes

1 T. Bennett, *Pasts Beyond Memory: Evolution, Museums, Colonialism* (London: Routledge, 2004), p. 14; K. Schubert, *The Curator's Egg: The Evolution of the Museum Concept from the French Revolution to the Present Day* (London: One-Off Press, 2000), p. 15.

2 C. McCarthy, 'Before "Te Maori": A Revolution Deconstructed', in S.J. Knell (ed.), *Museum Revolutions: Museums and Change* (London: Routledge, 2007), pp. 117–33; S.M. Mead, 'Te Maori in New York', *Art New Zealand*, 33 (1984), 24–7.

3 J. Harrison, 'The Spirit Sings: The Last Song?', *International Journal of Museum Management and Curatorship*, 7:4 (1988), 353–63; J. Harrison and B. Trigger, '"The Spirit Sings" and the Future of Anthropology', *Anthropology Today*, 4:6 (1988), 6–10; H. Devine, 'After the Spirit Sang: Aboriginal Canadians and Museum Policy in the New Millennium', in B. Beaty, D. Briton, G. Filax and R. Sullivan (eds), *How Canadians Communicate III: Contexts of Canadian Popular Culture* (Athabasca: AU Press, 2010), pp. 217–39; S.R. Butler, *Contested Representations: Revisiting Into the Heart of Africa* (Peterborough, Ontario: Broadview Press, 2nd edn, 2008); E. Schildkrout, 'Ambitious Messages and Ironic Twists: *Into the Heart of Africa* and *The Other Museum*', *Museum Anthropology*, 15:2 (1991), 16–23.

4 AFN and CMA, *Turning the Page: Forging New Partnerships between Museums and First Peoples*, Task Force Report on Museums and First Peoples (Ottawa: Carleton University, 1992).

5 Although not all museums have embraced the idea of facilitation and engagement.

6 Schubert, *The Curator's Egg*.

7 See for example: P. Schorch, 'Assembling Communities: Curatorial Practices, Material Cultures, and Meanings', in B. Onciul, M. Stefano and S. Hawke (eds), *Engaging Communities, Engaging Heritage* (Woodbridge: Boydell and Brewer, 2017).

8 For example, see G. Conaty (ed.), *We Are Coming Home: Repatriation and the Restoration of Blackfoot Cultural Confidence* (Edmonton: Athabasca University Press, 2015).

9 B. Onciul, *Museums, Heritage and Indigenous Voice: Decolonising Engagement* (New York: Routledge, 2015).

10 D.F. Cameron, 'The Museum, a Temple or the Forum', *Curator: The Museum Journal*, 14:1 (1971), 11–24.

11 R. Janes, *Museums in a Troubled World: Renewal, Irrelevance or Collapse?* (New York: Routledge, 2009), p. 31.

12 P. Schorch, 'Assembling Communities'. See also Introduction, above, McCarthy, Hakiwai and Schorch, Chapter 13 below, and Macdonald and Morgan, Chapter 2 above.

13 Such terms do not apply to all and over-simplify the complexities of historical curatorial relations with source communities, obscuring significant histori-cal collaboration, for example, C. McCarthy, *Exhibiting Māori: A History of Colonial Cultures of Display* (Wellington: Te Papa Press, 2007); C. McCarthy, *Museums and Māori: Heritage Professionals, Indigenous Collections, Current Practice* (Wellington: Te Papa Press, 2011); C. McCarthy, 'Carving out a Place in the Better Britain of the South Pacific: Māori in New Zealand Museums and Exhibitions', in J. McAleer and S. Longair (eds), *Curating Empire: Museums and the British Imperial Experience* (Manchester: Manchester University Press, 2012), pp. 56–81; I. Jackins, *The Storage Box of Tradition: Kwakiutl Art, Anthropologists, and Museums, 1881–1981* (Washington, DC: Smithsonian Institution Press, 2002); G. Isaac, 'We'wha Goes to Washington', in R. Harrison, S. Byrne and A. Clarke (eds), *Reassembling the Collection: Ethnographic Museums and Indigenous Agency* (Santa Fe: SAR Press, 2013); R. Torrence and A. Clarke, 'Creative Colonialism: Locating Indigenous Strategies in Ethnographic Museum Collections', in R. Harrison, S. Byrne and A. Clarke (eds), *Reassembling the Collection: Ethnographic Museums and Indigenous Agency* (Santa Fe: SAR

Press, 2013); A.K. Brown, *First Nations, Museums, Narrations: Stories of the 1929 Franklin Motor Expedition to the Canadian Prairies* (Vancouver: UBC Press, 2015).

14 Onciul, *Museums, Heritage and Indigenous Voice.*

15 *Ibid.* Brown, *First Nations, Museums, Narrations*; J.M. MacKenzie, *Museums and Empire: Natural History, Human Cultures and Colonial Identities* (Manchester: Manchester University Press, 2009), p. 24; S. Alberti, *Nature and Culture: Objects, Disciplines and the Manchester Museum* (Manchester: Manchester University Press, 2009).

16 See MacKenzie, *Museums and Empire*, 21–43; A. Gulliford, 'Bones of Contention: The Repatriation of Native American Human Remains', in S.J. Knell (ed.), *Museums in the Material World* (London: Routledge, 2007), pp. 284–91.

17 Mackenzie, *Museums and Empire*, 7–8.

18 Gulliford, 'Bones of Contention'; R.W. Hill Sr, 'The Indian in the Cabinet of Curiosity', in W.R. West (ed.), *The Changing Presentation of the American Indian: Museums and Native Cultures* (Washington, DC: Smithsonian Institution, 2000), p. 103.

19 TRC, *What We Have Learned: Principles of Truth and Reconciliation* (2015), http://nctr.ca/assets/reports/Final%20Reports/Principles_English_Web.pdf. Accessed 5 January 2017.

20 S. Deutschlander and L.J. Miller, 'Politicizing Aboriginal Cultural Tourism: The Discourse of Primitivism in the Tourist Encounter', *Canadian Review of Sociology*, 40:1 (2003), 27–44, 28.

21 Onciul, *Museums, Heritage and Indigenous Voice*, 60.

22 TRC of Canada, *Truth and Reconciliation Commission of Canada: Calls to Action* (2015) www.trc.ca/websites/trcinstitution/File/2015/Findings/Calls_to_Action_English2.pdf. Accessed 26 August 2016, 8.

23 Conaty (ed.), *We Are Coming Home!.*

24 T. Eccles, 'RAMM Meets Blackfoot Representatives', RAMM: World Cultures (2015), http://rammworldcultures.org.uk/ramm-meets-blackfoot-representatives/. Accessed 18 October 2016.

25 In 1990, the Provincial Museum (now known as Royal Alberta Museum) experienced an attempted 'grab and run' of a sacred bundle by a member of the Blackfoot Confederacy, which disrupted further repatriation negotiations with the museum at the time (see Onciul, *Museums, Heritage and Indigenous Voice*, 62).

26 On this point, see Phillips, Chapter 9 above. AFN and CMA, *Turning the Page: Forging New Partnerships between Museums and First Peoples*, Task Force Report on Museums and First Peoples (Ottawa: Carleton University, 1992); RCAP, *Report on the Royal Commission on Aboriginal Peoples* (Ottawa: The Commission, 1996), http://hdl.handle.net/1974/6874. Accessed 22 August 2016.

27 BBC, *Ghost Shirt Dances Back* (1999), http://news.bbc.co.uk/1/hi/uk/409876.stm. Accessed 28 August 2016; Glasgow City Council, 'Memorandum submitted by Glasgow City Council', *Select Committee on Culture, Media and Sport Minutes of Evidence* (UK Parliament, 2000), www.publications.parliament.uk/pa/cm199900/cmselect/cmcumeds/371/0051808.htm. Accessed 22 August 2016; S. Maddra, 'The Wounded Knee Ghost Dance Shirt', *Journal of Museum Ethnography*, 8 (1996), 41–58; P. Bienkowski, 'A Critique of Museum Repatriation and Restitution Practices', in C. McCarthy (ed.), *Museum Practice* (Oxford: Wiley Blackwell, 2015).

28 N. Curtis, 'Going Home: from Aberdeen to Standoff', *British Archaeology* (2005), 40–3; N. Curtis, 'Thinking about the Right Home: Repatriation and the University of Aberdeen', in M. Gabriel and J. Dahl (eds), *UTIMUT Past Heritage – Future Partnerships – Discussion on Repatriation in the 21st Century* (Copenhagen and Nuuk: IWGIA/NKA, 2007), pp. 44–54; N. Curtis, 'North America in Aberdeen: The Collections of Marischal Museum, University of Aberdeen', in A.K. Brown (ed.), *Material Histories: Proceedings of a Workshop Held at Marischal Museum, University of Aberdeen, 26–27 April 2007* (Aberdeen: Marischal Museum, University of Aberdeen, 2008); N. Curtis, 'Repatriation from Scottish Museums: Learning from NAGPRA', *Museum Anthropology*, 33 (2010), 234–48; Brown (ed.), *Material Histories*.

29 L. Peers and A.K. Brown, *Visiting with the Ancestors: Blackfoot Shirts in Museum Spaces* (Edmonton: AU Press, 2016); L. Peers, *Things We Have Learned from the Blackfoot Shirts Project*, Brave New World Curator (2013), http://pittrivers-americas.blogspot.co.uk/2013/04/things-we-have-learned-from-blackfoot.html. Accessed 28 August 2016.

30 A.K. Brown, T. Eccles and A. Herle, 'Storied Landscapes: Enlivening Blackfoot Collections in UK Museums', *Journal of Museum Ethnography*, 29 (2016), 29–52, 29–30.

31 *Ibid.*, 50; Eccles, 'RAMM Meets Blackfoot Representatives'; A. Dempster, 'Chief Crowfoot's Regalia to Return Home to Alberta', *CBC News* (26 May 2014), www.cbc.ca/news/canada/calgary/chief-crowfoot-s-regalia-to-return-home-to-alberta-1.2654211. Accessed 18 October 2016.

32 While actor network theory is growing in popularity in the way it is used to explain museum assemblages, it also echoes many Indigenous epistemologies that recognise the agency of items otherwise known as 'things'. See for example M. Zedeño, 'Bundled Worlds: The Role and Interactions of Complex Objects from the North American Plains', *Journal of Archaeological Method and Theory*, 15 (2008), 362–78.

33 See also Mallon, Chapter 17 below.

34 Cameron, 'The Museum, a Temple or the Forum'.

35 Onciul, *Museums, Heritage and Indigenous Voice*; B. Lynch, *Our Museum: A Five-Year Perspective from a Critical Friend* (London: Paul Hamlyn Foundation), http://ourmuseum.org.uk/wp-content/uploads/A-five-year-perspective-from-a-critical-friend.pdf. Accessed 4 January 2017.

36 On this point see Kahanu, Nepia and Schorch, Chapter 18 below.

37 L.T. Smith, *Decolonizing Methodologies: Research and Indigenous Peoples* (London: Zed Books, 1999), p. 124.

38 P. Schorch, C. McCarthy and A. Hakiwai, 'Globalising Māori Museology: Reconceptualizing Engagement, Knowledge, and Virtuality through Mana Taonga', *Museum Anthropology*, 39:1 (2016), 48–69, 54; MOA, *The Collections*, MOA (2016), http://moa.ubc.ca/collections/. Accessed 25 August 2016; see also Mallon, Chapter 17 below; McCarthy, Hakiwai and Schorch, Chapter 13 below; and Tapsell, Chapter 12 below.

39 M. Gibney, R.E. Howard-Hassmann, J.M. Coicaud and K. Steiner, *The Age of Apology: Facing Up to the Past* (Philadelphia: University of Pennsylvania Press, 2007), pp. 216–28.

40 TRC of Canada, *Truth and Reconciliation Commission of Canada*, 8.

41 Bill Reid Gallery, *Current Exhibitions* (2016), www.billreidgallery.ca/Exhibition/CurrentExhibition.php. Accessed 8 October 2016.

42 *Ibid.*

43 R. Kurin, *Reflections of a Culture Broker: A View from the Smithsonian* (Washington, DC: Smithsonian Institution Press, 1997), p. 19.

44 F. Cameron, 'Contentiousness and Shifting Knowledge Paradigms: The Roles of History and Science Museums in Contemporary Society', *Museum Management and Curatorship*, 20:2 (2005), 213–33. www.aspacnet.org/apec/case_studies/_pdfs/cameron_aspac.pdf.

45 Janes, *Museums in a Troubled World*.

46 Lynch, *Our Museum*, 5.

47 *Ibid.*, 7, 9–13.

48 Bennett, *Pasts Beyond Memory*.

49 Janes, *Museums in a Troubled World*, 166.

50 Lynch, *Our Museum*.

51 G. Conaty, 'The Effects of Repatriation on the Relationship between the Glenbow Museum and the Blackfoot People', *Museum Management and Curatorship*, 23:3 (2008), 251.

52 R. Janes, 'Prologue', in Conaty (ed.), *We Are Coming Home*, 4.

53 G. Conaty, 'Beginnings', in Conaty (ed.), *We Are Coming Home*, 24.

54 Interview Gerald Conaty (26 September 2007).

55 Interview Frank Weasel Head (13 November 2008).

56 F.W. Head, 'Repatriation Experiences of the Kainai', in Conaty (ed.), *We Are Coming Home*, 181.

57 Interview Frank Weasel Head (13 November 2008).

58 Interview Gerald Conaty (20 November 2008).

59 Janes, 'Prologue', 7.

60 Head, 'Repatriation Experiences of the Kainai', 181.

61 Interview Jerry Potts (10 October 2008).

62 Interview Gerald Conaty (20 November 2008).

63 Such as myself who was an intern at Glenbow. Also see J.C. Atkinson, *Education, Values and Ethics in International Heritage: Learning to Respect* (London: Routledge, 2014).

64 Interview Frank Weasel Head (13 November 2008).

65 See Glenbow Museum, *Report to the Community 2013/14* (2014), 4. www.glenbow.org/about/media/Glenbow%20Museum_Report%20to%20Community.pdf. Accessed 19 Sept 2017.

66 Onciul, *Museums, Heritage and Indigenous Voice*.

67 See for example C. Kreps, 'Indigenous Curation as Intangible Cultural Heritage: Thoughts on the Relevance of the 2003 UNESCO Convention' (Smithsonian, 2005), www.folklife.si.edu/resources/center/cultural_policy/pdf/ChristinaKrepsfellow.pdf. Accessed 7 January 2017; C. Kreps, *Liberating Culture: Cross-Cultural Perspectives on Museums, Curation, and Heritage Preservation* (London and New York: Routledge, 2003); N. Stanley, *The Future of Indigenous Museums* (Oxford: Berghahm Books, 2007).

68 Nuyumbalees, *Nuyumbalees … In the Beginning.* Nuyumbalees Cultural Centre, www.museumatcapemudge.com/the-centre-1. Accessed 24 October 2016; U'mista, *The Potlatch Collection History*, U'mista Cultural Society, www.umista.ca/exhibits/index.php. Accessed 30 August 2016; S.F. Racette, 'Confessions and Reflections of an Indigenous Research Warrior', in Brown (ed.), *Material Histories*, 57–67; G. Cranmer-Webster, 'The Potlatch Collection Repatriation', *University of British Columbia Law Review*, Special Issue:

Material Culture in Flux: Law and Policy of Repatriation of Cultural Property (1995), 137–41.

69 Onciul, *Museums, Heritage and Indigenous Voice.*

70 Kurin, *Reflections of a Culture Broker*, 19.

71 See Lythberg, Ngata and Salmond, and McCarthy, Hakiwai and Schorch, Chapters 14 and 13 below.

72 See Onciul, *Museums, Heritage and Indigenous Voice*, ch. 7 for further discussion.

73 N. Poole, *The Rise and Fall of the Curator*, Museum ID, www.museum-id.com/idea-detail.asp?id=275. Accessed 22 August 2016.

74 T. Ewin and J. Ewin, 'In Defence of the Curator: Maximising Museum Impact', *Museum Management and Curatorship*, 31:4 (2016), 322–30, 322.

75 Smith, *Decolonizing Methodologies*, 124. Though there are notable exceptions such as Conaty (ed.), *We Are Coming Home*; C. Krmpotich and L. Peers, *This Is Our Life: Haida Material Heritage and Changing Museum Practice* (Vancouver: UBC Press, 2013), and chapters in this volume.

76 Janes, *Museums in a Troubled World*, 64; L. Peers and A.K. Brown, *Museums and Source Communities: A Routledge Reader* (London: Routledge, 2003), pp. 11–12.

77 Poole, *The Rise and Fall of the Curator.*

78 J. Holt, 'The Curators', *Museums Journal. Museums Association*, 113:3 (2013), 30–3.

79 Ewin and Ewin, 'In Defence of the Curator', 322.

80 G. Kendall, 'MacGregor Warns of Erosion of Curatorial Strength in Regions', *News*, Museums Association (2016), www.museumsassociation.org/museums-journal/news/11052016-macgregor-warns-erosion-curatorial-strength. Accessed 22 August 2016.

81 R. Janes, 'The Blackfoot Repatriation: A Personal Epilogue', in Conaty (ed.), *We Are Coming Home*, 260.

82 Kendall, 'MacGregor Warns of Erosion of Curatorial Strength in Regions'; N. Merriman, 'The Future of Collecting in "Disciplinary" Museums: Interpretive, Thematic, Relational', in C. McCarthy (ed.), *Museum Practice* (Oxford and Malden, MA: Wiley Blackwell, 2015), p. 250.

83 Poole, *The Rise and Fall of the Curator.*

84 N. Sullivan, 'Communities Counting the cost of Museum Closures', *News Analysis*, Museums Association (2016), www.museumsassociation.org/museums-journal/news-analysis/01032016-communities-counting-the-cost-of-museum-closures. Accessed 20 August 2016.

85 Onciul, *Museums, Heritage and Indigenous Voice.*

86 Gibney et al., *The Age of Apology.*

Joining the club:
a Tongan *'akau* in New England

Ivan Gaskell

'Call me Ishmael.' These three words form one of the most famous opening sentences in world literature. Herman Melville published *Moby-Dick; or, The Whale* in 1851, taking his readers in New England, and well beyond, deep into the South Seas. Even before Ishmael and the ill-fated captain and crew of the whaling ship *Pequod* leave the safety of Nantucket, and even before Ishmael journeys to that island, he encounters wonders from Oceania. Writing of the southern Massachusetts whaling port of New Bedford, Ishmael recounts how, 'Entering that gable-ended Spouter-Inn, you found yourself in a wide, low, straggling entry with old-fashioned wainscots, reminding one of the bulwarks of some condemned old craft'. He continues:

> The opposite wall of this entry was hung all over with a heathenish array of monstrous clubs and spears. Some were thickly set with glittering teeth resembling ivory saws; others were tufted with knots of human hair; and one was sickle-shaped, with a vast handle sweeping round like the segment made in the new-mown grass by a long-armed mower. You shuddered as you gazed, and wondered what monstrous cannibal and savage could ever have gone a death-harvesting with such a hacking, horrifying implement.[1]

Ishmael learns from Peter Coffin, landlord of the Spouter-Inn, that he is to share a bed with a 'harpooneer' who, Coffin tells him, 'can't sell his head'.[2] It turns out that the harpooner had, in the landlord's words:

> just arrived from the south seas, where he bought up a lot of 'balmed New Zealand heads (great curios, you know), and he's sold all on 'em but one, and that one he's trying to sell to-night, cause tomorrow's Sunday, and it would not do to be sellin' human heads about the streets when folks is goin' to churches.[3]

Ishmael is apprehensive and fearful of his bed-mate, who turns out to be a tattooed Polynesian animist and cannibal. But he swiftly reasons, 'the man's a human being just as I am: he has just as much reason to fear me, as I have to be afraid of him. Better sleep with a sober cannibal than a drunken Christian.'[4] Ishmael and the South Sea Islander, whose name is Queequeg, ship for Natucket together and become fast friends as shipmates on the *Pequod*.

Melville's Queequeg, and the Oceanic characters of his first novel, *Typee: A Peep at Polynesian Life* (1846), suggest that, by the middle of the nineteenth century, the inhabitants of Oceania already occupied an equivocal role in the North American imaginary. In terms of material culture, this equivocation is exemplified by Oceanic clubs of the kind described by Melville's Ishmael in the Spouter-Inn. Such clubs had long been accessible to curious New Englanders.

The Peabody Essex Museum in Salem, Massachusetts, USA, contains more than twenty thousand Oceanic items in its vast collection. The collection began with donations by local sea captains and supercargoes to its predecessor institution, the East India Marine Society, founded in 1799. Its members conceived it to have a 'cabinet of natural and artificial curiosities' in accordance with contemporaneous museum practice.[5] Salem became the leading port in the Pacific trade from the North American eastern seaboard from the later eighteenth century onwards, opening routes to Hawai'i, Fiji and other Oceanic islands, Aotearoa New Zealand, the Philippines, Java, Canton, Zanzibar and even visiting the, then, closed nation of Japan.[6]

East India Marine Hall, the Federal-style building constructed for the East India Marine Society in 1825, has recently been restored to evoke its original appearance. Above one door is an array of Oceanic clubs in a fan-like arrangement familiar from nineteenth-century illustrations, in which the individual clubs are subordinated to a characteristically Western pattern (Figure 11.1). Such clubs were popular souvenirs brought back by New England traders and whalers who voyaged to the Pacific from the later eighteenth century onwards. Founding member William Putnam Richardson gave two of these clubs to the East India Marine Society in 1810.[7] A successful sea captain, Richardson commanded at least three Salem vessels, trading in the Pacific as far as Canton during a voyage between 1805 and 1806. His namesake nephew commanded the bark *Active*, which first opened trade between Salem and both Fiji and Aotearoa New Zealand in 1811.[8]

The associations that such things held for New Englanders are hard to pin down, but they included admiration for the intricate carvings that often characterised them, and identification with manly martial prowess that they seemed to signify. They could also prompt a prurient fascination with imputed cannibalism. In his 1846 novel *Typee*, Herman Melville evokes the popular notion of Oceanic cannibalism, the particular horror of contemporaneous North Americans, both South Sea voyagers and those who stayed at home but read popular accounts. He does so in order to challenge it. He wrote:

> According to the popular fictions, the crews of vessels, shipwrecked on some barbarous coast, are eaten alive like so many dainty joints by the uncivil inhabitants; and unfortunate voyagers are lured into smiling and treacherous bays; knocked on the head with outlandish war-clubs; and served up without any preliminary dressing.[9]

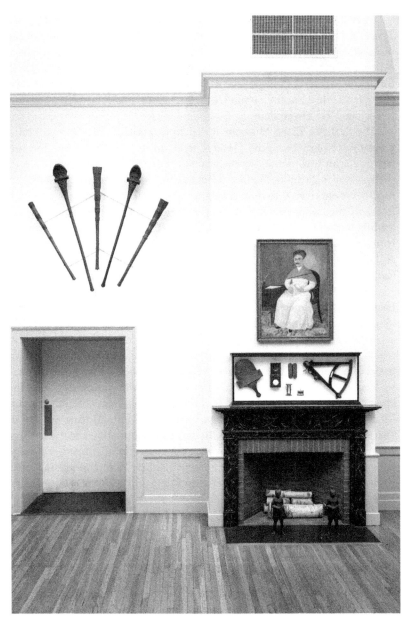

11.1 Five Oceanic clubs as displayed in East India Marine Hall, Peabody Essex Museum, Salem, Massachusetts, USA.

Such clubs, then, occupied an equivocal position in the nineteenth-century North American mental repertory as indices of savage sophistication on the one hand, and inhumanity on the other. Their arrangement in the East India Marine Hall, though, is unequivocally in accordance with eighteenth- and nineteenth-century Western decorative conventions.

Given that the premise of this volume is that Native thinkers and cultural guardians should be involved in the care and presentation of items that originated in their own cultural milieux when those items are in hegemonic Western museums – an ambition with which I have every sympathy – the most urgent curatorial question must surely be: How are such things to be cared for and presented in an emergent climate of scholarly opinion in which the concerns of contemporary members of originating communities are, at the very least, to be taken into account by those who look after them? A second and equally challenging curatorial question, not invariably also addressed, is: To what extent, if at all, should the lives of things subsequent to their acquisition from Native peoples be taken into account in their current and future care? The clubs in the Peabody Essex Museum have likely existed longer within its walls than anywhere else, and their current display expresses a historicising attitude that seeks to validate their early use in that collection. Is this legitimate?

Today in the USA, the 'vanishing Indian' has vanished, though it took Native American anger translated into political clout to push home the case.[10] Many US Americans take it for granted that Native thinkers and cultural guardians should be involved in the care and presentation of items that originated in their own cultural milieux but are now in hegemonic settler museums. This can be seen as a relatively new consensus, finally established in the little more than twenty-five years since the enactment of the Native American Graves Protection and Repatriation Act of 1990 (NAGPRA).[11] NAGPRA mandates the return on demand of items in various categories – human remains, funerary objects, sacred objects, and objects of cultural patrimony – from institutions in receipt of federal funds to federally recognised American Indian tribes and Hawaiian organisations.[12] Many people and things have been returned. The sky has not fallen in. Such has been the impact of NAGPRA that the old ethnological orthodoxy espoused by many settler scholars, that they have the unquestionable right to examine anything and anybody for their own exclusive scientific purposes, today seems as quaint as it does deluded. The watchword today is collaboration: collaboration between the faculty and staff of settler institutions, and Native scholars, thinkers and cultural guardians. It is worth briefly mentioning instances of just this kind of collaboration before looking critically but sympathetically at some of the practical difficulties that many settler institutions and their staffs face that inhibit this kind of ideal collaboration. Those who take a purely moralising stance regardless of circumstances, without acknowledging the practical challenges, may feel good, but no actual good follows.

At the Peabody Museum of Archaeology and Ethnology at Harvard University, Massachusetts, USA, Butch Thunder Hawk collaborated with the Peabody curator Castle McLaughlin to produce an innovative exhibition about a rediscovered ledger book. Butch Thunder Hawk is a Hunkpapa Lakota artist and scholar, and is the Tribal Arts instructor at the United Tribes Technical College in Bismarck, North Dakota. The ledger book in question, rediscovered in Harvard's Houghton Library, contains seventy-seven drawings by at least five Native warrior artists. *Wiyohpiyata: Lakota Images of the Contested West* opened at the Peabody in spring 2009, and offers a Native view of the events surrounding the defeat and death of George Armstrong Custer at the Battle of Greasy Grass or the Little Big Horn in 1876 at the hands of a Cheyenne–Lakota coalition.[13]

A second example of collaboration at the Peabody Museum is the project to study and conserve the only known surviving Alutiiq warrior kayak from the coast of Alaska. Visiting Alutiiq tribal members Sven Haakanson, then director of the Alutiiq Museum and Archaeological Repository in Kodiak, Alaska, and Alutiiq elder Ronnie Lind identified the kayak. The Alutiiq collaborated with conservators at the Peabody to study and conserve the kayak with the participation of Alfred Naumoff, the last traditionally trained Kodiak Alutiiq kayak maker. Much of the conservation work took place in a public gallery at the Peabody which was converted into a conservation laboratory for this purpose between 2011 and 2013.[14] The kayak is at present on long-term loan to the Alutiiq Museum and Archaeological Repository in Kodiak.[15]

Such ways of working are no longer novel or exceptional at the Peabody Museum. It is not at such institutions – which remain settler institutions, however collaboratively they conduct themselves – that the kind of challenges that concern me are to be found, though such projects are surely a vast improvement on superseded ways of doing things that ignored Native interests and concerns. I am concerned with what happens at institutions in which Native things are the exception, and where responsible staff members have little or no idea of what caring for such things might entail. This strikes me not as a matter of culpability or assigning blame for failures of knowledge or sensitivity on the part of such staff. The presence of Native things as minority items in varied collections can be a measure of their absorption into their adopting culture as things that – rightly or wrongly – have found a place there, regardless of Native concerns.

Returning to Salem, we have already seen that New England mariners, merchants and whalers took an, often considerable, interest in the peoples they encountered in the eighteenth and nineteenth centuries in the course of their lengthy voyages to the Pacific. In 1867, the banker and philanthropist George Peabody created the Peabody Academy of Science, which took over the holdings of the declining and financially troubled East India Marine Society. The collection was displayed systematically in the East Hall, adjacent to the East India Marine Hall. An early photograph shows a spectacular early nineteenth-century Hawaiian *heiau* (temple) figure in pride of place. This commanding figure is the deity mostly (and reductively) associated with warfare, Kū, or Kūkaʻilimoku.[16] Its scale as well as the character of its carving have long ensured its prominence in the collection, but not until 2006 was there speculation in the press that Native Hawaiians were engaging with it in a devotional manner. The museum then acknowledged that 'groups have made planned offerings at PEM'.[17] Kūkaʻilimoku at the Peabody Essex

Museum is one of only three known large-scale figures to have survived. The others are in the British Museum, London, UK, and the Bishop Museum, Honolulu, USA. In 2010, they were united at the Bishop Museum in an exhibition, *E Kū Ana Ka Paia: Unification, Responsibility and the Kū Images*, which was directed by Noelle Kahanu, one of the other authors in this volume.[18] The museum website noted that '[t]he images will be on display during the season of Kauwela, a time traditionally associated with Kū'.[19] On its return to the Peabody Essex Museum in October 2010, the figure of Kū was ritually escorted, honoured and reassured by a Native Hawaiian delegation, including staff from the Bishop Museum.[20] Since then, the museum has accommodated the devotions and offerings of Native Hawaiian visitors more openly than previously. Until its recent removal to storage for the duration of an expansion project, the figure was shown in a prominent gallery, but away from other items, emphasising its special status, and secluding any ritual attention or offerings paid to it.

This is the kind of accommodation and attention one expects at major US American museums that have such sacred or otherwise culturally charged things in their care. But things that require sensitive treatment, that should ideally be open to interpretation and use by knowledgeable members of originating communities, are to be found in institutions that have equally onerous obligations in this area, but are ill-prepared to meet them.

Historic New England is a group of thirty-seven house museums spread throughout New England, plus additional collections in a central storage location. It is one such ill-prepared institution. It was founded in 1910 by the privileged Bostonian William Sumner Appleton Jr as the Society for the Preservation of New England Antiquities.[21] Its purpose was to preserve historically significant properties, initially with an emphasis on the colonial and early US periods. The name it bore until recently indicates that its foundational values emphasise the dominant settler culture. It has long been and continues to be highly significant and respected in terms of historic preservation, interpretation and the production of excellent material culture scholarship. Yet, as one might expect, some New Englanders, whose properties have come into the care of Historic New England, acquired things from well beyond New England's borders.

One example concerns the Phillips family of Salem, Massachusetts. Although the building dates back to the early nineteenth century, the present appearance of the Phillips House is due to its colonial revival renovation soon after its purchase by the Phillips family in 1911.[22] Stephen Willard Phillips had been born in 1873 in Honolulu. His father Stephen Henry Phillips was serving as the first attorney general of the, then, still independent Kingdom of Hawai'i. Although the elder Phillips resigned his posts in Hawai'i in the year of his son's birth, the younger Phillips took a serious interest in Oceanic ethnography and art, in particular that of Hawai'i. He died in 1955 and Historic New England acquired the property from trustees as an already functioning house museum in 2006.[23] Stephen Willard Phillips collected various Oceanic items, including a number of clubs that remain in the house. Two Fijian *'i Ula tavatava* clubs can be seen on his desk in his library.[24] He owned a number of other Oceanic clubs from the Marquesas, Fiji, Samoa and Tonga. Among the clubs associated with varying degrees of probability with Tonga are three that are intricately patterned with incised relief carvings. One, most likely from Tonga, is cylindrical, tapering from handle to head.[25] A second, probably from Tonga, is carved with zigzag patterns, figures holding various implements, images of rifles and a brig, demonstrating an incorporation of Western power goods.[26] A third club, assuredly Tongan, is a variation of the *apa'apai* type with a four-sided faceted form.[27] The upper half of the club is carved with birds, a figure attacking another with a club, and geometrical forms. This club appears to have no Western-inspired imagery.

There are no records to show where Phillips acquired these and other Oceanic items, or even whether he acquired them himself or inherited some or all of them from his father. It would be hard to believe, though, that Stephen Willard Phillips would have taken such an interest in Oceanic things without his father's involvement in the Kingdom of Hawai'i as it came increasingly under US American influence, and the accident of his birth. His father played an important role in the assertion of interests in Hawai'i, though he left the islands long before the US American-inspired *coup d'état* which overthrew the monarchy in 1893, and the unlawful annexation in 1898. (The USA formally apologised for these actions by act of Congress in 1993.)[28] Back in Massachusetts, the Phillips clubs were absorbed into a New England household of wealth and privilege. These clubs thereby became tokens of the nostalgic and sentimental side of empire building. However unpalatable in the light of the firm identification of Native things with Native peoples, is that, whatever else they may once have been and whatever else they may yet be, they are now firmly New England antiquities, preserved in a Federal-style house in Salem, Massachusetts. Over its front door flies the flag of Hawai'i.[29]

A highly professional institution such as Historic New England clearly does not have staff with specialist knowledge to deal adequately with the issues raised by Stephen Willard Phillips's collection of Oceanic clubs. What chance does a tiny organisation, such as the Atwood House and Museum in Chatham, Massachusetts, have? Chatham is a small town on the outside of the elbow of Cape Cod, the sand bar peninsula that forms the southern side of Massachusetts Bay. It was settled by the English in 1664, and originally called by the Algonquian name of the area it stood upon: Monomoit. Although subject to occasional severe storms that can even break through the barrier beach, Chatham is now prosperous owing to summer folk whose purchase of properties for summer use has driven many ordinary people from the town. By contrast, in the eighteenth and nineteenth centuries Chatham was a hardscrabble port at the perilous and ever-shifting entrance to the sheltered waters of Pleasant Bay.

Most New England towns have a local historical society that serves as an unofficial archive and local history museum, and Chatham is no exception.

Local historical societies in New England are long-standing social institutions. The Chatham Historical Society was founded in 1923 on the initiative of the Chatham Ladies' Reading Club.[30] In 1926, the Chatham Historical Society acquired the Atwood House. This is a gambrel-roofed house built for a local ship's captain in 1752, and reputedly the oldest surviving house in town. The last expansion was completed in 2005, and the museum now has eight galleries devoted to local history. Among them is the Joseph Atkins Nickerson, Jr Portrait Gallery, devoted to – in the words of the museum website – 'portraits of sea captains, notable residents of Chatham and other mariner themed items from the Historical Society archives'.[31] These include a model of the clipper ship, the *Flying Cloud*, the figurehead of the 1846 barkentine *Altamaha*, wrecked off Chatham in 1893, and a variety of nineteenth- and twentieth-century portraits. Several are by Frederick S. Wight (1902–1986), who had a long and varied career as a painter and art museum director. He grew up in Chatham, where his family moved in 1910, and began there as a portrait painter and writer from 1925 onwards, following studies at the University of Virginia, and the Académie Julien in Paris. After service as a naval officer in the Second World War, he studied museum management and curatorship at the Fogg Art Museum, Cambridge, receiving his Master's degree from Harvard in 1946. He then worked at the Institute of Contemporary Art, Boston, and moved west to direct the new art museum at the University of California, Los Angeles, in 1953, staying for twenty years.[32]

Among the miscellany of things shown with the portraits is the object, described as a 'Micronesian War Club', shown in Figure 11.2. The label further notes that it had been presented to Fred Wight, the portraitist, by Darius E. Hammond.[33] Wight had in turn given it to the museum. Adding to its intrinsic interest, a single-page manuscript document hangs beside it. What is a Micronesian war club – if that is indeed what it is – doing among the portraits and curiosities in the Nickerson Gallery of the Atwood House and Museum in Chatham, Massachusetts? Does it not bear a certain resemblance to the Tongan clubs in the Phillips House in Salem, and the Tongan clubs in the nearby Peabody Essex Museum? Perhaps most importantly, does its presence impose any particular obligations on the institution that cares for it? That is, would the successors of those who made and first used this thing have legitimate expectations regarding its care? If so, how is a small museum devoted to the local history of one corner of Cape Cod, with only one professional staff member, to meet any such obligations?

The museum has no further information on the object or the manuscript beside it, which has not yet been transcribed for the object file.[34] The text is clearly in two parts, in the same hand, but for the signature and date at the bottom of the first part, which is shaky and hesitant in execution. The first part reads as follows:

> The war club – that was given to me by a man of the name of [M?]ick Russell
> South Manchester Conn. for saving his life from drowning. I fetched him off

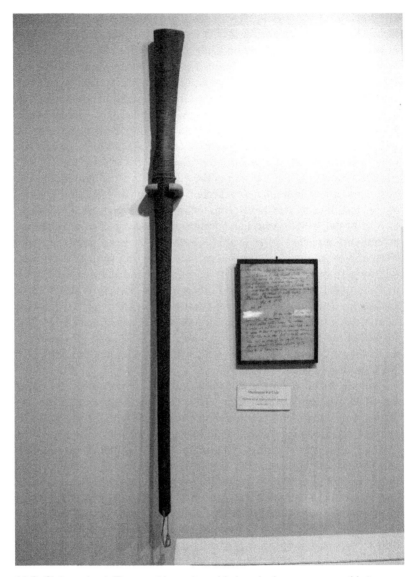

11.2 Club: apa'apai, Tonga, with carving added to the lower part possibly in Samoa or Kiribati, wood, Atwood House and Museum of the Chatham Historical Society, Chatham, Massachusetts, USA, X0679.

a blue fish trail [i.e. drail] off the bottom at Tuesday night about 6 o'clock & he never came too until Thurs. morning about 3 o'clock. He valued it pretty high –

Darius E. Hammond

Aug 12 1915

Age 80

We learn several things from this statement. First, that the owner was a man named Darius Hammond who was eighty years old in August 1915. Second, that Hammond had saved a man named Mick or Dick Russell from drowning; and, third, that Russell had given him the club as a token of his esteem and thanks, for Hammond reports that Russell 'valued it pretty high'.

The second part of the document gives an account of the rescue in Darius Hammond's voice:

> It was a party I led out sailing & he fell overboard & he never come up & I waited until I saw the bubbles a-comin' up & I leave a blue fish trail [i.e. drail] over the place & drew it gently & fetched him in the side & he was full of water down there but he come up as light as a pound weight & I come honestly by the club & so have you –

Hammond hooked Russell with a line used for catching bluefish, guided by the bubbles rising to the surface. He appears to be addressing this account to the person to whom he is giving the club, presumably Fred Wight, and his single greatest concern is to set down that he, Hammond, had acquired this extraordinary thing – extraordinary in Chatham, Massachusetts, that is – legitimately, and that his giving of it was in turn legitimate ('I come honestly by the club & so have you —').

Who was this man – this rescuer – who in old age was giving a prized exotic possession to Fred Wight, in 1915 still a teenage boy in high school? Seven years earlier, in 1908, the *Hyannis Patriot*, a Cape Cod newspaper, published an article on 'Capt. D.E. Hammond A Noted Cape Cod Life Saver, Rescued 24 Persons from Drowning'.[35] This article, plus US Census records, and his place of burial, gives sufficient information to identify Darius Hammond. He was a Chatham native bred to the sea who became a master mariner and who followed the coastal trade in schooners. He owned his own from 1861 onwards; and had a knack of being in the right place at the right time to rescue people from drowning. The article gives a slightly different account of the incident that led to Hammond receiving the club from the man he rescued. This makes it clear, though, that it hap-pened in August 1864 in Orient harbour, at the far north-east end of Long Island. Russell's first name is given as 'Mit', and his place of residence as South Manchester, Massachusetts. Given that there is no South Manchester in Massachusetts, and that the manuscript document gives his home as South Manchester, Connecticut, it seems likely that the man from whom Hammond received the club was from the latter town, then dominated by the Cheney Brothers Silk Manufacturing Company. The 1860 Federal Census records seven men named Russell who would have been adult in 1864. Milow Russell, whose occupation is given as 'Painter', and who would have been thirty-four years old in 1864, has the closest name, but this attempt at identification must remain inconclusive.[36]

In terms of ownership, it has proved possible to trace the club passing from a man from a silk manufacturing town in Connecticut in 1864 to a

Chatham schooner captain, who in turn gives it in 1915 to a local youth, who would become a painter and museum director, who finally gives it to the Chatham Historical Society. We can be confident that each 'valued it pretty high', as Captain Hammond put it. But what is it?

It is obviously comparable with the Tongan clubs we have already encountered in two collections in Salem. Lacking specialist knowledge, I consulted Jenny Newell, at that time curator of Pacific Ethnology at the American Museum of Natural History, New York.[37] Working from my photographs, she pointed out that carvers and styles moved back and forth among Tonga, Fiji and Samoa, so she could not be absolutely certain about its origin. She thought it most likely Tongan, though not as intricately carved as eighteenth- or most early nineteenth-century Tongan clubs.[38] She also pointed out a similar piece in the AMNH collection that entered in 1945, also probably Tongan.[39]

Having studied my photographs of the club in the Atwood House and Museum, the anthropologist and art historian Andrew Mills recognised it as a sub-type of *'akau tau* called *apa'apai* – like one of the examples in the Phillips House of Historic New England – most likely late eighteenth-century from the northern Tongan island group of Vava'u, possibly modified with further engraving in the lower part in a different style, though likely with a shark tooth implement rather than an iron trade nail. In Mills's opinion, the latter style is Samoan, or even linked with Kiribati, so the Tongan club may have been taken or traded to Samoa or Kiribati where it was modified.[40] The club therefore likely exemplifies exchange and cultural intercourse among Oceanic peoples over long distances even before a person of European origin acquired it. Oceanic peoples moved independently and also participated in the Western whale fishery – like Melville's Queequeg – so an earlier possessor may have been a trader or a Western-employed harpooner.

Such things are culturally very complex objects. In a 2009 article, Mills explains the status spectrum of the stave club or 'akau from tool to metaphysical entity:

> 'Akau were far from socially and spiritually inert tools. Significatively, they were inherently masculine and martial objects, with associations of successful competitive performance and chiefliness. Metaphysically, they incrementally developed an exalted status through performative use in warfare, dance and the hegemonic self-presentation of chiefly males. Through their biographical association with the *mana* of humans and deities, their deposition in the pre-Christian temple and their use as the manifest conduits and vessels of supernatural entities they gained exalted status. This status was manifested in an 'akau's progressive acquisition of an aggressive supernatural personhood, and a complement of its own *mana*, which it imparted to its user on (and off) the battlefield. This incremental, biographical process of 'akau coming to power and sentience may be labelled 'crystallising *mana* personhood' – a process that can also be recognised as the principal ennobling process undergone by fine mats, spears, bows and the variety

of ancestral relics that attained the status of manifestation vessels – an illustration of how initially ordinary items of material culture became extraordinary.[41]

Where does this leave the Chatham Historical Society in terms of responsibilities in respect of the extraordinary 'akau in its collection? Is it sufficient to present it as a curiosity associated with a local sea captain and a portrait painter?

Mills points out that European sailors acquired such things in considerable numbers from the eighteenth century onwards, suggesting not only their interest in weapons and the swift development of a market in such things but also their ready alienability from a Tongan point of view. In spite of any *mana* or sacred power an 'akau might have had, it was not necessarily inalienable. On passing into European or Euro-American hands, like the example that came into Darius Hammond's possession in 1864, it became, in Nicholas Thomas's terms, an entangled object.[42] We might even believe that each of its owners 'come honestly by the club', as Hammond asserted. We might thereby be in a position to respect its entire past as a transcultural object.

It is easy for outsiders – non-museum scholars – who have little idea about what curators have to do and what curators are actually able to do, to tell them what they should do. Ideally, the presence of a culturally highly charged item in a collection, such as the single 'akau in the Atwood House and Museum, might be the spur to those who look after it to initiate contact with scholars and other cultural guardians from the society of origin, Tonga in this instance. The staff of the Peabody Museum at Harvard, and the Peabody Essex Museum, Salem and even Historic New England all have the professional expertise, standing and cultural capital to bring this about. But – realistically – is the staff of the Chatham Historical Society in such a position? I doubt it. Until recently, their best information was that the object in question is Micronesian, though there is no indication where this idea may have come from. They begin from a position of real disadvantage, and have plenty of other, seemingly and indeed actually more pressing, things to do to keep the lights on and the doors open. That said, one day equally interested people from Chatham and from Tonga – presumably in the first instance from the Tonga National Cultural Centre in Nuku'alofa – might get together to discuss this wonderful thing that links them. Chatham might then join the club.[43]

Notes

1 Herman Melville, *Moby-Dick; or The Whale* (New York: Harper Brothers; London: Richard Bentley, 1851), pp. 12–13.
2 *Ibid.*, 19.
3 *Ibid.*, 20.
4 *Ibid.*, 27.

5 See K.K. Russell, 'Over 200 Years of Native American Art and Culture at the Peabody Essex Museum, Salem, Massachusetts', *Tulsa Law Review*, 45 (2009), 33. Russell cites *Bye-Laws and Regulations of the Salem East-India Marine Society* (Salem: Pool & Palfray, 1808), and E.S. Dodge and C.H.P. Copeland, *Handbook to the Collections of the Peabody Museum of Salem* (Salem: Peabody Museum, 1949). The British Museum, London, UK, had three departments until 1807 – Manuscripts, Printed Books, and Natural and Artificial Productions – when the latter was divided into departments of Natural History and Modern Curiosities, and Antiquities and Coins (E. Miller, *That Noble Cabinet: A History of the British Museum* (London: Deutsch, 1973), pp. 61, 100).

6 For aspects of the impact of Salem's ocean trade on American society, see P. Johnston and C. Frank (eds), *Global Trade and Visual Arts in Federal New England* (Durham: University of New Hampshire Press; Hanover, NH, and London: University Press of New England, 2014).

7 Club, wood, Tonga, Peabody Essex Museum, Salem, E4833 and E4834.

8 M. Malloy, *Souvenirs of the Fur Trade: Northwest Coast Indian Art and Artifacts Collected by American Mariners, 1788–1844* (Cambridge, MA: Peabody Museum of Archaeology and Ethnology, 2000), pp. 68–9.

9 H. Melville, *Typee: A Peep at Polynesian Life during a Four Months' Residence in a Valley of the Marquesas* (New York: Wiley and Putnam; London: John Murray, 1846), p. 262.

10 One key turning point was the building of the National Museum of the American Indian on the Mall in Washington, DC, which opened in 2004.

11 R. West et al., *The Changing Presentation of the American Indian: Museums and Native Cultures* (Washington, DC: Smithsonian Institution, University of Washington Press, 2006).

12 See, in the first instance, the National Park Service Website, *National NAGPRA*: www.nps.gov/nagpra/. Accessed 30 May 2016.

13 See C. McLoughlin, *A Lakota War Book from the Little Big Horn: The Pictographic Autobiography of Half Moon, Houghton Library Studies 4* (Cambridge, MA: Houghton Library and Peabody Museum Press, 2013).

14 See the Peabody Museum Website, www.peabody.harvard.edu/node/747. Accessed 30 May 2016.

15 Peabody Museum e-Newsletter, June 2016, www.peabody.harvard.edu/node/2658#story_3. Accessed 30 May 2016.

16 Hawaiian artist, *Kū*, breadfruit wood, early nineteenth-century, Gift of John T. Prince, 1846, Peabody Essex Museum, E12071. On this point, see T.K. Tengan, 'The Return of Kū? Remembering Hawaiian Masculinity, Warriorhood, and Nation' in L.R. Graham and H.G. Penny (eds), *Performing Indigeneity: Global Histories and Contemporary Experiences* (Lincoln: University of Nebraska Press, 2014), pp. 206–46. See also Kahanu, Nepia and Schorch, Chapter 18 below.

17 G. Edgers, 'Ritual Offerings, Peabody Essex Museum', *Boston Globe* (10 August 2006), quoting a museum spokesperson. I repeat this observation from I. Gaskell, 'Encountering Pacific Art', *Journal of Museum Ethnography*, 21 (2009), 202–10.

18 T.P. Kāwika Tengan, 'The Mana of Kū: Indigenous Nationhood, Masculinity and Authority in Hawai'i', in *New Mana: Transformations of a Classic Concept in Pacific Languages and Cultures* (Canberra: Australian National University Press, 2016); P. Schorch and N.M.K.Y. Kahanu, 'Forum as Laboratory: The Cross-Cultural Infrastructure of Ethnographic Knowledge and Material Potentialities',

in *Prinzip Labor: Museumsexperimente im Humboldt Lab Dahlem* (Berlin: Nicolai, 2015), pp. 241–8; P. Schorch and N.M.K.Y. Kahanu, 'Anthropology's Interlocutors: Hawai'i Speaking Back to Ethnographic Museums in Europe', *Zeitschrift für Kulturwissenschaften*, 1 (2015), 114–17.

19 *E Kū Ana Ka Paia: Unification, Responsibility and the Kū Images*, Honolulu: Bishop Museum.

20 'He's Back! Kū Returns Amid Honors from Hawaiian Delegation', www.pem. org/aux/pdf/collection/KuSmall.pdf. Accessed 30 May 2016.

21 See J.M. Lindgren, *Preserving Historic New England: Preservation, Progressivism, and the Remaking of Memory* (Oxford and New York: Oxford University Press, 1995).

22 For information on the Phillips House and family, see the web page of the Historic New England, www.historicnewengland.org/historic-properties/ homes/phillips-house. Accessed 30 May 2016.

23 The preservation of the house and its contents as a museum was the provision of Stephen Willard Phillips's son Stephen, who died in 1971.

24 Wooden throwing club or 'i Ula tavatava, from Fiji (two), Gift of the Stephen Phillips Memorial Charitable Trust for Historic Preservation, Historic New England, 2006.44.956, and 2006.44.1120. The identification of these and the subsequently cited clubs in the Phillips House is from the online catalogue of Historic New England, www.historicnewengland.org/collections-search/. Accessed 21 August 2017.

25 Club, likely from Tonga, possibly from Fiji or Samoa, Gift of the Stephen Phillips Memorial Charitable Trust for Historic Preservation, Historic New England, 2006.44.1488.

26 Club, probably from Tonga, Gift of the Stephen Phillips Memorial Charitable Trust for Historic Preservation, Historic New England, 2006.44.1487.

27 Club, Tonga, Gift of the Stephen Phillips Memorial Charitable Trust for Historic Preservation, Historic New England, 2006.44.1489.

28 'In 1993, then President Bill Clinton signed into law PL 103–150, a joint Congressional resolution which acknowledged and apologised for the role of the United States in the overthrow of the Kingdom of Hawai'i in 1893, a move which has not yet yielded political outcomes but confirms this legal argument [for illegal occupation]' (Schorch and Kahanu, 'Anthropology's Interlocutors', 115). See also N. Goodyear-Ka'ōpua, 'Introduction', in N. Goodyear-Ka'ōpua, I. Hussey and E.K. Wright (eds), *A Nation Rising: Hawaiian Movements for Life, Land, and Sovereignty* (Durham, NC, and London: Duke University Press, 2014), pp. 1–33.

29 The flag of the Kingdom of Hawai'i has been adopted by all succeeding governments: those of the short-lived Republic of Hawaii (1894–98), the US Territory of Hawaii (1898–1959) and the US State of Hawaii. I use the spelling that includes the *'okina* (glottal stop) for the kingdom, and without for subsequent governmental entities.

30 Information about the Chatham Historical Society is derived from its website, www.chathamhistoricalsociety.org/index.htm. Accessed 30 May 2016.

31 See Chatham Historical Society website, www.chathamhistoricalsociety.org/ Galleries/Galleries.htm. Accessed 4 March 2017.

32 See W. Wilson, 'Frederick S. Wight: Painterly Punch Lines', *Los Angeles Times* (3 August 1986), http://articles.latimes.com/1986–08–03/entertainment/ ca-1237_1_municipal-art-gallery. Accessed 30 May 2016. And 'Wight, Frederick

S[tallknecht Van Buren]', *Dictionary of Art Historians*, https://dictionaryofar thistorians.org/wightf.htm. Accessed 30 May 2016.

33 'Micronesian War Club, Atwood House and Museum, Chatham, MA, X0679.'

34 I noticed the club during my visit to the Atwood House and Museum (then called the Atwood House Museum) on 22 August 2014, and asked the staff present if any information about it was available. The very helpful volunteers on duty could tell me only that the museum had no further information on this piece, and that the document had not yet been transcribed.

35 'Capt. D.E. Hammond A Noted Cape Cod Life Saver, Rescued 24 Persons from Drowning', *Hyannis Patriot* (24 February 1908), 1.

36 See the image of the census document at: https://familysearch.org/ark:/61903/ 3:1:33S7–9YB2-FVN?i=44&wc=QZ2C-ZD1%3A1589422516%2C1589422632% 2C1589422971%3Fcc%3D1473181&cc=1473181. Accessed 30 May 2016.

37 Jenny Newell has since become associate director for Programs, Exhibitions, and Cultural Collections, Australian Museum, Sydney, Australia.

38 Email from Jenny Newell to the author, 17 September 2014.

39 Club, Tonga?, early twentieth century, Gift of William Williams, American Museum of Natural History, New York, 80.1/ 144.

40 Andy Mills, email to the author, 28 August 2014. Andy Mills is currently research associate in History of Art at the University of Glasgow.

41 Andy Mills, "*Akau tau*: Contextualizing Tongan War Clubs', *Journal of the Polynesian Society*, 118 (2009), 39–40.

42 N. Thomas, *Entangled Objects: Exchange, Material Culture, and Colonialism in the Pacific* (Cambridge, MA: Harvard University Press, 1991).

43 I delivered an earlier version of this chapter at the symposium *Curatopia: Histories, Theories, Practices, Museums and the Future of Curatorship*, Ludwig-Maximilians Universität-Munich, Germany, 2015. I delivered subsequent versions at a meeting of the Leonardo Art Science Evening Rendezvous, New York City, USA, 2015, and at the Institut für Ethnologie, Georg-August-Universität, Göttingen, Germany, in 2016. I am grateful to Philipp Schorch, Conal McCarthy, Patricia Olynyk and Roman Loimeier for the invitations, and to all those whose suggestions on those occasions led to improvements. I also owe debts of gratitude to Jenny Newell, Sean Mallon and Andy Mills. Steven Hooper and Nicholas Thomas have been long-term guides to the Pacific, and I should also like to acknowledge the generosity of Elfriede Hermann. I revised the chapter for publication during my annual residency as a permanent fellow at the Lichtenberg-Kolleg (Advanced Study Institute) of the Georg-August-Universität, Göttingen, and I am grateful to the director, Martin van Gelderen, the executive director, Dominik Huenniger, and their colleagues for their hospitality.

čəsnaʔəm, the City before the City: exhibiting pre-Indigenous belonging in Vancouver

Paul Tapsell

Introduction: nothing like now

The exhibition *čəsnaʔəm, the City before the City* is one of the most innovative exhibitions I have experienced.[1] It showed me a world that is 'nothing like now'. Known as čəsnaʔəm in the local hənɁəminəm̓ language, recalling the name of an ancestral village of the Musqueam First Nation, the exhibition raises questions about the tribal society that existed long before the modern city of Vancouver, what I call the 'pre-Indigenous'. As the exhibition website puts it:

> The curatorial premise of this project is simple: the bone, stone, and shell objects from čəsnaʔəm, which have survived thousands of years, are great catalysts for conversations about the relationship between Indigenous and settler societies in Vancouver. They are reminders of the connections between the history of colonialism, and the continuum of Musqueam culture … The exhibition asks, who's [sic] home is Vancouver? How have newcomers claimed Vancouver as their own? How do the Musqueam understand their lengthy connection to this place?[2]

In this chapter, I consider this extraordinary experiment in curating a First Nations exhibition in Canada from the tribal Māori perspective of Aotearoa New Zealand. As a tribal review of a tribal exhibition, this chapter is necessarily personal and reflective, as well as academic and analytical. First, by way of context I describe the general situation of tribal professionals working in and outside mainstream museums in the former settler colony of Aotearoa New Zealand, not unlike the situation in the USA and Canada, and specifically my own experience as a curator in the museum in my own tribal region of Rotorua, and in the country's largest city of Auckland. After I describe my visit to the čəsnaʔəm exhibition and my responses to its central themes, I consider the parallels and differences between Indigenous curatorship in Canada and Aotearoa New Zealand, before concluding by sketching out my own curatopia – what the future of pre-Indigenous curatorship might look like.

Background: tribal curators in Western museums

When I walked into the exhibition *c̓əsnaʔəm, the City before the City*, it occurred to me that it must have been one of the most logistically challenging projects ever curated. As most of my colleagues know, I am a harsh critic of any museum display; not least those purporting to represent Indigenous peoples, but which do not engage local and or visiting kin communities beyond consultative lip service.[3]

Its seems so long ago now that, when, in my youth, I was surrounded by tens of my tribal Te Arawa elders, raised in houses with dirt floors, who boasted about how old they were before they got their first pair of shoes, and when wealth was measured in grandchildren. In no small way, I was infused with the metaphorical soil from between their childhood toes. In due course, they presented me to the Rotorua Museum in 1990, and I became our tribe's first home-grown professional curator. From this very grounded ancestral space of belonging to the land on which I was conceived, lived, and worked, my fledgling career began. My curatorial practice was framed by the experiences of my elders with the very recent *Te Maori* exhibition, a remarkable phenomenon in which objects from local museum collections toured the USA and Aotearoa New Zealand between 1984 and 1987. What was unprecedented about this was the input of curator Hirini Moko Mead and other Māori leaders, such as Kara Puketapu, and the active participation of hundreds of Māori in opening ceremonies, guided tours, public programmes and so on.[4] My elders, the likes of Irirangi, Pateriki, Hamuera, Kuruotemarama and Kunikuni, had guided the Crown (i.e. the government) on the unprecedented ritual presentation and interpretation of artefacts, understood in Māori terms as *taonga* (ancestral treasures), in museum contexts.[5] The elders spoke about the debates and rationalisations that underpinned the methodology they engaged in to open *Te Maori* at all seven venues, beginning at the Metropolitan Museum in New York. By the time the exhibition closed in 1987 these ritualised practices became the new baseline *tikanga* (customary ceremonies) of Aotearoa New Zealand's newly evolving 'bicultural' museum practice.[6]

My learned elders have all passed on, but their gentle guiding lessons remain, shaping my curatorial purpose of guiding social groups, often referred to in the literature as 'source communities',[7] to find their voices and exercise leadership in museum contexts. As a curator, director and academic, I have been fortunate to travel the world, never ceasing to seek out new displays that might take our profession to new places and overtly challenge the legally constraining values of museum governance structures. Not for lack of volume, the past three decades have been generally disappointing. Many museums have attempted to replicate *Te Maori*, but time and again I came away from these 'Indigenous' exhibitions underwhelmed.

Although my career is more academically focused these days, I continue to ask myself why museums still feel the need to contain; to paternalise; to cast themselves as the authoritative over-writers of local and source kin community voices. I have written a number of papers exploring aspects of this theme, drawing on my own museological background.[8] In my work as a curator and director, I put this theory into practice. From the 1990s at the Rotorua Museum, I dared to invite local elders to co-produce exhibitions and give curatorial voice to their ongoing tribal stories – rights and responsibilities, colonial anguish and despair, hope and opportunity, from either host or visitor perspectives – which highlighted the growing disconnect with urban-raised grandchildren.[9] In the 2000s, my executive role at Auckland Museum facilitated bringing together a Māori values team, comprising urban-raised Māori curators, designers and researchers who, with expansive 'blue skies' thinking, built the *Ko Tawa* exhibition project comprising a travelling exhibition, website, database, book and related programmes (Figure 12.1).[10] Its cornerstone value was reciprocity, recognising the ancestral ties between museum-held taonga, landscapes and descendant communities, whether by elders at home on tribal marae or by their grandchildren raised in distant urban cities.[11]

Running hand in hand with *Ko Tawa*, and its (re)presentation of Auckland Museum-held taonga back to the living, was the Ancestral Human Remains (AHR) Repatriation to Source Project. They were two sides of the same coin: the living and the dead. My elders used to argue that if our dead – inappropriately acquired (stolen) from burial sites throughout Aotearoa New Zealand and the Pacific – remained trapped in museums then these institutions will for ever remain cemeteries. The release of AHR by museums and their host kin-community partners to source communities remains the gateway through which museums must first travel. After all, in

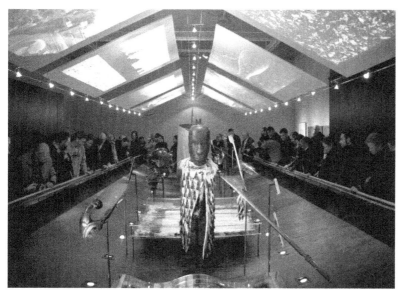

12.1 *Ko Tawa* exhibition on display at Rotorua Museum Te Whare Taonga o Te Arawa, Aotearoa New Zealand, 2007.

a Māori sense, we are our ancestors. In contrast to Western ideas about the living and the dead, the past and present, we see ourselves as connected to our ancestors from whom we are descended in a continuum of past/present becoming future.[12]

To say I came up against internal resistance, in trying to reverse the legal idea of ownership over taonga and AHR, and to set up a framework of belonging and reciprocity, would be an understatement. As reported elsewhere, my steadfastness to remaining in service to source communities and generational lessons of past elders was arguably a constant irritant to the Auckland Museum Trust Board all the way up to the Prime Minister.[13] As those close to me know, in late 2007 I was eventually challenged to choose between being a compliant employee of Auckland Museum and being Māori …

But this is the battleground of 'curatopia' where the old-world foundations, measured in terms of ownership, auction prices, market reach and fiscal bottom lines, continue to be valued as core museum business, and are in conflict with very different Indigenous ways of seeing things. In the Māori world, kin values are inherent in ancestral lands, tribal *marae* (ceremonial meeting places) and taonga – treasures which can include a wide range of natural, cultural, material and immaterial things. These taonga were included under Article II of the Treaty of Waitangi, Aotearoa New Zealand's founding document signed in 1840, which guaranteed Māori *tino rangatiratanga* (chieftainship or sovereignty) over '*ō rātou taonga katoa*' (all of their treasures or possessions).[14] These values were once meaningfully measured in terms of trusteeship, service and belonging. But in recent years they have been sidelined as footnotes in Treaty settlement-framed historical accounts and museum annual plans.[15] The days when belonging to a collective kin community – marae, representing the core social units or *hapū* – was essential to an individual's physical survival may have passed, but we still yearn to belong, to be valued, to be included and to meaningfully participate in the social milieu in which we find ourselves. For today's disconnected urban Māori majority, the last safe places they can physically reconnect to their ancestral past, without fear of rejection, ridicule or embarrassment, are museums.[16] But are museums really providing what these young people are seeking?

For New Zealand museums, the 1990s to 2000s were the post-*Te Maori* heyday of 'bicultural' experimentation, a government-led reform of the public service under the mantra of 'two peoples one country', which sought to incorporate Māori within the state.[17] A raft of Māori curators found careers in museums. But I felt that a new and more radical paradigm was needed, not least for curatorial practice, which pushed beyond the bicultural compromise to a more autonomous and independent Māori museology. *Ko Tawa* showed the way, giving audiences a glimpse of taonga through the associated genealogical relationships still represented in their originating kin community contexts or tribal marae, long before the modern notion of 'Indigenous' was developed.[18] In other words, it provided viewers with an insight to a world *before* the globalised idea of Indigeneity as framed by urban descendants took hold. *Ko Tawa* therefore represented a beacon lighting the path to an imagined curatopia, at least from a ground-up, pre-Indigenous perspective, that is to say, a Māori framework based on tribal values that predated the construction of 'Indigeneity' in the colonial period.

Recalling Michael Ames and the evolution of Indigenous exhibitions

From today's perspective, the era of bicultural engagement in New Zealand museums seems so long ago. With long grey clouds unfortunately hanging over the apparent sunset of co-curatorship in Aotearoa New Zealand, I directed my attention to see who else over the horizon had picked up where our museums had left off. What was the next step, and where was it being taken? Recently, I spent time with one of my mentors, Dr Rick West, former director of the National Museum of the American Indian in Washington, DC.[19] We both lamented the apparent flat-lining of Indigenous-led values in museums worldwide. He encouraged me not to give up hope – to look for lighthouses elsewhere in the apparent gloom of economic hardship and political transition. Was there some other place or institution of memory engaging and empowering local kin and source communities in museological co-production?

As it turned out, the answer lay in Vancouver, British Columbia. In the next section, I recount my visit to the ɔ́əsnaʔəm exhibition in 2014, and then analyse ɔ́əsnaʔəm and show how it has opened up new directions for Indigenous curatorship, but first I reflect on my conversations with the Canadian museologist Michael Ames in the 1990s about the development of Indigenous exhibitions.

Another of my museum mentors, the late Michael Ames was director of the Museum of Anthropology (MOA) at the University of British Columbia (UBC), Canada.[20] My first meeting with Ames was in Aotearoa New Zealand three years after *Te Maori*, when my elders hosted a crew of museum directors touring museums and Māori communities for the Taonga Māori Conference.[21] Ames later worked closely with the Māori museum director Mina McKenzie and pioneered the idea of Indigenous curatorship.[22] He came to understand the local Musqueam people's depth of humility and ongoing willingness to engage visitors on their lands despite their coloniser-imposed marginalisation. In no small way, the Musqueam assisted Ames in imagining a curatopia that mirrored all that the *Te Maori* exhibition promised, but arguably was not easily delivered in the following decades in Aotearoa New Zealand, as I argued above. Here, exhibitions not unlike *Te Maori* had been created, perhaps not on the same scale, but never reaching the dizzy heights of this benchmark. My curatorially framed observation – endorsed by Ames while mentoring me during my doctorate in the 1990s – was that this was a matter not only of political timing at a national or international level but also of the importance of grounded community engagement that recognised the specificity of the ancestors on display. *Te Maori* had demonstrated the critical importance of the local kin group maintaining the boundary between host and visitor, and the long-term negative effects if left un-negotiated or deliberately transgressed.[23]

Accessibility to ancestral belongings is one thing, but interpreting them to third-party visitors, especially on another kin group's ancestral domain, is a whole new level of engagement, rights and responsibilities. My conversation with Ames in 1996, decades ago, explored this curatorial complexity of co-production and the not so subtle unwillingness of museum governance to share power with descendants on whose ancestral lands their institutions stand. The recently legislated Indigenous (Māori) advisory committee (Taumata-a-Iwi) to the Auckland Museum's Trust Board was a key point of our discussion.[24] It was a world first, but was almost immediately paralysed when over thirty major tribes of Aotearoa New Zealand sought a seat each to exclusively protect their museum-held belongings. However, the impasse was resolved, both on the marae and in the boardroom when the local kin community of Orākei gently reminded the government of the day that it was they, not any other tribe on whose lands the Auckland Museum stood; and it was they with whom the government was invited to have an exclusive Treaty relationship over those lands, now known as Auckland City.

Why was this imagined curatopia being so elusive for us in Aotearoa New Zealand and our colleagues in Canada? The answer for us appeared simple and, perhaps by chance rather than design, we had stumbled upon the formula of success: we both felt that source kin, community-led co-curatorship was essential and the key to future museum success. Our agreement was based on direct experiential immersion with source communities; him with the Musqueam in MOA on their ancestral lands beneath UBC; and me with Ngāti Whakaue on Rotorua township lands. The complexity of kin politics intrigued us both; from an ethnicity perspective in terms of boundary maintenance, and the confusion this was creating, especially when museums attempted to engage iwi, tribes, not of the soil on which their institutions stood. At the time, I was Ames's curatopian ideal, an ideal which he dreamed one day would become Musqueam's reality. He envisioned a future where his partnership with the Musqueam community would one day produce Native leaders in MOA, co-curating and co-governing its important enthnographic collection. I can distinctly remember Ames stating that it was his hope that one day a whole raft of museum-trained Musqueam professionals from the neighbouring community would emerge, as I had for my people in Rotorua, and take MOA on a new journey across new horizons to a space of shared governance and curatorship.

So, what happened in Vancouver and at MOA after Michael Ames? Had his dream been realised? Had Indigenous curatorship taken the next step, and moved beyond the impasse that I had struggled to get around in Aotearoa New Zealand? On my visit to *c̓əsnaʔəm, the City before the City* in 2015 I was about to find out.

Visiting the ċəsnaʔəm exhibition

When in 2015 I arrived at the first of the three *ċəsnaʔəm* exhibition venues at the Museum of Vancouver (MOV), I knew, from the moment I crossed the threshold, that I was entering a new era of museology (Figure 12.2).[25] The next six hours of multiple venue engagement, as I went on to visit all three exhibition sites across the city, were, without exception, the most vibrant engaging museum experience of my life. It gave a grounded international example of what it means to be *pre-Indigenous* in twenty-first-century museum settings, countering the globalised noise of being ethnically glossed as the 'Indigenous Other'. This is my vision of curatopia.

The exhibition at MOV included artefacts, graphic and 3D modelling, videos, soundscapes and interactives which drew connections between Musqueam life in the past and present, as well as the colonial experience, and recent heritage politics.[26] But what stood out for me was the immediate

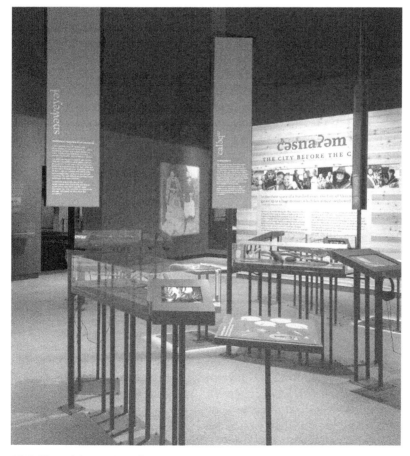

12.2 The exhibition *ċəsnaʔəm, the City before the City* at Museum of Vancouver, Vancouver, Canada.

and refreshing sense of being an honoured guest of the local Musqueam of Vancouver within a metropolitan museum.[27] And to be invited in their own voices to view their ancestral continuum, close up and personal, was a clear signpost that this was no museum 'telling me about the Other', but the Other sharing their own story through a museum with the world. It was a thrill to experience exhibition spaces filled with first-person narratives, and the lived community perspectives were palpable. I found myself journeying through the ancestral memories represented by what were called 'belongings', tangible and intangible connections to people and place, akin to what we would call taonga back home in the Māori tribal world (see section above). As a visitor, I felt that I was transformed from pre-Indigenous hitchhiker to an honoured guest through the 'belongings' digital interactive, which allowed visitors to share ancient and contemporary objects, and which elegantly defined the boundary between responsible kin insider and respected knowledge-bearing outsider.

c̓əsnaʔəm, the City before the City was a complex exhibition. It comprised three interconnected exhibitions at MOV, MOA at UBC and the Musqueam Cultural Educational Resource Centre (MCERC). The naming of the three exhibition venues as c̓əsnaʔəm, an ancient Musqueam community site, is itself a radical challenge to the orthodoxy of museums in Vancouver and their political complicity with settler conquest. When in 2012 the site of the village was rediscovered beneath the modern urban landscape, local people protested against the desecration of burial sites by developers and successfully stopped the construction and regained control of the land.[28] Situated on the shores of the Fraser River close to the international airport, this site became a site of protest and community occupation. The media may have aroused negative attention, but it also opened an opportunity to enlighten a wider city as to its local Native people.[29]

But c̓əsnaʔəm is more than one ancient village. It is a metaphor representing a complex kin network of pre-colonisation prosperity, settlement patterns and resource management across the wider metropolitan area of Vancouver – the city before the city that was 'not like now'. Since colonisation, the Musqueam people have been pushed to the fringes of this growing city. Giving this name to the exhibition project immediately challenges visitors to suspend any ideas of seeing this culture as a 'dead' display of the Other frozen in the ethnographic past.

The intimacy I sensed on visiting the MOV gained momentum on visiting the next two venues. Having begun my journey at MOV, the step-change of the exhibitionary complex that was c̓əsnaʔəm at MOA was breathtaking (Figure 12.3).[30] It broke all the rules and brought feelings of joy, frustration and sadness to my soul. For the first time in two decades, an exhibition challenged museum authority and its temporal space, situated in the here and now, and gave audiences another way of viewing time and place: sharing a space according to belonging, not ownership; acknowledging ancestral presence beyond physical containment and designer imposition. Curatopia engulfed me.

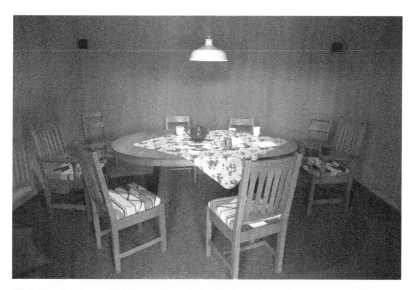

12.3 The 'kitchen table' interactive sq̓əq̓ip (gathered together) in the exhibition *ćəsnaʔəm, the City before the City* at Museum of Anthropology, University of British Columbia, Canada.

Whereas MOV had guided visitors with more orthodox labelling and display furniture, simulating a sense of authority and permanence; MOA provided a more ephemeral counterpoint of temporality, simplicity and recycling as once practised by all our ancestors. Here the multimedia exhibition dealt with identity, language, oral history and the Musqueam struggle to maintain their connections to the land. As the website states, the exhibition was 'told from the first-person perspectives of Musqueam community members both past and present' and sought to 'replicate aspects of Musqueam ways of educating', in part through a series of cultural exchanges.[31]

When I stepped into *ćəsnaʔəm* at MOA I immediately knew that what I was beginning to experience was breaking through the 'fourth wall' of museums. Not unlike in a children's movie, there was Musqueam elders' overt message of hosting and generosity, but underneath the obvious were more culturally nuanced messages, sometimes extremely humorous and artfully presented, or hidden more subtly, perhaps accessible to those who had lived within, or through or experienced elsewhere what it really means to be colonised, or part of a kin community, or to question elder wisdom.

Then the climax was the third exhibition venue I went to at MCERC (Figure 12.4). This version of the exhibition focused on the continuity of Musqueam culture past and present, drawing connections between traditional knowledge holders and contemporary tribal professionals today. Here the 'belongings' were curated for the kin community as an educational aid for elders to transfer knowledge. For me, this was the climax to

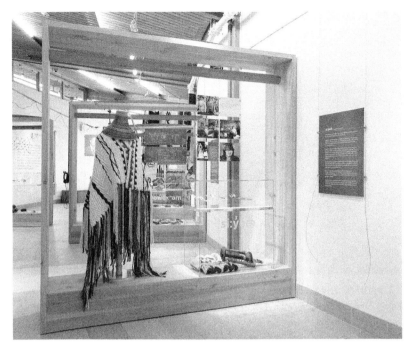

I2.4 The exhibition *c̓əsnaʔəm, the City before the City* at Musqueam Cultural Educational Resource Centre, Vancouver, Canada.

c̓əsnaʔəm. Without fear or favour, the curators overtly focused belongings to reach one audience, themselves.

My nephew accompanied me on our journey through the three components of *c̓əsnaʔəm*. We both noted time and again the uncanny parallels between Musqueam lived realities and our own Māori experiences. We literally forgot we were on the opposite side of the Pacific, let alone in a museum. We felt incredibly privileged entering into spaces where the intimacy of community voices, past and present, were being generously shared with outsiders.

Overall the highlight for us both was the 'kitchen table' interactive at MOA, called *sq̓əq̓ip* (gathered together) in the Musqueam language hən̓q̓əmin̓əm (Figure 12.3). We walked into a simple square, low-ceiling gallery (it might well have been one of our aunties' kitchens back in our home village on the other side of the Pacific). In this exhibit, visitors experience a sound installation in which they hear the after-dinner conversation of the advisory committee around the kitchen table. So, we took a seat and were stunned into an emotional silence as we heard elders' voices and laughter and everyday kitchen banter from the four corners of the room. Our presence made the exhibit complete, and on us departing, it was completed. So ephemeral, so minimalist, so elegant.

For my nephew, a 'pā boy' raised in the heart of our tribal village (*pā*) of Ohinemutu, it was a 'but of course' moment; while for me it was also an overwhelming concatenation of 'pre-Indigenous' being in a museum context. In *Ko tawa* we had turned the museum inside out and transformed the audience into the *object* of the ancestral view. But at the Musqueam kitchen table the exhibit was complete only when you took a seat at the table. That is co-curatorship.

Curating ćəsnaʔəm

The curatorial model for *ćəsnaʔəm* was innovative and collaborative. As well as with the cultural adviser Larry Grant, the co-curator Jordan Wilson, and a curatorial collective which brought together several Musqueam researchers, every aspect of the exhibition – research, content, design etc. – was developed alongside a Musqueam advisory group, along with other elders, community leaders and knowledge holders.[32] As I write this, I am still overawed by the courage and commitment of the three institutions, including two mainstream museums, who were prepared to submit to the simultaneous presentation of three exhibitions, and above all who were pre-pared to release curatorial veto to their local kin/source community. They, and not the institution, had the 'final cut'.

The exhibition's central concept was ground-breaking. It explored the pre-Indigenous values and vitality – kin-accountability on ancestral landscapes of origin – of a globally interconnected twenty-first-century tribal community. Rather than being the authoritative voice of postcolonial modernity, the museum spaces of Vancouver submitted to becoming vehi-cles by which the local Musqueam community might converse directly with visitors within galleries on their alienated ancestral lands. At each venue, visitors were carefully guided across the exhibition threshold by community voices, from a timeless ancestral past up to today's critical challenges for Musqueam who are trying to maintain a sense of identity within a city that has all but consumed their long history.

But despite the apparent urban encroachment of Western-framed 'Otherness', the 'belongings' brought to light in the exhibition effectively animated and validated the inherent rights of the Musqueam people's unin-terrupted thousands of years' association to and with Vancouver. *ćəsnaʔəm, the City before the City* therefore metaphorically speaks to the complexity of kin belonging on landscapes, each venue carrying the Musqueam voice to three very different audiences: MOV (downtown Vancouver) catered to the more orthodox non-Indigenous museum visitor; MOA (on the peninsula at UBC) challenged its academically inclined visitors with an ephemeral approach and the Musqueam Cultural Centre (aimed at the Musqueam community) became complete only when elders and grandchildren occu-pied the exhibition space.

At one end of the spectrum, the MOV became the gateway exhibition to the global or urban coloniser audience, whether living in Vancouver or on the other-side of the world; and at the other end was the MCERC exhibition designed specifically to reach deep into their own kin. And the nexus of the continuum was MOA, straddling the world of pre-Indigenous being, urban-framed Indigenous identity and legally framed coloniser descendant belief systems. Each exhibition provided an insider-curated glimpse to the multiple challenges the past one hundred and fifty years of colonial exclusion has presented to Musqueam identity. Focused by the common theme of kin accountability to 'belongings,' *c̓əsnaʔəm* is not unlike a three-movement symphony. Central to each of the three kin-framed narratives was the inclusive concept of community belonging as represented by 'belongings' or ancestral treasures to which *we belong.* The juxtaposition of exterior global modernity and engulfing ancestral presence was direct, engaged and, at times, for me as a visitor, overwhelming.

The challenges to orthodoxy were everywhere: from a digital exhibition of a Musqueam curator by another Musqueam curator; use of outdoor vistas to demonstrate the museum's responsibility to maintain kin accountability to surrounding landscapes; newsprint-quality paper labels presented in authoritative, unsanitised first-voice quotes of community members; and the exhibiting of *belongings* as ancestors. But the co-curators were always generous and respectful to the hosting institution, leaving space for community elders to animate their existence in a continuum dependent on both sides – host and visitor – recognising, negotiating and maintaining the fluid boundaries of social interaction in an ancestrally collapsed museum space, not unlike a tribal marae in the South Pacific. As a visitor, I could not resist drawing comparisons to the plight of Ngāti Whātua o Orākei, the Māori tribe in central Auckland, Aotearoa New Zealand. But in spite of marginalisation, the Musqueam never ceased demonstrating their rights and obligations to all outsiders through hospitality – a measure of service and leadership that is still maintained throughout the pre-Indigenous world.

So, had the Musqueam progressed to Ames's imagined space of shared governance and co-curatorship; to a space where being pre-Indigenous still matters; and, when fused into a museum context, a space within which we can well imagine a future 'curatopia'? These were the thoughts racing through my mind during my visit to *c̓əsnaʔəm.* Certainly, there were positive signs of a closer relationship between museums and local Native people in recent years. As part of a recent physical redevelopment, MOA had modernised its entrance, a spectacular hall of towering ancestors in the form of totem poles, an open storage area, and new and exciting exhibition spaces. These extensive renovations were completed in 2012, digitally enhancing Ames's uniquely transformational open storage system established in the 1980s.[33] This time, however, MOA honoured the pre-Indigenous space of belonging by shifting away from typological ordering of objects to what I would describe as an exhibitionary style of open storage spaces, drawers and cases clustered according to community origin, radiating outward across the Pacific, North America and beyond. A major driver of this shift was the realisation that many thousands of MOA's twenty-first-century visitors are urban-raised Native (aboriginal) peoples *not* of Vancouver origin, but nevertheless keen to find and reconnect to their ancestral identity. While the entrance introduces the Musqueam as the local aboriginal people, the open storage exhibits reinforce their customary responsibility of hosting *all* visitors as honoured guests while on their lands.

The co-hosting responsibility with Musqueam underpinned MOA's 2012 redevelopment, though it was not explicit. It evolved directly out of Ames's recognition back in the 1980s of their colonial marginalisation throughout Vancouver, not least the peninsula where UBC is located. He forged what has since become a cross-generational relationship, originally built on an academic course – Musqueam 101. By 2012, UBC and its customary hosts had become so entwined that it was a matter of course to recognise Musqueam as the host kin community of the UBC peninsula.

Beyond UBC, however, confusion reigned over kin authority in spaces of memory and protocol, despite the obvious cues provided by Musqueam and supported by the wider Squamish nation, for example, during the 2010 Vancouver Winter Olympics. The relatively recent arrival of thousands of Native immigrants from wider Canada has provided an ongoing and not inconvenient layer of confusion. Not unlike post-Second World War Orākei in Auckland, Aotearoa New Zealand, Vancouver City has also defaulted to engaging the numerically larger immigrant tribal and pan-tribal communities that swamped the locals.

Post-2012, MOA further built on its redevelopment and sent a powerful message to wider Vancouver regarding the primacy of local kin. It began establishing a whole new level of curatorial engagement with Musqueam, drawing on degree-qualified and curatorial-trained descendants to take a lead in the production of an imagined exhibition that might highlight the accelerating crisis of urban development inundating communities like Musqueam. One such curator turned out to be Jordan Wilson, a graduate student in anthropology and museum studies at UBC, who worked on the *ċəsnaʔəm* exhibition. When the *ċəsnaʔəm* project began, it assisted MOA to clarify and articulate the boundaries of kin-host insider/visitor outsider within an innovative digital domain of kin identity and belonging. Running parallel to the evolving Musqueam/MOA co-curatorship of *ċəsnaʔəm* was the reformation of ancestral belongings within the Reciprocal Research Network (RRN), a digital gateway portal which packaged and delivered knowledge and images of source community ancestral belongings beyond MOA's four walls.[34]

Not surprisingly, for the Musqueam nation itself *ċəsnaʔəm* became a call to arms. It evolved into an exhibitionary challenge over the next three years, keeping both the lessons of protest and reconnection alive while seeking to reach three disparate audiences: visitors from afar; resident immigrants; and own descendants. The boundaries established were clear and simple: either you were an insider (Musqueam living either in or beyond the village community); or outsider (resident on Musqueam lands or visitor to Musqueam lands). It did not matter from which ethnic or tribal community any outsider originated: if you are not Musqueam, then you are a guest on land that has been occupied continuously for more than five thousand years.

These elements of insider and outsider according to Musqueam values permeated throughout the c̓əsnaʔəm project's development and in time manifested themselves throughout the three venues as a concurrent tension being offered three times over. The one overarching core value apparent at all sites was the Musqueams' guiding relationship of empowering MOA to share in the responsibility of hosting all visitors entering c̓əsnaʔəm. Initiated by Ames, three decades earlier, the Musqueams' leadership role in MOA now radiated beyond UBC and into MOV, thus enabling their belongings to become the primary vehicle by which the ancestral voice of c̓əsnaʔəm was conveyed to multiple outsider audiences.

Conclusion: lessons from the Musqueam curatorial process

Through c̓əsnaʔəm, it seems to me that the Musqueam people are now on the verge of transformation, not unlike the way Auckland Museum's Orākei community were in the mid-2000s. Through the inclusive efforts of past and present leadership in (real) partnership with UBC/MOA and MOV, the Musqueams' home status is again coming to the fore after years of brutal marginalisation. The very fact this band was rendered invisible, not unlike Ngāti Whātua o Orakei in Auckland, has fuelled the shared purpose not just of surviving but of revitalising the Musqueam's deep sense of identity as the founding population of Vancouver City. This chapter spoke to and explored this shared Musqueam crisis, and how museums have come to play a major role in the re-establishment of the Musqueams' First Nation status.

But, despite this progress and the success of c̓əsnaʔəm, has Ames's dream of Musqueam and museum co-production from a pre-Indigenous-led value system of belonging been realised? Did the c̓əsnaʔəm exhibition measure up? The answer is a resounding 'yes'. c̓əsnaʔəm, the City before the City was, to my mind, a world first: it broke out of an orthodox Western-framed, museum-prescribed straitjacket and gave serious voice to serious issues from lived, local kin-community (Musqueam) perspectives of survival. The exhibition took me through that curatopian fourth wall as only pre-Indigenous curators can, if afforded the opportunity: the exhibition remains a powerful tribute to co-production as it should be – two value systems (Native and Western) co-existing in a space of clear boundaries under one roof, one voice leading, then passing over to the next, from community elders to museum curators to urban-savvy youth to Musqueam knowledge holders. It is no coincidence that the grandchildren of those elders Ames invited across the MOA threshold in the 1980s are today's curators, guides, designers and educators of c̓əsnaʔəm.

c̓əsnaʔəm was a daring exhibition concept that simultaneously engaged three differentiated target audiences across three very different venues in one metropolis through a collaborative curatorial process. It heralded a new pre-Indigenous frontier of curatorial co-production in North America, building on the *Ko tawa* platform set by Auckland Museum in the mid-2000s. Although *ċəsnaʔəm* is a temporary exhibition, it provides a new level of kin-led curatorial innovation; a step-change for museums emerging out of colonial paradigms to engage and reach those audiences who matter most: *our* guests (whoever walks on our ancestral land) and *our* grandchildren (future guardians of kin-framed *belongings*).

Where *Ko tawa* reversed Otherness, *ċəsnaʔəm* turned Otherness on its head by inviting the audience to become part of an ongoing ancestral landscape continuum – *belonging. ċəsnaʔəm* demonstrates that joint curatorship – co-production – by kin-qualified specialists is not just possible, but essential, if we are to appreciate the sophisticated depth of knowledge still being carried by pre-Indigenous or kin communities fighting to survive the ongoing challenges of colonisation in the twenty-first century.

Notes

1 *ċəsnaʔəm, the City before the City*, Museum of Vancouver, Canada, 2010–2015, www.museumofvancouver.ca/exhibitions/exhibit/c%CC%93%C9%99sna%CA%94%C9%99m-city-city. Accessed 10 December 2016.

2 *Ibid.*

3 See for example P. Tapsell, *Pukaki: A Comet Returns* (Auckland: Reed, 2000); P. Tapsell, 'Taonga, Marae, Whenua – Negotiating Custodianship: A Maori Tribal Response to Te Papa: The Museum of New Zealand', in A. Coombes (ed.), *Rethinking Settler Colonialism: History and Memory in Australia, Canada, Aotearoa New Zealand and South Africa* (Manchester: Manchester University Press, 2006), pp. 86–99; P. Tapsell, 'Aroha Mai: Whose Museum? The Rise of Indigenous Ethics in Museum Contexts', in J. Marstine (ed.), *The Routledge Companion to Museum Ethics* (London and New York: Routledge, 2011), pp. 85–111.

4 S.M. Mead (ed.), *Te Maori: Maori Art from New Zealand Collections* (New York: Heinemann: American Federation of Arts, 1984).

5 On the use of the word taonga, and more information on the cultural dimensions of this term, see P. Tapsell, 'The Flight of Pareraututu: An Investigation of Taonga from a Tribal Perspective', *Journal of the Polynesian Society*, 106:4 (1997), 323–74.

6 For developments in museums post *Te Maori* see C. McCarthy, *Museums and Māori: Heritage Professionals, Indigenous Collections, Current Practice* (Wellington: Te Papa Press, 2011).

7 See L. Peers and A.K. Brown (eds), *Museums and Source Communities: A Routledge Reader* (London: Routledge, 2003).

8 Key exhibitions and associated publications: 1991 *Te korimako tangi ata* (The New Dawn), 1993 *Te ohaaki o Houmaitawhiti* (The Legacy of Houmaitawhiti), 2005 *Ko Tawa*, 2010 *Te Ara: Pathways of Leadership*.

9 Rotorua Museum Te Whare Taonga o Te Arawa website. www.rotoruamuseum.co.nz/. Accessed 5 January 2017.

10 Auckland War Memorial Museum Tāmaki Paenga Hira website, www.auck landmuseum.com/about-us. Accessed 5 January 2017.

11 For an overview of this exhibition see the catalogue: P. Tapsell et al., *Ko Tawa: Maori Treasures of New Zealand* (Auckland: David Bateman: Auckland Museum, 2006). For my thoughts on the lessons of this project, see P. Tapsell, 'Ko Tawa: Where Are the Glass Cabinets?', in R. Silverman (ed.), *Museum as Process: Translating Local and Global Knowledges* (London and New York: Routledge, 2015), pp. 262–78.

12 See Tapsell, 'The Flight of Parerauututu'.

13 See Tapsell, 'Aroha Mai: Whose Museum?'.

14 On the Treaty of Waitangi and its contemporary application to Māori cultural rights, see H. Kawharu, *Waitangi: Maori and Pakeha Perspectives of the Treaty of Waitangi* (Auckland: Oxford University Press, 1989); D. Butts, 'Maori, Museums, and the Treaty of Waitangi: The Changing Politics of Representation and Control', in S.J. Knell, S. Watson and S. MacLeod (eds), *Museum Revolutions: How Museums Change and Are Changed* (London and New York: Routledge, 2007), pp. 215–27.

15 M. Kawharu, 'Indigenous Governance in Museums: A Case Study, the Auckland War Memorial Museum', in C. Fforde, J. Hubert and P. Turnbull (eds), *The Dead and Their Possessions: Repatriation in Principle, Policy and Practice* (London: Routledge, 2002), pp. 293–330.

16 P. Tapsell, 'Tribal Marae: Crisis? What Crisis?' in M. Kawharu (ed.), *Maranga Mai! Te Reo and Marae in Crisis?* (Auckland: Auckland University Press, 2014), pp. 35–64.

17 D. O'Sullivan, *Beyond Biculturalism: The Politics of an Indigenous Minority* (Wellington: Huia, 2007).

18 On marae and non-tribal marae in the cities, see Paul Tapsell, 'Marae and Urban Tribal Identity in Aotearoa New Zealand', *Pacific Studies*, 25:1–2 2002, 141–71. On the modern development of Indigeneity, see Rodney Harrison, 'Reassembling Ethnographic Museum Collections', in R. Harrison, S. Byrne and A. Clarke (eds), *Reassembling the Collection: Ethnographic Museums and Indigenous Agency* (Santa Fe: SAR Press, 2013), pp. 6–11.

19 R. West et al. *The Changing Presentation of the American Indian: Museums and Native Cultures* (Washington, DC: Smithsonian Institution, University of Washington Press, 2006).

20 M. Ames, 'Free Indians from Their Ethnological Fate', *Muse*, 5:2 (1987), 14–25; M. Ames, *Cannibal Tours and Glass Boxes: The Anthropology of Museums* (Vancouver: University of British Columbia Press, 2nd edn, 1992).

21 M. Lindsay (ed.), *Taonga Maori Conference New Zealand November 18–27 1990* (Wellington: Cultural Conservation Advisory Council, Department of Internal Affairs, 1991). See also McCarthy, Hakiwai and Schorch, Chapter 13 below.

22 M. Ames and M. McKenzie (eds), *Curatorship: Indigenous Perspectives in Postcolonial Societies* (Ottawa: Canadian Museum of Civilization, 1996). On Māori–Indigenous Canadian connections, see also C. McCarthy, 'Historicising the "Indigenous International": Museums, Anthropology, and Transpacific Networks', in E. Durr and P. Schorch (eds), *Transpacific Americas: Encounters and Engagements between the Americas and the South Pacific* (London and New York: Routledge, 2016), pp. 3–26.

23 P. Tapsell, 'Taonga: A Tribal Response to Museums' (PhD thesis, University of Oxford, 1998).

24 M. Kawharu, 'Indigenous Governance in Museums'.

25 For the background to the exhibition see the website, www.thecitybeforethecity. com/. Accessed 5 January 2017.

26 For background, images and further information on this award-winning exhibition at the Museum of Vancouver, see Museum of Vancouver website: Musqueam, www.museumofvancouver.ca/programs/blog/tags/musqueam. Accessed 1 September 2017.

27 The community to which I refer, the the founding population of Vancouver City (and surrounding municipalities), is made up of the key elders, leaders, fathers and mothers, youth and children of the 1300-plus band who live at Musqueam with a longhouse, tribal administration, cultural and recreation facilities at its heart. Of the original 144,888 hectares of their territory, only 0.2 per cent makes up their current land holdings. I had the pleasure to get to know these people when hosted by them over a period of five years. Like any community there are always rival family factions and tensions. Many more Musqueam, like the curator of this exhibition, live beyond the village, but this does not make them any less Musqueam. For more on this community, see Darryl Hol, 'Using Traces from Vancouver's Past, a Vibrant Community Is Recognized', *The Globe and Mail*, Vancouver (16 January 2016), https://beta.theglobeandmail.com/news/ british-columbia/using-traces-from-vancouvers-past-a-vibrant-community-is-recognized/article22497261/?ref=http://www.theglobeandmail.com&. Accessed 1 September 2017.

28 See Musqueam First Nation website, www.musqueam.bc.ca/c%CC%93%C9%99 sna%CA%94%C9%99m-city-city-exhibition. Accessed 5 January 2017.

29 For the background to this topic, including media coverage, see Musqueam: A Living Culture – *ȼəsnaʔəm* website, www.musqueam.bc.ca/c%CC%93% C9%99sna%CA%94%C9%99m. Accessed 5 January 2017.

30 For *ȼəsnaʔəm, the City before the City* at MOA, see the Museum of Anthropology website, http://moa.ubc.ca/portfolio_page/citybeforecity/. Accessed 5 January 2017.

31 Quotation from website, cited above. For the exchange programme, see MOA website, http://moa.ubc.ca/portfolio_page/cultural-exchanges/. Accessed 5 January 2017.

32 The co-curator at MOA was Susan Rowley, and at MOV was Vivien Gosselin. For the background to the exhibition development see The City Before the City, www.thecitybeforethecity.com/. Accessed 5 January 2017.

33 See the MOA website, http://moa.ubc.ca/. Accessed 5 January 2017.

34 See the RRN website, www.rrncommunity.org/. Accessed 5 January 2017.

PACIFIC

 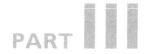

13

The figure of the kaitiaki: learning from Māori curatorship past and present

Conal McCarthy, Arapata Hakiwai and Philipp Schorch

Introduction: curating differently

At an international conference in Canada on Indigenous curatorship in 1996, Awhina Tamarapa, then a Māori curator from the Museum of New Zealand Te Papa Tongarewa (Te Papa), spoke about the display of the *pātaka* (food storehouse) called *Te Tākinga* in the exhibition *Mana Whenua* (Figure 13.1). From her description of how she worked with her tribal community Ngāti Pikiao to develop and interpret the exhibit, it was clear that her practice as a curator, while recognisably curatorial, reflected a distinctively Māori perspective. According to Tamarapa, she did not speak *about* or *for* the people, rather she spoke *with* them. She stressed that the object was not an inert artefact but a *taonga* (treasure), a living object-being; and that the exhibit did not talk only about the tribal past, but also about the present and future. In sum, her conception of the curator's role was not that of the authoritative expert speaking from within an academic discipline, but of the facilitator working within and between both a museological and an Indigenous framework.[1] As a curator, she aimed to reconnect the community with their alienated cultural heritage, helping them to reclaim it as their own, and in the process deliberately marginalising her role as curator-expert and minimising the ethnographic authority of the national museum. The label text for the finished exhibit stated modestly that the research, the planning and the reconstruction of the pātaka was the work of 'our elders', who worked in a 'co-operative relationship' with Te Papa. The people have 'made this house our own again' under the patronage of *Tāne-whakapiripiri* (Tāne-who-unites), the spiritual guardian of these and all other wooden carvings in the museum.[2]

The museum, James Clifford reminds us, 'is an inventive, globally and locally *translated* form, no longer anchored to its modern origins in Europe'.[3] In this volume we argue that curatorship may similarly be recalled and remade through collaborative relationships with communities and 'experiments in culture'.[4] What can museums of ethnography in the Americas and Europe learn from the experience of nations where distinctive forms of Indigenous museology are emerging and reshaping the

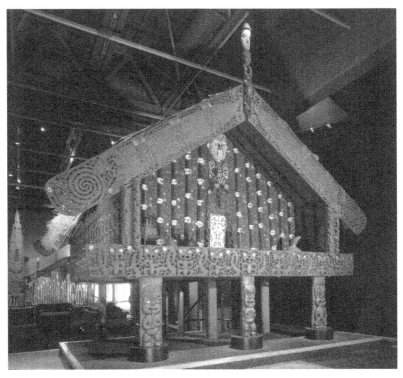

13.1 The food store house or pātaka called *Te Tākinga* on display in the Māori exhibition *Mana Whenua* at the Museum of New Zealand Te Papa Tongarewa, Wellington, 1998.

conventions of curatorial practice? In attempting to address this question, the current chapter draws on research by the authors, including interviews with Māori curators, museum professionals, academics and community leaders throughout Aotearoa New Zealand, exploring connections with the wider Pacific and the world.[5] In doing so, we consider the 'figure of the *kai-tiaki*', the Māori 'guardian', as a particular local development of the 'figure of the curator'.[6]

An extensive literature is available on curatorial theory and practice in contemporary art, and to a lesser extent about curators working in anthropology and history museums, but little on explicitly Indigenous curating.[7] We seek to build a broader interdisciplinary curatorial framework for a range of museums that incorporates not just *what* is being curated (e.g. the object) but also the politics and poetics of *how* it is being curated, i.e. the practice itself, embedded in wider social relations.[8] This chapter shows, through examples of curatorial work in exhibitions, community engagement, research projects and repatriation, that a Māori curatorial practice has been emerging within a range of cultural institutions – museums, galleries, libraries and archives – which intersects with Western ideas but also draws on customary concepts offering different views of material culture, ways of being and knowing, and space and time. In addition, we suggest that this contemporary phenomenon is part of a long history of Māori engagement with anthropology, ethnology and the culture of collecting and display, which was always intensely political and performative, but also cosmopolitan, seeing value in 'the things and thoughts of Europe' and beyond.[9] We turn now to the rich histories of Māori participation in, and challenges to, European museology which arrived in Aotearoa New Zealand with *Pākehā* (European) settlers in the nineteenth century.

Looking in and facing out: curatorial histories in Aotearoa New Zealand

In the South Pacific nation of Aotearoa New Zealand, the history of museums and heritage practices such as curatorship reflect their British antecedents, but owing to close proximity to local Indigenous models these practices have been gradually inflected by Polynesian ways of doing things. Established in the mid- to late nineteenth century along colonial lines, museums and art galleries developed quickly to the point where, by the mid-twentieth century, they had become professional scientific organisations that were in many ways indistinguishable from their counterparts in the UK and North America.[10] Within these institutions, curators – in the scholar or connoisseur mould – went about their work, which typically

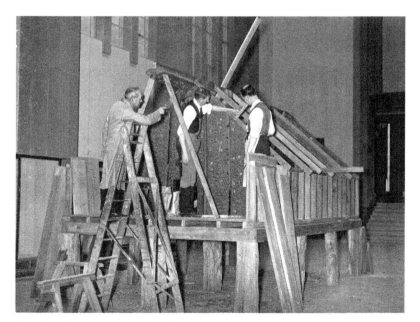

13.2 The Māori carver Thomas Heberley directing work on the carved store house *Te Tākinga* in preparation for the opening of the Dominion Museum, Wellington, New Zealand, mid-1930s.

involved an inward-looking preoccupation with the acquisition, documentation, care, management, research and exhibition of art, history, natural history and, of course, Māori material culture (the latter variously analysed within the Western frameworks of ethnology, ethnography, anthropology and art history).

However, this otherwise Eurocentric history was punctuated at various points by Māori people who worked in and around museums to insert Indigenous perspectives that opened up institutions to face outwards to communities. In the 1920s and 1930s at the Dominion Museum in Wellington, for example, the Māori carver Thomas Heberley played a key role in collecting and exhibiting – here he can be seen directing work on restoring *Te Tākinga* (the same storehouse discussed by Tamarapa above) in preparation for the opening of the new museum building (Figure 13.2). At the same time, the Māori politician and scholar Āpirana Ngata, while not on the museum staff like Heberley, nevertheless played a leading role in the display of the meeting house *Te Hau ki Tūranga* at the centre of the Maori Hall, sat on the museum board and also directed government research and publishing through the Board of Maori Ethnological Research.[11] Ngata's leadership in reviving 'traditional' arts and crafts, employing museum objects and other resources as a springboard, was aligned with tribal cultural and social development and aimed at the improvement of life for Māori and the betterment of their position in New Zealand society.[12] In reflecting on these historical precedents for her work as a kaitiaki Māori today, Tamarapa comments:

> The meeting house *Mahinaarangi* [built in the 1920s] at Tūrangawaewae [seat of the Māori King movement] is a special place where taonga are looked after, and [since the 1970s] the Whanganui *iwi* [tribe] at Koroniti have had special places where taonga were and are held. So, the museum is not a foreign concept to many Māori, they've always practised the care of cultural treasures. Te Rangihīroa was an amazing person who has always been regarded on my Taranaki side as a *rangatira* [chief]. To us, we've grown up knowing him, as well as Ngata and other graduates of Te Aute [Anglican Māori college].[13]

The 'practical' or 'empirical' anthropology of Ngata, and his ally Peter Buck (Te Rangihīroa), who became a prominent scholar of the Pacific and director of the Bishop Museum in Honolulu, has strong parallels with what has been referred to as the 'ontological turn'. In drawing on Indigenous concepts such as *whakapapa* (genealogies), scholars have employed different ways of being and knowing as tools to analyse the past in the present. The ultimate aim was and is the preservation of material culture for its own sake but also the task of improving the material conditions of the people to whom that culture belonged.[14]

These remarkable early interventions into museum practice were expanded from the 1970s. At the Dowse in Lower Hutt, for example, the Māori artist and curator Selwyn Muru turned the art gallery into a *marae*

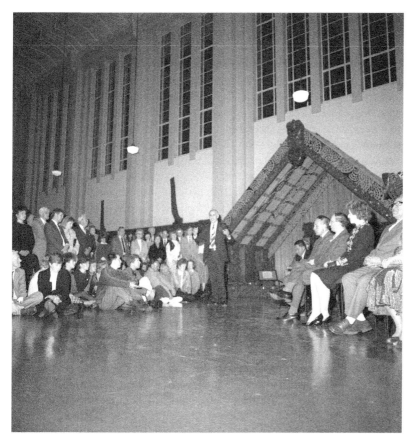

13.3 Professor Hirini Moko Mead, academic and curator of the exhibition *Te Maori*, seen giving a talk at the National Museum, Wellington, Aotearoa New Zealand, 1986.

(communal meeting house) where guests slept on the floor among the paintings in the exhibition *Parihaka*. In the 1980s, the academic Hirini Moko Mead took a leading role in the exhibition *Te Maori* which toured the USA and Aotearoa New Zealand and brought about sweeping changes in local museums, including the adoption of *tikanga* (Māori practices) in conservation, collection management and other areas, the hiring of Māori staff and the repatriation of human remains and artefacts.[15] As a curator-activist, Mead saw the exhibition and its related public programme as a way of liberating Māori cultural heritage and returning it to tribal control under the tribes' own frameworks (Figure 13.3). He stated this view in the following unequivocal terms:

> The Maori people want to control their own heritage; they want to be the people who handle their *taonga*; they want to have the knowledge to explain them to other cultures; they want to explain them to their own people; they want to define their past and present existence, they want to control their

own knowledge (*matauranga Maori*) and they want to present themselves their way to the world and to themselves.[16]

By the 1990s, the curatorial framework for Māori collections and exhibitions in museums had shifted from ethnology and anthropology to what is today referred to as '*kaitiakitanga*' (see below). Broadly, the changes meant adopting elements of *tikanga taonga*, or traditional Māori protocols and practices for managing ancestral treasures; and shifting from sole institutional control of collections to kaitiakitanga, customary guardianship, operationalised inside the museum by employing Māori people as kaitiaki and externally by co-management of taonga in partnership with iwi.[17] On this last point, institutions, from trustees and senior management down to curatorial and collections staff, acknowledged that museums did not 'own' the taonga but looked after them on behalf of, and in partnership with, iwi. This idea of partnership reflected the principles of the Treaty of Waitangi (1840), which from the 1980s were used as a blueprint for a process of reconciliation in the public sector dubbed 'biculturalism'.[18]

Until recently, the last 'ethnologist' working under that rubric was Roger Fyfe at the Canterbury Museum in Christchurch. Elsewhere, the curatorial responsibility for taonga Māori rests almost exclusively with Māori staff who work in departments called Mātauranga Māori (Te Papa), Māori values (Auckland War Memorial Museum), or some equivalent title recognising an Indigenous framework. Nevertheless, the work of Fyfe and his immediate predecessors has also been influenced by Māori paradigms and ideas, seen in the way that they readily work with source communities, share intellectual authority and incorporate Māori perspectives into the ways they do things. Fyfe, for instance, works with Māori people in prisons using carving and other collection objects as a form of social work.[19] Indeed, a feature of Māori museum practice, which can be seen in this reconfiguration of curatorial work, is that it has leaked out of Māori units to influence other non-Māori staff in museums, such as Pacific and history curators working with communities in a similar collaborative fashion.[20]

Kaitiakitanga: a Māori curatorial framework

In this section, we describe the components of the new Māori curatorship. It is important to stress that this is a diverse phenomenon taking various forms in different places, and which has not been codified in a formal way. There has been some academic analysis of the work of Māori art curators,[21] although the field of contemporary art is perceived – rightly or wrongly – as different from museums which deal with collections of social history and taonga Māori, comprising, in the main, customary carving, weaving and other 'heritage' arts. It is also important to emphasise that, despite this differentiation between contemporary art galleries and other institutions, aspects of Māori curatorship can be observed across the heritage sector in galleries, libraries and archives, as well as museums. For example, the Māori curator Paul Diamond, who works at the Alexander Turnbull Library in Wellington with manuscripts, books and other documentary heritage, employs a term for curatorship which he sees as being common to all Māori curators regardless of the format of the material they work with. This term is *kairaupī*, coined by the Māori scholar Timoti Kāretu, literally meaning one who takes care of, or cherishes tenderly.[22] It stresses the care of cultural treasures, analogous to collection management, rather than other aspects of curatorial work such as research or developing exhibitions. However, Diamond explains that many different kinds of objects (and indeed intangible heritage) can be understood as taonga regardless of whether the object is made by Māori or something manufactured by Europeans of value to Māori – material, immaterial, natural, digital or otherwise.[23]

Current models of Māori museum curatorship share four main concepts.[24] First, curators, as well as collection managers, archivists and others, usually refer to themselves as kaitiaki, which suggests the caring (*tiaki*) dimension of the role akin to conservation, collection care and management, or curation traditionally defined (that is to say before collection managers or registrars took over that physical function from curators in recent decades). Collectively, kaitiaki Māori refer to their role as that of kaitiakitanga, which points to the cultural and spiritual aspects of the position and its collective or shared responsibility. Kaitiakitanga carries with it many obligations, and kaitiaki Māori are acutely aware that they are working with ancestral Māori treasures or *taonga tuku iho* (see below) of iwi, *hapū* (subtribes) and *whānau* (extended family). Great respect is required to ensure that the *taha wairua* or spiritual dimension is catered for as much as the *taha tinana* or physical dimension.[25]

However, Māori museum professionals also see public outreach as important, whether it is through exhibitions or community engagement. Tamarapa recently described her understanding of kaitiakitanga in these terms:

> As a Māori curator, I'd describe myself more as a facilitator. In hindsight, I think I have worked as a bridge between the community and the taonga that I am caring for in the museum. In the past, I have called myself a kaitiaki, sort of a custodian of the taonga, looking after them in a cultural sense. But over the years I have realised that the position of the Māori curator is to introduce people to their taonga, and to their culture, through the mātauranga around that taonga, and also being able to bring about change and stimulate opportunities in Māori communities, which is the most exciting part of being a Māori curator.[26]

Interestingly, these ideas overlap with Western concepts to a degree, such as the recent idea of co-curation. Māori models are not necessarily at odds with international museological practices, but at times they fundamentally differ. As scholars have noted, a Māori understanding of collective ownership fundamentally challenges the convention of museum ownership and cultural property.[27]

Second, Māori museum staff generally refer to the objects they look after not as artefacts or art but as taonga. Huhana Smith defines it as '[a]nything tangible or intangible to do with accumulated value with regards to peoples' relations to it, including objects, stories, *whenua* (land), *awa* (rivers), in a whole-of-person, whole-of-entity context'.[28] There is a significant literature on this word.[29] The associated term often heard in Māori speeches on the marae is *taonga tuku iho* (a precious heirloom handed down from the ances-tors). Importantly, while sometimes used interchangeably with 'artefact' or 'object', the word 'taonga' expresses a different epistemology and ontology, encompassing the natural and human worlds, the past and present, living and dead. The linguist Richard Benton defines taonga as 'property' or 'any-thing highly prized', while the anthropologist Anne Salmond calls it a 'fixed point in the tribal network of names, histories, and relationships'.[30] On a political level, the word functions as an act of reclamation, what Mead called a 'tool of explanation' and 'means of enculturation', which allows Māori people today to repossess their ancestral culture in museums, as witnessed dramatically with the *Te Maori* exhibition we alluded to above.[31]

An important modern extension of this concept is the phrase *mana taonga* (community authority over treasures), which joins the word taonga with that of *mana* (power, authority, responsibility, respect, reputation). Recent research has shown how this concept has guided Māori curato-rial work at Te Papa, such as the ongoing iwi exhibitions co-curated with tribes around the country, and at regional museums.[32] It has been argued that mana taonga 'aims to restore the rights of Māori to their material culture and thus awards the museum the interpretive authority through its connectivity and meaningful relationships with the communities of origin'.[33]

Third, mātauranga Māori is the overarching framework within which Māori curatorship operates. The following policy statement at Te Papa captures its meaning:

> *Mātauranga Māori* is a dynamic and evolving system of knowledge used by
> *tangata whenua* [people of the land] to explain, interpret and understand
> the world in which they live. It is framed by *whakapapa* (genealogy) and
> *whanaungatanga* (kinship connections) between all things and is evidenced
> through *kōrero* (narratives and history).[34]

As suggested in the quote from Mead above, and reinforced in many inter-views with Māori professionals, mātauranga Māori highlights the Māori worldview within which cultural customs, and by extension museum tech-niques and procedures, are practised. The Māori scholar Te Ahukaramu Charles Royal, now Director Ngā Manu Atarau at Te Papa, argues that mātauranga Māori as a modern term refers not only to traditional knowl-edge but also to *new* knowledge actively created today within a Māori para-digm and in response to other influences.[35] Māori curatorship acknowledges this dynamism within the Māori world both in historical and in contemporary times, so that knowledge and understanding of the Māori language and its continuous evolution are as vital to nurture as material expressions and the associated cultural practices.

Lastly, we come to tikanga, or customary Māori practices. In museums today, Māori people refer to tikanga taonga, or cultural protocols for managing, interpreting and caring for taonga. These include fundamental concepts such as: *mana* (see above); *tapu* (sacred, restricted), *noa* (everyday, unrestricted); *mauri* (life force, essence); and *whakapapa* (genealogy, relatedness).[36] Despite a tendency to codify these concepts in terms of museum work, Royal emphasises the 'contemporary dynamism' of Māori culture, reminding us that tikanga are living and evolving practices.[37] This last point is critical for understanding how these cultural practices are employed by Māori curators, and potentially *any* curator looking after taonga, not just in local but also in global settings, as we explore below.

Beyond the museum: social development and cosmopolitan futures

In this section, one of the authors of the current chapter, who has worked at the national museum for over twenty years and is now *kaihautū* or Māori co-director of Te Papa, reflects on his practice in relation to the Māori curatorship sketched out above. Arapata Hakiwai has curated major permanent exhibitions like *Mana Whenua* (1998), and has been involved in numerous iwi exhibitions, as well as projects offshore, such as the restoration of the meeting house *Ruatepūpuke* at the Field Museum in Chicago, USA.[38] Here we review a series of projects associated with the Ngāi Tahu people of the South Island of Aotearoa New Zealand, and consider the ways in which curatorial work, as a method and practice, moves beyond the walls of the museum to support the process of tribal cultural, social and economic development. It goes without saying that this style of curation, working alongside the tribe and in line with their perspectives and expectations, would not be possible without the cultural frameworks of kaitiakitanga, taonga, mātauranga Māori and tikanga.

Ngāi Tahu, a small tribe who suffered greatly from the loss of land, language and culture during European colonisation in the nineteenth century, were one of the first to settle their claim with the Waitangi Tribunal in the 1990s, and have since embarked on an ambitious process of cultural revitalisation and economic development including tourism, fisheries, forestry and farming. Twenty years on they have become a major player on the national stage, quickly moving beyond categories such as colonial and even postcolonial, as well as traditional notions of Indigeneity, towards what the anthropologist Jeffrey Sissons has called 'postindigenous'.[39] In the cultural sphere, as Hakiwai's PhD thesis demonstrates, the same resilience, tenacity and dynamism is apparent in programmes for music, language, visual arts and heritage, all of which shape and are shaped by the evolving identity of

Ngāi Tahu people.[40] Hana O'Regan, for example, sees her Ngāi Tahu identity as constantly shifting and relational: 'identity is about feeling, belief and perception. It is about … one's relationships and interactions, one's experience within the world.'[41] One of the most extraordinary examples of this outward-oriented internationalism occurred when Ngāi Tahu represented Aotearoa New Zealand at the forty-ninth Venice Biennale: there contemporary artists Jacqueline Fraser and Peter Robinson were joined there by a performing arts group (*kapa haka*) called Pounamu Kāi Tahu.

It is only natural that, in order to support this quest for tribal self-determination, Indigenous museum curators cannot operate as disinterested academic observers, who typically reserve the right to select and arrange objects for exhibitions over and above communities, but must become intimately involved in co-curation of what are effectively political projects aimed at the betterment of those communities. One of Hakiwai's case studies is the iwi exhibition *Mō Tātou, ā, Mō Kā Uri ā Muri Ake Nei* (*For us and those following after us*) which shows how tribal development is affected through the agency and efficacy of their tribal taonga. Co-curated by museum staff and iwi, it was staged at Te Papa in Wellington 2006–2009, and then toured the tribal homelands (*Te Waipounamu*) at museums in Christchurch, Dunedin and Invercargill, acting as a bulwark for the tribe in establishing fruitful relationships with local heritage institutions. Although the exhibition drew on the past, it was essentially (and crucially) about cultural futures. Megan Tāmati-Quennell, the curator and concept developer (herself Ngāi Tahu), set out 'to make sure that it was not a classical social history narrative, "who we are", "what we are"'. Instead, she 'wanted to use a different curatorial model. I wanted to talk about us as a people historically', Tāmati-Quennell stressed, 'but also in modernity and ensure our present was acknowledged and seen as important, that there was not only a focus on our past.'[42] As one review notes: 'The *Mō Tātou* exhibition also paid tribute to the historical moments that changed the tribe … [but] [o]verall Ngāi Tahu emerge as a vibrant and dynamic tribe with strong roots in tradition, but well informed and engaged in contemporary economic, political, and cultural affairs.'[43]

The logical extension of this curatorial outreach in the tribal regions, operating within a framework of independent 'post-settlement' development (that is to say, *after* the settlement of claims to the Waitangi Tribunal concerning colonial grievances), is the work that Hakiwai and other Te Papa staff have been involved in overseas, including travelling exhibitions and repatriation. A recent example was the voluntary return of a famous feather cloak, given to Captain Cook by the Hawaiian leader Kalaniʻōpuʻu in 1779, as an act of restitution underpinned not by (post)colonial redress but by Pan-Pacific notions of gift and reciprocity shared by Māori and Pacific Islanders.[44] Experiencing the return of the *mahiole* (cloak) and *ʻahuʻula* (headdress) back to their *āina* (homeland) and people will, according to Hakiwai, remain a highlight of his professional career. These *taonga whakahirahira* or magnificent treasures will be anchors in the revitalisation of Hawaiian language, culture and identity, and enduring symbols for the ongoing journey towards Hawaiian self-determination. The relationships (re-)established between the three organisations that made this possible (Te Papa, Bernice Pauahi Bishop Museum and the Office of Hawaiian Affairs) were reflected in the title of the exhibition – *He Nae Akea: Bound Together*. As used in the formal invitation to the opening, the title was symbolic of the ties that bind – the *hulu* (feathers) bound to the *nae* (netting) of the ʻahuʻula, the past to the present, and the individuals and institutions that have honoured Hawaiian culture through the care for the ahuʻula and mahiole of High Chief Kalaniʻōpuʻu.

Our last example illustrates the essentially cosmopolitan nature of this Indigenous curatorial activism. Awhina Tamarapa, who used to work at Te Papa as we have seen above, is now a freelance curator working with a diverse team that is running a Māori, Dutch and local community cultural centre in Foxton, a small town north of Wellington. Called Te Awahou Nieuw Stroom, this multi-purpose facility – incorporating an information centre, library, café, gallery and education centre – aims to provide a 'new cultural heart' for this small, economically depressed community.[45] Opened in late 2017 and designed around an existing windmill and flax museum, the centre tells stories of *mana whenua* (the people with customary authority over the land), local Pākehā (European, mostly British settlers), and the Dutch community in Aotearoa New Zealand.[46] It is clear that, far from having a narrow nativist, settler or migrant focus, this project is broad, transnational and cosmopolitan, collapsing the local and the global.

Conclusion: curatopian visions and global potentialities

The experiences of Māori curators, such as Arapata Hakiwai and Awhina Tamarapa, who have been working with their own people *and* other diverse constituencies over the last twenty years, have shown that there *is* a *curatopia*, a future vision (however idealised) of Indigenous cultural independence which can be realised through curatorial work. This imperative makes it necessary for Māori curators to work as facilitators, activists and culture workers, as well as scholars, in order to reposition the museum as an active supporter of the development aspirations of their people. The tribal case studies presented in this chapter support Sissons' argument that 'Indigenous reappropriations represent futures redirected'.[47] Māori see their taonga in museums not as disconnected from the past but rather as enduring symbols of cultural identity that connect the past with the present and future.

What, then, are the implications of the 'figure of the kaitiaki' for museums housing Māori treasures around the globe? First, if taonga can travel, then the associated Indigenous philosophies, theories and concepts also travel and can potentially speak back to foreign frameworks, such as anthropology or art, to which they are commonly subjected in

Euro-American institutions. In other words, wherever taonga are held, the practice of kaitiakitanga can be deployed, thus changing curatorship from the outside and from within, as has happened in Aotearoa New Zealand and across the Pacific. Such epistemological and ontological reframing can transform the mutual, asymmetrical relations underpinning global, scientific entanglements of the past and turn them into reciprocal, symmetrical forms of cross-cultural curatorship and anthropology in the present, a task we have advocated recently and to which this volume is devoted.[48]

In fact, this process began over twenty-five years ago. In November 1990, the Taonga Māori Conference in Wellington consolidated the dramatic changes in New Zealand museums and embedded them in curatorial practice at home and abroad. Curators from overseas museums with Māori collections in the USA, UK and Europe, along with local professionals and more than thirty kaitiaki Māori, came together to learn from the local experience.[49] There were several keynote speakers, including Hirini Mead who gave the important paper cited above on the nature of taonga. At this time, the word 'taonga' replaced 'artefact' and 'art' in common usage, and participants of the conference, international visitors included, used this word to describe their Māori objects and collections.[50] International delegates were impressed with the big turnout of Māori people at the conference, and commented on 'their willingness to assert their *rangatiratanga*' (chieftainship or sovereignty). They learned from meeting Māori and left with a 'new framework' to view their collections. Many spoke of their plans to change displays, facilitate community access and acquire contemporary Māori art.[51] According to the conference proceedings:

> They could see and hear how taonga grow out of Māori history, symbolise Māori belief and represent Māori mythology. They could also come to understand that what they may see simply as objects are in fact an important part of contemporary Māori life and belief.[52]

Second, such conceptual moves cannot be confined to the past or present but have to be geared towards Indigenous futures, as the above examples have shown. Current discussions around the evolving Humboldt Forum in Berlin, for example, point to the intensity of (post)colonial demands for moral redress, political concessions and legal reparations. While legitimate issues may exist with regard to the initial collection of material treasures and whether ethical limits were reached or exceeded, another, at least as important, conversation is whether the journey of these ancestral figures is indeed over.[53] Backward-oriented provenance research alone – currently the main strategy of Euro-American institutions to pacify Indigenous claims – is not enough; even if it can be proved historically that so-called museum objects were not looted but gifted, then there still remains the responsibility for future reciprocity. Museums across the world, then, can learn from the remarkable return of the feather cloak from Aotearoa New Zealand to Hawai'i, alluded to above, and strive to become active agents in shaping cultural revival and future potentialities on a global scale. We leave the final words to Tamarapa, who, when asked what a curator in Europe could learn from her work, replied:

> If these people so far away looking after our taonga can see that they are living treasures and need to have a connection to the people, then that's enough in order to take care of them. But if they accept this living connection and allow it to generate the kinds of social change that we are doing here, then that's awesome![54]

Notes

1 We would like to thank Awhina Tamarapa for reading and commenting on a draft of this chapter, as well as agreeing to be interviewed. See also A. Tamarapa, 'Museum Kaitiaki: Māori Perspectives on the Presentation and Management of Māori Treasures and Relationships with Museums', in M. Ames and M. McKenzie (eds), *Curatorship: Indigenous Perspectives in Postcolonial Societies*, Proceedings of Conference, May 1994 (Ottawa: Canadian Museum of Civilization, 1996), pp. 160–9. Available from ICOM website, http://icom.museum/resources/pub lications-database/publication/curatorship-indigenous-perspectives-in-post-colonial-societies-proceedings/. Accessed 15 September 2016.

2 Label for *Te Tākinga*, *Mana whenua* exhibition, Museum of New Zealand Te Papa Tongarewa, Wellington, 1998.

3 See Clifford, Chapter 7 above.

4 C. Healy and A. Witcomb (eds), *South Pacific Museums: Experiments in Culture* (Melbourne: Monash University ePress, 2006); V. Golding and W. Modest (eds), *Museums and Communities: Curators, Collections and Collaboration* (London and New York: Bloomsbury, 2013).

5 C. McCarthy, *Museums and Māori: Heritage Professionals, Indigenous Collections, Current Practice* (Wellington: Te Papa Press, 2011); P. Schorch and A. Hakiwai, 'Mana Taonga and the Public Sphere: A Dialogue between Indigenous Practice and Western Theory', *International Journal of Cultural Studies*, 17:2 (2014), 191–205; P. Schorch, C. McCarthy and A. Hakiwai, 'Globalizing Māori Museology: Reconceptualising Engagement, Knowledge and Virtuality through Mana Taonga', *Museum Anthropology*, 39:1 (2016), 48–69.

6 P. Schorch, 'Assembling Communities: Curatorial Practices, Material Cultures, and Meanings', in B. Onciul, M. Stefano and S. Hawke (eds), *Engaging Communities, Engaging Heritage* (Woodbridge: Boydell and Brewer, 2017), pp. 31–46.

7 For an overview of the writing on curating, see the Introduction, above. For Indigenous curating see Ames and McKenzie, *Curatorship*; C.F. Kreps, 'Non-Western Models of Museums and Curation in Cross-Cultural Perspective', in S. Macdonald (ed.), *A Companion to Museum Studies* (Malden, MA: Blackwell Publishing, 2006), pp. 457–72.

8 C. McCarthy, 'Theorising Museum Practice through Practice Theory: Museum Studies as Intercultural Practice', in P. Burnard, L. McKinlay and K. Powell (eds), *Routledge International Handbook of Intercultural Arts Research* (London and New York: Routledge, 2016), pp. 24–34.

9 J. Belich, 'Myth, Race and Identity in New Zealand', *New Zealand Journal of History*, 31:1 (1997), 12, www.nzjh.auckland.ac.nz/docs/1997/NZJH_31_1_04. pdf. Accessed 1 December 2016.

10 J.M. MacKenzie, *Museums and Empire: Natural History, Human Cultures and Colonial Identities* (Manchester: Manchester University Press, 2009); C. McCarthy, 'Museums', in *Te Ara: Encyclopedia of New Zealand* (Wellington: Ministry for Culture & Heritage, 2014), www.teara.govt.nz/en/museums. Accessed 1 November 2016.

11 C. McCarthy, *Exhibiting Māori: A History of Colonial Cultures of Display* (Oxford and New York: Berg; Wellington: Te Papa Press, 2007); Schorch, McCarthy and Hakiwai, 'Globalizing Māori Museology: Reconceptualising Engagement, Knowledge and Virtuality through Mana Taonga'.

12 C. McCarthy, '"To foster and encourage the study and practice of Maori arts and crafts": Indigenous Material Culture, Colonial Culture and Museums in New Zealand', in J. Helland, B. Lemire and A. Buis (eds), *Craft & Community: The Material Culture of Place & Politics, 19th–20th Century* (Aldershot: Ashgate, 2014), pp. 59–82; C. McCarthy, '"Empirical anthropologists advocating cultural adjustments": The Anthropological Governance of Āpirana Ngata and the Native Affairs Department', *History and Anthropology*, 25:2 (2014), 280–95.

13 Conal McCarthy and Philipp Schorch, interview with Awhina Tamarapa, Victoria University, 5 July 2016.

14 A. Henare, 'Nga Rakau a te Pakeha: Reconsidering Maori Anthropology', in J. Edwards, P. Harvey and P. Wade (eds), *Anthropologies and Science: Epistomologies in Practice* (Oxford and New York: Berg, 2007), pp. 93–113. See also A. Salmond, 'Transforming Translations (Part 1): The Owner of These Bones', *Hau: Journal of Ethnographic Theory*, 3:3 (2014), 1–32.

15 S. (Hirini) M. Mead, 'Indigenous Models of Museums in Oceania', *Museum*, 35:139 (1983), 98–101; S.M. Mead (ed.), *Te Maori: Maori Art from New Zealand Collections* (New York: Abrams: American Federation of Arts, 1984); S.M. Mead, 'Concepts and Models for Maori Museums and Culture Centres', *AGMANZ Journal*, 16:3 (1985), 3–5.

16 S.M. Mead, 'Te Maori Comes Home: The Walter Auburn Memorial Lecture', presented to the Friends of the Auckland City Art Gallery, 31 July 1985, 4. E.H. McCormick Library, Auckland Art Gallery Toi o Tāmaki, Auckland.

17 McCarthy, *Exhibiting Māori*, 168.

18 McCarthy, *Museums and Māori*, ch. 5 'Reforming Museology at Te Papa'; A. Fleras and P. Spoonley, *Recalling Aotearoa: Indigenous Politics and Ethnic Relations in New Zealand* (Auckland: Oxford University Press, 1999); P. Adds, B. Bönish-Brednich, R. Hill and G. Whimp (eds), *Reconciliation, Representation and Indigeneity: 'Biculturalism' in Aotearoa New Zealand* (Heidelberg: Universitätsverlag, 2016).

19 Conal McCarthy interview Roger Fyfe, Canterbury Museum, Christchurch, 1 December 2008. A good example was the ethnologist and archaeologist Roger Duff (1912–1978), the director of the Canterbury Museum in the postwar period, who not only spoke Māori and worked closely with Māori people but whose casket, when he died, lay in state in the museum according to Māori funeral customs. See J. Davidson, 'Roger Shepherd Duff', *Te Ara – The Encyclopedia of New Zealand*, updated 7 June 2013, www.teara.govt.nz/en/biographies/5d27/ duff-roger-shepherd. Accessed 15 January 2017.

20 See Sean Mallon in McCarthy, *Museums and Māori*; see also Mallon, Chapter 17 below.

21 A.M. White, 'Māori Curatorship at Auckland Art Gallery Toi O Tāmaki 1998–2001' (MA thesis, Massey University, 2006).

22 H. Williams, *A Dictionary of the Maori Language* (Wellington: GP Books, 7th edn, 1971), 330.

23 Interview Conal McCarthy with Paul Diamond, Alexander Turnbull Library, Wellington, 1 November 2016.

24 McCarthy, *Museums and Māori*. This book was compiled from interviews with over sixty museum professionals, most of them Māori, between 2008 and 2010.

25 Note that in Māori phrases used in New Zealand English the order of noun and adjective observes Māori grammar, so 'kaitiaki Māori' not 'Māori kaitiaki'. Though it is widespread, there is debate among Māori professionals about the term 'kaitiaki', and who is looking after whom. Some observe that kaitiaki in museums do not stand in for local iwi, who are the real kaitiaki, while others point out that, in times past, it was the taonga that was the kaitiaki that looked after people, not the other way around.

26 Tamarapa interview 2016.

27 C. McCarthy, E. Dorfman, A. Hakiwai and Ā. Twomey, 'Mana Taonga: Connecting Communities in New Zealand Museums through Ancestral Māori Culture', *Museum International*, 64:3 (2015), 5–15; J. Marstine, 'Introduction: The Contingent Nature of the New Museum Ethics', in J. Marstine (ed.), *The Routledge Companion to Museum Ethics* (London and New York: Routledge, 2011), pp. 3–25.

28 Interview Conal McCarthy with Huhana Smith, Te Papa, Wellington, 15 January 2009.

29 H. Mead, 'The Nature of Taonga', in M. Lindsay (ed.), *Taonga Maori Conference* (National Museum, Wellington: Department of Internal Affairs, 1990), pp. 164–9. P. Tapsell, 'The Flight of Pareraututu: An Investigation of Taonga from a Tribal Perspective', *Journal of the Polynesian Society*, 106:4 (1997), 323–74; A. Henare, 'Taonga Maori: Encompassing Rights and Property in New Zealand', in A. Henare, M. Holbraad and S. Wastell (eds), *Thinking through Things: Theorising Artefacts in Ethnographic Perspective* (London and New York: Routledge, 2007), pp. 47–67.

30 A. Salmond, 'Nga huarahi o te ao Maori / Pathways in the Maori World', in S.M. Mead (ed.), *Te Maori: Maori Art from New Zealand Collections* (New York: Heinneman, 1984), p. 118.

31 Mead in Lindsay, *Taonga Maori Conference*, 168.

32 Schorch and Hakiwai 'Mana taonga and the Public Sphere'; McCarthy, Hakiwai, Dorfman and Twomey, 'Mana Taonga'.

33 Schorch and Hakiwai, 'Mana taonga and the Public Sphere', 197. This concept has also come under criticism from some scholars, see for example P. Tapsell, 'Taonga, Marae, Whenua – Negotiating Custodianship: A Maori Tribal Response to Te Papa: The Museum of New Zealand', in A. Coombes (ed.), *Rethinking Settler Colonialism: History and Memory in Australia, Canada, Aotearoa New Zealand and South Africa* (Manchester: Manchester University Press, 2006), pp. 86–99.

34 *Mātauranga Māori Strategy: He Ara Whainga* (Wellington: Museum of New Zealand Te Papa Tongarewa, 2004) (adapted from original).

35 K. Johnstone, 'Mātauranga Maori and Museum Practice', *He Rauemi: Resource Guides Issue No. 31* (Wellington: National Services Te Paerangi, Museum of New Zealand Te Papa Tongarea, 2006).

36 See the glossary drawn from various sources in McCarthy, *Museums and Māori*, 263–70. See also H.M. Mead, *Tikanga Māori: Living by Māori Values* (Wellington: Huia, 2003).

37 C. Royal, *Mātauranga Maori and Museum Practice: A Discussion* (Wellington: National Services Te Paerangi, 2007), p. 1.

38 A. Hakiwai, 'Kaitiakitanga – Looking after Culture: Insights from "within" – Two Curatorial Perspectives', *ICOM Ethnographic Conservation Newsletter*, 19 (1999), 10–12; A. Hakiwai, 'Ruatepupuke: Working Together, Understanding One Another', *New Zealand Museums Journal*, 25:1 (1995), 42–4.

39 J. Sissons, *First Peoples: Indigenous Cultures and Their Futures* (London: Reaktion, 2005); C. McCarthy, 'Postcolonial Pasts and Postindigenous Futures: A Critical Genealogy of "Māori Art"', in J. Anderson (ed.), Proceedings of *Crossing Cultures: Conflict, Migration, Convergence* (Melbourne: The Miegunyah Press, 2009), pp. 829–34.

40 Hakiwai, *He mana taonga*, ch. 3, 'Mō tātou: The Politics of Ngāi Tahu Tribal Identity and Development'.

41 H. O'Regan, *Ko Tahu, ko au: Kai Tahu Tribal Identity* (Christchurch: Horomaka Publishing, 2001), p. 27.

42 Tamati-Quennell quoted in Hakiwai, *He mana taonga*, 140. For a more recent account, see Te Papa blog, http://blog.tepapa.govt.nz/2016/04/07/indigenous-art-curatorial-practice-ideas-and-observations/. Accessed 15 September 2016. See also A. Sciascia, 'Iwi Exhibitions at Te Papa: A Ngai Tahu Perspective' (Master's dissertation Museum and Heritage Studies, Wellington: Victoria University, 2011).

43 M. Alivizatou, 'From Artefacts to Communities: Participation and Contestation at Te Papa Tongarewa', in M. Alivizatou (ed.), *Intangible Heritage and the Museum: New Perspectives on Cultural Preservation* (Walnut Creek, CA: Left Coast Press, 2012), pp. 60–1.

44 See Mallon, Chapter 17 below.

45 Te Awahou Nieuw Stroom website, www.tans.org.nz/. Accessed 20 October 2016.

46 The term *mana whenua*, in this case the local iwi (tribe) in this specific location (Ngāti Raukawa ki te Tonga), is distinguished from the more general *tangata whenua* (people of the land) which usually refers to Māori people as a whole.

47 Sissons, *First Peoples*, 11.

48 Schorch, McCarthy and Hakiwai, 'Globalizing Māori Museology'.

49 Lindsay, *Taonga Maori Conference*.

50 Mead in Lindsay, *Taonga Maori Conference*, 164–9.

51 *Ibid.*, 9–10.

52 *Ibid.*, 7.

53 P. Schorch and N. Kahanu, 'Forum as Laboratory: The Cross-Cultural Infrastructure of Ethnographic Knowledge and Material Potentialities', in *Prinzip Labor: Museumsexperimente im Humboldt Lab Dahlem* (Berlin: Nicolai, 2015), pp. 241–8.

54 Conal McCarthy and Philipp Schorch, interview with Awhina Tamarapa, Victoria University, Wellington, 5 July 2016.

Curating the uncommons: taking care of difference in museums

14

Billie Lythberg, Wayne Ngata and Amiria Salmond

This chapter considers approaches to 'curating the uncommons' carried out by and with the Māori tribal arts management group Toi Hauiti and with Paikea, a carved wooden ancestor figure of the Te Aitanga a Hauiti *iwi* (tribe). It focuses on the 'uncommon' qualities of *taonga* (Māori treasures) such as Paikea, and the way Toi Hauiti are inflecting curatorial practice with their own distinctive *whakapapa* or heritage.

'Toi Hauiti' literally means Hauiti Arts, Hauiti being the eponymous ancestor of the Te Aitanga a Hauiti people of Ūawa-Tolaga Bay in Aotearoa New Zealand. Established in 1999, Toi Hauiti is a collective of tribal artists who create, initiate and manage art projects and activities with a view to building and reinforcing tribal awareness and expression of their cultural knowledge. Over this period, they have developed constructive working relationships with a range of academic and cultural institutions within Aotearoa New Zealand and internationally. The knowledge framework of Toi Hauiti is built on the premise of articulating and applying ancestral Hauiti – and more generally Māori – knowledge in modern situations. Their work has encompassed a range of activities including the mounting of local exhibitions as well as museum-based education and research, and also extends well beyond the traditional heritage sphere into a wide-ranging programme of cultural and artistic revitalisation that has attracted international attention for their skilful interweaving of innovative technological experimentation with the meeting of community responsibilities and needs. In this sense, Toi Hauiti's activities are curatorial in the earliest meaning of the concept 'to curate' as pastoral care.[1]

Through their mobilisation of whakapapa, the group's initiatives may be seen to challenge some of the ways that multiculturalist discourses have helped domesticate difference by making it fit into predetermined categories, not least those we are accustomed to thinking of as cultures.[2] Such ways of conceiving relations within and between groups of people – common to anthropology and museums, as well as to liberal democratic regimes of governance – assert that differences are relatively superficial in the sense that our cultures overlie a fundamental and universal sameness. Museums showcasing so-called cultural artefacts have thus helped domesticate difference by promoting world-making visions of (natural) unity in (cultural) diversity. We are all human after all, one in our shared biological heritage as *Homo sapiens*. In light of this fundamental sameness, whatever differences may arise between us are manageable and resolvable within a single scale, since attributes like our common capacity for language (which separates us from other species) guarantee the possibility of mutual understanding.

Yet some 'things' within museums resist these strategies of domestication. In 2013, members of Toi Hauiti made a week-long curatorial visit to one such 'artefact', their ancestor Paikea, at the American Museum of Natural History (AMNH) in New York, USA. There, they shared his story and their connection to him with the museum's curators, collections managers and educators. Through these interactions and a series of performative workshops with the museumgoing public,[3] they established his presence and rights as an ancestor.

Toi Hauiti's visit, discussed below, brought to the fore the living relational fabric in which Paikea endures as an integral nexus, acting as a catalyst for his figure to be taken care of differently by AMNH staff, and paving the way for further visits by his descendants. Four years later it is still possible to discern the curatorial hand of Toi Hauiti in how Paikea is perceived and cared for in New York, gently but persistently asserting that he exceeds the multicultural categories designed to contain him; that his figure, and the dynamic matrices of whakapapa of which it is part, oblige thought and handling beyond the usual requirements of contemporary curatorial practice.[4]

Multicultural discourse and the new museology

Discourses of multicultural diversity (including biculturalism and other culture-based thinking) of course emerged for important reasons – not least to counter earlier theories of racial superiority, which held that differences between peoples could be correlated hierarchically to absolute measures of intelligence, adaptability and physiological advantage. Multiculturalism has played a critical role in despatching such theories to the realms of pseudo-science, and in effecting some legal and moral improvements in the treatment of minority and colonised peoples within former imperial powers and in former colonies. It has also been mobilised by minorities and by colonised peoples themselves as tools in struggles for sovereignty and self-determination – having a distinct culture has been a powerful way in which Indigenous peoples, for instance, have been able to assert rights and the acknowledgement of wrongs suffered under colonisation.[5]

Yet, as Indigenous scholars[6] and theorists like Elizabeth Povinelli have pointed out, multiculturalist policies have at the same time served as powerful strategies of commensuration deployed to smooth out distinctions between groups to the advantage of ruling elites.[7] In defining certain kinds of difference as 'cultural' (as opposed to, say, political), multiculturalism mobilises a powerful ontology of sameness that can be used to dismiss those who insist on the fundamental importance of things that might exceed its realms of possibility as radicals or fanatics, thus banishing differences it finds unpalatable to the realms of extremism, even madness. On a more prosaic level, multiculturalism is frequently deployed in disputes to relegate certain kinds of views seen to clash with others as 'merely cultural' (as in 'well it might be wrong according to their culture to lay a pipeline or highway across this land but in my culture it's quite acceptable'). There is also a thriving industry of cultural commentators (particularly active in the Pacific) who continue to explain away certain kinds of claims made by present-day Indigenous peoples as aspects of 'invented' (or 'creatively imagined') cultural traditions – because obviously (the story goes) a mountain like Mauna Kea in Hawai'i, for instance, or a wooden figure like Paikea in New York, cannot *really* be an ancestor.[8]

Museums have been seeking for a number of decades to transform themselves from monuments of imperial power into cross-cultural 'contact zones' that can help us all to understand each other better and generally get along.[9] In some ways they have led the charge of multiculturalism across Europe's former empires, in a sort of pattern of reverse intellectual colonisation, from the so-called settler colonies of Canada, Aotearoa New Zealand and Australia, as well as the USA, back to the former imperial centres. In particular, it seems that national museums in those places – as spaces dedicated to culture – were among the first government institutions to fully implement liberal democratic state-sponsored multiculturalism, beginning in the 1970s and 1980s.[10] And if the earliest museums to adopt strongly multiculturalist policies and administrative structures were outside Europe, then it is at least partly through the influence of curatorial practice in those regions (and of individual curators from there) that such policies have taken off more recently in Britain and on the European continent.[11]

Again, the implementation of multiculturalist policies and structures in museums was achieved partly as an important corrective to earlier regimes that were hierarchical and unbalanced in the treatment meted out to different peoples. As public educational institutions, museums delivered effectively for over a century on their mandate to instruct citizens in the correct order of things, not least on who were the planet's best and most deserving denizens, a status asserted three-dimensionally in evolutionary displays underlining essential differences (biological, technological and cultural) between 'primitive' and 'civilised' races. And, as over three decades of Foucauldian scholarship continues to remind us, the linguistic turn in museums that brought 'many voices' and 'diverse stories' in to break up such hegemonic master narratives was above all intended as a means of democratising museums and opening their doors to diverse groups of people.[12] On multiple measures and indicators it has succeeded; many museums today are utterly different, far more welcoming and accommodating places to different constituencies than the imperial temples of the past.

Yet, as much recent research is showing, the advent of the 'New Museology' did not after all prove a panacea for the still often strained relations between museums and many of the people(s) whose treasures they store and exhibit. Well-intentioned efforts to invite Indigenous and minority groups to participate in exhibitions, object cataloguing and outreach activities often have great results; they also sometimes backfire, leaving museum staff and participants alike nursing dashed expectations and diminished *mana* (status, prestige, credibility); even where goodwill is evident, unanticipated differences can lead people to talk past each other. Where museums have actually employed members of Indigenous and minority communities they appear to have had more consistent successes, but even then the difficulties faced, for example, by New Zealand Māori curators in regional museums who are required to mediate disputes between local tribal factions, show that some differences overflow those envisaged by multicultural or bicultural management strategies.[13] These are people at the coalface of what we are calling 'taking care of difference' in museums, and the ways of working they are actively developing often draw on repertoires of expertise that far exceed definitions like 'cultural'. For this reason, some of the most interesting theories and methods for taking care of difference – ones that offer promising alternatives to multiculturalist approaches – are currently emerging from the field of Indigenous curation, whether in locally managed tribal cultural centres or in 'mainstream' regional and national museums.[14]

The curatorial practice of Toi Hauiti

The authors of this chapter have collaborated for more than a decade on a series of ongoing projects involving museums and Toi Hauiti, initiatives designed to benefit Te Aitanga a Hauiti alongside the heritage and academic institutions with which they work.[15] Toi Hauiti's curatorial practice – like their work in general – is innovative in combining cutting-edge technologies with an approach defined, above all, according to principles of whakapapa (glossed as genealogy).[16] Pioneers in developing digital solutions that deliver on tribal aspirations, they invented the 'tele-*tangi*' to allow far-flung relatives to participate in mourning for deceased tribal members by broadcasting *tangihanga* (funerals) live over the Internet and enabling instant message-based interaction with those gathered at Ūawa (Tolaga Bay, East Coast).[17] Since 2000, a focus of their projects has been to reunite tribal treasures, digitally and materially, so that people living in Ūawa and beyond can learn about, come into contact with and be inspired by their ancestral heritage. They have worked with and in Auckland War Memorial Museum, Museum of New Zealand Te Papa Tongarewa, and Tairāwhiti Museum, all in Aotearoa New Zealand; and, further afield, Cambridge University's Museum of Archaeology and Anthropology, the British Museum, the Hancock Museum (part of Newcastle's Great North

Museum) in the UK, Museum der Universität Tübingen, Germany, Florence's Muzeo Nazionale di Antropologia ed Etnologia, Italy, and the American Museum of Natural History in New York, USA.

In dealing with museums and other institutions Toi Hauiti present themselves as the living faces of particular ancestors, rather than as representatives of a generic Māori culture. This whakapapa orientation informs every aspect of their negotiations and educational engagements, and sometimes unsettles curatorial assumptions about what it means to take care of difference in museums. For, while whakapapa is typically translated as 'genealogy' (so that to whakapapa back to eponymous ancestor Hauiti, for example, is to claim a cognatic relationship of descent from him), whakapapa is at the same time Toi Hauiti's 'fundamental relationship manager and enabler' in a more general sense.[18] Far from merely defining interpersonal and intergenerational ties between Hauiti's descendants, it is an all-encompassing methodology that gives form and direction to every aspect of life, including dealings with natural phenomena, the sacred and the spiritual, and realms of thought, philosophy and ideas. Toi Hauiti's way of approaching museums that house their taonga is thus as much informed by principles of whakapapa as are their experiments with digital technology or their practice of ritual encounters on *marae* (meeting areas, focal points of engagement with others). Every aspect of their *kaupapa* (their project and purpose, *raison d'être*) is dedicated to the continued flourishing and ongoing generative existence of Hauiti's legacy.

Up until Wayne Ngata's appointment as Head of Mātauranga Māori at Te Papa Tongarewa, New Zealand's national museum, Toi Hauiti had mainly worked collaboratively with museums rather than inside them.[19] While the group's earlier plans anticipated the building of a multifunctional arts, museum, information and technology centre at Ūawa, this 'bricks and mortar' approach is currently on hold due to the high level of resourcing such a facility would demand. Since many of their most important ancestral taonga are in museums that are unlikely – at least in the foreseeable future – to release them, furthermore, Toi Hauiti resolved in the first instance to pursue digital solutions to repatriation alongside a strategy of cultivating face-to-face relations with their taonga and the people who now care for them. In service of this, as project partners on the Artefacts of Encounter project based at Cambridge University's Museum of Archaeology and Anthropology (2010–2013), and through Te Ataakura, a project led by Ngata and funded by University of Auckland research institute Ngā Pae o te Māramatanga (2010–2012), [20] the group has worked together with anthropologists, art historians and technical experts to develop a digital research network called Te Rauata, to house their taonga in digital form and to repatriate the knowledge thus instantiated. Their commitment to this strategy, combined with regular trips by iwi members to visit, greet and study particular ancestral treasures overseas, has enabled the group to successfully establish and develop mutually beneficial relationships with the current caretakers of some of their most highly valued taonga.

Taonga

Taonga is an old Māori concept that has been translated as: 'a treasure, something precious; hence an object of good or value. The object or end valued may be tangible or intangible; material or spiritual.'[21] The broad range of things that may be considered taonga means that the term offers an insightful lens onto concepts of cultural and intellectual property.[22] While they are often thought of as objects of the kind found in museums, such as Paikea at the AMNH, Te Aitanga a Hauiti's taonga include images, video footage, sound files and documents, both historical and contemporary, relating to their whakapapa (genealogies and oral histories); their traditional arts of *karakia* (ritual incantations), *haka* (performing arts), and *mōteatea* (chants and songs); as well as *tā moko* (tattoo), *whakairo* (carving), *whatu* (weaving) and *raranga* (basketry), all of which are incorporated in Te Rauata, their digital system, and all of which may instantiate ancestral presence.

Taonga are uncommon things in the sense of being unusual or not quotidian, and also in the sense of not being held in common – according to Toi Hauiti, they appear as taonga only within certain relationally defined perspectives. There is a tendency nowadays to use the term 'taonga' indiscriminately – any cloak, carving or greenstone pendant can apparently be described as a taonga, regardless of its history, its whakapapa (lineage) or meaning. For people in Hauiti, however, the taonga-ness of an object, digital or otherwise, is determined by the quality of its relationships, so that something that to one person might appear as 'just an artefact' could be a taonga to someone who knows and/or is part of its history and kinship networks. Artefacts that have become detached from their stories and whakapapa are only potential taonga until these connections are reanimated and the object is restored as the living face of those relationships.[23]

As such, taonga demand particular modes of attention and care. In working with Hauiti and their taonga we have found ourselves and our roles defined by forms of relational subjectivity (whakapapa) that both encompass and exceed the kinds of rights conventionally associated with intellectual property and creative authorship, which might otherwise govern what an anthropologist or curator might make out of taonga conceptually. The taonga of Te Aitanga a Hauiti are uncommon in the way they resist appropriation (intellectual and otherwise); they cannot be extracted from the relations within which they emerge – and which they help constitute – without effectively ceasing to exist as Hauiti taonga. Attention to such uncommon things as taonga thus raises different questions of different subjects; their refusal to behave objectively elicits relational forms (not-quite-subjects-nor-objects) that are not always expected. In this sense taonga can open up anthropology, curatorial practice, and other disciplines to differences other than those they already anticipate: unexpected modes of creativity; other truths or politics; different (kinds of) relations among different (kinds of) people and things.

The challenges of working within a dynamic, whakapapa-defined relational fabric became particularly evident in our work together to create the digital system Te Rauata. Toi Hauiti made clear from the outset that, unlike museum collection management systems which are decidedly *object-centric*, Te Rauata's ontology would be driven by a different, *relationship-centric*, complex set of protocols and practices. Everything within Te Rauata would emerge from the genealogies and oral histories that weave together Te Ao Hauiti (the Te Aitanga a Hauiti 'world'). Whereas museum content management systems often contain objects in digital form about which little is known and to which nothing else can be related, Te Rauata does not. Everything in Te Rauata is *already related* to Te Aitanga a Hauiti people and their taonga via whakapapa on a formal basis, prior to entering the system. A similar approach is taken to reconnecting with taonga face-to-face. Tracking down their artefacts like the figure of Paikea in museum collections and working out and through relationships of whakapapa prior to such visits is one way in which Toi Hauiti goes about reclaiming a knowledge base that allows each Hauiti descendant to 'know [themselves] so [they] can get on with life'.[24]

Paikea

Paikea is an enigmatic and important ancestor for the tribes of the eastern seaboard of Aotearoa New Zealand's North Island, including Te Aitanga a Hauiti. Popularly referred to as The Whale Rider, and immortalised in a book and film of that name,[25] according to oral narratives Paikea was a man and a whale, and a great commander of the realm of the sea. Attacked by his brother whilst out on a fishing trip, Paikea escaped certain death by calling to his living ancestors, the whales, who aided his journey from the coastal waters of the Māori ancestral homeland of Hawaiki to Aotearoa New Zealand. As an ancestor, himself – in both human and whale form – he is the subject of chants and action songs that continue to be regularly performed to acknowledge and strengthen living connections with and between his descendants.

Paikea simultaneously appears in the form of several carved wooden gable figures that are or have been mounted on particular tribal meeting houses, past and present, on the East Coast of Aotearoa New Zealand's North Island. The Paikea with which we are concerned here was earlier mounted on the ancestor-house Te Kani a Takirau that stood in Ūawa (Tolaga Bay) (Figure 14.1), named after one of the last *ūpoko ariki* (high chiefs) of the East Coast region, a descendant of several of Hauiti's senior lines, who lived from c. 1790 to 1856.[26] Erected in 1880, Te Kani a Takirau was dismantled in the early twentieth century and the house's carvings – including Paikea – and *tukutuku* (woven latticework panels) were acquired by European collectors and taken overseas, some surviving today in museums in Aotearoa New Zealand, Britain and North America. A series

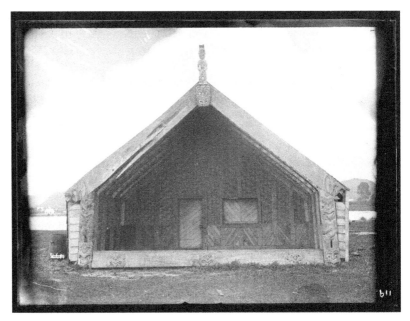

14.1 Paikea on the apex of the meeting house Te Kani a Takirau, Aotearoa New Zealand Photo by Augustus Hamilton.

of Toi Hauiti-led projects has been dedicated over the last decade to locating these taonga, building relationships with their present-day custodians, incorporating them into Te Rauata and planning for the full-scale digital – and perhaps, one day, physical – return to Ūawa of Te Kani a Takirau in its entirety.

Paikea the *tekoteko* or gable figure from Te Kani a Takirau currently resides at the American Museum of Natural History as a carved wooden object (80.0 / 615) and as an entry in the Museum's online Anthropology Collections Database, in which aspect he is regarded as a digital taonga.[27] In his wooden form he arrived in the USA via England in 1908 via the collecting practices of Major-General Horatio Robley, best known for his interest in *moko*, the distinctive Māori facial tattoo, an example of which Paikea wears so prominently. Such is the importance of Paikea the figure in New York that East Coast children are said to be 'born' performing a *haka* (action song) composed for him that instantiates potent meaning amongst his descendants even in the absence of the tekoteko itself.[28]

Uia mai koia whakahuatia ake	Ask and you will be told
Ko wai te whare nei e?	What is the name of this house?
Ko Te Kani[29]	It is Te Kani
Ko wai te tekoteko kei runga?	And who is the sentinel on top?
Ko Paikea! Ko Paikea!	It is Paikea! It is Paikea!

This is the first stanza of the haka with which fifteen members of Toi Hauiti greeted Paikea face-to-face in New York, on a bright autumn day in

April 2013, some one hundred and five years after he left Ūawa. Newly mounted on a plinth for the occasion, Paikea was wheeled through a door towards Toi Hauiti by collections management staff of the museum, who then withdrew to effect a handover of their ancestor to some of the Hauiti men. Months of digital communications, aspirations and assumptions were brought into sharp relief in the pivotal moment when Paikea was given over, albeit temporarily, to the care of his kin.[30] Able, finally, to perform the haka in the presence of Paikea, one of the teenagers later commented, 'It was like my whole life finally made sense!';[31] a literal reclaiming of the knowledge Paikea instantiates for Hauiti descendants.

Following this haka, Toi Hauiti approached the wooden figure. Some gently caressed his face and shoulders, while others boldly placed their forehead and nose to Paikea's to share breath through the Māori greeting known as *hongi* (Figure 14.2). Sung to, touched, and sharing *hau*, the breath of life with his descendants, the tekoteko became, once again, the activated presence of Paikea the ancestor. In this moment and for the week that followed, Paikea was a face of *te hunga mate*, the deceased. It was vital that those past ancestors be acknowledged and greeted by their descendants through haka, formal address, conversation, tears and touch. As Lythberg, Newell and Ngata explain (emphasis added),

> The genealogy, the life force (*mauri*) and the stories that are attached to taonga are what draw their descendants to engage with them. To touch, to talk with, to cry over, to reconnect with them; these are important facets of cultural behaviour, and in fact all human behaviour. *These behaviours make the object a taonga, they bring it back to life, and in doing so, bring life to the descendants of those taonga.*[32]

In other words, the activation of Paikea by his descendants was a curatorial act; an act of pastoral care with life-giving ramifications. In the days that followed, Paikea was greeted each morning, talked to, embraced, lifted gently on and off stage for public performances, and shaken by stirring renditions of his haka (Figure 14.3), then carefully and somewhat reluctantly returned to the anthropology stores each afternoon. Had they been allowed, his relatives would have slept alongside him, as *tūpāpaku*, the bodies of deceased persons, are treated during *tangihanga* or mourning ceremonies on marae. Aside from this restriction, throughout proceedings, as Paikea and his descendants revitalised their relationships and cared for one another, the AMNH staff maintained a discreet background presence, not dictating whether or how the figure was to be handled. This was an uncommon situation, brought about by an uncommon thing.

That staff at a national institution would let visitors caress and weep over artefacts in their collection is a result of some fundamental shifts in mainstream museum practice that in countries like the USA, Canada and Aotearoa New Zealand have been unfolding over several decades. For example, the British Museum and Cambridge University Museum of Archaeology and Anthropology in the UK, have on a number of recent

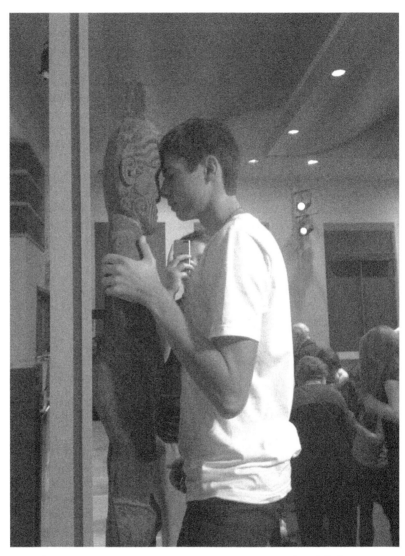

14.2 Owen Wharekaponga Rayner shares a hongi (greeting) with Paikea, American Museum of Natural History, New York, USA.

occasions allowed eighteenth-century Polynesian musical instruments and weapons to be played and ceremonially brandished by contemporary practitioners;[33] similarly, some American museums now have dedicated smudge rooms for Native American purification practices; and museums in Aotearoa New Zealand often have water available for cleansing after exposure to potent artefacts. Such developments have to a large extent been enabled and encouraged by multiculturalist theory and policy. Yet, taking care of difference is done differently in different museums and by different kin groups, and in its 'doing' yields results that can confound multicul-

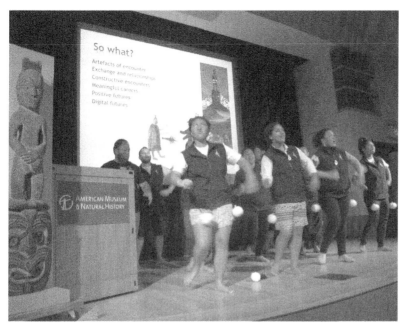

14.3 The Toi Hauiti group perform Paikea's haka (posture dance). American Museum of Natural History, New York, USA.

turalist expectations. An understanding of how Māori might generically respond to taonga within museum environs – popularised within America in the 1980s for instance by the touring exhibition *Te Maori* – is complicated by nuances and particularities of taonga and whakapapa that are not necessarily anticipated or admitted by culturally informed curatorial practice.

When Toi Hauiti encounter Māori things that are not Te Aitanga a Hauiti things, for example, these are carefully handled just long enough for physical observations to be made. Photographs are taken and descriptions are written to be shared with people for whom these might indeed be ancestral taonga. There is no haka for such things; no tears are shed; in short, no reconnection is made since these are neither taonga nor ancestors of Te Aitanga a Hauiti people.

In our work together, we have observed that wherever such quotidian reactions are elicited by the things carefully laid out for Toi Hauiti to view there is a sense that the curators and other museum staff are somewhat relieved but also mildly disappointed that this is not the day on which their collection will inspire the kinds of deeply moving responses that their own efforts to take care of difference have anticipated and possibly even desired.

In New York, the various ways in which relationships with Paikea might be actualised and revitalised – which had been discussed beforehand via email and in Skype conversations between museum staff, Hauiti members and the anthropologists with whom they work – played out over a full week, and were made explicit in presentations by Hauiti to groups of American schoolchildren and their parents. Beyond introducing audiences to Paikea and not only impressing them with but also teaching them the haka and action songs composed and sung for him, Toi Hauiti skilfully recruited their audiences into the enactment of the whakapapa meshwork animated by Paikea as a living face of Hauiti relationships.

Volunteers from the audience were paired with Toi Hauiti members to learn the names of antecedents that link Te Aitanga a Hauiti – the progeny of Hauiti – to their eponymous ancestor, including Paikea himself and Te Kani a Takirau, the chief whose house gable Paikea adorned. Lined up on the stairs of the Museum auditorium and shouting out their names in order of descent, the audiences in New York themselves enlivened the whakapapa of Paikea and Hauiti.

At the conclusion of their week in New York, Toi Hauiti bid Paikea farewell with further words, songs, tears and caresses, and by placing a special pendant around the figure's neck. Carved from a whale's tooth, it had been especially made for Paikea – the man, the whale and the figure – and worn by one of the Hauiti men throughout the visit.

Significantly, prior to Toi Hauiti's visit, Paikea had been stored on his back on a shelf in the museum stores, tucked away from sight, his own line of vision focused on the shelf above him. When it was known that his kin were coming and had asked to give performances with him, negotiations began which culminated in his being mounted upright on a plinth, and placed on castors for easy mobility. Toi Hauiti's curatorial approach to Paikea required that he be properly introduced to his community in New York. Just as it was vital that Toi Hauiti be allowed to care for – to curate – Paikea whilst in his presence, so too was it vital that he be upright, mobile and secure in order for their curatorial plans to proceed.

The impact that a week spent with Paikea and Toi Hauiti had on his New York caretakers crystallised in the museum's decision to return him to the stores mounted in this way, leaving him permanently upright in order – among other things – to receive subsequent visitors. It appeared that his presence and perhaps even his personhood had been acknowledged in a way that was not addressed whilst he lay prone and shelved. Thanks to the curatorial acts of his kin, in other words, Paikea seemed to have been recognised and treated by museum staff as not a mere object in storage but as an ancestor to whom visits would continue to be made and gifts would be given; he was being taken care of as an uncommon thing.

Imagine the museum curator's disappointment, then, when upon returning to her office the week after Toi Hauiti's departure, she found the pendant on her desk along with a note from a collections manager explaining that it could not remain in the stores without being formally accessioned. Towards actioning the accession process the note also asked what the pendant was made from. Following subsequent, somewhat awkward communications with Paikea's descendants, the gifting of the whale tooth pendant was deemed to breach the Convention on International Trade in

Endangered Species of Wild Fauna and Flora (CITES), an international treaty drawn up in 1973 to ensure that international trade in specimens of vulnerable wild animals and plants (including whales) does not threaten their survival.[34] Paikea, despite his apparently acknowledged personhood, despite his being an ancestor who was also a whale, was not permitted to keep the pendant gifted to him by his descendants.

The pendant has since been returned to its maker. In accordance with CITES, it was placed around the neck of another of Paikea's descendants who came to visit him at AMNH, and worn home on a flight to Aotearoa New Zealand. Negotiations are still under way to secure CITES authorisation for its return to Paikea, and alongside these discussions a conversation has developed between Toi Hauiti and museum staff about Paikea himself and his rights, as an ancestor and a living face of Te Aitanga a Hauiti and other East Coast iwi, to receive and retain gifts that are his due, if not easily accommodated by international treaties. These ongoing exchanges are generating new insights into uncommon things – not-quite-subjects-nor-objects – and how best to take care of difference in museums.

Conclusion

In New York, Paikea remains as a cultural ambassador for Te Aitanga a Hauiti and other East Coast iwi – what Toi Hauiti refer to only half-jokingly as a 'globally positioned resource'. Still mounted on his plinth so as to move more freely from one vantage point to another within the anthropology stores, he is well known to the collections management team and curatorial staff who now regularly accommodate requests from his descendants to spend time with him. His visitors include first-time and repeat visitors to New York, and his presence is sought in times of joy as well as sadness. On at least one occasion he has cared for the recently bereaved; a descendant unable to return home for a tangihanga who instead found a family member in New York (Paikea) with whom to grieve. Such is his uncommon presence in the stores that – unlike other artefacts – it seems preferable for him to remain off-display and able to be touched by his visitors rather than on display and locked behind glass. Indeed, some of those who have been working with him now consider the stores to be his *whare* (house), and imagine Paikea the tekoteko surmounting the apex of the museum's grand entrance on Central Park West, now not only the figurehead of Te Kani a Takirau but also of a new embassy for his descendants.

Exemplifying what can be achieved when Indigenous people interpret their own culture or curate their uncommons or take care of difference within museums, Paikea also raises questions about what taonga and other artefacts might be or become and the kinds of possibilities they can open when alternative ways of relating things and people – for instance through whakapapa – assert themselves. In considering such different approaches to curating the uncommons and taking care of difference in museums we are interested in the varied kinds of relationships Paikea elicits; whereas he relates to his people first and foremost as an ancestor (in human and whale form), to the Museum's curatorial, conservation and collections teams he remains primarily an artefact. At the same time, however, repeat visits by his descendants are challenging this latter conception in ways that are affecting both his categorisation and his care within this institution.

Quite deliberately, then, the strategies employed by Toi Hauiti to curate their taonga in digital and material form, within and beyond Ūawa, raise at least as many questions as they answer. How does taking care of difference in museums reveal the limitations of multicultural discourse and its projects of domestication? What might museum collection management systems gain from an understanding of the workings of Te Rauata, Toi Hauiti's digital artefact system? What are the implications of the expansive, generative qualities of whakapapa for the categories usually relied upon to classify and contain artefacts within museums? In New York, how are Te Aitanga a Hauiti concepts driving and problematising the way Paikea is understood and cared for at AMNH as not-quite-subject-nor-object? What pressures might his presence as an ancestor who receives visitors and gifts place on museum staff and resources, and for how long will these be accommodated? Put another way, might the day conceivably arise when Paikea and his visitors are deemed too uncommon a presence in the museum stores; when this ancestral figure and his entanglement in a relational fabric defined by whakapapa so far exceed the multicultural categories designed to contain him that his physical return to Ūawa is desired by the museum itself? And might his descendants resist this repatriation, preferring instead to keep AMNH within the expansive reach of their whakapapa? Might this, in fact, be Curatopia?[35]

Acknowledgements

The authors thank Toi Hauiti; staff at the American Museum of Natural History who have facilitated visits to Paikea with warmth, enthusiasm and curiosity, especially former AMNH curator Jennifer Newell; and this volume's editors whose wise counsel assisted greatly in the preparation of this chapter.

Notes

1 On this point see Clifford, Chapter 7 above.
2 A. Henare [Salmond], M. Holbraad and S. Wastell (eds), *Thinking through Things: Theorising Artefacts Ethnographically* (Oxford: Routledge, 2007); A. Salmond, 'Transforming Translations (Part II): Addressing Ontological Alterity', *Hau: Journal of Ethnographic Theory*, 4:1 (2014), 155–87.

3 For a full account of this visit and its educational strategies see B. Lythberg, J.Newell and W. Ngata, 'Houses of Stories: The Whale Rider at the American Museum of Natural History', *Museum and Society*, special issue 'Museum education today: synergies and innovations in multicultural contexts', 13:2 (2015), 195–220.

4 We do not mean to suggest that Paikea's figure is a mere pawn in the schemes of people, rather than (at least partially) driving the process himself. This point may easily be lost on those unaccustomed to regarding people like Toi Hauiti as the living face of ancestors; most of whom would be inclined to understand the process in terms of present-day strategic social constructions or cultural inventiveness, applied to an obviously inert material object. There is a difference, we mean to suggest, between a taonga-in-potentia on one hand and an empty vessel animated through human social interaction on the other.

5 B. Bönish-Brednich and R. Hill, 'Fitting Aotearoa into New Zealand: Politico-Cultural Change in a Modern Bicultural Nation', in M. Berg and B. Schaeffer (eds), *Historical Justice in International Perspective: How Societies Are Trying to Right the Wrongs of the Past* (Washington, DC, and Cambridge: German Historical Institute and Cambridge University Press, 2009), pp. 239–63.

6 For Māori and North American examples, see C. Allen, *Blood Narrative: Indigenous Identity in American Indian and Maori Literary and Activist Texts* (Durham, NC: Duke University Press, 2002), pp. 110–13; for a range of critical Māori curatorial perspectives on multiculturalism and biculturalism, see C. McCarthy, *Museums and Māori: Heritage Professionals, Indigenous Collections, Current Practice* (Wellington: Te Papa Press, 2011), especially ch. 8, 'Biculturalism and Its Discontents'.

7 E. Povinelli, 'Radical Worlds: The Anthropology of Incommensurability and Inconceivability', *Annual Review of Anthropology*, 30 (2001), 319–34, and E. Povinelli, *The Cunning of Recognition: Indigenous Alterities and the Making of Australian Multiculturalism* (Durham, NC: Duke University Press, 2002).

8 See for example B. Rousseau, 'In New Zealand, Lands and Rivers Can Be People (Legally Speaking)', *New York Times* (13 July 2016), www.nytimes.com/2016/07/14/world/what-in-the-world/in-new-zealand-lands-and-rivers-can-be-people-legally-speaking.html?_r=0. Accessed 15 January 2017. See also note 4 above on the status of Paikea.

9 J. Clifford, *Routes: Travel and Translation in the Late Twentieth Century* (Cambridge, MA, and London: Harvard University Press, 1997).

10 A. Henare [Salmond], *Museums, Anthropology and Imperial Exchange* (Cambridge: Cambridge University Press, 2005).

11 C. Durand, *Anthropology in a Glass Case: Indigeneity, Collaboration, and Artistic Practice in Museums* (Saarbrücken: VDM Verlag Dr Müller, 2010).

12 See for example R. Mason, 'Cultural Theory and Museum Studies', in S. Macdonald (ed.), *A Companion to Museum Studies* (Oxford: Blackwell, 2006), pp. 17–32.

13 McCarthy, *Museums and Māori*.

14 M.K. Dupreez, 'Eia Hawai`inuiākea: Reflections on the Protocol for the Opening of the *Pacific Encounters* Exhibition', *Journal of Museum Ethnography*, 21 (2009), 103–9; A. Hakiwai and H. Smith, *Toi Ora: Ancestral Māori Treasures* (Wellington: Te Papa Press, 2008); S. Mallon, 'Afterword', in McCarthy, *Museums and Māori*, pp. 248–53; McCarthy, *Museums and Māori*; P. Schorch and A. Hakiwai, 'Mana Taonga and the Public Sphere: A Dialogue between

Indigenous Practice and Western Theory', *International Journal of Cultural Studies*, 17:2 (2014), 191–205; P. Schorch and N.M.K.Y. Kahanu, 'Forum as Laboratory: The Cross-Cultural Infrastructure of Ethnographic Knowledge and Material Potentialities', in *Prinzip Labor: Museumsexperimente im Humboldt Lab Dahlem* (Berlin: Nicolai, 2015), pp. 241–8; P. Schorch and N.M.K.Y. Kahanu, 'Anthropology's Interlocutors: Hawai`I Speaking Back to Ethnographic Museums in Europe', *Zeitschrift für Kulturwissenschaften*, 1 (2015), 114–17; P. Schorch, C. McCarthy and A. Hakiwai, 'Globalizing Māori Museology: Reconceptualising Engagement, Knowledge and Virtuality through Mana Taonga', *Museum Anthropology*, 39:1 (2016), 48–69; C.F. Kreps, *Liberating Culture: Cross-Cultural Perspectives on Museums, Curation, and Heritage Preservation, Museum Meanings* (London and New York: Routledge, 2003); B. Onciul, 2013. 'Community Engagement, Curatorial Practice, and Museum Ethos in Alberta, Canada', in V. Golding and W. Modest (eds), *Museums and Communities: Curators, Collections and Collaboration* (London and New York: Bloomsbury, 2013), 79–109; see also Kahanu, Nepia and Schorch (Chapter 18 below), and McCarthy, Hakiwai and Schorch, Chapter 13 above.

15 As (former) Chair of Toi Hauiti, Ngata (at the time of writing the Head of Mātauranga Māori at the Museum of New Zealand Te Papa Tongarewa) has led a number of these projects and represented Toi Hauiti as one of the main research partners on other projects based in universities. Lythberg is a Pacific art historian who has been a researcher as well as face-to-face liaison between museums and Toi Hauiti on several projects. Salmond, formerly a senior curator at the Museum of Archaeology and Anthropology at the University of Cambridge, devised one of the projects while supporting others through consultation and research.

16 But see A. Salmond, 'Transforming Translations (Part I): "The Owner of These Bones"', *Hau Journal of Ethnographic Theory*, 3:3 (2013), 1–32; V. Walker, 'Te Aitanga a Hauiti and the Transit of Venus', *Journal of the Royal Society of New Zealand*, 42:2 (2012), 105–12.

17 W. Ngata, S. Ngata-Gibson and A. Salmond, 'Te Ataakura: Digital Taonga and Cultural Innovation', in A. Salmond and B. Lythberg (eds), *Digital Objects, Cultural Subjects* (proceedings of a workshop of the same name), special issue of the *Journal of Material Culture*, 17:3 (2012), 229–44.

18 Walker, 'Te Aitanga a Hauiti and the Transit of Venus', 106.

19 Prior to the establishment of Toi Hauiti in 1999, however, a number of members of Te Aitanga a Hauiti held museum positions in local and national museums. In the late 1980s, for instance, the Hauiti artist John Walsh was employed as Exhibitions Officer at Gisborne Museum (today the Tairāwhiti Museum), before being appointed as the first Curator of Māori Art at Te Papa. In the late 1990s Cynthia McCann was Museum Education Officer at Tairāwhiti Museum and Anne McGuire was Hauiti's representative on the Museum's Trust Board (David Butts, 'Maori and Museums: The Politics of Indigenous Recognition' (PhD thesis, Museum Studies, Massey University, 2003). Irihāpeti Walters (Auntie Bessie) was a kaiārahi (Māori guide) and then a kaitiaki (collection manager) at the national museum for many years, from as early as the late 1980s.

20 N. Thomas, J. Adams, B. Lythberg, M. Nuku and A. Salmond (eds), *Artefacts of Encounter: Cook's Voyages, Colonial Collecting and Museum Histories* (Dunedin and Cambridge: Otago University Press and Cambridge University Museum of Archaeology and Anthropology, 2016), http://maa.cam.ac.uk/aofe/, www.

maramatanga.ac.nz/project/te-ataakura-re-connecting-voyage-collections-archives-and-museums-through-creation-digital. B. Lythberg, C. Hogsden and W. Ngata, 'Relational Systems and Ancient Futures: Co-Creating a Digital Contact Network in Theory and Practice', in B. Onciul, S. Hawke and M. Stefano (eds), *Engaging Communities* (Heritage Matters series) (London: Boydell and Brewer, 2017).

21 Māori Marsden, *The Woven Universe*, ed. Te Ahukaramū Charles Royal (The Estate of Rev. Māori Marsden, 2003).

22 See also McCarthy, Hakiwai and Schorch, Chapter 13 above.

23 Ngata, Ngata-Gibson and Salmond, 'Te Ataakura', 14.

24 W. Ngata, 'Te Ataakura: Re-Connecting Voyage Collections in Archives and Museums through the Creation of Digital Taonga', presentation to Ngā Pae o te Māramatanga, 30 May 2012, http://mediacentre.maramatanga.ac.nz/content/digitisation-and-research-part-two-dr-wayne-ngata. Accessed 15 January 2017.

25 The Māori novelist Witi Ihimaera wrote *The Whale Rider* (1985), which was adapted into the very successful film of the same name by Niki Caro (2003).

26 V. Walker, 'Te Kani a Takirau – He Ariki' (MA Thesis, Massey University, 1997); Lythberg, Newell and Ngata, 'Houses of Stories', 198.

27 American Museum of Natural History, Anthropology Collections Database, www.amnh.org/our-research/anthropology/collections/database. Accessed 15 January 2017; B. Lythberg, 'The American Museum of Natural History Anthropology Database', *Journal of Museum Ethnography*, 26 (2013), 181–6.

28 Lythberg, Newell and Ngata, 'Houses of Stories', 201.

29 'Ko Whitireia' is also used as Paikea sits on the house *Whitireia* in Whāngārā, north of Gisborne, today.

30 Lythberg, Newell and Ngata, 'Houses of Stories', 205.

31 *Ibid.*

32 *Ibid.*, 201.

33 R. Raymond and A. Salmond (eds), *Pasifika Styles: Artists inside the Museum* (Cambridge and Dunedin: University of Cambridge Museum of Archaeology and Anthropology [MAA] and Otago University Press, 2008).

34 CITES website, www.cites.org/. Accessed 15 January 2017.

35 As this book goes to press the pendant has been returned to New York, with all international conventions satisfied, and accepted as a gift to Paikea by the American Museum of Natural History.

15 Collecting, curating and exhibiting cross-cultural material histories in a post-settler society

Bronwyn Labrum

Introduction: a history curator looks back (and forward)

This chapter is a 'think piece' about history curating in a postcolonial context through a focus on objects. My field is Aotearoa New Zealand, a former British colony in the South Pacific. I want to raise issues to do with *Pākehā* (European, non-Indigenous) curatorship in relation to, and also in contrast with, Indigenous collections and displays. I pose the questions: What does a twenty-first-century history curator look like in a society like Aotearoa New Zealand? Does the history curator continue the mutual asymmetry that has characterised relations between 'settler' and 'native', or is there a way to recognise cross-cultural material histories in collecting and exhibiting?

But first a word on the following slippery words: history, curator, post-settler and Pākehā. In this chapter, I problematise the notion of history *in* museums and the history *of* museums, which, somewhat ironically, lacks a specific *historical* analysis. 'History' is often left out of debates about museums which are dominated by studies of art, science and anthropology, and usually conducted through frameworks borrowed from social and cultural theory, among others, but not history. 'Curator' is a term we have puzzled over in the two seminars that led to this book, in which authors are again grappling with different and changing definitions, models and methods. As a historian and former history curator, and now someone who manages teams of curators, I see a curator as someone who works across the overlapping and interdependent fields of exhibitions, collections, writing and communication through public programmes and digital platforms. Yet in most of the literature, and certainly in the (now outdated) handful of books about history curatorship, this multifaceted role of concept development, assembly, interpretation, research and dissemination is virtually absent.[1] Attention is usually paid to either exhibitions *or* collections, not both, and little space is given to cross-cultural modes of working within social history.

What is also surprising is the low profile of history as a *discipline* in a multidisciplinary institution, as I show below. History struggles to make a place for itself in museums, standing in the shadows cast by the disciplines with more cultural or intellectual capital, and with more vociferous advocates within the community. As Larissa Förster and Friedrich von Bose argue (Chapter 3 above), different disciplines and institutions often do not talk to each other, and you could equally argue that, within a national or civic museum, even disciplines within the same institution do not talk to each other either. I am particularly concerned with this problem right now, as I have returned to work at the Museum of New Zealand Te Papa Tongarewa (Te Papa) to lead a team of history and Pacific cultures curators, after some years in the university system teaching and researching history, visual and material culture, and design.

One factor which contributes to the lower profile of history as a discipline is the historical amnesia of many museum staff who often do not know much about the recent past of the institution they work in; even history curators themselves may be ignorant of their histories. This can create further problems. Moreover, while the collections may be well documented, archived and interpreted, the records of the institution and, crucially, the records of past exhibitions are scanty and encourage presentism amongst curatorial staff. We seem to lack a historical consciousness: there does not appear to be a strong sense of historical change within Te Papa and its collection, and also the intersection with those material things which remain constant through all those changes. What may have been attempted in the past is not always remembered, nor what did not work and why. These issues are exacerbated in the current situation in which Te Papa is undergoing a whole-of-museum renewal, replacing all its long-term exhibitions, refreshing its collecting strategies and plans, and implementing a new digital strategy. Yet there is pressure on the new historical exhibitions, like the museum itself, to be 'future-focused'. The museum's one hundred and fiftieth anniversary in 2015 was barely recognised in the efforts to enact another 'new' museological revolution, just as the opening of Te Papa in 1998 in a new building with new exhibitions provided a startling incarnation of the 'new museology'.[2]

Another term to unpack is 'post-settler'. I refer to Aotearoa New Zealand as a post-settler society, which can be taken to mean a society after the settlement phase of colonisation, in which settlers renegotiate their relationship with the colonised people.[3] But I want to clarify that the 'post' in post-settler does not mean *after* in a chronological sense, but refers to the continuing conditions, as in my case study, of the phenomenon and the associated practices of settler colonialism within what is often called, somewhere inwardly, the 'British world'. As has been pointed out in this book, our language and vocabulary are left wanting as we try to describe the ambiguous situations we find ourselves in.

Finally, I want to explain the focus in this chapter on the non-Indigenous, on that complicated mixture of British settlers and later migrants which is referred to loosely today as Pākehā, New Zealand or Kiwi culture.[4] By Pākehā I mean white New Zealanders of European descent.

As will become clear in this chapter, I believe there has been, in the New Zealand context, a problematic separation of the two histories of Māori and Pākehā (or what is sometimes now called non-Māori, which incorporates recent non-white migrants), and its materialisation in museums. This is the perhaps unintended result of Māori sovereignty discourses, and the emergence of the philosophy of *mana taonga* in museums, amongst other issues.[5] The Pākehā response to this Indigenous assertiveness, a Māori Renaissance which has gained pace since the 1970s, is not unproductive. For example my team are now exploring how mana taonga applies to non-Māori material culture and community engagement, and this work may provide interesting models for museums who want to connect more with their diverse communities, audiences and publics.[6] However, the current separation of New Zealand society into Māori and Pākehā, based in part on the contemporary interpretation of the nation's founding document the Treaty of Waitangi (1840), is problematic, not least because it oversimplifies a history of mutual engagement and exchange. These New Zealand histories, in all their messy entanglements, and the curating of them, need to be mixed up much, much more. A fundamental reason for my argument is the extraordinary interaction apparent in New Zealand society then and now, quite distinctive in an international context, which belies the separation demanded by (post) colonial politics. The intermingled histories of Māori and Pākehā over the twentieth century, and the ways in which they are materialised in everyday objects, call for a particular kind of curator in the twenty-first century, a role I sketch out in the conclusion.

A history of history (and history curating)

I would like to begin with an overview of the characteristics of history curatorship. Here I am drawing on my published and ongoing research into the development of history as a discipline, and its parallel role in the arena of collections and exhibitions in museums.[7] It seems to me that the default model of current scholarship in museum studies, curatorial studies and other fields, is overwhelmingly focused on either anthropological collections and colonialism/postcolonialism; or art and its very particular concerns; or natural history and science.[8] There are examinations of the exhibition and collection of official histories of national institutions in the wake of contemporary debates about 'the nation', national anniversaries and the importance of official collective memory.[9] We can see this particularly in the huge five-year programme of centenary commemorations of the First World War going on right now in the former British world. The historical shaping of the modern museum is also a focus of much inquiry, but not always examined from a historical perspective. These studies privilege metropolitan centres and the experiences of the related developments of ethnology, anthropology, archaeology and art history or fine arts, which all stem from the late eighteenth and early to mid-nineteenth centuries.[10]

They take precedence over the formative period of the shaping of history as a museum discipline in the twentieth century. This manifested itself, interestingly, in a wide variety of styles, from period rooms to colonial streets, historic sites and geographical locations.[11] Yet many studies of museums appear to leap from the imperial/colonial period straight to the postmodern era, as the two key periods of change, with little sense of historical development in between. This academic analysis is also somewhat isolated from current professional practice in museums in which history curators grapple with everyday issues to do with collections, display, digital technology and public programmes.[12] The problem is, in other words, that history as history easily disappears from consideration.

The resulting invisibility of history in museums leads to the strange situation in which history curatorship lacks a framework of its own, let alone a historiography. I have been pondering this as I write with the curatorial teams at Te Papa the strategy documents for Pacific cultures and New Zealand history. What does it mean to be the national museum and the institution charged with telling national stories about our past, both as a set of Pacific Islands and as a former colonial power in the Pacific, with close and ongoing ties to former colonies? With a 150-year-old collection originally built on colonial and encyclopaedic museum principles – which has more silver, ceramics, dress and furniture than objects that materialise migration, growing super-diversity or urban experiences – how do we rationalise and focus a diverse 'catch-all' set of historical objects? How do we include contemporary Pasifika experiences within Aotearoa New Zealand,[13] whether in the rural South Island attached to rugby team franchises, or in Auckland, which claims to be the largest Polynesian city in the world? How can the global and local be collected and exhibited when they are so intertwined?

For a post-settler nation like Aotearoa New Zealand, part of the explanation for what has happened, and what has not happened, lies in more general historical developments and the very recent emergence of a sense of national history. History as a museum discipline is a twentieth-century phenomenon in Aotearoa New Zealand, more so particularly after the Second World War. The postwar period of the 1950s and 1960s, which, contrary to many stereotypes, was not only a time of conformity, drabness and turning inwards but also a time of variety, change and experimentation, demands a more critical and close investigation in relationship to museums. Very important patterns and changes were apparent at this time, decades before the larger shifts in museology and other cultural institutions of the late twentieth century (the 'new museology') which have received so much publicity and analysis. History, in this more specific sense, is most often considered in terms of history curatorship and in examinations of discrete objects and material culture, but is not always linked to broader historical narratives and people's sense, and uses, of the past.

Until quite recently New Zealand museums, along with those in other former British settler colonies, were devoted to natural history, ethnography or art rather than 'history' per se. There were very few non-Indigenous historical collections until the 1970s.[14] This reflected a narrow sense of national historical consciousness that began to change only after the Second World War. Pākehā New Zealanders were content to see themselves as 'better Britons of the South Pacific' and were late in discovering that they had a history at all.[15] Then in the late 1950s and 1960s, there was a cluster of crucial developments borne on a wave of cultural nationalism: the teaching of New Zealand history at universities; the establishment of The Historic Places Trust (the government-supported national heritage organisation); and the growth and reinvigoration of local historical societies. The sense of having an interesting, localised past that is worth representing and preserving in a museum had clearly come into being.[16]

As well as a lack of recognition of this history, other gaps in the existing literature include the connections between social history and regional or local histories, which are so intertwined with Indigenous histories, where many encounters are played out on the ground in specific local arenas, as other chapters in this volume show so clearly. In what follows I consider these issues in relation to the development of history in museums, specifically social history, along with the new category that I advocate, namely *material history*. This category of material history covers a broad range of things, including fashion and clothing, and design.

Case study: Te Awamutu Museum

The late emergence of history in museums, especially in regional rather than national institutions, is clearly seen in the example of Te Awamutu Museum in the Southern Waikato region in the North Island of Aotearoa New Zealand. This museum grew from the formation in 1935 of the Te Awamutu Historical Society, which aimed to 'collect specimens of ancient Maori weapons, implements, carvings, etc. with the idea of later forming a museum'.[17] Members assiduously recorded local Māori and Pākehā history and historical sites although the society went into recess during the Second World War. The collection kept growing and the museum opened on a part-time basis in 1954 (Figure 15.1). In the 1960s, an archaeological group was formed, the society began to publish a journal and members took part in community activities for the centenary of the Battle of Orākau in 1964, a major event in the war between Waikato Māori and government forces which took place not far from Te Awamutu. In 1967, the interior of the museum was completely reorganised.[18] Members felt it 'should confine itself to being a very good folk museum, telling only the history of its own district'.[19] While the 'collections illustrate the history of the district, Maori, Missionary, Waikato War and pioneering periods',[20] over half of the entire display space was devoted to 'Maori culture', and there were four cases devoted to the 'Colonial Exhibit'. Many displays had been cut drastically or removed completely, including 'large Boer War and World War' displays,

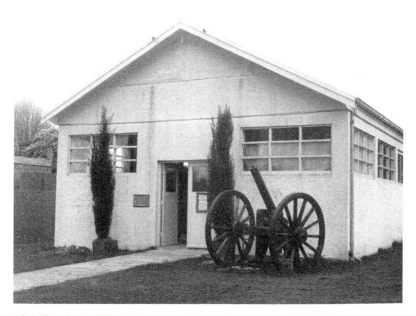

15.1 The Gavin Gifford Museum, which was later renamed the Te Awamutu Museum, Aotearoa New Zealand, in the 1950s. The gun wheel in the foreground signals the importance of the local military history to the institution and its collections.

'which attract very little local interest'.[21] By the 1970s, the Te Awamutu and District Museum was in a new building, which was still described as a local 'folk' museum, dedicated to 'preserving and demonstrating the history and cultural growth of the area'.[22] Its 'collections mainly related to Maori culture, Missions, Land Wars and the pioneer period of the district'.[23] The upper gallery was used for craft demonstrations, recitals and temporary exhibitions of photography, painting and carving.[24]

Today, the museum still has a Māori/settler focus, but also features displays of local contemporary popular culture (Figure 15.2). As the hometown of the Finn brothers, who led the internationally renowned pop bands Split Enz and Crowded House, one of its main attractions is the family piano and other memorabilia. Its current mission is to 'preserve and promote Waipa District's diverse culture, and its environmental and social heritage in order to engage, inform and inspire our community and visitors'.[25] An important part of this role is the provision of an archive, run by trained archivists rather than a local history society. Staff are now paid professionals, rather than volunteer amateurs, and their practices are in line with developments in New Zealand museums more generally.

This brief survey of collection and display at the Te Awamutu Museum reveals a rather more complex situation than is often recognised in the literature on museum history, history in museums and history curating. There

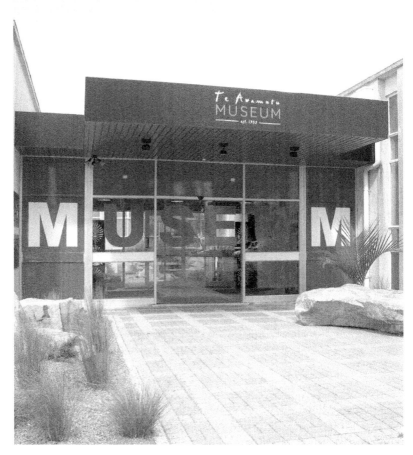

15.2 Currently, the Te Awamutu Museum, Aotearoa New Zealand, is in a purpose built building from the 1970s, situated next to the town library.

are conventional understandings of history and historical importance, with a strong emphasis on pioneering, war and politics. Yet we see here, in this post-settler context, a long-term interest in Māori culture and objects which are mixed up with Pākehā people and society.[26] This is in strong contrast to other colonial contexts in which the Indigenous are absent from museum collections, except as literally dead objects of ethnology and anthropology.[27] The historian Chris Hilliard has described this as a 'textual museum', the product of systematic and dedicated collecting and recording of both Māori and Pākehā ways of life within an ideology of rescue.[28] In this respect, the importance of Te Awamutu Museum's physical location, in terms of its proximity to past mission stations and battle sites, is crucial, as this historic heritage was literally all around the museum's staff and supporters.

This emphasis on history 'from below' showing the interaction of Māori and Pākehā, in contrast to the national museum as we see below, raises the question of what kind of curatorship was operating here. Presumably one that was attuned to the specificity of the local past and its material culture, and that responded to community interests and concerns, which have long been cross-cultural and reflected differences as well as similarities, and deviated as needed from an overarching or 'national' story. The extraordinary thing about this case study is that the Te Awamutu Museum did not even have curators as such until very recently, and the 'curatorial' work of researching, collecting and exhibiting was done by other staff and volunteers in a non-professionalised, but no less effective, way. The development of the professional role of history curator, like the notion of academic history, is a relatively recent phenomenon.

Curating Te Papa 1998

By the time New Zealand's national museum was being developed into what would become Te Papa, with an avowed focus on multidisciplinary displays, the curating and exhibiting of history looked very different. The form of this 'new' history was shaped by a range of factors familiar to those in other revamped national museums in Canada and Australia at this time: the wider political and social context, ideas about popular culture and new media, conceptual planning, budgets and marketing, an interest in personal stories and engaging interpretation for a mass audience.[29]

Te Papa claimed to be, in policy and practice, a 'bicultural' museum.[30] Since opening in 1998 it has had physically and conceptually distinct spaces for displaying Indigenous and non-Indigenous art, history and culture. On level four of the building, which houses galleries and displays of human culture, Pākehā (non-Indigenous) art, history and culture are on one side and Māori art, history and culture on the other. The two areas are separated by a wedge-shaped exhibition space in the middle devoted to a long-term display about the Treaty of Waitangi (Figure 15.3). Popular and academic comment on Te Papa at the time of opening and since has focused on the role and function of Indigenous history and the politics of art at the institution, as it continued the policy of the 1992 Act which combined the former National Museum and National Art Gallery. Yet much of the initial criticism during construction and establishment expressed anxiety about the representation of Pākehā history, although this has since abated and been overshadowed by the continuing complaints about the place of art.[31]

At Te Papa's opening, there was a suite of three interconnected history exhibitions. The noted historian Jock Phillips, the concept leader of the history team, had conceived them as being, in turn, about the stories and experiences associated with the arrival of Pākehā New Zealanders over time (migration); those associated with aspects of daily life (everyday experiences); and those associated with how New Zealanders saw themselves (identity). Consequently, *Passports* included the experiences of migrants in the places they lived before coming to Aotearoa New Zealand, their journey

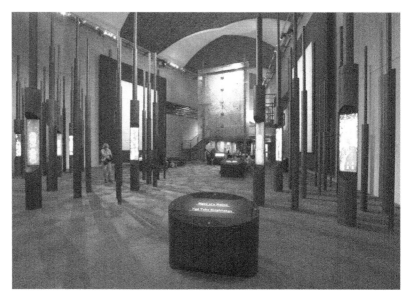

15.3 The entrance to *Signs of a Nation: Ngā Tohu Kotahitanga*, the Treaty of Waitangi exhibition, at Te Papa, Wellington, Aotearoa New Zealand, 2015.

by ship or later aeroplane, their impressions of the 'new country' and the contributions they made to Aotearoa New Zealand in their communities and more generally. Attached to the main exhibition space is a changing 'community gallery', which has featured, in turn, the stories and experiences of Chinese, Dutch, Indian, Italian and Scottish migrants. The first and only exhibition about daily life was *On the Sheep's Back*, which I worked on as concept developer, about the many stories of wool in New Zealand life, including many everyday objects. The third exhibition in the suite was an original take on the thorny question of national identity, which I also worked on. *Exhibiting Ourselves* reproduced in individual gallery spaces the New Zealand courts at selected International Exhibitions and Expos from the Crystal Palace in 1851 to the 1992 Seville Expo. As Phillips has noted, 'it makes obvious how much projections of New Zealand identity were constructions – the visitor walks into constructed architectural spaces'.[32] These shows were my first experience as a history curator, fresh from academia and learning first-hand what doing history with objects might constitute. It really made me think about conveying the past in three dimensions in space and the place of museums in terms of public communication, and led to ongoing exploration about what we should be collecting and how we could and should materialise the past.[33]

I learned another lesson in the development of the other key exhibition mounted by the history team: *Signs of a Nation Ngā tohu kotahitanga.* Intended as a contemporary commentary on the Treaty of Waitangi and its central place in the nation, this display contains a giant facsimile of the original document, set like a rose window up high in a cathedral, with

the words of the English and Māori versions set in large letters on opposite walls. The religious ambience is intentional, as the display setting is
intended for quiet contemplation, underneath a high vault-like ceiling in an
'imposing wedge shaped space' directly between and separating the Māori
and Pākehā sections. This controversial exhibit has drawn much commentary (Figure 15.3).[34]

What many academic critics of the opening exhibitions do not realise is
that the board and management paid a great deal of attention to fears that
Te Papa would be a PC (politically correct) 'Māori Museum' and would
omit or denigrate settler culture by being more critical and questioning
of New Zealand's Pākehā experiences than it would of Māori experiences.
Separations within the museum between teams working on individual
exhibitions, particularly between what was called the Tangata Tiriti and
Tangata Whenua[35] sections, led to unconnected displays in conceptual
as well as experiential terms. Nervousness amongst the leadership about
whether Pākehā culture was being celebrated enough – despite continuing
debate about what Pākehā culture and history actually consisted of – led to
the downplaying and deletion of the exhibitions about the interconnected
experiences of the two population groups. For example, a planned display
in the 'wedge' between Māori and Pākehā zones was turned into a café, with
the only object featured a motorcycle designed by the DIY (Do It Yourself
or non-expert/professional) folk hero John Britten.

Phillips commented in an interview on the complexities of developing
the non-Māori exhibitions: 'Pākehā, let alone all non-Māori, do not think
of themselves as having a separate identity … they think in terms of New
Zealand identity.'[36] He believed the exhibitions were 'New Zealand identity,
not Pākehā identity', because many Pākehā included Māori culture within
their definitions and symbols of New Zealand identity, and many Māori
in turn participated within a broad New Zealand identity. Phillips set out
to include Māori elements within these exhibitions, where appropriate.[37]
However, despite some interaction in the history exhibitions, and Māori
art works appearing in New Zealand art exhibitions, overall a clear Māori/
Pākehā divide was maintained, a bicultural segregation noted in the writing
about Te Papa.[38] Owing to practical pressures and other factors, it seemed
that the curators' lofty aim of an integrated history of Aotearoa New
Zealand was not to be.

Diluting Te Papa 2008–2015

In 2001, I left Te Papa and returned to teaching and writing history in the
university. Ironically, this distance from the museum enabled me to develop
new ideas about material history. Meanwhile back in Wellington, Te Papa
had now been open for almost twenty years and the original intention
of a suite of interconnected but changing history exhibitions has disappeared within its dynamic environment because of shifting institutional

priorities.[39] Attempts were made to deal with the issues surrounding the conceptual, narrative and spatial consequences of Te Papa's particular form of biculturalism. Key curatorial personnel were no longer involved, underlining the importance of institutional structure and work processes in the making of history exhibitions, a factor which is seldom acknowledged in the scholarly literature.[40]

Passports is now the only long-term 'history' exhibition at Te Papa remaining from day one. Determined visitors will find historical representations in the Pacific exhibition, *Tangata o le Moana*, which charts the ways in which Aotearoa New Zealand can be seen as a Pacific Island. However, given the overall layout of level four, visitors may be forgiven for thinking that the portrayal of history in general, and the Pākehā past in particular, has been reduced both physically and conceptually. A new show dealing with twentieth- century New Zealand history opened in 2010, called *Slice of Heaven? Twentieth Century Aotearoa*, in an area which formerly contained art and design displays, adjacent to *Passports*.[41] The rationale for the opening exhibitions was that they would deal with 'narratives of culture and place',[42] and would be thematic, rather than taking the form of a conventional, chronological narrative which 'would be boring'.[43] The pendulum had now swung the other way with a desire to be more comprehensive and chronological. Changes were also afoot with the Community Gallery adjoining *Passports*. In 2010, the first exhibit that was not defined in ethnic terms opened. *The Mixing Room: Stories from Young Refugees in New Zealand* features 'stories of growing up in New Zealand by young people who have come here as refugees'. In the absence of any objects, curators facilitated a series of workshops to 'enable these young people to record – through words, film, photography, and visual art – the joys and difficulties of their experience as they settle into a new way of life in New Zealand'.[44]

History at Te Papa in 2017 consisted of a rather conventional periodisation of migration, with a heavy focus on the nineteenth century, and a twentieth-century overview that covers the conventional 'big' themes and events of New Zealand history. This, in part, was a product of problems with history curatorship. For example, subsequent directors put their own stamp on the curatorial portfolios, and two of the history team members were reoriented towards 'contemporary' collections as well as communities and diversity. History curatorship became focused on ethnic community identity and engagement, social issues, diversity and other themes which, it could be argued, were not fundamentally historical, or at least the connection needed to be more explicit. Collecting and displays were increasingly driven by contemporary concerns and subjectivities, which has long been the case, but at Te Papa were particularly set adrift from notions of national historical significance.

This will change when a new suite of exhibitions, currently in the early stages of conceptualisation, open in both the New Zealand history and Pacific cultures zones. A museum-wide 'renewal' aims to provide a further step-change in museology, in a digitally driven world. At the same time, there has been a huge amount of scholarship in New Zealand history and, to a lesser extent, in Pacific history. The interest in hybridity and mixed heritage of peoples, in transnational stories, and in how not just personal stories but people's histories can be incorporated, as well as a more wide-ranging 'material turn' (see below) have left deep marks on curatorial theory and practice. New ideas about what national histories are and might be, and how they are materialised, not just 'collected' or 'interpreted', drive the new strategies, collecting plans and exhibition development. For our team some of the key questions are: How can we collect and display the national life of Aotearoa New Zealand and New Zealanders, as well as its impact on daily life? What exactly is the form of public history in a museum that we are engaged in? How do we communicate that history in myriad ways for diverse audiences?

Material histories

In this section, I consider how material histories might work as a curatorial method in collecting and exhibiting to address the issues raised above.[45] By material history I do not mean conventional static material culture as in archaeology and anthropology or ethnology, but the whole range of things that people in the past had around them, that they used, wore, consumed and discarded. So, for clothing and fashion, for example, the garments *and* their various wearings, the designer *and* the everyday, would be key.[46] Objects are put back into their context of activities so that the focus is on social routines, habits and patterns, as well as the things themselves. The materialisation of the past in the round becomes the aim.[47] The trouble is that ordinary, everyday objects have often not found their way into museum collections.

If we consider fashion and design, as part of either social history or decorative arts, we find another set of challenges facing curating history in contemporary museums in Aotearoa New Zealand and elsewhere. Across social history or material history or fashion/design there seem to be great chasms and voids. These different disciplines and objects are all aspects of daily life, yet conventional history museums separate them out. I am interested in 'the fashionable', as well as high fashion and design.[48] Many displays of colonial history focus on dress and fashionable society yet they are seen as decorative arts displays rather than being about history and daily, or should I say 'evening', life. At many museums, including Te Papa, there are separate galleries and exhibitions about dress and textiles, which may have their avid fan base of female textiles lovers, but which leave long-term narrative exhibitions to other historical narratives and materialisations.

At this point, I would like to consider new approaches for curating material histories as presented in my recent book *Real Modern*.[49] It tries to put the current vogue for mid-twentieth-century design, vintage and retro, as well as stereotypes about the drab, boring and conservative nature of Aotearoa New Zealand in the 1950s and 1960s into a wider perspective. It is a *material* as well as a social and cultural history, which tries to write history with objects and materialise the past in a broader sense, activities that museums *should* be doing, or *say* they are doing, but are less successful at. It draws upon museum collections, which have had to be supplemented by private collections, because they often do not include the everyday. Most history museum collections in Aotearoa New Zealand focus on the nineteenth and early twentieth centuries. Energetic activity is taking place to collect the more recent past, the material culture of which is all around us, as are the stories and provenance, unlike many older objects.

My book illustrates a range of material objects and their uses, considers Pākehā–Māori interaction, and tries to challenge the 1980s orthodoxy of museum and other kinds of historical representations and materialisations. It spans the whole of daily life from home to school and work, getting around, recreation, going out and going shopping, to a consideration of the rituals and traditions of the period and their materialisations. Figure 15.4 shows a 1957 '78' recording of 'Pie Cart Rock and Roll', written and sung by Johnny Cooper, known as the Māori Cowboy. The song describes a pie cart

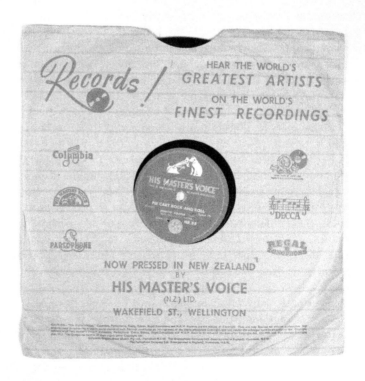

15.4 The Māori Cowboy Johnny Cooper's 1957 recording of 'Pie Cart Rock and Roll'. Te Papa, Wellington, Aotearoa New Zealand.

in the small town of Whanganui where Cooper would often eat late at night after a talent quest or dance. This object materialises local inflections of international popular culture, demonstrates the interaction between Māori and Pākehā in regional towns and centres, and reflects Māori appropriation of Western musical styles. Going out on the town is central to daily life in this period and takes distinct forms according to age, gender and locality.

Most history exhibitions in New Zealand museums largely reproduce the standard interpretation of the period. They say little about some of the key things in my book: schooling (I had to borrow a common school boy's satchel from a private owner); gardening and lawn mowing (great New Zealand obsessions); transport; daily dressing, and routines of cleanliness, both bodily and household. After all, famous United States cosmetic firms used *te reo* (Māori language) in their advertisements aimed at Māori women and placed them in the Māori Affairs Department magazine *Te ao hou* that was delivered to Māori households.

A host of other things are excluded from history exhibitions and collections, including urbanising Māori and greater postwar migration from Europe and the Pacific. Is this silence the result of the burden of having to tell a 'national' story? Where are ordinary people's experiences? Where, I always ask, and not just facetiously, is shopping? Urbanising Māori were as avid followers of fashion and got dressed up to go to dances and downtown on Friday night, as the images in my book show. I am now planning to use material history as a curatorial method through a collection plan and exhibition, instead of a book. This influences every choice of interpretation and communication, from collecting to selecting the object to materialise a particular storyline, to web exhibitions, blogs and beyond. This approach breaks down the bicultural division between Māori and Pākehā by focusing on everyday objects and their messy and entangled production, consumption, use and exchange. It realises the aim of recognising that (sub) urbanisation and popular culture are great drivers of change, and telling cross-cultural histories in a post-settler society is both historically more accurate and museologically more necessary than ever.

Conclusion: the twenty-first-century history curator

So, this brings me back to a persistent question: How do contemporary curators in museums deal with everyday life and its material aspects, when they are still to a large extent focused on discrete objects and forms of material culture, and when they carry the burden of the historical development of their collections? My answer would be that history curators use material history as a method to practise contemporary public history in a museum setting. The figure of the social history curator would thereby move from being trapped within their collections and institutional demands, restricting their work to non-Indigenous stories, to being freer to realise the past that needs to be materialised. Their work would have a social and cultural focus that encompasses everyday habits and practices. It would not shy away from showing the messy, entangled nature of the past in all its cross-cultural richness, diversity and ambiguity. After all, we do that for the present, so why do we not allow that for our historical representations: Indigenous, non-Indigenous and those that fall between?

Notes

1 Most of the literature deals with collection care, acquisitions and the selection and arrangement of objects in exhibitions, aspects of the traditional curatorial role which have in the last few decades been devolved to collection managers, conservators, designers and others within museums. See J.B. Patrick, 'The Museum Profession', in S. Macdonald (ed.), *A Companion to Museum Studies* (Malden, MA: Blackwell, 2006), pp. 415–30; G. Kavanagh, *A Bibliography for History, History Curatorship, and Museums* (Aldershot and Brookfield, VT: Scolar Press, 1996); G. Kavanagh (ed.), *Making Histories in Museums* (New York: Leicester University Press, 1996). A recent exception is V. Gosselin and P. Livingstone (eds), *Museums and the Past: Constructing Historical Consciousness* (Vancouver: University of British Columbia Press, 2016).

2 There was a modest temporary exhibition acknowledging the anniversary on level three, focused on Te Papa's scientific and taxonomic heritage, www.tepapa.govt. nz/visit/whats-on/exhibitions/you-called-me-what-150-years-scientific-discov ery-te-papa.

3 See J. Sissons, *First Peoples: Indigenous Cultures and Their Futures* (London: Reaktion, 2005). See also Michael King on 'settling and unsettling' in relation to Pakeha settler nationalism and reconciliation with *tangata whenua* (the people of the land). M. King, *The Penguin History of New Zealand* (Auckland: Penguin Books, 2003). Another related phrase often heard today is 'post-settlement', referring to the period after the settlement of Treaty claims. For Aroha Harris's research on post-settlement iwi, see Te Taiwhakaea: Treaty Settlement Stories, at the Ministry for Culture and Heritage, www.mch.govt.nz/treatystories. Accessed 1 November 2016.

4 According to the anthropologist Anne Salmond, Pakeha means 'extraordinary', coined by Māori in contrast to the word they used to refer to themselves upon contact with Europeans, namely 'Māori', meaning ordinary, or natural. A. Salmond, *Two Worlds: First Meetings between Maori and Europeans 1642–1772* (Auckland: Viking, 1991).

5 See McCarthy, Hakiwai and Schorch, Chapter 13 above.

6 P. Schorch, C. McCarthy and A. Hakiwai, 'Globalizing Māori Museology: Reconceptualizing Engagement, Knowledge, and Virtuality through Mana Taonga', *Museum Anthropology*, 39:1 (2016), 48–69.

7 B. Labrum, 'Making Pakeha History in New Zealand Museums: Community and Identity in the Post-War Period', in S.J. Knell, S. MacLeod and S. Watson (eds), *Museum Revolutions: How Museums Change and Are Changed* (London and New York: Routledge, 2007), pp. 149–59; Laabrum, 'Reliving the Colonial Past: Histories, Heritage, and the Exhibition Interior in Postwar New Zealand', *Interiors: Design, Architecture, Culture. Special Issue: Living in the Past*, 2:1 (2011), 27–44; Labrum, 'Historicising the Museum's Recent Past: History

Exhibitions at the Museum of New Zealand Te Papa Tongarewa, 1998–2008', *Museum History Journal*, 5:1 (2012), 29–52.

8 C.F. Kreps, *Liberating Culture: Cross-Cultural Perspectives on Museums, Curation, and Heritage Preservation* (London and New York: Routledge, 2003); S. Longair and J. McAleer (eds), *Curating Empire: Museums and the British Imperial Experience* (Manchester: Manchester University Press, 2012); H.U. Obrist, *A Brief History of Curating* (Zürich and Dijon: JRP / Ringier & les Presses du Reel, 2008); T.E. Smith, *Thinking Contemporary Curating* (New York: Independent Curators International, 2012); S. Macdonald (ed.), *The Politics of Display: Museums, Science, Culture* (London and New York: Routledge, 1998).

9 F.E.S. Kaplan (ed.), *Museums and the Making of 'Ourselves': The Role of Objects in National Identity* (London and New York: Leicester University Press, 1996); J. Evans and D. Boswell, *Representing the Nation: A Reader: Histories, Heritage and Museums* (London and New York: Routledge Open University, 1999); S. Knell, P. Aronsson, A.B. Amundsen et al. (eds), *National Museums: New Studies from around the World* (London and New York: Routledge, 2010).

10 T. Bennett, *The Birth of the Museum: History, Theory, Politics* (London: Routledge, 1995); S. Conn, *Museums and American Intellectual Life, 1876–1926* (Chicago: University of Chicago Press, 1998); B. Kirshenblatt-Gimblett, *Destination Culture: Tourism, Museums, and Heritage* (Berkeley: University of California Press, 1998).

11 W. Leon and R. Rosenzweig, *History Museums in the United States: A Critical Assessment* (Urbana: University of Illinois Press, 1989); G. Kulik, 'Designing the Past: History-Museum Exhibitions from Peale to the Present', in W. Leon and R. Rosenzweig, *History Museums in the United States* (Urbana and Chicago: University of Illinois Press, 1998), pp. 3–37; B. Labrum, 'The Female Past and Modernity: Displaying Women and Things in New Zealand Department Stores, Expositions and Museums, 1920s–1960s', in B.F. Tobin and M. Goggin (eds), *Material Women 1750–1950: Consuming Desires and Collecting Practices* (London: Ashgate, 2009), pp. 315–40.

12 F. Cooper, 'Postcolonial Studies and the Study of History', in A. Loomba, S. Kaul, M. Bunzl, A. Burton and J. Esty (eds), *Postcolonialism and Beyond* (Durham, NC, and London: Duke University Press, 2005), pp. 401–22; C. McCarthy, 'Grounding Museum Studies: Introducing Practice', in C. McCarthy (ed.), *Museum Practice: The International Handbooks of Museum Studies* (Oxford and Malden, MA: Wiley Blackwell, 2015), pp. xxxv–lii. For a notable exception see Macdonald and Morgan, Chapter 2 above.

13 See Mallon, Chapter 17 below.

14 K.W. Thomson, *Art Galleries and Museums of New Zealand* (Wellington: Reed, 1981); J. MacKenzie, *Museums and Empire: Natural History, Human Cultures and Colonial Identities* (Manchester: Manchester University Press, 2009); C. McCarthy, 'Museums', in *Te Ara – The Encyclopedia of New Zealand* (Wellington: Ministry for Culture and Heritage, 2015): www.teara.govt.nz/en/ museums. Accessed 1 November 2016.

15 J. Belich, *Making Peoples: A History of the New Zealanders from Polynesian Settlement to the End of the Nineteenth Century* (Auckland: Allen Lane, Penguin, 1996); *Paradise Reforged: A History of the New Zealanders from the 1880s to the Year 2000* (Auckland: Allen Lane and Penguin, 2001).

16 K. Gentry, *History, Heritage, and Colonialism: Historical Consciousness, Britishness, and Cultural Identity in New Zealand, 1870–1940* (Manchester:

Manchester University Press, 2015). A remarkable number of museums were founded or revived in the postwar period, especially the 1960s and 1970s. K. Thomson, *Art Galleries and Museums of New Zealand* (Wellington: Reed, 1981). See also B. Dalley and J. Phillips (eds), *Going Public: The Changing Face of New Zealand History* (Auckland: Auckland University Press, 2001).

17 A.J. Evans, 'New Museum at Te Awamutu', *Journal of the New Zealand Federation of Historical Societies*, 1:4 (1974), 29.

18 *Ibid.*, 31.

19 J.G.G., '"New Look" at the Museum. Extensive Alterations and Improvements', *The Journal of the Te Awamutu Historical Society*, 2:3 (1967), 78.

20 B. Gamble and R.C. Cooper (eds), *Art Galleries & Museums of New Zealand* (Auckland: Art Galleries and Museums Association of New Zealand, 1969), p. 24.

21 J.G.G., '"New Look" at the Museum. Extensive Alterations and Improvements', 79.

22 'Historical Society Looks Back on Over 60 Years of Achievement', *Footprints of History*, 15 (November 1995), 21.

23 Evans, 'New Museum at Te Awamutu', 64.

24 *Ibid.*, 65.

25 Website, http://tamuseum.org.nz/about-2/.

26 A. Henare, *Museums, Anthropology and Imperial Exchange* (Cambridge: Cambridge University Press, 2005).

27 T. Griffiths, *Hunters and Collectors: The Antiquarian Imagination in Australia* (Melbourne: Cambridge University Press, 1996).

28 C. Hilliard, 'Textual Museums: Collection and Writing in History and Ethnology, 1900–1950', in B. Dalley and B. Labrum (eds), *Fragments: New Zealand Social and Cultural History* (Auckland: Auckland University Press, 2000), 118–39.

29 A. Witcomb, *Re-Imagining the Museum: Beyond the Mausoleum* (London and New York: Routledge, 2003); K. Message, *New Museums and the Making of Culture* (Oxford and New York: Berg, 2006).

30 C. McCarthy, *Museums and Maori: Heritage Professionals, Indigenous Collections, Current Practice* (Wellington: Te Papa Press, 2011). See T.S. McArthur, 'Walking the Talk: An Ethnography of Biculturalism at Te Papa' (PhD thesis, Victoria University of Wellington, 2015). See also P. Adds, B. Bönisch-Brednich, R. Hill and G. Whimp (eds), *Reconciliation, Representation and Indigeneity 'Biculturalism' in Aotearoa* (Heidelberg: Universitätsverlag Winter, 2016).

31 C. Macdonald, 'Two Peoples, One Museum: Biculturalism and Visitor "Experience" at Te Papa Our Place, New Zealand's New National Museum', in D.J. Walkowitz and L. Maya Knauer (eds), *Contested Histories in Public Space: Memory, Race, and Nation* (Durham, NC, and London: Duke University Press, 2009), pp. 49–70.

32 J. Phillips, 'Our History, Our Selves: The Historian and National Identity', *New Zealand Journal of History*, 30:2 (1996), 107–32.

33 B. Labrum, 'Thinking Visually: Doing History in Museums', in B. Labrum and J. Phillips (eds), *Going Public: The Changing Face of New Zealand History* (Auckland: Auckland University Press, 2001), pp. 176–86.

34 B. Attwood, 'Difficult Histories: The Museum of New Zealand Te Papa Tongarewa and the Treaty of Waitangi Exhibit', *The Public Historian*, 35:3 (2013), 46–71.

35 Defined as People of the Treaty (those here by right of the Treaty of Waitangi) and People of the Land (those by right of first discovery or Indigenous).

36 J. Waite, 'Under Construction: National Identity and the Display of Colonial History at the National Museum of Singapore and the Museum of New Zealand Te Papa Tongarewa' (Master's dissertation, Victoria University of Wellington, 2009).

37 *Ibid.*

38 J.M. Gore, 'Representations of Non-Indigenous History and Identity in the National Museum of Australia and Museum of New Zealand Te Papa Tongarewa', *The Electronic Journal of Australian and New Zealand History* (2003), www.jcu.edu.au/aff/history/articles/gore.htm. P.Williams, 'Reforming Nationhood: The Intersection of Free Market and Biculturalism at the Museum of New Zealand Te Papa Tongarewa', in C. Healy and A. Witcomb (eds), *South Pacific Museums: Experiments in Culture* (Melbourne: Monash E-Press, 2006), 2.1–2.16; K. Message, 'Representing Cultural Diversity in a Global Context: The Museum of New Zealand Te Papa Tongarewa and the National Museum of Australia', *International Journal of Cultural Studies*, 8:4 (2005), 465–85.

39 In this section I draw on Labrum, 'Historicizing the Museum's Recent Past'.

40 R. Gillespie, 'Making an Exhibition: One Gallery, One Thousand Objects, One Million Critics', *Meanjin*, 60:4 (2001), 118–19.

41 This exhibition has now closed to make room for more art gallery space within Te Papa. This can be seen as further dilution of both the opening vision and the less secure place for New Zealand history within the institution, as well as ongoing anxiousness about the place of art.

42 Phillips, 'Our History, Our Selves: The Historian and National Identity'.

43 *Ibid.*

44 www.tepapa.govt.nz/visit/whats-on/exhibitions/mixing-room-stories-young-refugees-new-zealand.

45 This section draws on B. Labrum, 'Material Histories in Australia and New Zealand: Interweaving Distinct Material and Social Domains', *History Compass*, 8:8 (2010), 805–16; B. Labrum, S. Gibson and F. McKergow (eds), *Looking Flash: Histories of Clothing in Aotearoa New Zealand* (Auckland: Auckland University Press, 2007).

46 Labrum, McKergow and Gibson, *Looking Flash*.

47 Labrum, 'Material Histories in Australia and New Zealand' and B. Labrum, *Real Modern: Everyday New Zealand in the 1950s and 1960s* (Wellington: Te Papa Press, 2015), 16. See also T.J. Schlereth, *Material Culture Studies in America* (Lanham: Altamira Press, 1999); D. Miller (ed.), *Material Cultures: Why Some Things Matter* (London: University College London Press, 1998), and K. Harvey (ed.), *History and Material Culture: A Student's Guide to Approaching Alternative Sources* (London and New York: Routledge, 2009).

48 B. Labrum, 'Expanding Fashion Exhibition History and Theory: Fashion at New Zealand's National Museum since 1950', *International Journal of Fashion Studies*, 1:1 (2014), 95–115, doi: 10.1386/infs.1.1.95_1.

49 Labrum, *Real Modern*.

16 Curating relations between 'us' and 'them': the changing role of migration museums in Australia[1]

Andrea Witcomb

> I would also like to ask two related things … which have puzzled me since a brief visit to the museum some years ago. One is to ask if you want donations of crafts and small items used in households in South Australia during [the] last century? These are from the wave of first settlers, ie. Anglo-Celtic. The related question is whether the museum is mainly about the subsequent waves of settlers or is the history of the early mainly Anglo-Celtic people given appropriate space? Perhaps when I was there I missed some rooms where their history is featured but ever since my visit I have thought of the museum as being about the migration to South Australia of the various ethnic minorities – I am correct in thinking this?[2]

Written in 1995, nine years after the opening of the Migration Museum in Adelaide, Australia, the question posed by Evelyn Wallace-Carter in her letter to the museum reflects some of the central problems faced by migration museums in a settler country like Australia – who are migration museums for, and how do they negotiate relations between different population groups? This chapter argues that the answer to these questions does not simply require an analysis of the ways in which museums have represented these relations over time, for the answers are not only about the politics of representation. The answers also require a recognition that there is a history to curatorial practices, and that this history has an impact on the ways in which relations between 'us' and 'them', 'self' and 'other' play out. Furthermore, the history of these practices is not only a function of developments in historiography and changing political contexts but a matter of curatorial approaches to collecting and interpretation that have also evolved in response to various technological possibilities.

These approaches make differing uses of the working elements of exhibitions – objects, images, text and sound – to create a range of exhibition experiences, each of which prioritises different senses and activities on the part of the visitor. Individually and in combination with each other, these approaches shape the production of different sets of relations between 'us' and 'them', 'self' and 'other', effectively producing four very different 'pedagogies' in the way museums manage relations between different population groups. The first of these is a 'pedagogy of looking', the second a 'pedagogy of reading', the third a 'pedagogy of listening' and the fourth a 'pedagogy of feeling'. Migration museums are particularly rich sites for identifying the curatorial strategies involved in each, given they are, as intimated by the opening quote, centrally concerned with defining relations between different cohorts of people. The arguments will be developed with reference to two Australian museums – the Migration Museum in Adelaide, which uses the more conventional pedagogies of looking, reading and listening, and the Immigration Museum in Melbourne which is experimenting with a pedagogy of feeling alongside the other three.

The inspiration for describing interpretative approaches as a form of 'pedagogy' comes from Tony Bennett's[3] work on late nineteenth-century exhibitions and his focus on the way in which they embodied their pedagogical aims through the activity of walking alongside linear taxonomies of display. For Bennett, this form of pedagogy embodied a particular approach to collecting and display, based on formal taxomomic systems which were a reflection of the prevailing social Darwinian theories which took the theory of evolution and applied it to human society, giving it a linear temporality from primitive to advanced. This was supported through a linear mode of display, so that, as people walked alongside these displays, they took in an embodied evolutionary lesson which ended with themselves at the apex – audiences at this time being almost invariably white and middle- to upper-class and rarely the object of display themselves. Those on display, however, were objectified and thus framed as the other to those who were viewing them. While looking was important to the way this form of public pedagogy was produced, it was walking alongside a taxonomically displayed collection, supported by the theory of evolution, that allowed an embodied approach to the construction of relations between self and other to take form, making this a performative act.[4]

Bennett's argument suggests that there is a relationship between the curatorial practices of collecting, display and interpretation which, when looked at as an assemblage, constitute a form of public pedagogy aimed at the management of relations between 'self' and 'other' and 'us' and 'them'. This chapter takes this idea and uses it to identify and analyse the development of a range of collecting and display practices from the 1980s to the early 2000s that have led to a suite of new forms of 'pedagogy' and to other ways of embodying relations between 'self' and 'other', 'us' and 'them'.

Exhibiting the history of migration and settlement at the Migration Museum, Adelaide

When the Migration Museum opened in 1986, it did so as the world's first migration museum, in a context when the official Australian government policy governing the ways in which the nation understood itself was framed by multiculturalism. Under this policy, explicit attempts were made to reframe the public understanding of Australia's migration history away from an understanding that migrants were 'others' who had to assimilate into the dominant Anglo-Celtic society into the idea that Australia was a nation of immigrants, and that therefore its cultural identity was the result of the rich tapestry woven together by all the different groups that had come to settle here.

The museum was the result of a recommendation made in the Edwards report[5] into the state of museums in South Australia which recommended the need for a suite of museums dealing with history. The result was the South Australian History Trust,[6] which had, as part of its remit, an 'ethnic' museum. As the name 'ethnic' museum indicates, however, multicultural heritage was understood as non-Anglo-Celtic. The issue was quickly identified as problematic by a working party set up to develop the parameters for the Ethnic Museum. They argued that the name would set up distance between all the ethnic groups and the dominant Anglo-Celtic population. As a result, the working group 'proposed a "display programme developed around the interlocking themes of migration and settlement" as an "exciting alternative" to the proposed displays representing different ethnic groups'.[7] The museum thus opened as the Migration and Settlement Museum, intent on using the history of migration to showcase the existence of cultural diversity from the moment of settlement.

As our letter writer's question to the curators of the museum indicates, however, the tensions were not so easily dealt with in the public imagination, as there, the history of settlement is an Anglo-Celtic story largely based on the pioneer myth in which British settlers opened up an uninhabited and uncultivated landscape, bringing civilisation with them, while the history of migration is an ethnic story. This is due to three issues: first, the idea of *terra nullius* which created a myth that despite the presence of Indigenous people the land itself was regarded as empty; second, the legacy of assimilationist thinking in which postwar migrants were expected to conform to Australian (i.e. settler) values and give up their own; and third, any attempt to narrate the story of Australia as a nation of migrants has to deal with the fact that only one group brought the existing system of governance with them – the English. From this perspective, the desire to narrate the nation, or in this case South Australia, as a nation of migrants elides the very real and unequal power relations between the various groups. Furthermore, such an approach to the history of the nation focuses the attention on each new arrival, inevitably presenting a history of increasing diversity but also an increasing focus on the 'other', as the original groups which make up the Anglo-Celtic majority disappear into the background.

As will become clear below, the curators who put together the initial suite of exhibitions at the Migration Museum were not unaware of these problems. Their response – to develop a strategy that combined a radical politics with pluralist representational strategies – was not, however, entirely successful, if the tension captured by our letter writer is any indication. To understand why this was so we need to delve into the structural characteristics of each of the pedagogies of looking, reading and listening in order to analyse how they embodied social relations as relations of 'us' and 'them'.

The first suite of exhibitions at the Migration and Settlement Museum was based on four key points that its original curators – Director Margaret Anderson and curator Viv Szekeres – wanted to make as part of their attempt to deal with the problems discussed above. The first was that the history of South Australia reflected a continual process of migration whose impact on Indigenous people was one of dispossession.[8] In this, they were reflecting and supporting new developments in Australian history writing which were turning the conventional pioneer narrative upside down. The second point was that the history of migration reached back into the nineteenth century and thus included the dominant majority – those of British background – and was not to be understood simply as the influx of non-British migrants in the postwar period, challenging the association between migration history, multiculturalism and ethnicity. The third was that nineteenth-century migration also included non-British migrants, and thus that cultural diversity had always been part of the Australian social fabric. The fourth was a desire to look at this history from the point of view of the dispossessed as well as the ordinary person rather than the establishment, reflecting the new social history then emerging and its focus on class, race and gender.

Thus, as a piece written to advertise the new museum and call for donations in a variety of South Australian newspapers put it, visitors:

> will start at a port of departure in England in the 19th Century, and then move into a gallery about early settlement. There, they can discover the number of different groups and individuals who made the long journey to settle in South Australia like the Germans, Poles, and Chinese, or the Afghan traders who with their camels opened up the northern areas of the colony … One can not tell these stories without also looking at the impact of white settlement on the Aboriginal population.[9]

These stories, the article went on to explain, are told from a social history perspective which meant that 'the focus is on "ordinary" people; the life experiences of the average man, woman, and child. What it felt like to make the journey from a far off land, arrive in a new and strange country and to begin to build a home and a future here.'[10] The twentieth century was covered in a further two galleries called respectively *Division and Dislocation: War, Depression and More War*, and *The Crest of the Wave: Immigration 1950s–1970s*, which looked at the experiences of postwar migrants, changes to immigration legislation and the arrival of refugees from Indo-China and South America in the 1970s.

To achieve their reinterpretation of conventional narratives and redraw the relationship between the history of colonisation, migration and our understanding of multiculturalism, however, there were a number of practical problems that the curators and their design team had to overcome. One was the lack of an existing historical collection dealing with either the history of settlement or indeed the history of migration.[11] Moreover, as both

Margaret Anderson[12] and Viv Szekeres[13] have remarked, not only did the poor, the dispossessed and the marginalised leave little behind in the way of material culture, what did remain did not conform to traditional expectations of what should be in a museum – these were not valuable objects from a monetary or artistic perspective. Furthermore, such material, when it could be found, was largely unprovenanced, making it very difficult to anchor thematic displays in personal stories, particularly for the nineteenth century. More recent migration history was still within living memory and the relevant communities could be accessed, but this would take a few years to build. In response to these issues, the curators developed three very different forms of social history collecting which in themselves led to three of the different interpretative pedagogies referred to above.[14]

Collecting the representative and building a pedagogy of looking

The first, used mainly in the nineteenth-century galleries, was a pedagogy of looking. It literally built a series of windows into the past that communicated thematic content through the use of well-known images and representative objects or even props, rather than using provenanced objects to tell individual personal stories. While this was not uncommon in social history exhibitions being developed in the early to mid-1980s, the use of this window into the past interpretation technique at the Migration and Settlement Museum was unusual at the time for the depth of its critical aim – to question the pioneer narrative by naming settlement as colonisation, invasion and genocide while also firmly placing settlers as migrants. Its aim was an activist one – to erase differences between 'us' and 'them' by narrating Australian history as migration history while recognising that one group was still fighting for inclusion – Indigenous people.

This interpretative approach begins in Gallery three[15] in the introductory area called *Farewell Forever*. The space consists of a scene from East London, showing the poverty people were leaving behind as well as a re-creation of two domestic scenes – one a middle class family, the other working class – packing to leave. The re-creation of the docklands area of London was done by sourcing images from the *Illustrated London News*. This practice effectively set up a process of recycling images that carried well-known narratives, such as, in this case, leaving desperate circumstances behind. Props such as nautical ropes suggested the journey the people in the images were about to take in search of a better life – the long voyage, by ship, to South Australia (see Figure 16.1).

To the left of these images, windows – for that is literally how they are described in the curatorial folders and what the designers alluded to in their design (see Figure 16.2) – allow visitors to peek into family parlours, looking into the decision-making process of what to take and what to leave behind, introducing the idea that these immigrants came with particular kinds of 'cultural baggage' which were used when they got to Australia to re-create home.

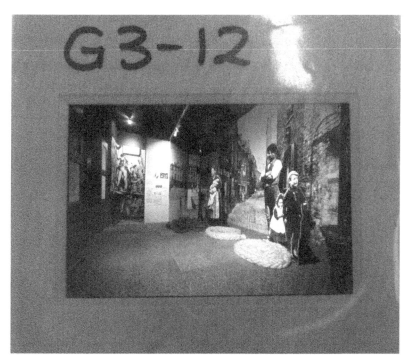

16.1 Entry area to Gallery 3, Migration Museum, Adelaide, Australia, 1986.

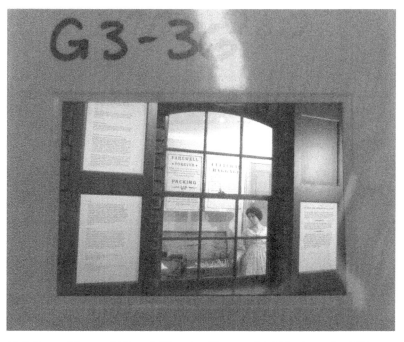

16.2 *Farewell Forever*, Gallery 3, Migration Museum, Adelaide, Australia, 1986.

These interpretative strategies enabled the curators to deal effectively with the lack of provenanced material culture with most items bought through auction or through local antique shops.[16] Their value was not in an individual person's story but in the ideas that they could be made to embody. In this particular display, this was the idea of cultural baggage, or as the label puts it: 'their life in a "new" land will take not only a great deal of baggage, but also the cultural traditions of a middle-class background'.[17]

This notion of cultural baggage is what enabled the curators to develop a critical edge to their interpretation of a pedagogy of looking, enabling them to take it beyond a romanticised view of the past – a view they recognised many in their audiences would have. Thus, in another label for the window next to this one, they attempted to work against this possibility by asking their visitors to consider the following question:

> What does it all mean?
>
> For us the gun case represents the conflict between colonists of the British Empire and the Aboriginal people. For others the gun case is a testimony to the courage and bravery of the pioneers and explorers.
>
> Do the Bible, prayer books and christening gown show the steadfast faith of Christians in a new land? Or are they evidence of the way that Christians ignored the spirituality of Aboriginal people?[18]

As this label indicates, much of the critique was carried by words and direct mode of address which had, at times, a rather didactic tone. As Margaret Anderson, the inaugural director of the Migration Museum, put it in a recent interview, 'We were pretty earnest!'[19] But the point was also made through the power of juxtaposition, by placing a series of jarring windows side by side.

This was the case in Gallery four where the suggestion made in the introductory gallery that fashion, the Bible and the gun were all instruments of colonisation was literally embodied in a series of displays. Titled 'Colonization or Invasion? Nineteenth Century settlement', the gallery used strong visual juxtapositions alongside uncompromising language to make its points.

The distance between past and present, however, was maintained by the use of the third-person curatorial voice and the use of the past tense as the label in Figure 16.3 demonstrates. The effect is to implicitly suggest that 'we' know better at the same time as to continue to 'other' Aboriginal people by not giving them their own voice.

Mining the archive to construct a pedagogy of reading

The second strategy, mainly used in the twentieth-century galleries, is a pedagogy of reading. In Gallery five, for example, which dealt with the history of the White Australia policy[20] and the wider context which eventually saw its demise, the curators used images and documents from public

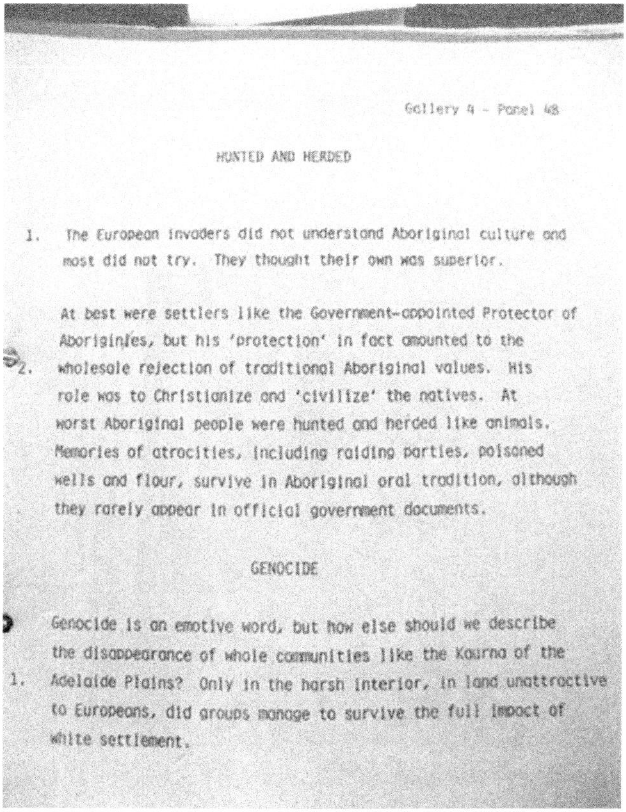

Gallery 4 - Panel 48

HUNTED AND HERDED

1. The European invaders did not understand Aboriginal culture and most did not try. They thought their own was superior.

At best were settlers like the Government-appointed Protector of Aborigines, but his 'protection' in fact amounted to the
2. wholesale rejection of traditional Aboriginal values. His role was to Christianize and 'civilize' the natives. At worst Aboriginal people were hunted and herded like animals. Memories of atrocities, including raiding parties, poisoned wells and flour, survive in Aboriginal oral tradition, although they rarely appear in official government documents.

GENOCIDE

Genocide is an emotive word, but how else should we describe the disappearance of whole communities like the Kaurna of the
1. Adelaide Plains? Only in the harsh interior, in land unattractive to Europeans, did groups manage to survive the full impact of white settlement.

16.3 Typewritten label. Gallery 4, Migration Museum, Adelaide, Australia, 1986.

archives and newspapers to convey the contrast between official policies on migration and attempts to market Australia as a migrant destination with accounts of racism during the Depression; displaced people's camps in Europe to indicate the wider context for postwar migration with images of internment camps for 'enemy aliens' during both world wars; ethnic workplaces and businesses to signal migrant contributions to Australian society with newspaper-based examples of racism during the Depression.

The approach reflects a different social history practice from that used in the pedagogy of looking. Rather than representative objects, curators wanted to anchor the history of migration in official records which would help them to give weight to the tensions between inclusion and exclusion – a point that they could make through their own curatorial voice in guiding readers and visitors through the 'evidence' as well as their choice of case studies. The approach allowed them to move through large swathes of time while pausing on particular vignettes whose inclusion prevented the chronological narrative from becoming an unreflective narrative that erased conflict and contradiction. In Figure 16.4, for example, curatorial attention was given to the ethnic tensions that arose during the

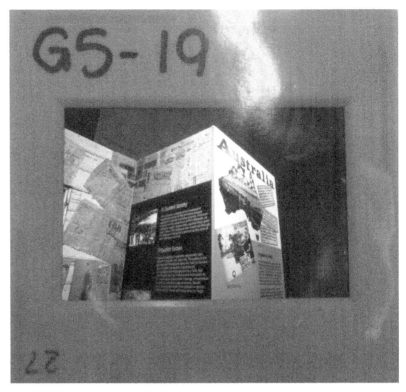

16.4 From a display titled the 'War to end all Wars' in the listing of images for gallery 5, Migration Museum, Adelaide, Australia, 1986.

Depression which were then contrasted with the need to populate or perish in the period after the Second World War in the next face of the graphic panels.

The chronological approach, however, supported the overall aim of documenting and interpreting the increasing cultural diversity of the population, adding to the impression that the main narrative at the museum was about 'the ethnics'. Furthermore, the impersonal nature of these displays did not provide a space for building empathy, making it clear that the function of a pedagogy of reading is the provision of information, which, while key to providing a holistic understanding of the history of migration, does not connect the past to the present or provide bridges between 'us' and 'them'. If anything, this approach is firmly about 'them' as a group of people that needed to be managed so as to ensure the boundedness of 'us'. To break that effect down, a *pedagogy of listening* was needed.

Oral history and the pedagogy of listening

This is effectively what occurred through an audiovisual display on the experiences of Polish survivors from the Second World War which used oral history as the basis of the narrative. According to Szekeres,[21] the aim of the project was not to present another war story but 'to re-create the atmosphere, experience and horror of those times in order to explain to the museum visitor the reason for the influx of large numbers of homeless refugees who came after the war from Europe to settle in Australia'. Placed within a display that sought to suggest the horror of concentration camps through the use of barbed wire, prisoner of war (POW) uniforms and dark colours, the film followed the lives of each of the individuals until they came to Australia, in their own voices, aided by various objects they had managed to keep from that time.

Apart from showing how oral history became intimately associated with collecting objects, what this display suggests is the emotional power of combining the pedagogy of looking with that of listening as a counter to the drier pedagogy of reading. Essential to this was the ability to reproduce the images and sounds of those interviewed within the context of exhibitions. The introduction of multimedia into the exhibition space is what made a pedagogy of listening possible. By providing personal accounts of historical experiences, other visitors who had shared similar experiences were able to see themselves within the museum. Furthermore, such displays asked visitors to extend tolerance to those who are 'other' by asking them to recognise their humanity.

A second strategy for giving voice to the experiences of new migrants was to use actors to read extracts from primary sources such as letters or diaries (or alternatively to quote from them in labels). This was used in a display in the final gallery about Elizabeth, a suburb of Adelaide specifically designed to house British postwar migrants. The display, called 'Letters home', used letters written in the 1960s and 1970s between British migrants and their friends and family back home to explore a range of themes, including the cost of living and the weather, as well as more intimate feelings like homesickness. In one extract, for example, visitors heard Shirley Gutteridge saying to her mother Olive Snuggs that 'I had my first little homesick cry the other night but I'm alright now'.[22] Instructed to 'Lift the handset. Listen to what it feels like to leave your home and start a new life in another country',[23] visitors could follow Shirley's emotional journey which indicated that it actually took her quite a long time to be 'alright'. While this approach facilitated the promotion of tolerance and understanding, however, it left the structural relations between migrant and host untouched. This was not the case with the final interpretative approach – a pedagogy of feeling at the Immigration Museum in Melbourne.

Anchoring the past in the present, or a pedagogy of feeling

Opened in 1998, this museum had the benefit of being able to study the Migration Museum in Adelaide. While dealing with similar thematic terrain, the Immigration Museum in Melbourne privileged a thematic approach over a chronological one, focusing on leavings, journeys and arrivals to begin with and adding the history of immigration policy in 2003 and, most recently, an exhibition on practices of inclusion and exclusion called *Identity – Yours, Mine, Ours*.[24] Personal stories, or a pedagogy of listening are the museum's strongest interpretative approach, which is used to deal with the limitations of the pedagogies of looking and reading. Here however, I want to explore how a pedagogy of listening is turned into a pedagogy of *feeling*, using an interactive developed for the *Getting In* Gallery – a gallery which uses a pedagogy of reading to provide information on the history of immigration policy in Australia.

Just as the Migration Museum in Adelaide used personal stories to provide a human anchor to the drier history of immigration policies, the Immigration Museum also knew that it had to use personal stories to interpret the significance of immigration policies to the lives of real people. Unlike at the Migration Museum, however, curators chose not to use oral histories but to stage an interactive 'play' based on hypothetical but historically accurate case studies with a part for visitors that could be acted out through an interactive screen. It is the nature of this interactive space and the way it connected visitors with the history of immigration policies that we need to focus on next.

The piece opened in 2003 – the year in which the National Museum of Australia found itself embroiled in the history wars for its stance on colonial history and its elevation of multiculturalism[25] – as well as two years after 9/11 and, for Australians, the ugly *Tampa* incident in which the conservative Australian government refused to accept a boatload of asylum seekers picked up by the Norwegian merchant ship *Tampa*.

This multimedia interactive enables those who engage with it to occupy the position of immigration officer, making decisions on who can and cannot enter or stay in Australia. Each applicant is played by an actor. Visitors have access to a dossier that contains information about each one – the same dossier used by the immigration official, played by an actor whom visitors temporarily replace at the decision moment. Visitors witness their interview and are asked to evaluate whether or not, on the basis of their answers and the information in the dossier, they would allow them to remain in the country. Those seeking residency range from Chinese citizens at the start of the twentieth century to recent asylum seekers from the Middle East – a process that was already taking place in 2003. Visitors then witness the actual decision which is made on the basis of immigration policies at the time of application and the emotional reaction of the applicant to that decision. The contrast between visitors' decisions and those of the information officer is what enables visitors to confront the ethical and political overtones of Australia's immigration policies and their own relationship to them.

This emotional engagement is achieved through the close-ups of peoples' faces and their tone of voice – the impassive face of the immigration officer who nevertheless conveys his own values through this tone of voice, the stressed, emotional faces of the applicants for whom this means life and death or the ability to be with their families. Visitors experience outrage when the immigration officer remains impassive while excluding a Chinese migrant from remaining in Australia at the turn of the last century who will be deported and have to leave her husband and children behind; betrays no empathy for an Iraqi asylum seeker who fails to get in on the count that he cannot produce official papers; but welcomes a British couple despite the fact that the wife is not as enamoured of coming to Australia as her husband. They are distressed by both the cruelty and unfairness of the system and the officer's coldness. Empathy is the last thing that is present in immigration policies and their application in practice. The net result is a recognition that policies concerning immigration are based on cultural values that define who are 'us' and who are 'them' and that these values have a long history in Australia which is very difficult to dislodge.

Collecting practices are not key to a pedagogy of feeling. What is key is the form of display which reflects the self through the other. In other words, the form of interactivity on offer is a reflection on the 'self' or 'us', rather than an insight into the other. This is done through a focus on people's emotions. Applicants are presented in a *mise-en-scène* that encourages eye-to-eye contact, or some form of bodily sensation or connection so as to establish a sense that direct communication is going on, that there is a conversation happening.

This intense form of sensory engagement, in which meanings are emergent rather than didactic, and which necessitates both emotional and

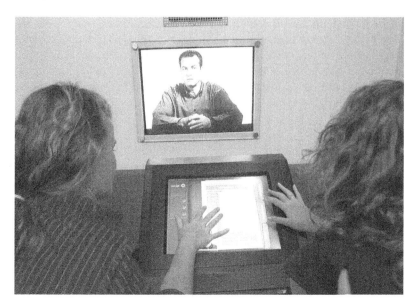

16.5 Interview interactive with Iraqi applicant in view, *Getting In* Gallery, Immigration Museum, Melbourne, Australia.

cognitive labour on the part of visitors, takes this form of pedagogy into the realm of affect, making it more than a matter of representation. This becomes clear if we understand what is going on as a process of mimetic communication.[26] As Anna Gibbs explains it, this is a form of communication practice that embodies relations between people, rather than the communication of information. It involves 'corporeally based forms of imitation, both voluntary and involuntary', producing a tendency for those involved 'to converge emotionally'.[27]

It seems to me this is exactly what is happening in this interactive as visitors 'witness' the emotional journeys of the applicants and the impassivity of the official. Responding to the facial expressions of the applicants, as well as their voices, they become embroiled in their emotional predicaments, responding negatively to the impassivity of the immigration officer in the presence of these very same emotions, and ultimately bonding with the applicants – as Gibbs puts it, the 'facial expressions and the tonal quality of the human voice spread contagion like, across bodies, building emotional landscapes that build as well as break social bonds'.[28] At that moment, the distance between 'us' and 'them', 'self' and 'other' is minimised, and empathy, rather than tolerance, becomes a possibility. At the same time, an insight into the cruelty and politics of a system, in this case policies of immigration, also become apparent, making critique a possibility.

Although visitor research is not part of the current study, the power of a pedagogy of feeling to challenge traditional understandings of relations between us and them was suggested in a recent audience study by Philipp Schorch which looked at this same interactive,[29] pointing to the need for further research into how visitors experience each of the pedagogies discussed above. In his discussion of various visitors' reflections about this interactive, Schorch points to the ways in which the face-to-face encounters experienced by these visitors led them to think critically about the impact of present-day immigration policies, prompting them to respond to the emotional landscape which the interviews performed on the screen elicited for them.

Analysis and conclusion

What emerges from this brief analysis of these migration exhibits at two Australian museums is the fact that curatorial methods of collecting and research have a bearing on the form of display. In turn, these forms of display privilege different activities – looking, reading, listening and feeling – which elicit a different set of relations between visitors and the subjects of display. In so doing, these forms also use different pedagogical modes, from outright didacticism to more constructivist and interactive modes based on more affective forms of interpretation.

Thus, in a 'pedagogy of looking', the lack of a curatorial methodology for sourcing provenanced personal objects, leads to a collecting practice that locates representative objects that can then be used to illustrate already established narrative tropes. Any critique of those tropes requires a very didactic form of text which uses the second person to direct how visitors look at the displays and what thoughts to take away from them. The display is image-rich, whether from reproductions of images or theatricalised settings which invite visitors to look into the past and at others, effectively producing what Barbara Kirshenblatt-Gimblett[30] refers to as an 'in-situ display'. The window effect, however, literally separates 'them' from 'us', as does the use of past tense and third-person curatorial voice in the labelling. The effect of a pedagogy of looking is thus of producing a notion of the past which is framed as distinct from the present and as separate from 'us'. This is because those who inhabit that past are types rather than individual people with whom we can have a personal relationship.

In contrast to the immersive qualities of a 'pedagogy of looking', a 'pedagogy of reading' is a non-immersive, two-dimensional environment, dominated by graphic panels with images and text. Based on archival research from sources such as institutional archives, the approach is more likely to reflect official narratives, unless there is an explicit curatorial attempt to counteract such narratives through the use of juxtapositions or direct critique. It too uses the third-person curatorial voice to produce institutional authority and the second person to provide direct and didactic modes of address to visitors to get them to reflect on particular points of interpretation. Reflecting a shift away from collecting representative objects, it points to the way in which history curators began to use archives to build the narrative structure of their exhibitions rather than simply illustrating received historiographies with representative images already available in books. While in the 1980s curators had to physically travel to the archive, limiting their ability to access a wide variety of sources, digitisation has enabled a much wider access to institutional and public archives, aiding the ability to juxtapose contrasting and competing narratives and introduce a more pluralistic curatorial practice. However, the lack of personal stories as well as the institutional voice means that it is hard to establish close relations between past and present and between 'self' and 'other', 'us' and 'them'.

In a 'pedagogy of listening' however, personal stories are what drive the larger narrative. Based largely on oral history projects, curators focused on collecting stories, with objects playing a secondary role.[31] This meant that suddenly it was possible to provoke more critical insights into the past by using the first-person narrative voice – rather than the third-person voice of curators trying to ask challenging questions themselves or presenting contrasting institutional perspectives.

Visually, the look of exhibitions also changed. Rather than either dioramas or strong graphic design using image and text, telephones, video booths and later touch screens appeared next to supporting objects or even without them, pointing to the importance of multimedia in display practices. Photographs of individual people, or video of them, are central, as is their voice – either through a recording or quoted directly in labels (as opposed to the curator using the information contained in the oral history to renarrate the story in third-person voice). The voice of those being represented is thus prioritised leading to a pluralist curatorial practice that encourages visitors to listen. Visitors are not, however, implicated as witnesses. This means that while the increase in voices lends itself to a recognition of the politics of identity, a 'pedagogy of listening' leaves untouched the ways in which these politics are embedded in the power relations between self and other. Indeed, quite often it reasserts such relations.[32]

A 'pedagogy of feeling' attempts to address this problem by making the subjectivity of the visitor the ground for inquiry as well. Here the objective is not just to represent diversity but to make the space between 'self' and 'other', 'us' and 'them', the subject of inquiry. The curatorial practice is dialogic in that visitors are required to engage with the aims of the display using their own identities and collective memories in order to rethink relations between themselves and others. Oral histories become testimonies and visitors become witnesses leading to a curatorial practice that invites a rethinking between 'self' and 'other', 'us' and 'them'.

Notes

1 The research for this chapter was funded by the Australian Research Council (DP 120100594) and I gratefully acknowledge their support. I also wish to acknowledge the support of the Migration Museum and Museum Victoria for allowing me access to their archives and to Conal McCarthy and Philipp Schorch for their supportive and incisive engagement as I developed my argument, as well as the research assistance of Karen Schamberger.

2 Migration Museum, Adelaide, *Chops & Changes* Gallery 8 curatorial folder '1995–1997' Bread, Sweets. Meets, Towers, *Letter to the Migration Museum* by E. Wallace-Carter, 13 October 1995.

3 T. Bennett, *The Birth of the Museum* (London: Routledge, 1995).

4 T. Bennett, 'Museums and Progress: Narrative, Ideology, Performance', in *ibid.*, 179–86.

5 R. Edwards, *Museum Policy and Development in South Australia, Final Report* (Adelaide: Government Printer, 1981).

6 This Trust was composed of the Constitutional Museum, the National Motor Museum, the Migration Museum and the South Australian Maritime Museum.

7 History Trust of South Australia and the Ethnic Museum Working Party, *Ethnic Museum Working Party Report* (Adelaide: History Trust of South Australia, 1982), p. 12, in E.J. Henrich, 'Whose Stories Are We Telling? Exhibitions of Migration History in Australian Museums 1984–2001' (PhD Dissertation, University of New South Wales, 2012), p. 32.

8 V. Szekeres, 'The Problems of Collecting and Interpreting our Multicultural Heritage', in M. Birtley and P. McQueen (eds), *New Responsibilities: Documenting Multicultural Australia: A Record of the Conference for Museums,*

Libraries, Archives and Historical Collections: Towards a National Agenda for a Multicultural Australia (Melbourne: Museums Australia Inc. Victorian Branch and Library Council of Australia, 1989); V. Szekeres, 'Representing Diversity and Challenging Racism: The Migration Museum', in R. Sandell (ed.), *Museums, Society, Inequality* (London and New York: Routledge, 2002).

9 Migration Museum, Adelaide, 'The Migration and Settlement Museum – A New Museum for South Australia and a First for Australia', in File P2, History Trust of South Australia, *Appeals through Media MM*.

10 *Ibid.*

11 V. Szekeres, 'The Use of Oral History in Museum Displays', *Oral History Association of Australia Journal*, 9 (1987), 112–16; V. Szekeres, 'The Problems of Collecting and Interpreting Our Multicultural Heritage'. See Labrum, Chapter 15 above, for a further discussion of this point.

12 M. Anderson, 'Museums, History and the Creation of Memory, 1970–2008', in D. Griffin and L. Paroissien (eds), *Understanding Museums: Australian Museums and Museology* (2011), http://nma.gov.au/research/understanding-museums/MAnderson_2011.html. Accessed 4 January 2017.

13 Szekeres, 'Oral History in Museum Displays'.

14 The exhibitions discussed here no longer exist. The discussion is based on archival sources at the Migration Museum, particularly the working files for each gallery of the initial suite of exhibitions developed between 1984 and 1986.

15 Gallery 1 provided a history of the site, which was a former destitute asylum, and Gallery 2, the Forum Gallery, had a changing programme of community-based exhibitions.

16 Migration Museum, Adelaide, Gallery 3 Working files, individual object sheets.

17 *Ibid.*

18 *Ibid.*

19 Andrea Witcomb, oral history interview with Margaret Anderson, 22 November 2016.

20 For the White Australia policy see the National Museum of Australia website, www.nma.gov.au/online_features/defining_moments/featured/white_australia_policy_begins. Accessed 15 January 2017.

21 Szekeres, 'Oral History in Museum Displays', 113.

22 Migration Museum, Adelaide, Panel 24, Working file for Gallery 6, Letters Home.

23 Migration Museum, Adelaide, Working file for Gallery 6, Letters Home.

24 See A. Witcomb, 'Cultural Pedagogies in the Museum: Walking, Listening and Feeling', in M. Watkins, G. Noble and C. Driscoll (eds), *Cultural Pedagogies and Human Conduct* (London: Routledge, 2015).

25 G. Davison, 'What Should National Museums Do? Learning from the World', in M. Lake (ed.), *Memory, Monuments and Museums: The Past in the Present* (Melbourne: Melbourne University Press, 2006).

26 A. Gibbs, 'After Affect: Sympathy, Syncrony, and Mimetic Communication', in M. Greg and G.J. Seigworth (eds), *The Affect Theory Reader* (Durham, NC: Duke University Press, 2010).

27 E. Hatfield, J.T. Cacioppo and R.L. Rapson quoted in Gibbs, 'After Affect', 186; E. Hatfield, J.T. Cacioppo and R.L. Rapson, *Emotional Contagion Studies in Emotion and Social Interaction* (Cambridge: Cambridge University Press, 1994), p. 5.

28 A. Gibbs, 'After Affect', 191.

29 P. Schorch, 'The Cosmohermeneutics of Migration Encounters at the Immigration Museum Melbourne', *Museum Worlds: Advances in Research*, 2:1 (2014), 81–98.
30 B. Kirshenblatt-Gimblett, 'Objects of Ethnography', in *Destination Culture: Tourism, Museums and Heritage* (Berkeley: University of California Press, 1998).
31 See Macdonald and Morgan, Chapter 2 above.
32 See Witcomb, 'Cultural Pedagogies in the Museum'.

Agency and authority: the politics of co-collecting

Sean Mallon

There is a seashell in the Museum of New Zealand Te Papa Tongarewa (Te Papa) that was collected on one of the coral atolls of Tokelau in the 1990s and gifted to the museum in 2006 by a Tokelauan man called Kupa Kupa.[1] We do not have a collection of unmodified seashells in the Pacific Cultures storeroom in the museum. We have shell cultural valuables, shell necklaces, shell trumpets, shell decorated shields and canoes, but no seashell collection. Yet this shell is one of our most interesting cultural acquisitions in recent years for how it helps tell a story of Pacific Islanders in Aotearoa New Zealand, of migration, transnational ties, cultural memory and loss, and the politics of co-collecting. It is an item that would not have come into the Pacific Cultures collections if Kupa Kupa did not have some sense of ownership, responsibility or an opinion about what was important, and what *should* be collected to represent Pacific peoples in the national museum.

As in most museums, curators are responsible for developing Pacific Cultures collections at Te Papa. I am one of them, being of Samoan Irish descent, and I share the curatorial responsibility with fellow curator Nina Tonga (who is Tongan).[2] Grace Hutton (who is Cook Islander and Welsh) is the Collection Manager of Pacific Cultures. Our role is to develop, research and exhibit the museum's Pacific Cultures collections within the parameters of collection policies, strategies and plans. To do this, we examine auction catalogues and monitor online auction sites. We attend cultural festivals and events, and visit art galleries and exhibitions. We consider and accept gifts or donations, and we go out into our communities and purchase things. We also initiate and maintain relationships with artists, academics and Pacific communities, for it is their cultures and histories we are representing through our work. However, while we bring specific knowledge and skills to our role as curators, the development of collections is not a curatorial preserve. Te Papa has a long history of activity extending over many years that sheds light on how our communities have shaped the collections and sometimes the curatorial work around them. Kupa Kupa's act of presenting the seashell to Te Papa is one of many interactions where Pacific peoples have played an active role in our collecting practices.

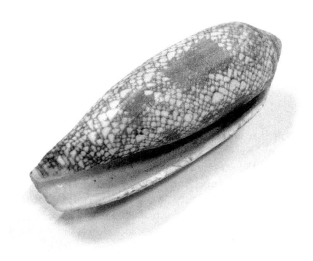

17.1 Seashell from Tokelau in the Pacific Cultures Collections. Museum of New Zealand Te Papa Tongarewa, Wellington. Gift of Kupa Kupa, 2015.

Collecting in context

The subject of this chapter is the history of Pacific people contributing to the development of the cultural collections in Te Papa. I look back over twenty-five years and analyse how donating, gifting and selling cultural artefacts to the museum might be considered *co-collecting* or a *collaborative collecting* activity. I argue that these transactions make visible the individual and collective agency of Pacific peoples in their engagement with and within the museum.

There is some historical background specific to the museological and cultural context I discuss in this chapter. From 1865, Pacific peoples[3] were represented in New Zealand's Colonial Museum (Te Papa's predecessor) mainly because we were foreigners and/or colonial subjects. For the founding director James Hector and staff who followed, it was our exoticism as Pacific peoples that made us interesting and a subject of study. The Pacific Cultures collections, as we know them today, are evidence of a range of collecting activities undertaken by travellers, colonial administrators, missionaries, teachers and business people throughout the early to late twentieth century.[4] Museum curators acquired items from networks of these people, friends and contacts, and they sometimes undertook field collecting by working directly with Pacific peoples. They also purchased artefacts from private collectors and auction houses.[5] For much of the late nineteenth and twentieth centuries, the museum's collecting of the Pacific was part of a project of ethnology – of documenting and comparing cultures. This was a process that had occurred in other parts of the world and was 'associated with the projects of colonialism, imperialism, and the development of the professional field of anthropology'.[6] The Pacific material culture acquired for the Colonial, Dominion and National Museums were in part artefacts of New Zealand's own ambitions to be an empire of the south.[7]

At the end of the Second World War, the museum's relationship with the Pacific changed as the numbers of Pacific people living in Aotearoa New Zealand steadily increased. From the 1950s, people from New Zealand's Pacific Islands colonies migrated to New Zealand in greater numbers than before to find employment and fill labour shortages, others came to seek further education or to travel. Many ended up settling permanently and raising families whose members went on to raise families of their own. These growing populations of Pacific people transformed the social, cultural and economic landscape in Aotearoa New Zealand.[8] They comprise a very diverse group of communities from Samoa, Tonga, the Cook Islands, Niue, Tokelau, Tahiti, Kiribati, Tuvalu and elsewhere. Collectively, their histories and highly visible cultural proximity present very different reasons for their inclusion in the national museum. Today, material culture from the Pacific that was once part of the Foreign Ethnology Collection is organised into a separate Pacific Cultures collection. This differs from ethnographic museums in Europe and the United States, who store Māori and other Pacific Cultures collections together. The Pacific Cultures collection at Te Papa is managed separately from Mātauranga Māori collections in recognition that Māori are the Indigenous *tangata whenua* or the first settlers of the land.[9]

Since the opening of Te Papa in 1998, the cultural influence of Indigenous Māori in shaping and decolonising museology within Te Papa has been ground-breaking.[10] Guiding a great deal of our curatorial work is *mana taonga* – the power and authority associated with *taonga*, or cultural treasures – a key concept for activating access, collaboration and sharing authority with stakeholder communities.[11] Although mana taonga is grounded in and expressed through Māori culture and language, it is a concept that applies to *all* the communities that Te Papa represents and interacts with.[12] Put into practice through exhibition, event and publication development, it is an important concept for guiding all kinds of collaborative activity including collection development. Mana taonga is a catalyst for discourse and debates that have transformed our curatorial work and is the impetus behind our efforts to establish co-collecting practices.

The term co-collecting does not appear to have much currency in academic and museum-related literature although there are many examples of collaboration and co-curating between museums and communities worldwide. I first came across it in 2015, as part of the publicity for a work-shop on co-collecting at the Research Center for Material Culture in Leiden, the Netherlands.[13] However, citizen curating and crowd curating have played a role in some high-profile collecting and exhibition projects for the Museum of London (protest placards) and the Brooklyn Museum (photography).[14] New Zealand History curators at Te Papa have initiated their share of formal collaborative collecting projects within New Zealand communities. In 2011, Stephanie Gibson worked with a group called Lyttel Stitches (Lyttelton Stitches spirit-raising hearts from the Canterbury earthquakes) who spearheaded a brooch-making project in the aftermath of a major earthquake.[15] Since 2012, Lynette Townsend has worked with children and their families to build a collection of objects representing the lives and experiences of children from different backgrounds growing up in Aotearoa New Zealand.[16] In 2016, Pacific Cultures curators collaborated with Humanities Guåhan[17] on a co-collecting project focused specifically on the culture of Guam's Indigenous Chamorro people, including works by master carvers, weavers and blacksmiths. This was followed by a longer-term (and ongoing) experimental project on materialising German-Samoan Colonial Legacies. Finally, in 2017, we undertook a field worker programme among Tongan communities in Auckland, Aotearoa New Zealand, with the aim of developing contemporary Tongan cultural collections for the museum.[18]

There are precedents for formal co-collecting involving museums and communities in the wider Pacific region. One of the most significant collaborative collecting projects is a volunteer field worker programme started in the mid-1970s by the Vanuatu Cultural Centre.[19] Each year, field workers from across this expansive archipelago attend a two-week workshop held at the cultural centre. Then over the course of the next twelve months, the participants collect cultural materials and document knowledge relating to a predetermined topic or theme such as land, performance, food, governance or environment. At the annual workshops, the field workers return to present their research findings to the cultural centre and each other.[20] The Vanuatu field workers programme is the inspiration for our own Tongan field workers programme mentioned above, and it was a network we utilised to collect a male dance costume for the exhibition *Culture Moves! Dance Costumes of the Pacific* curated in 2005 by the former staff member Kolokesa U. Māhina-Tuai.[21]

The Te Papa New Zealand History curator Stephanie Gibson considers co-collecting to run from the 'informal and organic to the organised and strategic'.[22] This is a useful description signalling the potential complexity as much as the simple and unexpected aspects of our co-collecting practices. It is the informal and organic aspects of co-collecting that I am most interested in analysing in the rest of this chapter. I am referring to the unsolicited approaches from individuals or groups who want to donate, gift or sell items to us, rather than the organised and strategic activity, where we go out and purposefully acquire material as part of a predetermined programme or collecting plan.

Communities, agency and co-collecting

As part of a history through which the museum appropriated Pacific cultures, I am curious about how Pacific peoples may have in turn appropriated the museum. In terms of co-collecting and other collaborative collecting practices, what does the community get out of donating, gifting and selling to the museum? In projects of co-collecting, where do issues of authority and agency arise? Objects do not always find their way to the museum according to a curatorial agenda or a strategic plan. If we consider the decision of a donor to donate an item as the first step in a process of collecting by the museum, then we acknowledge power of a donor to initiate a series of actions by curators.

In my career, one of the earliest examples of a Pacific person stepping forward and making a statement of what he considered should be collected by the museum involved the Reverend Lagi Sipeli of the Niuean community. In 1996, and in the lead up to the opening of Te Papa and its new suite of exhibitions, he offered the museum a *palau*, a drum made from a recycled British Paints™ tin, and smeared with a random splash of white paint. I have written about this object elsewhere, explaining how it was a challenging object to collect, because of its contemporary materials and lack of aesthetic appeal.[23] It was even more confronting for visitors to the collections, including our own Pacific communities who questioned me as to why we had collected and displayed such an object, suggesting it showed our lack of respect for the other items on display. When I told them that Rev. Lagi Sipeli, a Niuean elder on our Pacific Advisory Committee, had presented the drum to Te Papa they were surprised and somewhat silenced – because in many Pacific societies elders are custodians of cultural knowledge and expertise. Sometimes who collects (or donates) is as important as what is collected. I think that we as curators and our visitors have been conditioned through books and exhibitions to think about Pacific material cultures in highly aestheticised, and often essentialist and non-historical ways – with the present being somehow less authentic than the past. Rev.Lagi Sipeli's donation of a barely modified paint tin forced us to confront this issue in a most public way in the opening exhibitions of Te Papa. We were barely ready to do so, but how could we say no?[24] Our commitment to the concept of mana taonga meant there was a certain obligation for us to say yes to our experts' donations. To say no would be to question our experts' cultural authority and their credibility as community representatives.

Te Papa's Pacific Advisory Committees were set up as mechanisms to facilitate mana taonga through the advice from and connections to communities they provided. If there were incentives for the committee members' participation, it may have been in the social capital of being involved with one of the most high-profile cultural projects the country had ever seen. It may have been in the many ways that they could demonstrate their cultural competency and expertise. The task of identifying and donating items to the museum not only activated the relationship between the community and the museum, it quite literally gave material form to the committee members' knowledge and expertise. As a cultural adviser, Rev. Lagi Sipeli used his community mandate to make suggestions and direct the museum in aspects of its work related to Niue. The donation of the palau is an example of how an expert cultural adviser influenced our commitment to contemporary collecting. In hindsight, it was a small but influential action. Later, and before he passed away in 2008, Rev. Lagi Sipeli submitted to us a list of other Niuean items he thought should be in the collections.

However, there are other people outside cultural adviser or leadership roles, and without the mandate of community, who have made similar and very direct moves to influence what the museum collects. They demonstrate that having a sense of history, and recognising what is culturally significant, are not a talent or responsibility restricted to the cultural elite. In 2015, a member of the public made an unsolicited donation of a pair of road running shoes to the Pacific Cultures collection. They had been worn and were offered by Vasa Tasele: he and Joe O'Neill were the first Pacific Islanders to walk the length of Aotearoa New Zealand. Vasa and Joe undertook their Walk the Talk project to raise awareness of child abuse and raise funds for a charitable foundation. The international shoe company New Balance (NZ) supplied the shoes to Vasa in support of his cause. We accepted Vasa's donation because his achievement was a first by a Pacific Islander, but also because it represented a popular form of social activism or enterprise undertaken by a number of New Zealanders over a couple of

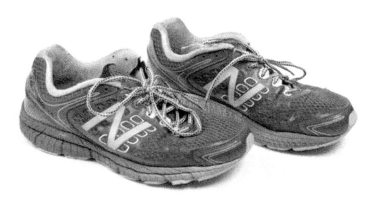

17.2 New Balance running shoes in the Pacific Cultures Collection at the Museum of New Zealand Te Papa Tongarewa, Wellington. Gift of Vasa Tasele, 2015.

decades. Vasa's donation highlights how people outside the museum think about the representation of Pacific peoples in the museum – beyond the ethnographic cultural representations we are most familiar with and sometimes more curatorially invested in.

On occasion, people have donated items to Te Papa because they have identified objects they have a connection with already in the Pacific Cultures collection. By donating or leaving something behind after a cultural event or interaction with the collections, they claim or establish relationships with ancestors who donated or formerly owned items now in the museum. Some of the visitations by descendants and the gifts they leave behind are a reconnecting of 'kin' which is a conceptualisation explored by Hays-Giplin and Lomatewama in relation to the Hopi and their interactions with cultural artefacts in museums.[25] Examples at Te Papa include a family's discovery of a stunning blue woollen cloak with golden hibiscus fibre fringing, gifted to the New Zealand government by Teai'a Mata'iapo, a Cook Islands leader who visited Aotearoa New Zealand in 1872. Teai'a's descendants learned of its presence in Te Papa in 1997, and they donated a special Cook Islands *tivaevae* (patterned quilt) and *moenga* (woven pandanus leaf mat) to honour and continue the relationship between the family and the museum.[26] Similarly in 2004, two descendants of the eighteenth-century Hawaiian chief Kalani'ōpu'u came to Te Papa to view the *'ahu'ula* (feather cloak) he gifted to the English explorer James Cook in 1779. Neither of them had visited the *'ahu'ula* before, and they and a party of warriors and officials who accompanied them marked the occasion with a special *awa* (kava drinking) ceremony and left two *apu* (cups) they used to be part of the Pacific Cultures collections. It was the beginning of a significant sequence of visitations and gifting associated with the *'ahu'ula* that is documented elsewhere.[27]

A third example is from 2006, when Mr Kora Kora, the mayor of Manihiki in the Cook Islands, visited Te Papa as part of celebrations marking one hundred years since the museum acquired a *vaka* (canoe) decorated with pearl shell inlay – one of only three remaining in the world. He donated to Te Papa a necklace of pearls from Manihiki, honouring the museum's connection with the Cook Islanders that goes back a century to 1906 when the vaka was acquired during the New Zealand International Exhibition of Arts and Industries in Christchurch. As with the previous examples, some of the ancestors who had accompanied the vaka to Aotearoa New Zealand a century before were known. The vaka was a remnant of their experiences at that time, a present-day symbol for their descendants of a treasured and distant past. The necklace was perhaps a contemporary token closing some of that distance, and healing a sense of loss.[28]

These events show how objects in museum collections can maintain a life cycle within the institution that sees them connect, reconnect and disconnect with people. Some scholars use the metaphor of biography to describe this process and talk of objects as having biographies or social lives despite being in museums and supposedly static.[29] One may be able to imagine the pressure museum staff come under to accept donations and honour the histories and relationships that are very much alive, or reinvigorated through these exchanges. These acts of giving are also acts of reclaiming objects, histories and ancestors. We are familiar with these processes outside the museums and in our community life. They are well documented and theorised.[30] As Pacific peoples, we are less used to experiencing them in museums where, until recent decades, our engagement has been more sporadic and less on our terms. They are occasional interactions and transactions in the everyday business of the museum, yet they bring the collections to life and enrich them. They connect descendants with ancestors, contemporary people with their histories. And in return, the museum becomes relevant to people and part of their lives.

I have talked about donating, but what about selling? People sell to the museum for many of the same reasons that they donate. An obvious difference is they would like financial compensation for the items they are parting with. Some people have sold objects to us to raise money for cultural projects like church building, or to meet financial and social obligations within extended families or communities. On one occasion, when word got around a community that we were purchasing a certain type of cultural object, we were inundated with offers of similar items. It was almost as if the community saw the museum as a Cash Converters or pawnshop, providing quick access to cash. We had a glimpse of how vital these transactions could be to sellers, judging by the telephone calls we received requesting that x payment was made urgently so a seller could meet their obligations for a wedding. This conversion of supposedly sacred cultural valuables into cash, or cultural gifts into commodities, is not unusual in some of the Pacific communities we represent. For example, the buying and selling of Tongan *ngatu* (decorated barkcloth) through *kautaha nō paʻanga* (pawnshops) is common in Tonga and Aotearoa New Zealand.[31] Similarly, in Fiji, pawnshops buy and sell Indigenous cultural valuables to assist people with their urgent social and cultural commitments.[32] It may not sound very glamorous, but in some ways the museum, like a pawnshop, is also a resource utilised by people to meet their own purposes and needs.

The museum's deep potential as a social and cultural resource sometimes puts curators in difficult positions. The intentions of donors and sellers can shape the collection in positive ways but can also burden the museum. People have offered us items because they are psychologically or culturally affected by them. They may have become uncomfortable with them because of their cultural significance or because they obtained them illegally. For example, I had one donor who brought along a small haul of material collected by a deceased family member who had worked in the Pacific Islands. Included in the material was a human skull, heavily decorated with clay, fibre, paint and shells. I could not accept it for the collections as Te Papa has a policy of not collecting human remains.[33] However, the donor responded by declaring 'Well if you don't take it from me now, I am going to dispose of it at the rubbish dump!' In the end, we took the skull but did not formally register it in the collections. It rests with other human remains in a holding area at Te Papa until future research facilitates its return to its country of origin.

People have also offered us a wide range of items ranging from stone adze blades to textiles to full-size sailing canoes because people do not know what to do with them, are too afraid to destroy them or, in the case of the sailing canoe, have run out of resources to maintain them. They have become burdens that they wish to pass on to somebody else. However, we should also recognise that people donate to the museum because there is prestige associated with having items in a museum. The museum has the power to legitimise. We have accepted donations from cultural groups who have come to us directly with presentations because our acceptance of their objects validates their group's existence or identity. I mentioned above how the cultural elite can leverage their interactions with the museum for these purposes, but so too can people outside these groups. If the incentives for the social and cultural elite are about social and cultural capital, the same is true for non-elites seeking to establish a relationship with the museum.

Curators, agency and co-collecting

Co-collecting is as much about enhancing the institutional prestige as it is about working with communities and curators are the agents for this process. Co-collecting can have valuable flow-on effects for the museum, enhancing its reputation within the museum world as a socially conscious organisation, engaged with its communities and increasing the depth and value of its collections. Mana taonga and collaborative collecting projects allow us to share authority, and bring authenticity, historical precision and ethnographic detail to the museum collections. Co-collecting improves our documentation and facilitates the recording of makers' names, biographies, associated places of origin and Indigenous terms for materials or object types. We are not collecting objects just as specimens any more, they are objects that connect people, places and events, and represent histories of continuity and change. Even simple but often overlooked details such as dates of birth that for too long have been absent in our ethnographic collections are valued now, as key building blocks in the recording and writing of Pacific peoples' histories.[34] In 2011, we were offered and acquired a birthday gown, made for a young Tongan woman's sixteenth-birthday celebrations. It is the first of its kind in the collection, and a stunning example of a European-style gown made from Indigenous tapa (barkcloth) material. We have documented who wore it, who designed and made it; we have the invitations for the birthday and the party favours supplied to guests. The acquisition is a comprehensive snapshot of a key moment in a teenager's life. Potentially, co-collecting will allow us to develop collections representing a wider spectrum of the societies that are part of the Pacific Cultures collections; we should hope that it would bring to the fore a diverse range of experiences in terms of age, gender and social class, allow us to be more inclusive and to acquire the work of people and groups outside the often over-represented social and cultural elites (who admittedly have the most interactions with museums).

Co-collecting challenges and reconfigures our role as Indigenous curators of collections. In a museum where we are at such close physical, cultural and digital proximity to our communities, it is difficult (and in our case not culturally desirable) to be a curator of the ivory tower variety, the all-knowing connoisseur. You can never be sure whom you are talking to. Often the experts in our communities do not have business cards or name tags identifying themselves. The person you are dealing with might be a leading Tongan composer, but work as a computer programmer most days of the week. However, I understand that an expert version of the curatorial role *is* possible, maybe even necessary, in other institutions with ethnographic collections where distances from, and levels of engagement with, source communities are different. While ideas and concepts can travel, the financial cost of regular face-to-face engagement means that turning concepts into actions can be difficult to sustain.

As curators of Tongan, Samoan and Cook Islands descent, our experience as museum workers is that we are sometimes not worthy in the eyes of our communities to be curators. It may be because culturally we are considered too young to be talking about such things; we are the wrong gender, too intellectual, unskilled or unknowledgeable in cultural matters such as specific languages and customs. We may be of Pacific Islands descent but not the appropriate cultural group. There have been occasions where we have had to stand by and listen respectfully as elders provide incorrect identifications or histories of particular objects for groups they are accompanying. However, there are rewarding moments, such as the time I was about explain to a group how to use a coconut shell shark rattle, when a man stepped forward who had actually fished for sharks using such rattles in his youth. Cultural proximity to our communities often presents such surprises, which are also opportunities to be constantly on alert for, even if it is just so we can share them.

Why are we pursuing co-collecting? It is because we recognise that, while we as curators have expertise, we are not experts on everything. Co-collecting or collaborative collecting enables us to share authority as well as the responsibility and opportunity to collect with those communities we are supposed to represent. Co-collecting decentres us, and makes us less the focus of attention. Decentring ourselves presents opportunities to empower others. However, we still need to be skilled as curators, maintain a bird's-eye view and bring discipline, critical thinking and knowledge of research methods to our work.[35] A postgraduate tertiary education is often hard to come by, but it usefully prepares the way. As professional curators, we still need to curate, and develop a knowledge base to inform our decision-making and interactions with our communities. We need to constantly improve our ability to manage relationships, to listen and learn, as well as educate and lead. While it is helpful that collaborations can protect us from criticism from our communities, they do not absolve us from responsibility and they often come with risk. As one of my colleagues has reminded me, 'if something goes wrong we risk getting fired, not our co-collaborators!'[36]

Te Papa's commitment to mana taonga protects our presence and work as staff of Pacific Islands descent and as agents for certain types of activity in the museum. In the face of limited resources there is an economy in co-collecting activity that facilitates our agency as Pacific Cultures curators. In titling this section 'Curators, agency and co-collecting', I was referring to co-collecting as a strategic and empowering process for Te Papa as an institution operating in society, but also for us as Pacific Cultures curators within the culture and politics of the museum. As much as we share the responsibility of collecting with others outside the museum, curating is a political activity and a strategic and organised strand of our work. It shapes the collections and influences the distribution of resources in the museum, and in the long term it shapes the museum's future. Within the museum there is often inequity in access to resources. There is a cultural hierarchy and different levels of opportunity for different curatorial departments. We develop proposals in alignment with the museum's strategic interests but we are competing with projects from other parts of the museum to fund them. When we decide to create a Tongan field workers programme, or experiment with co-collecting the German-Samoan Colonial Legacy, we are making curatorial decisions based on our research, our analysis of the strengths and weaknesses of the existing collections, and the interests and politics of our times. They are opportunities that come with limitations.

Co-collecting and its limits

We are realistic about co-collecting and what opportunities it offers. If it is to be part of our strategy of increasing collaboration and honouring the principle of mana taonga, then we understand it has its limits *and* its politics. Mana taonga and co-collecting are a partnership but an unequal one. The curatorial choices we make in framing our projects, electing to collect from one community and not another, are controlling mechanisms that can all be challenged. Curators are just one party in the politics of these negotiations. Co-collecting is a sharing of authority, but also a sharing of people's knowledge, time and energy. These are limited resources in the museum as well as our communities. In terms of time and resource, we in museums often hold the power, the purse strings and ultimately the right to say 'yes' or 'no'.[37] However, communities also have their own controllers, decision-makers and politics about what intellectual and cultural resources go where and when. The 'challenges and tensions' of mana taonga are only briefly acknowledged elsewhere.[38]

The sombre reality is that it is difficult to untangle ourselves from the colonial origins of the museum and decentre ourselves as the authority. The politics involved in co-collecting and the limits of mana taonga in practice (as opposed to theory) make it difficult to talk about specific cases of when we have said 'no' to donations, gifts and offers to sell. However, without going into specifics, one that sticks in my mind involved the proposed acquisition of a full-size sailing canoe. We were originally discouraged from pursuing it by a third party because the group who constructed it still occasionally used it. The third party was angry that the museum would even attempt to acquire it, taking it out of the community. However, some years later, the same third party let us know it was available for the museum. While the canoe was still a valuable cultural artefact for the makers, who wanted it cared for and restored, we discovered that in the time that had passed since we expressed our original interest, it had deteriorated significantly on the front lawn of someone's property through lack of maintenance. It was too late to save it. Despite the community interest in re-engaging the museum on the future of the canoe, we were unable to start a formal conversation about acquiring it. The canoe's great size and the time and cost of repair made it unfeasible to pursue as an acquisition. It was a difficult curatorial decision to make, but mana taonga has its limits.

What is valuable about the concept of mana taonga is that it formally imbeds in the institutional culture an orientation towards the sharing of authority with our communities. Co-collecting, as a significant expression of mana taonga, is an opportunity for empowerment of our people and a catalyst for agency. However, in some ways co-collecting is a difficult term as it obscures the politics of an activity that in practice and in name appears to be an equal relationship but is actually asymmetrical in its power relations. Robin Boast argues that this asymmetry is 'determined by our funding regimes, by our proscribed professional practices ... by the very roles that we fulfil – collecting, documenting, and displaying'.[39] He goes on to call for a redrafting of the museum, a confronting of its neocolonial practices and a letting go of resources 'even at times of the objects, for the benefit and use of communities and agendas far beyond its knowledge and control'.[40] I can imagine letting go of things more (and we do already), but we would need to do more to reimagine the relationship management and financial models to make these processes happen more frequently. Museums will still require people to facilitate and create or curate connections between people and objects as well as bring informed critique to these processes. For now, curators often take on this role and, on many occasions, it is a shared role. However, not all curators are interested in community-related work in the same way, and they have different views on the relationship between collaborative approaches and scholarship.[41] Similarly, communities may be not be interested in working with curators if the former are making all of the decisions.

Conclusion: co-collecting and co-developing the future museum

In conclusion, I want to return to the seashell picked up in Tokelau. The shell is a *Conus aureus*, a species of seashell found throughout the tropical Indo-Pacific region. This specimen was picked up in Tokelau and brought to Aotearoa New Zealand in 1989 by Kupa Kupa, who migrated to New Zealand with his family from the atoll of Fakaofo, Tokelau, in 1969. He was five years old at the time. In 1989, an opportunity came up for him to go back to Tokelau on a holiday with an aunt and cousin. They intended to visit for only a few weeks but they enjoyed the experience so much that they ended up staying there for nearly twelve months. The week before Kupa returned to Aotearoa New Zealand, he looked for something to bring back that would help him feel connected to Fakaofo. He picked this shell up along the edges of the lagoon close to his house and took it with him. In 2007, Kupa gifted his precious shell from Tokelau to Te Papa Tongarewa, at the opening ceremony of the exhibition *Tangata o le Moana: The Story of Pacific People in New Zealand*.[42] Today it is part of Te Papa's collection as an example of how people can make important connections to distant places, and preserve and share experiences through seemingly ordinary things. It is also an example of an object that we might not have identified or imagined as being part of such narratives, but Kupa Kupa did that work for us.

At stake in the politics of co-collecting and other collaborative collecting practices is the relevance of our museum to the communities we serve. Indigenous peoples in museums (and not just curators) often exercise agency within the machinery of the institution, where we are resisting something or challenging the museum or our colleagues on an issue. If we are occasionally resisting or obstructing, we are also agents for the museum in its renewal, transformation and growth. I believe our communities will come to us if we do our work well, build a good reputation around our practice and help people understand that they can utilise the museum in a range of ways. Increasingly we in the Pacific Cultures team talk about ourselves as part of an ecology of institutions, centres of knowledge and cultural producers. Looking after, documenting and exhibiting the history of objects and people is one thing we are reasonably good at. For us as Indigenous curators, the museum is a resource, it is a toolkit; and co-collecting is one activity that encourages us to empower and get closer to our communities. It means that sometimes we will have to take the lead, and sometimes we will have to let go, look and listen. Co-collecting encourages sharing and reworking of one aspect of our curatorial role, and I do not think we or the museums we work for should feel threatened by this, because in decentring ourselves we might actually recentre our museums as places that are relevant to the communities we represent. If we are committed to history, material cultures and the people that make them, then a co-collected, co-curated future must surely be a crucial dimension of the twenty-first-century museum.

Notes

1 Tokelau consists of four atolls: Fakaofo, Nukunonu, Atafu and Olohega.

2 My current role is Senior Curator of Pacific Cultures. I joined the staff at Te Papa as a Pacific collection management intern in 1992.

3 The term 'Pacific people' has been used in Aotearoa New Zealand synonymously with 'Pacific Nations people', '*tangata pasifika*', '*tagata pasefika*', 'Pasefika people' and 'Pacific Islanders', though the latter carries with it pejorative connotations. Most commonly, the terms refer to people of Samoan, Cook Island, Tongan, Fijian, Tokelauan, Niuean and Tuvaluan descent; these are the seven Pacific national categories disaggregated in the New Zealand census. However, there are also significant populations of migrants from other Pacific nations, including French Polynesia, Kiribati, Papua New Guinea and Solomon Islands. See T. Teaiwa and S. Mallon, 'Ambivalent Kinships? Pacific People in New Zealand', in J.H. Liu, T. McCreanor, T. McIntosh and T. Teaiwa (eds), *New Zealand Identities: Departures and Destinations* (Wellington: Victoria University Press, 2007).

4 J. Davidson, 'Pacific Collections: The National Museum of New Zealand/ Te Whare Taonga o Aotearoa', *Pacific Arts: The Journal of the Pacific Arts Association*, 3 (1991), 9–13; Museum of New Zealand Te Papa Tongarewa, M. Trewby, P. Walker, M. Schwass, A. Carew, H. Jacob, S. Bailey, I. Cormack and C. Taylor (eds), *Icons Ngā Taonga from the Museum of New Zealand Te Papa Tongarewa* (Wellington: Te Papa Press, 2004).

5 R. Livingstone, 'The History and Development of Foreign Ethnology Collections in the Museum of New Zealand Te Papa Tongarewa', *Tuhinga: Records of the Museum of New Zealand Te Papa Tongarewa*, 10:1–29 (1998), 3–7; S. Akeli and S. Pasene, 'Exploring "the Rock": Material Culture from Niue Island in Te Papa's Pacific Cultures Collection', *Tuhinga: Records of the Museum of New Zealand Te Papa Tongarewa*, 22 (2011), 101–24.

6 R. Harrison, S. Byrne and A. Clarke (eds), *Reassembling the Collection: Ethnographic Museums and Indigenous Agency* (Santa Fe: SAR Press, 2013), p. 8.

7 See D. Salesa, 'A Pacific Destiny: New Zealand's Overseas Empire, 1840–1945', in S. Mallon, K.U. Māhina-Tuai and D. Salesa (eds), *Tangata o le Moana: New Zealand and the People of the Pacific* (Wellington: Te Papa Press, 2012); K. Pickles and C. Coleborne (eds), *New Zealand's Empire* (London and New York: Manchester University Press, 2016).

8 S. Mallon, K.U. Māhina-Tuai and D. Salesa (eds), *Tangata o le Moana: New Zealand and the People of the Pacific* (Wellington: Te Papa Press, 2012); D.I. Salesa, 'New Zealand's Pacific', in G. Byrnes (ed.), *The New Oxford History of New Zealand* (Melbourne: Oxford University Press, 2009), pp. 149–72.

9 See McCarthy, Hakiwai and Schorch, Chapter 13 above.

10 C. McCarthy, *Exhibiting Māori: A History of the Colonial Cultures of Display* (Wellington: Te Papa Press, 2007); C. McCarthy, *Museums and Māori: Heritage Professionals, Indigenous Collections, Current Practice* (Wellington: Te Papa Press, 2011).

11 See also P. Schorch, C. McCarthy and A. Hakiwai, 'Globalizing Māori Museology: Reconceptualizing Engagement, Knowledge and Virtuality through Mana Taonga', *Museum Anthropology*, 39:1 (2016), 48–69; P. Schorch and A. Hakiwai, 'Mana Taonga and the Public Sphere: A Dialogue between Indigenous Practice

and Western Theory', *International Journal of Cultural Studies*, 17:2 (2014), 191–205; H.M. Smith, 'Mana Taonga and the Micro World of Intricate Research and Findings around Taonga Māori at the Museum of New Zealand Te Papa Tongarewa', *Sites: A Journal of Social Anthropology and Cultural Studies*, 6:2 (2009), 7–31.

12 For examples of successful non-Māori museum projects underpinned by the concept of mana taonga see S. Gibson, 'Te Papa and New Zealand's Indian Communities – A Case Study about Exhibition Development'. *Tuhinga: Records of the Museum of Te Papa Tongarewa*, 14 (2003), 61–75; S. Gibson, and S. Mallon, 'Representing Community Exhibitions at the Museum of New Zealand Te Papa Tongarewa', *Tuhinga: Records of the Museum of Te Papa Tongarewa*, 21 (2010), 43–58; S. Gibson, and S. Kindon, 'The Mixing Room Project at Te Papa: Co-Creating the Museum with Refugee Background Youth in Aotearoa / New Zealand'. *Tuhinga: Records of the Museum of Te Papa Tongarewa*, 24 (2013), 65–83.

13 *SWICH Co-Collecting Workshop*. Research Center for Material Culture, National Museum of World Culture, Leiden, Netherlands, 19–20 October 2015.

14 'Museum of London Collecting Cuts Protest Placards', BBC (2 April 2011), www.bbc.com/news/uk-england-london-12921158. Accessed 20 November 2016; *Click!* A crowd-curated exhibition, www.brooklynmuseum.org/exhibitions/click/. Accessed 20 November 2016.

15 S. Gibson, 'Case Study: Museum of New Zealand Te Papa Tongarewa', in O. Rhys and Z. Baveystock (eds), *Collecting the Contemporary: A Handbook for Social History Museums* (Edinburgh: MuseumsEtc, 2014), pp. 440–6.

16 L. Townsend, 'Collecting Childhood – in More Than One Way', *Uni News, The University of Auckland News for Staff*, 44:8 (2015), 5. See also http://collections.tepapa.govt.nz/Topic/8828. Accessed 15 November 2016. Objects and stories collected as part of Te Papa's Collecting Childhood project link to the findings of the University of Auckland's Growing Up in New Zealand longitudinal study – a research project following the lives of seven thousand children in New Zealand.

17 Humanities Guåhan is an independent non-profit organisation that presents public humanities programmes and projects relating to the history, arts and cultures of Guam.

18 At the time of writing these projects were in progress and will be the subject of future publications.

19 Vanuatu Cultural Centre, www.vanuatuculturalcentre.vu/. Accessed 15 September 2017.

20 L. Bolton (ed.), 'Fieldwork, Fieldworkers, Developments in Vanuatu Research', Special issue of *Oceania*, 70:1 (1999); L. Bolton, *Unfolding the Moon: Enacting Women's Kastom in Vanuatu* (Honolulu: University of Hawaii Press, 2003), pp. 44–50.

21 K.U. Mahina-Tuai, 'Intangible Heritage: A Pacific Case Study at the Museum of New Zealand Te Papa Tongarewa', *International Journal of Intangible Heritage*, 1.1 (2006), 13–24.

22 Stephanie Gibson (Curator History) personal comment, 17 November 2016.

23 S. Mallon, 'Still Vastly Ingenious? Globalization and the Collecting of Pacific Material Cultures', in A. Anderson, K. Greene and F. Leach (eds), *Vastly Ingenious: The Archaeology of Pacific Material Culture* (Dunedin: Otago University Press, 2007), pp. 291–309; S. Mallon, 'Against Tradition', *The Contemporary Pacific*, 22:2 (2010), 362–1.

24 The national museum had collected contemporary Pacific material before, with the archaeologist and curator Dr Janet Davidson being particularly influential in making it a collecting focus.

25 K. Hays-Giplin and R. Lomatewama, 'Curating Communities at the Museum of Northern Arizona', in R. Harrison, S. Byrne and A. Clarke (eds), *Reassembling the Collection: Ethnographic Museums and Indigenous Agency* (Santa Fe: SAR Press, 2013), pp. 259–84. Indeed, when the 'ahu'ula of Kalani'ōpu'u returned to Hawai'i on a long-term loan in 2016, I heard several people in Hawai'i at the time refer to the return of Kalani'ōpu'u as if the 'ahu'ula was a person.

26 See C. Tetley, 'Lifting the Cloak of Silence: Redramatising Clothing as Material Culture, through an Object Analysis of Te Aia's Cloak', *Tuhinga: Records of the Museum of New Zealand Te Papa Tongarewa*, 21 (2010), 125–34.

27 S. Mallon, R. Te Kanawa, R. Collinge, N. Balram, G. Hutton, T.W. Carkeek, A. Hakiwai, E. Case, K. Aipa and K. Kapeliela, 'The 'Ahu 'Ula and Mahiole of Kalani'ōpu'u: A Journey of Chiefly Adornments', *Tuhinga: Records of the Museum of New Zealand Te Papa Tongarewa*, 28 (2017), 3–22; S. Mallon, 'Kalani'ōpu'u's Gift to Cook: A Sacred Cloak and Its History of Display', http://blog.tepapa.govt.nz/2016/02/18/kalaniopuus-gift-to-cook-a-sacred-cloak-and-its-history-of-display/. Accessed 5 January 2017. See also McCarthy, Hakiwai and Schorch, Chapter 13 above; Kahanu, Nepia and Schorch, Chapter 18 below.

28 Pearl Necklace, Cook Islands, maker unknown. Gift of Mr Kora Kora, 2010. Te Papa (FE012492).

29 I. Kopytoff, 'The Cultural Biography of Things: Commoditization as Process', *The Social Life of Things: Commodities in Cultural Perspective*, 68 (1986), 70–3; C. Gosden and Y. Marshall, 'The Cultural Biography of Objects', *World Archaeology*, 31:2 (1999), 169–78.

30 For examples from the Pacific, see N. Thomas, *Entangled objects: Exchange, Material Culture, and Colonialism in the Pacific* (Cambridge, MA: Harvard University Press, 2009), and P. Schoeffel, 'Samoan Exchange and Fine Mats', *Journal of the Polynesian Society*, 108:2 (1999), 117–48.

31 P.A. Addo and N. Besnier, 'When Gifts Become Commodities: Pawnshops, Valuables, and Shame in Tonga and the Tongan Diaspora', *Journal of the Royal Anthropological Institute*, 14:1 (2008), 39–59.

32 S. Mallon 'Following Tapa: New Contexts and Global Culture', in P. Mesenhöller and A. Stauffer (eds), *Made in Oceania: Proceedings of the International Symposium on Social and Cultural Meanings and Presentation of Oceanic Tapa* (Newcastle upon Tyne: Cambridge Scholars Publishing, 2016).

33 See Te Papa's Repatriation programme Karanga Aotearoa, www.tepapa.govt.nz/about/repatriation. Accessed 10 January 2017.

34 It should be noted that the standards for this work in Te Papa's Pacific Cultures Collections had been set by the archaeologist and curator Dr Janet Davidson.

35 On this point see Onciul, Chapter 10 above.

36 Personal comment, Nina Tonga, 17 March 2016.

37 On this issue see B. Lynch, 'Whose Cake Is It Anyway?', Paul Hamlyn Foundation website, 2011, www.phf.org.uk/reader/whose-cake-anyway/. Accessed 15 January 2017. See also B. Onciul, *Museums, Heritage and Indigenous Voice: Decolonising Engagement* (London and New York: Routledge, 2015).

38 P. Schorch and A. Hakiwai, 'Mana Taonga and the Public Sphere: A Dialogue between Indigenous Practice and Western Theory', *International Journal of Cultural Studies*, 17:2 (2014), 199.

39 R. Boast, 'Neocolonial Collaboration: Museum as Contact Zone Revisited', *Museum Anthropology*, 34:1 (2011), 56–70, 66.

40 *Ibid.*, 67.

41 C. McCarthy, E. Dorfman, A. Hakiwai and A. Twomey, 'Mana Taonga: Connecting Communities with New Zealand Museums through Ancestral Māori Culture', *Museum International*, 65:1–4 (2013), 5–15, 6.

42 See exhibition page on Te Papa website, www.tepapa.govt.nz/visit/whats-on/ exhibitions/tangata-o-le-moana-story-pacific-people-new-zealand. Accessed 10 January 2017.

18 He alo ā he alo / kanohi ki te kanohi / face-to-face: curatorial bodies, encounters and relations

Noelle M.K.Y. Kahanu, Moana Nepia and Philipp Schorch

In spring 2016, two of the authors, Noelle Kahanu and Moana Nepia, boarded a plane from Honolulu, Hawai'i, to Auckland, Aotearoa New Zealand, destined for the Pacific Arts Association conference. Kahanu had previously initiated a consultation project between the Bernice Pauahi Bishop Museum, Hawai'i, Native Hawaiian cultural practitioners and museums in Aotearoa New Zealand and Australia. The most significant consequence of the project was a long-term loan of the *'ahu'ula* (feathered cloak) and *mahiole* (helmet) of the Hawaiian high chief Kalani'ōpu'u from the Museum of New Zealand Te Papa Tongarewa (Te Papa) to the Bishop Museum and the Office of Hawaiian Affairs.[1] Back on the plane, Kahanu felt regret for arriving in Aotearoa New Zealand a day after the completion of ceremonies to mark the physical and spiritual return of these *mea waiwai ali'i* or chiefly adornments to Hawai'i. She envisioned their planes crossing in mid-flight and it was only upon arriving that she realised that the Hawaiian and Māori delegation had not yet left; rather, they were waiting at the gate to board the very same Hawaiian Airlines plane that she and Nepia had just disembarked from. Separated by thick tempered glass, Kahanu and Kamana'opono Crabbe, Ka Pouhana (CEO) of the Office of Hawaiian Affairs shared a *honi*, a greeting that embodied an understanding of the magnitude of the moment of Kalani'ōpu'u's return, and the multitudes whose *mana* (power, authority, reputation) had made it possible.

Nepia captured the moment (Figures 18.1 and 18.2), an image that reveals the illusory nature of cultural, spiritual, and intellectual separation which can be overcome through the physical and emotional connectivity of a simple and genuine act of ritual encounter: a *honi* that has compressed both time and distance across generations. In the Pacific, interpersonal encounters are characterised by a deep level of physical intimacy and engagement – from the *honi/hongi*, the face-to-face greeting, to the *ha'a/ haka wero*, these rituals of encounter also serve as an acknowledgement of living ancestral presences. In these physical exchanges, relationships are built, tended and tested through an embodied confirmation of values, practices and ethics. For museums holding Pacific collections, the importance

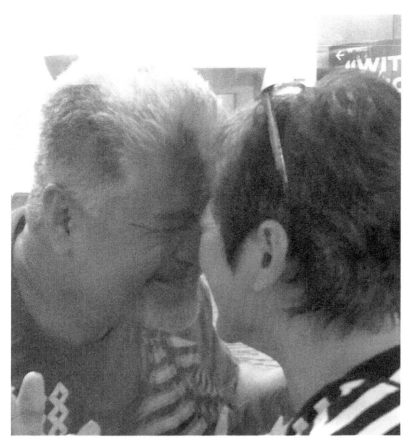

18.1 Office of Hawaiian Affairs Pouhana and Chief Executive Officer Dr Kamanaʻopono Crabbe and Noelle Kahanu share a honi (greeting) at Auckland Airport, Aotearoa New Zealand, March 2016.

of relationships, *and their physicality*, persist. The increasing acknowledgement of, and interaction with, communities of origin, whose works reside in museums throughout the world, is thereby not a new practice but merely the current phase of a continuum of relations that have ebbed and flowed over centuries.[2]

Indeed, perhaps no other cultural treasure symbolise the meeting between Hawaiʻi and the Western world more profoundly than the chiefly adornments presented to Captain James Cook by Chief Kalaniʻōpuʻu on 26 January 1779. They are the tangible representations of this extraordinary meeting, of the significance of ceremonial gifting, and of individual intentionality. While the pathways and travels of these chiefly adornments are of critical importance in ensuring their provenance, what is significant to many in Hawaiʻi is simply this: they left by an act of Pacific generosity, and they returned by an act of Pacific generosity. Both acts were of lasting cultural and political importance, and both were magnificent gestures of faith,

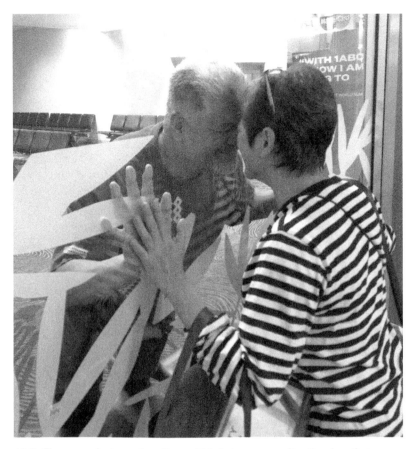

18.2 The same photograph as Figure 18.1, but now revealing the glass that separated Crabbe and Kahanu.

trust and, one might argue, commitments intended to bind future generations. They were *he alo ā he alo* (face-to-face) encounters.

This chapter involves three scholars whose research, interests and collaborations coalesce around concepts of Indigenous creative and curatorial practice.[3] Kahanu focuses on Bishop Museum's exhibition *E Kū ana ka paia*: *Unification, Responsibility and the Kū Images* (2010), which featured important Hawaiian temple images loaned from the British Museum, UK, and the Peabody Essex Museum, Salem, Massachusetts, USA. She utilises the Hawaiian framework of he alo ā he alo to illustrate Indigenous curatorial practices, and to show how it underpins the development of key cross-cultural relationships and encompasses encounters between people and their cultural treasures as ancestral embodiments.[4] Kahanu emphasises how he alo ā he alo facilitated these exhibitions across cultural boundaries, thereby ultimately enabling extensive community engagement.

Nepia proposes a choreographic approach to curation in his discussion of two related exhibitions he has been involved with: *Binding and*

Looping: Transfer of Presence in Contemporary Pacific Art, curated by Deborah Waite for the University of Hawai'i (UH) at Mānoa Art Gallery in 2014, and *ArtSpeak: Languages of Creativity*, a month-long programme of exhibitions and events coinciding with *Binding and Looping*. Philipp Schorch, then, rounds off this last chapter of *Curatopia* by speaking back to the introduction and highlighting the significance of interpersonal relationships, including the one between the three authors, for the development of academic initiatives, such as this book and its preceding conferences. The chapter is thus both an exploration of Indigenous curatorial practices across the Pacific and itself a manifestation of Euro-Pacific relations.

He alo ā he alo: curating as transformative practice of encounter

In her seminal poem, *He alo ā he alo*, Puanani Burgess writes about face-to-face encounters: '[t]hat's how you learn about what makes us weep … [t]hat's how you learn about what makes us bleed … [t]hat's how you learn about what makes us feel'.[5] She distinguishes these personal encounters from those derived from a book, article or other 'reliable source' and ultimately invites the reader to 'come down here and learn of the big and little current, face-to-face'.[6]

This poem brings us to the essence of this chapter – the importance of face-to-face encounters that are at once physical, spiritual, emotional and intellectual, yet fraught with colonial complexities and tragedies. Within a museum context, these encounters occur across a great divide: the passage of hundreds of years, the deaths of generations, thousands of miles of distance and the unquantifiable loss and separation of people from their ancestral treasures as empires crossed the Pacific. Seen as 'contact zones',[7] museums 'invoke the spatial and temporal copresence of subjects previously separated by geographic and historical disjunctures and whose trajectories now intersect'.[8] This perspective enables a relational emphasis on 'copresence, interaction, interlocking understandings and practices' while also considering asymmetrical power relations.[9]

But what happens when such cross-cultural encounters not only happen just across the proverbial consultation table but are brought even closer? Can he alo ā he alo serve as a means of describing and enacting a new kind of personalised interaction that is based on mutual trust, shared authority and ultimately collective healing and well-being? What happens when we literally face one another and share the same breath, as we do by pressing noses in the ritual greeting of the honi? He alo ā he alo encounters are incredibly personal – difficult terrain in cross-cultural and global professional arenas – made more so for those cultures who are uncomfortable with such intimate proximities. But despite these difficulties, Puanani Burgess ends with a profound invitation, a *kahea*, a call, to come and help us 'dig, the lo'i, deep',[10] to join us in the rich, moist and fertile *taro* patches, planting for our collective future. In this sense, he alo ā he alo means more than facing one another: it means facing forward together.

As museum professionals and academics, we are often instructed to be impartial and objective, yet that which is personal can be most powerful. Our cultural knowledge as individuals and community members shapes our professional philosophy and practices on a daily basis. So too do we develop, cultivate and tend to a myriad of personally professional and professionally personal relationships within and among our institutions and communities that are often kept internal. How can these practices be shared rather than kept in the shadows? This is my, Noelle Kahanu's, attempt, as both a Native Hawaiian and a fifteen-year veteran of the museum profession, to reflect on and illuminate these deeply personal practices through the lens of he alo ā he alo.

The last several decades have seen a shift in power relations between US American museums and Indigenous communities whose cultural material is ensconced within them, a move clearly attributable to the passage and implementation of the Native American Graves Protection and Repatriation Act of 1990 (NAGPRA).[11] Much has been written about whether these consultations, initially forced, have truly evolved into willing and mutual collaborations.[12] Nonetheless, through experiences working with NAGPRA as a member of Congressional staff, a Native Hawaiian claimant organisation and at Bishop Museum, I have witnessed the development of truly profound museum relationships based not necessarily on philosophical alignment but on professional respect and mutual trust. Beginning in 1999, a series of federal grants enabled Bishop Museum and the Peabody Essex Museum (PEM) in Salem, Massachusetts, to work collaboratively together on numerous cross-cultural educational endeavours, including an annual travelling storytelling programme, artist exchanges and travelling exhibitions. This recent relationship, however, paled in comparison to one built upon the nineteenth-century merchant and whaling industries, which regularly plied Pacific waters, leading PEM to assemble the largest collection of Hawaiian ethnographic material outside of Bishop Museum, including a large wooden temple image referred to as Kūkaʻilimoku. Bishop Museum also possessed a similar figure or image, as did the British Museum. All three are embodiments of the Hawaiian deity Kū, the male principal of chiefly governance and politics.[13] In previous times, such images would have been arranged into a *kūkalepa*,[14] a crescent-shaped assemblage – but such a gathering had not been witnessed since the mid-1800s for, in the aftermath of the ending of the state religious system and the coming of the US American Protestant missionaries in 1820, most of the images had been removed or destroyed.[15]

Hawaiian carvers, artists and *lua* (Hawaiian martial arts) practitioners had long since dreamed of a unification of these three Kū images, and the grand reopening of Bishop Museum's Hawaiian Hall served as the impetus to voice such a collective desire. A myriad of challenges, logistically and financially, resulted in Bishop Museum abandoning the idea, but, as our ancestors have taught us, dreams are powerful. In 2008, I was presented with a rare opportunity to deliver a paper on the Hawaiian Hall renovation at a Paris symposium, and called forth this vision of a Kū unification within *his* very presence, as the British Museum Kū image was a part of the *Pacific Encounters* exhibition simultaneously being held at the Musée du Quai Branly. 'Perhaps some day', I posited, 'we will stand in their presence and reflect on the divine. They will look down upon us, these sacred vessels, and we will see ourselves in their eyes.' Relationships born between key staff of the British Museum and Bishop Museum at that symposium ultimately led to a loan request which breathed life back into the exhibition idea. *E Kū Ana Ka Paia: Unification, Responsibility and the Kū Images* was thus planned for 2010 to coincide with the two-hundredth anniversary of the unification of the Hawaiian Islands and the second 'Aha Kāne Men's Conference, in which hundreds of Hawaiian men gathered to consider issues of health, wellness and responsibility.[16]

While movement was occurring on the international front, there was hesitancy on the part of the Peabody Essex Museum, and this was not without reason. As a member of the NAGPRA review committee, the director and CEO Dan Monroe had witnessed first-hand numerous contested cases including those involving deep conflicts among Native Hawaiian claimants. It was entirely possible that such an exhibition might prompt a NAGPRA claim, or cause further discord in what some viewed as an already fractured Hawaiian community. The practice of he alo ā he alo is premised upon the establishment and evolution of a relationship over time that has been tried, tested and tended, and it requires a level of compassion based on an understanding of each other's cares, concerns, passions and fears. It requires mutual respect and trust, and it requires physical access – which was provided through the federal grant that enabled Bishop Museum and PEM staff to sit together at the table. Over a shared meal in Washington, DC, Monroe and I spoke about allowing this Kū image to return home, saying that such an exhibition would be the cause for unification and healing, bringing people together, not apart. In response, he challenged me to do my homework, to talk to Hawaiian leaders, scholars, artists and practitioners, and bring him back such evidence.

This then was the *'a'a*, the gift of the challenge, and so I engaged mostly Hawaiian men in difficult conversations about these Kū images that had long since been taken, about the persistence of *mana* (efficacy) and their contemporary relevance, about what it would mean to have them home, only to see them leave once again. For Hawaiians, mana represents the life force. In the context of these Kū, it invoked notions of residual mana, of what remains residing within these images, of what might be reawakened, and, ultimately, of agency. The results of these extended conversations were summarised in the following letter to Monroe:

> Time passes, yet it does not. Today, just as there were centuries ago, there are language and cultural barriers, but also deep and abiding interest in one another, respect, and even affection, that led to the most treasured

of possessions being gifted away. These loans provide a rare and wonderful opportunity to build upon this foundation of trust, to move past
objectification towards a deeper understanding of culture and meaning, and
to demonstrate the ability of our institutions to be leaders in this process of
healing and cooperation.[17]

In the end, the Kū images from both the British Museum *and* the PEM
came to Hawai'i. Despite all odds, they came, overcoming financial obstacles, legal concerns about confiscation and repatriation, and international
travel and insurance issues. They came because individuals moved mountains, especially our Native Hawaiian advisory team, some of whom were
among those initially consulted, as well as staff from all three participating
museums. These Kū came because we needed them. In the words of the
Hawaiian scholar and practitioner Keone Nunes: 'Their coming together,
despite all the obstacles, reminds us that we too can come together in a
sacred way.'[18]

On the day of the exhibition opening, Bishop Museum presented
Jonathan King, Research Keeper of Anthropology at the British Museum,
and Dan Monroe of Peabody Essex Museum with *pāhoa*, Hawaiian
daggers, embodiments of Kū's warrior manifestation, but also King's and
Monroe's own responsibilities as representatives of museums with custo-
dial care over these images (Figure 18.3). When it came time to present
these pāhoa, I asked my Hawaiian martial arts group if I might be allowed
to make the presentation to Monroe. The challenges for a woman facilitating a largely male-centred project is a subject for another essay, but it
suffices to say that this particular request was not easily made or granted.
Crossing the length of the cement walkway on bent knees, prostrating
before Monroe with humility and gratitude for that which had been collectively achieved, might appear to an outsider as a placation and subjugation
of the Native in a postcolonial context, but, for me, it was a privilege. As an
expression of he alo ā he alo, this gifting acknowledged our personal histories and perspectives, our strengths and vulnerabilities, and our commitment towards a future of continued engagement, of shared breath, earnest
challenges and responses.

My great-grandfather, George Kealoha Kahanu, was a *kahuna lā'au
kahea*, a healer who used words and prayers rather than medicinal plants.
If the stricken person was unavailable, he would call in his son to serve
as *noho*,[19] or proxy. Then a child of perhaps eight or nine, my grandfather would sit at his father's feet, his head between his father's hands, not
knowing who was being ministered to, or why. My grandfather, George
Hawae Kahanu, Sr, even into his nineties could still recall feeling the spirits
that would pass through him as he became the focus of this ritual healing.
In this traditional practice of noho, I also see a connection to the role that
many curators carry out. In its medieval Latin context, a *curatus* cured
or tended to the souls of those within his parish, but, in a contemporary
museum context, the curator has become the custodian or guardian of a

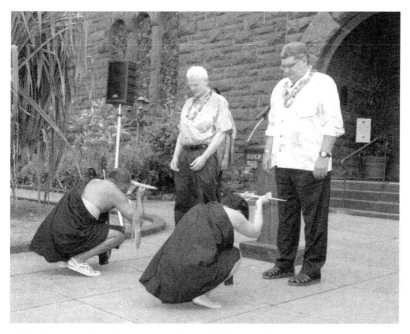

18.3 Members of Pā Kuʻi A Lua, including Kahanu on the right, present gifts on behalf of Bishop Museum, Honolulu, USA, to representatives of the British Museum and Peabody Essex Museum.

physical collection. Yet, for Indigenous curators, our responsibilities are for the spiritual health and well-being of our collections, which are an extension of our very communities. There is no separation between Native Hawaiian collections and those who made them, who wore them, who used them; and, as ancestral embodiments, these collections are directly connected to their descendants, current-day Native Hawaiians. The role of a curator is thus to maintain the health of these connections and to tend to their spiritual dimension. Just as my grandfather was the link between the physical and spiritual, so too do Indigenous curators facilitate the relations between multiple realms even if, at time, we are not fully aware of the full import of that which we are engaged in.

In a very real sense, *E Kū Ana Ka Paia* enabled face-to-face encounters between the three Kū and the more than seventy thousand people who came to visit them in the course of four months. Others have written of the power of exhibitions to bring about peace and reconciliation through collaborative endeavours, by bridging divided communities and institutions, or by engaging in difficult subject matter[20] but the healing I speak of is within the context of the physical he alo ā he alo, between the Kū themselves and the Hawaiians of today. Such experiences are not merely figurative or metaphorical for just as we looked upon them, they returned our gaze. I bore witness to those who sat mesmerised for hours, sharing space at the feet of Kū, who expressed anger and rage at having had them taken away, who cried tears of joy at their reunion, who were moved to offer spontaneous chants, who sat quietly in the still of the night, capturing each moment with pen and paper, who threatened liberation by helicopter. As the exhibition drew to an end, Bishop Museum invited access by Hawaiian cultural groups during closed hours, so that they might engage with Kū collectively in private. A final public programme was held, attended by dozens and with senior /management in attendance, so that the community could express their gratitude, anger, sadness, frustration and grief.

On the day that the Kū on loan from Peabody Essex Museum and the British Museum were brought down from their specially made pedestals and returned to their respective wooden crates, I watched as our Native Hawaiian community advisers and museum staff did the physical labour. At first, I stood on the side, and then from the second floor, witnessing each unbearable moment, audibly weeping in agony. Just as it was my role to voice the dream two years prior, so too was it my job to *uwē*, to cry that day for those who could not, to be the noho, within whose body flowed the *'uhane*, the soul or spirit, of those not present – just as my grandfather once did. Such is the role of any curator engaged in the practice of he alo ā he alo, to bear the joy and sorrow of the connective tissues that bind our museum collections and communities together. Four years later, the journalist Sonny Ganaden, exploring the residual legacy of the Kū exhibition, observed the irony that 'advocating for the return of the god of war and conquest is, in a way, an act of peace and reconciliation'.[21] Keone Nunes agreed: 'I knew the impact they [Kū] had on me, and that the impact on Hawai'i would be ten-fold. There's nothing that can rectify the atrocities that any indigenous peoples have suffered. But bringing them back signifies what is pono,

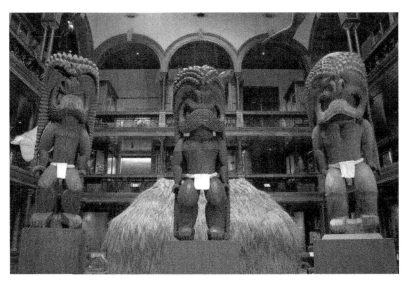

18.4 The exhibition *E Kū Ana Ka Paia: Unification, Responsibility and the Kū Images* on display at the Bishop Museum, Honolulu, USA, 2010.

what is appropriate, and who we are as Hawai'i now.'[22] Looking upon our singular Kū today at Bishop Museum, it is with a profound sense of sorrow to experience the tangible *physicality* of the absence of his two brethren. I used to say that bringing the three Kū together was a once in a lifetime opportunity, but no longer is that the case. Instead, I know that they will be united once again, and that there are those near and far who will make it so when the time comes, he alo ā he alo.

Kanohi ki te kanohi: a choreographic approach to curation

At the 5 October opening of the 2014 exhibition *ArtSpeak: Languages of Creativity*, at the University of Hawai'i at Mānoa's (UHM) Commons Art Gallery, master *ka kakau* (traditional Hawaiian tattoo) artist Keone Nunes completed a Hawaiian *uhi* (tattoo) in full view of an audience including faculty and students from the university, visiting artists and members of different Pacific Island communities (Figure 18.5). People could sit in the gallery, listen to the sound of him tapping, watch and ask questions, or view the action from outside through large glass windows. As curator and photographer, I, Moana Nepia, was also part of the audience, shifting focus between my responses to the performance in front of me, what my camera was recording and how others were responding.

As he worked, Nunes revealed how sustaining the customary practice of kakau is part of a much larger personal commitment he has made to Native

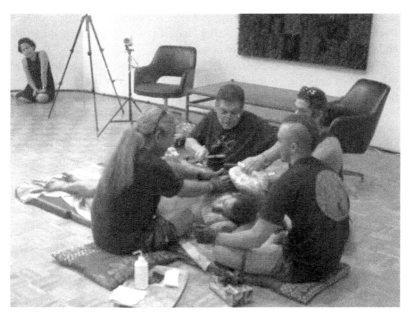

18.5 Keone Nunes and assistants at work in the University of Hawai'i at Mānoa Commons Gallery opening of the exhibition *ArtSpeak*, 5 October 2014.

Hawaiian communities, to Hawaiian visual and performing arts, to hula, to the Native Hawaiian language and to education. While discussing the origins and significance of different patterns and influences upon his work, he traced ancestral and contemporary patterns of movement and cultural connection across the Pacific, including his own travels to Samoa to learn from Sua Sulu'ape Paulo II, the master Samoan *tā tatau* artist, and journeys to Aotearoa New Zealand to connect with Māori artists similarly committed to issues of decolonisation and cultural sustainability.

I sat listening and was taken on another more personal journey as he worked. Faces from my past came into view, embracing memories of others they may have seen in me, layering my understanding of his words with their voices and touch. While I watched the stretch and puncture of someone else's skin, my stomach and chest tensed, then relaxed to exhale. A trace of blood flowed into memories of an oak leaf curled into *koru* (Māori spiral pattern) and *nikau* (native New Zealand palm) on the shoulders and back of an English friend. I remembered Ngāropi White, the last surviving member of our extended *whānau* (family) to have received a customary *moko kauae* (chiselled chin tattoo), and the image of my baby brother reaching to touch her chin as she sat teaching my mother to weave. Memories of other whānau and friends who wear contemporary *moko, uhi, pe'a* or *malo* with pride faded into the sound of her laughter.

The face-to-face encounter with Nunes set a precedent for how I had envisaged other *ArtSpeak* events might offer similar opportunities for intimate conversations and encounters with artists. While foregrounding the issues, concerns and language Pacific Island artists use to describe their work, *ArtSpeak* aimed to offer audience opportunities to connect with Pacific artists, take part in events they had helped to organise, and experience their work in emotional and sensory ways.

Perceived through the Māori concept of *kaitiakitanga*, curatorship in this context aligns with the Latin terms *cura*, meaning 'care', *curare*, 'to take care of', and an ecclesiastical understanding of the curator as someone who takes care of people and their souls.[23] This emphasises relationships between people, their concerns, stories, histories, emotional experiences, spiritual beliefs and values, as well as their objects. In the Māori language, *huihuinga* describes the process of gathering people together. In the curatorial context, I extend this to include the process of gathering stories, objects and ideas in preparation for collaborative, creative and curatorial encounters. Meeting *kanohi ki te kanohi*, face-to-face, helps to build trust, gather support, foster relationships and secure meaningful outcomes that are mutually beneficial.[24] Meeting in this way, we honour our different cultural and academic lineages and learn to understand and respect one another as part of a continuum – related to those who have gone before, those who make us who we are.

This approach draws upon customary Māori understandings of kaitiaki-tanga, which in my own whānau and *iwi* (tribal) context includes adopting the roles and responsibilities of custodians, caretakers, minders, protectors, interpreters and guardians for our ancestral *taonga* (treasures), including our land, seas, language, arts and creative, political and educational institutions. I also draw upon my interdisciplinary background as a visual and performing artist, and privilege a choreographic way of knowing in which the choreographer, artist or curator is a facilitator, or conduit for knowledge and meaning to emerge, rather than its primary source.

Two theoretical investigations inform this approach – my interdisciplinary PhD thesis exploring the Māori concept of *Te kore* (void, nothingness and potentiality) that features a creative methodology incorporating other Māori concepts derived from ancestral narratives and cosmologies,[25] and an article on creative collaboration co-written with the choreographer Carol Brown,[26] in which we extended the notion of choreographic collaboration, as an 'encounter through the body – sharing connections to place, histories and personal experience kanohi ki te kanohi',[27] to include collaborative writing as a 'remote collaboration calibrated by Wi-Fi connectivity and the erratic rhythm of emails, skype conversations and words shared between different time zones'.[28] While writing about these encounters, screens formed 'the interface for [our] collaboration. Keys nuance[d] touch and kinaesthetic exchanges'; and while 'tracking between spaces that are physically real, virtually distant and palpably present to each other demand[ed] of us an elastic perception of time and space',[29] we acknowledged bonds that tie us together. While writing this chapter with Noelle Kahanu and Philipp Schorch, I recognise a similar series of turns and transformation of ideas between our meetings and geographic separations.

To describe the dynamic layering, interaction, collaboration and analysis a choreographic approach to curation entails, I also utilise the Māori concepts *whakapapa* and *hurihuritanga*. Whakapapa can be understood as a genealogical or relational way of knowing: the action or process of making or establishing connections between people, objects, the natural and immaterial worlds; the beliefs, concerns and emotional connections people have with objects within cultural and curatorial contexts; and the analysis of those connections. Hurihuritanga, the choreographic action of turning, or turning ideas over in one's mind, can be substituted for the more optically oriented notion of reflection to indicate the potential for turning and realigning ideas, objects, bodies and oneself in order to consider things from multiple perspectives or positions.[30]

While developing the initial proposal for *ArtSpeak*, I was a new faculty member in the Center of Pacific Island Studies (CPIS) at UHM. I was keen to develop collaborative teaching and learning opportunities with other faculty members, including colleagues from Theatre and Dance, Fine Arts, the Academy for Creative Media, American Studies and the English creative writing programme. Face-to-face meetings between us were an important step towards realising this possibility. The proposal also responded to two opportunities – a gap in the UHM Commons Gallery calendar, and the chance to develop something that would complement another exhibition in the main UHM Art Gallery, titled *Binding and Looping: Transfer of Presence in Contemporary Pacific Art.*

Binding and Looping was curated by the art history Professor Deborah Waite, and brought together artists and their work from Papua New Guinea, Aotearoa New Zealand, the Cook Islands, Hawai'i, Samoa, Tonga and the Marshall Islands. Some of the work incorporated binding and looping as a physical process in the weaving or twining of natural materials to make cloaks, *bilum* (bags) and mats while representing the spiritual connections and emotional ties that bind people together. Other works drew on customary forms and processes but interpreted these with modern materials. Some of Bernice Akamine's suspended jewel-like pieces, for example, were modelled after traditional Hawaiian *hina'i*, or fish traps, but were delicately woven with glass, copper and sterling silver wire. Threading together material elements in one of these works offered a nuanced interpretation of social connection as a source of strength and something precious to be treasured and nurtured with care: 'Ua hilo 'ia i ke aho a ke aloha. Braided with the cords of love. Held in the bond of affection.'[31] Filipe Tohi's *Nikoniko* replicated *lalava*, or lashing patterns found in Polynesian boat building and architectural contexts, with wooden slats to create a spiral, architectural scaled form around one of the columns supporting the gallery roof. For Tohi, lalava patterns 'were a mnemonic device for representing a life philosophy' and 'balance in daily life' – they were 'metaphorical and physical ties to cultural knowledge'.[32]

The binding and looping theme that Deborah Waite aimed for[33] was further reiterated in the spatial configuration of exhibits within the gallery that encouraged a circular movement through the space, around, and between adjacent works. This theme resonated with *ArtSpeak*'s goal to provide space and opportunities for audiences and artists to meet kanohi ki te kanohi, join in conversations that would move and be reconfigured in relation to different works on display in both galleries. Face-to-face meetings were also an integral part of the planning process between Deborah Waite and myself, the gallery director Rod Bengston, the head of the Department of Art and Art History Gaye Chan and other gallery staff.

Binding and Looping and *ArtSpeak* opened together on the same day with a ceremonial Hawaiian launch, introductory talks from the curators, live music, food and impromptu dancing (Figure 18.6). A large number of community members from outside the university attended the opening and a joint programme of public events helped to sustain good attendance figures throughout the duration of the installations. There had not been a major exhibition of art work by Pacific Island artists at the UH Mānoa art gallery for more than twenty years, and many felt that such programming, especially with its emphasis on securing Pacific Island community support and engagement with artists, was long overdue.

One of my video installations, *Kēhua Wahangū*,[34] was included in *Binding and Looping*. In this work, the camera pans across a surface, outlines an edge moving slowly against a dark background and down towards us – the viewers – like a wave, before turning to reverse our perception of movement up and over something darker, shifting our centres off balance towards and away from the wall. With this larger than life-sized video loop that repeats and inverts itself, I wanted to convey the sense of uncertainty and self-reflection that can accompany investigative thinking within a creative practice prior to the completion of an art work – as *whakatītahataha,* a teetering sensation, as if being perilously positioned on the edge of an abyss while peering into the unknown.

Devised as part of my doctoral investigation into how Te Kore might be represented and explored through different media and in different contexts, *Kehua Wahangu* embodies at one level a choreographic and digital manipulation of video data. Hurihuritanga – understood here as shifting modes of perception from visual to spatial and kinaesthetic dimensions – was part of the making process and sensory experience I wanted viewers to have while engaging with the work. This in turn evoked one of the ways in which Te kore can be described – as *Te Kore-te-rawea* – a void where nothing is entwined or bound together. In creative and curatorial contexts, this understanding of Te kore-te-rawea can be likened to the sense of being incomplete, including the state of anticipation and anxiety felt prior to the successful resolution or completion of an art work or installation, and the possibility for meaning to be generated that is not yet fully resolved until an audience moves through, interacts with, and responds to the exhibition.

Hurihuritanga in a curatorial context is thus more than a form of analysis; it is a process that enhances curatorial potential through emphasising multiple rather than singular perspectives and opportunities for audiences to connect with the work. As an exploratory approach, hurihuritanga also aims to draw audience attention to detail as well as broader contextual information – variations in texture, rhythm, scale and use of space in installations can be used to highlight and shift attention from one historical, aesthetic or cultural layer within an exhibition to another. Where audiences, including artists and performers, are invited to respond to exhibitions, their feedback and conversations generate new layers of meaning that can be returned to the communities the objects originate from. They can offer frank advice and also challenge curators to rethink their strategies. Textual variation in label descriptions can also be perceived as choreographic prompts or directions to move our thinking in new directions, to consider different voices and multiple interpretations, and unsettle entrenched views.

Hurihuritanga further entails reflection upon our own curatorial practice – how we might position ourselves in relation to the objects and communities we work with, evaluate and improve the quality of our working relationships, and remain open to the potential for new meanings to emerge. This emphasis on process and relationship building, within relevant cultural contexts and with relevant cultural experts, aims to highlight the significance of cultural objects, art works, and practices to their respective cultural communities. It also enables them to be part of the ongoing caretaking of these works, and for the works themselves to remain part of those extended communities. Curatorial anxieties about retaining a sense of control can be replaced in this way with a more fruitful and generative focus on building and sustaining networks of relationships that recognise the sense of agency, dignity and mana of people and their art.

On the final night of *Binding and Looping*, students from a class I had been teaching joined forces with visiting students from the Australian National University in Canberra to devise a collaborative response to that exhibition. Their brief was to make a series of habitable dwellings from recycled materials that would be installed adjacent to selected work in the *Binding and Looping* exhibit. The work would then be deconstructed during the performance or immediately afterwards. One group installed a cardboard home beneath my video, complete with a coral pathway, an original sound score and a garden of painted signs protesting against the level of homelessness in Hawai'i. Empathising with the experiences of loss, physical and emotional trauma that members of the local homeless community experience, students making this work created a personal response to a socio-political condition made all the more poignant for its domestic touches and design detail. Another group chose to weave a mat that doubled as a tent, out of plastic bags, for a performance featuring Māori chant and contemporary dance next to Tina Wirihana's *Kahu weka*, a cloak woven from New Zealand flax and *weka*[35] feathers. In this work, Wirihana's understanding of cloaks being metaphorically twined with *makawe*, or ancestral hair, to offer spiritual, ancestral and physical protection,[36] was transposed through material substitution and scale from clothing imbued with cultural significance into a theatrical set.

A third group responded to the commercialisation and corruption of customary Pacific cultures, and institutional restrictions placed on their attempt to introduce natural plant materials into the gallery, with costuming that included a finely made cloak of oiled leaves, Samoan chant, a knife dance that paid homage to a spot-lit cross of Diet Coke cans, and a ritual procession that exited the gallery and finished outside. Considered in relation to the concept of hurihuritanga, aims to raise awareness of the multilayered physical, metaphorical, emotional, philosophical and spiritual nature of contemporary Pacific Island art were reflected in the complexity of student work created for this event and the level of conversation the exhibitions generated.

Binding and Looping had opened two months earlier with a choreographed procession and entrance that circled through the gallery led by Hawaiian chanters (Figure 18.6), and the students' final performance and exhibition culminated in a procession that spiralled out of the gallery in the opposite direction. While reflecting the spirit of the ceremonial opening, their work honoured curatorial themes of *Binding and Looping* and *ArtSpeak* and extended potential readings of them in new directions.

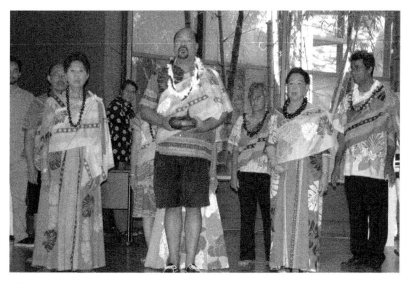

18.6 Native Hawaiian chanters, led by Keali'i Gora, leading opening proceedings for the *Binding and Looping: Transfer of Presence in Contemporary Pacific Art* exhibition, 5 October 2014.

Coda: Curatopia face-to-face

There is a growing body of literature in anthropology, museum studies and related fields that draws attention to more nuanced dimensions of the human experience, such as senses, feelings, emotions, affect and embodiment.[37] Attending to these qualities while working on this book, which is devoted to curatorial histories, theories and practices, I was instinctively drawn to think about 'audiences' and their sensory and visceral engagements with curatorial *products*, such as exhibitions. Yet, I also wondered about the physicality of the curatorial *process*, that is, the curatorial bodies, encounters and relations which inescapably shape, but are often excluded from, conventional definitions of 'the scientific'. Noelle Kahanu and Moana Nepia have countered this tendency by presenting he alo ā he alo / kanohi ki te kanohi as an Indigenous curatorial principle and method.[38] I, Philipp Schorch, want to add to this line of argument by suggesting how the face-to-face has brought a scholarly network, gathered and expressed through *Curatopia*, into being.

This book, like any intellectual endeavour (even so-called abstract reasoning), is the outcome of face-to-face encounters and interpersonal engagements. It would not have been possible without the remarkable hospitality with which Kahanu and Nepia welcomed me into their lives while doing fieldwork at Bishop Museum and research at the University of Hawai'i at Mānoa in 2014. Nor would it have been possible without Arapata Hakiwai introducing me to staff at Bishop Museum, and Billie

Lythberg putting me in touch with Amiria Salmond, who connected me with more people at Bishop Museum and the University of Hawai'i – all before I even arrived in Honolulu. When the idea of a symposium spontaneously erupted over lunch with Kahanu and Nepia, I reached across the 'sea of islands'[39] to Aotearoa New Zealand and Conal McCarthy, who immediately jumped on board to launch a second edition of the initial *Curatopia*, which he had organised a few years earlier at Victoria University of Wellington. Last but not least, I reached the other way across the globe to my colleagues Eveline Dürr and Gabriele Herzog-Schröder at the Ludwig-Maximilians-Universität München in Germany, who also jumped on board the *waka* (canoe) and supported the initiative from inception to fruition. For me, *Curatopia* is, both personally and intellectually, the highlight of the last decade of living, travelling, working, thinking and feeling between European and Pacific worlds.

Choosing these words to finish this book, I might easily be criticised for not complying with often rigidly defined academic criteria because I have addressed personal affairs and indulged in a sort of nostalgic and sentimental navel-gazing exercise. I simply respond that I do not care and will not apologise. Much more than the personal, however, is at stake here. Feminist thought has quite successfully taught us that the personal is political. In a similar vein, then, the personal is intellectual or academic too. Instead of trying hard to move the audience to a sympathetic or even empathetic response, these closing words clearly map the place, or rather places, from which *Curatopia* evolved and from which I speak and write. *Tūrangawaewae*, a powerful Māori concept and word – literally meaning standing place (*tūranga*) and feet (*waewae*) – is often translated as 'a place to stand', referring to places where one feels empowered and connected as one's foundation and place in the world, or rather worlds. Approaching *Curatopia*, and understanding myself in this context, through the concept of tūrangawaewae makes sense for several reasons.

First, on an intellectual level the concept resonates well with so-called Western notions such as Pierre Bourdieu's 'epistemic reflexivity',[40] which denotes reflection on the conditions under which knowledge comes into being. *Curatopia* should therefore be seen not as an attempt to issue a kind of legislative prescription but, instead, as a particular moment in a process which is *at once* personal and intellectual/academic, a critical attitude emerging through cross-cultural encounters and engagements between biographies, bodies and imaginations. Something that could be called, using a cross-cultural label, an 'epistemic tūrangawaewae' can help to humanise curatorship by pulling 'the curators' out of their often obscure role as an 'invisible actor behind the scenes'[41] of the production of knowledge, and thus of the execution of power.

Second, the concept of tūrangawaewae brings us back to the thematic focus of this edited volume. Importantly, I do not appropriate tūrangawaewae as a sign of jubilant postmodern or postcolonial celebration, or as a gestural accommodation of the subaltern before its eventual

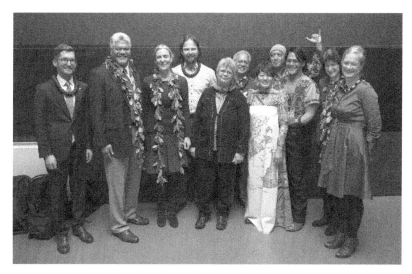

18.7 A group of German and Hawaiian participants – including authors Noelle Kahanu (fifth from right) and Philipp Schorch (fourth from left) – in the historic repatriation of iwi kūpuna (ancestral remains) from the State Ethnographic Collections Saxony, Germany, to Hawai'i, 23 October 2017.

assimilation within the dominant whole, but rather mobilise it on the conceptual plane to make sense of the inherently cross-cultural quality of the place that I stand, speak and write from. While it is undisputable that this argument presented here departs from my position as an (East) German scholar of the Pacific and museums (among other things) who is now based in Leipzig, (East) Germany, it is equally undisputable that both places, Germany and Leipzig, are – through the perpetual travelling of people, objects, ideas, theories, concepts, practices and meanings – unavoidably intertwined with other places. In short, Germany, Leipzig and my own biography are integral parts of Pacific (and other) worlds, as demonstrated anew in the historic repatriation of iwi Kūpuna (ancestral remains) from the State Ethnographic Collections Saxony, Germany, to Hawai'i (Figure 18.7). *Curatopia*, the book, the events, the models of curatorship presented here, and the various relationships with people from different parts of the globe instantiated by them, lend further empirical weight to this assertion. *Curatopia* offers a conscious initiative that resists territorial confinements through so-called national intellectual traditions.

If these personal comments appear too utopian, one could ease any note of caution by referring to an intellectual reality most readers would likely agree with: if we accept that curatorial histories, theories and practices are socially constructed, then they can also be deconstructed and reconstructed. *Curatopia*, then, is for ever up for grabs; and it will for ever depend on, and be enacted through, the he alo ā he alo / kanohi ki te kanohi / face-to-face.

Notes

1 See McCarthy, Hakiwai and Schorch; and Mallon, Chapters 13 and 17 above.

2 See L. Peers and A.K. Brown, *Museums and Source Communities* (Oxford and New York: Routledge, 2003); N. Thomas, *Entangled Objects: Exchange, Material Culture, and Colonialism in the Pacific* (Cambridge, MA, and London: Harvard University Press, 1991).

3 P. Schorch and N.M.K.Y. Kahanu, 'Forum as Laboratory: The Cross-Cultural Infrastructure of Ethnographic Knowledge and Material Potentialities', in *Prinzip Labor: Museumsexperimente im Humboldt Lab Dahlem* (Berlin: Nicolai, 2015), pp. 241–8; P. Schorch and N.M.K.Y. Kahanu, 'Anthropology's Interlocutors: Hawai'i Speaking Back to Ethnographic Museums in Europe', *Zeitschrift für Kulturwissenschaften*, 1 (2015), 114–17; P. Schorch, 'Assembling Communities: Curatorial Practices, Material Cultures, and Meanings', in B. Onciul, M. Stefano and S. Hawke (eds), *Engaging Communities, Engaging Heritage* (Woodbridge: Boydell and Brewer, 2017), pp. 31–46.

4 For a related Māori example of this approach, see P. Tapsell, 'The Flight of Pareraututu: An Investigation of Taonga from a Tribal Perspective', *Journal of the Polynesian Society*, 106:4 (1997), 323–74.

5 P. Burgess, 'He alo ā he alo', in R. MacPherson (ed.), *He alo ā he alo: Face to Face: Hawaiian Voices on Sovereignty* (Honolulu: Hawai'i Area Office American Friends Service Committee, 1993), p. xii.

6 *Ibid.*

7 J. Clifford, *Routes: Travel and Translation in the Late Twentieth Century* (Cambridge, MA, and London: Harvard University Press, 1997), p. 188.

8 M.L. Pratt in Clifford, *Routes*, 188.

9 *Ibid.*

10 The lo'i is an irrigated terrace or paddy where the native root vegetable *kalo*, or *taro*, is grown. Kalo is the traditional staple of the Hawaiian people and is genealogically considered the older sibling of the Hawaiian people. Burgess's invitation to work together in the lo'i is not a light matter. Not only is such work difficult labour, but it also requires an understanding of protocol regulating appropriate behaviour, such as not speaking ill of others.

11 Pub. L. 101–601, 25 U.S.C. 3001 et seq., 104 Stat. 304. This act creates a process whereby Native American tribes and Native Hawaiian organisations can petition for the repatriation of human remains, funerary objects, sacred objects and objects of cultural patrimony from federal agencies and institutions receiving federal funding.

12 K.S. Fine-Dare, *Grave Injustice: The American Indian Repatriation Movement and NAGPRA* (Lincoln and London: University of Nebraska Press, 2002); M. Graham and N. Murphy, 'NAGRPA at 20: Museum Collections and Reconnections', *Museum Anthropology*, 33:2 (2010), 105–24.

13 T.K. Tengan, 'The Return of Kū? Re-membering Hawaiian Masculinity, Warriorhood, and Nation', in L.R. Graham and H.G. Penny (eds), *Performing Indigeneity: Global Histories and Contemporary Experiences* (Lincoln and London: University of Nebraska Press, 2014), pp. 206–46; T.K. Tengan, 'The Return of Kū', in *E Kū ana ka paia: Unification, Responsibility and the Kū Images* (Honolulu: Bishop Museum, 2010).

14 S.M. Kamakau, *The Works of the People of Old* (Honolulu: Bishop Museum Press, 1976), p. 136.

15 T.P.K. Tengan, 'The Mana of Kū: Indigenous Nationhood, Masculinity and Authority in Hawai'i', in M. Tomlinson and T.P.K. Tengan (eds), *New Mana: Transformations of a Classical Concept in Pacific Languages and Cultures* (Canberra: Australian National University, 2016), p. 57.

16 *Ibid.*

17 This excerpt appears in M. Tomlinson and T.P.K. Tengan, *E Kū ana ka paia: Unification, Responsibility and the Kū Images* (Honolulu: Bishop Museum, 2010), and was attributed to the then President and CEO of Bishop Museum, Tim Johns.

18 *E Kū ana ka paia: Unification, Responsibility and the Kū Images* (Honolulu: Bishop Museum, 2010).

19 Literally translated, *noho* means 'the possession of a medium by a spirit or god', or, in other words, that the spirit sits or resides within the individual. See P. Elbert, *Hawaiian Language Dictionary* (Honolulu: Bishop Museum Press, 1986), p. 268.

20 See, for example, A. Lonetree, *Decolonizing Museums: Representing Native America in National and Tribal Museums* (Chapel Hill: University of North Carolina Press, 2012); S. Sleeper-Smith (ed.), *Contesting Knowledge: Museums and Indigenous Perspectives* (Lincoln and London: University of Nebraska Press, 2009); V. Gosselin and P. Livingstone (eds), *Museums and the Past: Constructing Historical Consciousness* (Vancouver and Toronto: University of British Columbia Press, 2016).

21 S. Ganaden, 'The Last Statues of Ku', *FLUX Hawaii Magazine* (24 November 2014).

22 *Ibid.*, 55.

23 See Introduction, above.

24 This aligns with practices other Māori researchers have proposed for Māori researchers. See L. Tuhiwai Smith, *Decolonising Methodologies: Research and Indigenous Peoples* (New York: Zed Books:; Dunedin: Otago University Press, 1999).

25 M. Nepia, 'Te kore: Exploring the Māori Concept of Void' (PhD dissertation: Auckland University of Technology, 2012), http://aut.researchgateway.ac.nz/handle/10292/5480.

26 C. Brown and M. Nepia, 'Te kore and the Encounter of Performance – Collaboration as a Mode of Labour', in N. Colin and S. Sachsenmaier (eds), *Collaboration in Performance Practice: Premise, Workings and Failures* (London and New York: Palgrave Macmillan, 2016).

27 *Ibid.*, 197.

28 *Ibid.*, 198.

29 *Ibid.*

30 Nepia, 'Te kore', 2012, 125, 129, 153, 159, 200, 254.

31 M.K. Pukui, *'Ōlelo no'eau Hawaiian Proverbs & Poetical Sayings* (Honolulu: Bishop Museum Press, 1983), p. 307; saying 2786 in Bernice Akamine (2014), *Binding and Looping* label text for *Pahele 1 – Portrait* (2013), University of Hawai'i at Mānoa Art Gallery, 3.

32 *Binding and Looping* label text.

33 University of Hawai'i Museum Studies Sound Cloud (1014). Curator's Introduction by Deborah Waite, https://soundcloud.com/uh-museum-studies/sets/binding-looping-transfer-of-presence-in-contemporary-pacific-art. Accessed 15 April 2017.

34 Originally titled *Sheets*, this work was created as part of my 2012 PhD thesis and is available for viewing online at AUT University's Scholarly Commons website, http://aut.researchgateway.ac.nz/handle/10292/5480. Accessed 15 April 2017.

35 Weka (*Gallirallus australis*) is a flightless native New Zealand bird with brown feathers.

36 Personal communication, Gallery Walk Through with Maile Andrade and Tina Wirihana, Tuesday 21 October 2014, UH Mānoa Art Gallery, Honolulu, Hawai'i, USA.

37 The literature is voluminous so here I am referring only to my work: P. Schorch, E. Waterton and S. Watson, 'Museum Canopies and Affective Cosmopolitanism: Cultivating Cross-Cultural Landscapes for Ethical Embodied Responses', in D. Tolia-Kelly, E. Waterton and S. Watson (eds), *Heritage, Affect and Emotion: Politics, Practices and Infrastructures* (London and New York: Routledge, 2017), pp. 93–113; P. Schorch, 'Cultural Feelings and the Making of Meaning', *International Journal of Heritage Studies*, 20:1 (2014), 22–35.

38 See Onciul, Chapter 10 above.

39 E. Hau'ofa, 'Our Sea of Islands', *The Contemporary Pacific*, 6:1 (1994), 147–61.

40 P. Bourdieu, *In Other Words: Essays towards a Reflexive Sociology* (Cambridge: Polity Press, 1994).

41 H. Arendt, *The Human Condition* (Chicago: University of Chicago Press, 1958).

AFTERWORDS

Curating time

19

Ian Wedde

Reading the chapters in this book I was struck by how often issues of time were critical to the discussions. 'Time', of course, is a very complex word that James Clifford parses with great economy in 'The Times of the Curator' (Chapter 7); but I was interested also in the ways in which issues of time were present as a kind of haunting in the texts assembled here, present (so to speak) by implication rather than by intent; and sometimes it was the absence of reflection on time that struck me as another kind of haunting, as if issues of temporality could be taken for granted as givens within the framing concept of a 'curatopia'.

The neologism 'curatopia' around which this book is organised is, of course, a temporal portmanteau within which *progress* – in the form of an evolving trajectory of curating practices or an ideal curatorial future – is proffered as a conceptual lure; or, more optimistically, as a *present* in which an ideal state of affairs has, finally, reached a destination in which current curatorial practices can be framed in utopian time. But then we all know that utopia by its nature does not exist except as an emergent or, as it may be, aspirational condition, and that what Clifford calls 'the times' are always at once fixed in a historical context and 'a-changing'; and a-changing for the better in the curatopian scenario. There may be, or may have been, utopian pasts – 'golden ages' etc. – but these are clearly not relevant to the current project, except as reminders of the slippery nature of the temporalities variously under discussion here.

Among several key passages in which Clifford probes and case studies these issues, the following are critical:

> In what follows I evoke two senses of temporality: 1. 'The Times': as in the historical moment or context, 'the life and times of x' 2. 'Times' plural: a sense of the curator's task as enmeshed in multiple, overlapping, sometimes conflicting times.

And:

> My primary concern is the discrepant temporalities (sometimes I want to say 'histories', or even 'futures') that are integral to the task of the curator today.

What this formula allows for is the possibility that a historically fixed instance of 'the times' in the past might be folded into an apparently 'discrepant' temporality: the present. This happens routinely when a museum object continues to be displayed within what we deem to be an outmoded or even inappropriate interpretative narrative – for example a colonialist one. A progressive curatopian impulse may want to remove or rescue this object from degrading anachronism. Left in this anachronistic state, the object will however yield knowledge not only about 'the [historical] times' from which it can or should be liberated but also about 'the [present] times' in terms of which we now believe it should be understood. And, I want to add, even if this object is re-presented in 'the [revisionist] times' of a progressive present, it will still continue to bear witness to its past or, indeed, pasts.

Curators themselves are likely to embody such over- or in-foldings of times: the curator's temporal presence and consciousness will be furnished not just by contemporary theories and beliefs and their associated practices but also by accumulated evolutionary and developmental steps along the way – by co-present temporalities and instances of 'the times'. The progressive and improving impulse of curatopia may seem to be linear but it will also, inevitably, be accumulative; and, we should expect, accumulative in a critically dialogic way. The curator will be the repository of these critical accumulations and even of sheddings and disavowals of them, and will move through time *with*, not just despite or on from or beyond such accumulations, sheddings and disavowals.

As well as thinking about things as historicised subjects 'with stories to tell', and about curators as subjects with accumulated knowledge about ways of telling those stories or enabling them to be told, we need to think about participating subjects in the form of diverse communities of interest, as many writers in this book do: traditional or customary owners of things including their stories, general as well as scholarly audiences, and even future audiences, as Sharon Macdonald and Jennie Morgan suggest in 'What not to collect? Post-connoisseurial dystopia and the profusion of things': 'But at the same time, we have a duty to future generations to actually try and show the way things are today'.

What is suggested here is a curatorial duty to project a model of 'the [today] times' into the future. Macdonald and Morgan are talking not quite about 'the times' in Clifford's sense but about the embodiment of 'the times' in their historically specific material cultures: in things – objects, images, texts, sounds, technologies, archives – that curators will have to make decisions about collecting or not collecting *today*. However, these things cannot be detached from collection development policies and priorities for the accumulation of things. Equally, such policies cannot be detached from 'the times' of curatorial practices 'at the time' of collection; nor from 'the [accumulated historical] times' of past practices known to the curator; nor from the accumulated stories the things-as-subjects have told and will be able to tell to 'future generations', including stories about the ways in which curators have treated them 'over time'. This at once over-arching and cumulative time might best be characterised as archival or memory-time – and as such, time that will inevitably be political, in as much as it will have encompassed ongoing contests and negotiations over ownership, including ownership of truth and truth-values, and therefore over power and knowledge; over class, taste and privilege; and, indeed, over contesting knowledge systems or epistemologies.

In 'Concerning curatorial practice in ethnological museums: an epistemology of postcolonial debates' (Chapter 3), Larissa Förster and Friedrich von Bose cite several writers including Macdonald, and introduce the challenging term 'memory politics'. Paul Tapsell's statement that, 'in a Māori sense, we are our ancestors' (Chapter 12) is a political framing of embodied memory. Memory, of course, is not inert: in 'The figure of the kaitiaki: learning from Māori curatorship past and present' (Chapter 13), Conal McCarthy, Arapata Hakiwai and Philipp Schorch refer to Awhina Tamarapa's statement that 'the display of the *pātaka* (food storehouse) called *Te Tākinga* in the exhibition *Mana Whenua*' at the Museum of New Zealand Te Papa Tongarewa 'did not talk only about the tribal *past*, but their *present and future*'. A Polynesian concept of time predicated on facing the past in order to move into and understand the future is mentioned several times in this book. The epistemologies of memory and of time have long, fractious histories in metaphysics and, more recently, in cognitive science, with the question of whether memory can ever be disconnected from systems of belief a persistent point of contention.[1] In addition, as well as the problem of truth values in relation to memory and belief, the factual reliability of individual memory is hardly certain in matters of public record. How memory functions is, also then, an inherently political issue, a provocation or irritant at the juncture of social or cultural and political histories since the cultural turn of the mid-1970s.[2]

The question of how memory may inform or shape the future is also, currently, reshaping how we might think about conservation – a word that has a rapidly expanding and urgent remit. The UK Arts and Humanities Research Council's project *Heritage Futures* (with which both Sharon Macdonald and Jennie Morgan are involved) is a good example of work that challenges 'heritage' to take legacy responsibility for impacts of 'the [today] times' on the future.[3] *Heritage Futures* asserts in its oxymoronic name and in its mission statements that the work of 'designing the future' goes well beyond conserving cultural memory for consumption by future audiences. The project's multidisciplinary goals are expressed in activist terms; memory is given explicit agency in a future imagined as potentially dystopian.

> Current global crises and transformations (from climate change to mass migration) highlight the need to develop more sustainable and resilient future making practices, and encourage different areas of interest to pursue common goals and learn from one another.[4]

'The [political] times' of the curator is, it seems to me, the prevailing theme of this book, and the context within which variously improving, revisionist and critical curatopian scenarios are discussed, analysed, critiqued and played out. A majority of these scenarios are concerned in one way or another with aspects of decolonisation, which of course involves a folding of time: interventions in the present on 'the times' of past or persisting colonialist practices, belief-systems or mind-sets; and all scenarios gathered in this book draw to some extent on memory resources with, inevitably, varying degrees of politicised belief-system affiliations.

Inevitably and appropriately, the scenarios cluster around museum work and discourse, both curatorial and academic. As I began to draw together the themes and scenarios of the chapters collected here, I increasingly felt the need to move outside points of view determined and contained to greater or lesser extents by the politics of museum practices and, indeed, by the locations and institutions that conventionally or unconventionally constitute museums. When teaching curatorial practice, I used to remind my students that an audience's museum experience begins some time before they enter the museum as such, and will not end the moment they leave: all museums are, so to speak, 'museums without walls'. The affective, cognitive and psychomotor components of a visitor's pre-visit time, not to mention the latest news item they read or heard, the varieties of excitement or indifference with which they approach the visit over preceding hours or days, their existing knowledge, interest or indifference – their cultural capital, if you will – the weather, the ease or difficulty of transportation, the company they are in: all of these (and more) times, temporalities and conditioning experiences come in to the museum with them. What they encounter in the museum will probably add to, challenge or affirm aspects of this pre-loaded mélange of times, moods, beliefs and memories. What they encounter and *perceive* may also influence how existing memories are stored, prioritised and framed: the museum visit may 're-mind' the visitor of something that happened in their past and may draw that 'long-term' memory into 'short-term', front-of-consciousness awareness – awareness based on sense and perception. From there, the 'short-term' memory will soon retire once again to its 'long-term' brain-space, but may do so in an altered or edited state.

To state the obvious in this way is only to remind ourselves that the temporalities of the museum experience exist within and in relation to the expanded field of the diverse subjectivities, including memories, of subjects-as-audiences. Despite the generous and diverse reach of curatopian thinking in these chapters, I found myself wanting to reorient my point of view outside 'the [institutional] times' of the curator, to find a subjective view-shaft on the urgent issues discussed under the heading Curatopia.

There is a personal story that I have shared a few times over the years in essays and occasional writing, and this may be a way of pivoting from the museum-centric focus of curatopia. But first, some preparatory thoughts. Looking back across the occasions on which I have told the story and the motivations for returning somewhat obsessively to it, I now notice a predictable set of conditions. These include the fact that I am usually trying to find a point of departure from which to understand and discuss the apparently paradoxical relationship of memory to a present, and at the same time trying to understand why abjection – an anxiety about self-identity or authenticity – also seems to be in play; this comes down to a self-doubting question: 'Am I telling the truth?' Or, to put it another way, does a narrative based in memory do credit to my consciousness, which I believe to be responsible not only for representing who I am, but how I got to be this way – how I got to be *present*?

The issue of whether or not the presence of memory is paradoxical will always be both a phenomenological and an epistemological one: what and how do I perceive, how do remembered perceptions inform the constitution of a present, and what and how do I learn from this? And what, indeed, do I learn from being conscious of – perceiving – the phenomenon of memory as a reticulation of the past in the present?

The German writer W.G. Sebald made this paradoxical dynamic the basis of much of his work, in particular his 1992 novels *Die Ausgewanderten*, published in English as *The Emigrants* in 1996; and *Austerlitz* (English translation 2001).[5] In *Austerlitz* the eponymous character, obsessed with memory and how he came to be who he is in a time he cannot fully comprehend as 'present', addresses a long disquisition on time to his unnamed companion (who resembles Sebald himself). In the course of this monologue, the ageing art historian Austerlitz, who was the emigrant child of Jewish parents murdered during the Holocaust, says this:

> I shall find that all moments of time have co-existed simultaneously, in which case none of what history tells us would be true, past events have not yet occurred but are waiting to do so at the moment when we think of them.[6]

Despite its tragic and traumatic historical context, the experience of time that Sebald describes through Austerlitz will be familiar to many of us. In my own case, I remember a particular moment in which a set of vivid sensory experiences caused a hallucinatory flashback to a time in my childhood, a kind of experience shared by many people I have spoken to about it, and made famous, of course, in Volume 1, 'Swann's Way', of Marcel Proust's *À la recherche du temps perdu*. The experience is phenomenological in as much as, *pace* Merleau-Ponty,[7] it consists of an apparently empirical record of perceptions, where memory is the recording agent. It is epistemological in as much as it discloses knowledge about the past that I have no reason to doubt, though that rationality is subverted to some extent by abjection; and it also shows me a kind of neurological or mentality experiment whose yield is how sensory perceptions such as smell can directly access knowledge we call 'memory' – can, in fact, recall the past into the present, producing that apparently paradoxical palimpsest.

So, the story. In 1969, I was twenty-three and recently married. Rose and I were travelling out of Colombo in what was then still known as Ceylon, to stay overnight in Kandy up in the mountains. We were in a battered, dark green Austin Cambridge with a driver whose name I cannot remember, though I am sure I have in the past. Let's call him Ricardo, a plausible Portuguese name, since our driver told us that he was a Roman Catholic whose family could be traced back to the Portuguese who had once colonised much of Ceylon in the sixteenth and seventeenth centuries. We made a deal with him to drive us up to Kandy and back that would cost a bit more than the bus, but that would return us in time for our flight out the next day. The deal included us staying in his cousin's hotel in Kandy and having a pre-departure meal in his brother's restaurant in Colombo.

It's odd that I can remember the car because I am not interested in them, but this banal detail seems to be the key with which to open the time capsule of memory. As part of his sales pitch, 'Ricardo' smacked the bonnet of his Austin Cambridge and assured us that English cars were the best, assuming that we were English or at least Anglophile. Entering the superior English car and driving out of Colombo on the left-hand side of the road, we were conveyed by colonial history as well as by Ricardo – at that time as New Zealanders we shared the same Commonwealth monarch and rules of the road, despite Ricardo's Portuguese ancestors and my German ones. In 1969, I belonged to a generation of New Zealanders that increasingly rejected traces of colonialism in our society, such as the designation of England as 'home', varieties of settler privilege and imperialisms marked for us by the war in Vietnam; and so, I felt somewhat ashamed of having a private car with a driver, a shame evidenced by our willing concessions to Ricardo's bargaining on behalf of his extended family.

However, part of my childhood had been spent within the Austin Cambridge, as it were, of colonialist protocols and privileges: when my twin brother and I were between the ages of seven and ten, our family lived in a remote part of East Pakistan, now Bangladesh. Despite coming from the frugal, post-Depression small-town home of our maternal grandmother in the South Island of Aotearoa New Zealand, we became accustomed to a household with servants and clear demarcations between the 'us' of a management elite and a 'them' of Bengali people living in the township by the paper mill where our father worked in one of the start-up projects planned to accelerate the country into industrial modernity. This was a past that, in 'the times' of 1969, I wished to banish or at least repudiate – but could not forget.

In 1954, the township of Chandraghona near the paper mill, the banks of the Karnafuli river and the dusty roads through the surrounding countryside were filled with a rich variety of pungent smells: dust, wood-smoke and the smoke of dried cow dung, drying fish, jasmines and frangipani flowers, shit. Fifteen or so years later, as we were driven in the green Austin Cambridge through villages and countryside on the road to Kandy, these same smells blew into the car and triggered a hallucinatory memory of the floral patterning of my mother Linda's frock when I was about seven. I turned to look at Rose and was momentarily shocked to see not my dark-haired mother Linda in her patterned frock but a slight, fair-haired young woman wearing jeans. This disconcerting effect came and went for the duration of our stay in Ceylon and only dissipated once we got back on the plane. The place and time I was in for about forty-eight hours, the senses and phenomena I encountered there, even the person I was with, all seemed to be shifting back and forth across another set of conditions that were at once vividly present and from the past. The effect, though, was not of separation but of a kind of simultaneity.

Were I now to curate this simultaneity as a Sebald-like social and political history project, its key artefact might well be the battered green Austin Cambridge driven in the late 1960s by the Sinhalese descendant of a sixteenth-century Portuguese trader or soldier or colonial administrator. The car's passenger narratives would fold together a childhood in small-town Aotearoa New Zealand during the late 1940s and early 1950s, the experience of colonialist expatriate privilege in post-partition East Bengal during the mid- to late 1950s, a counter-narrative of youthful radicalisation and postcolonial chagrin in the late 1960s, and a 'present' rather like that described by Sebald's character Austerlitz, in which 'the moment when we think of them' is when events happen.[8]

This contingent and uncertain 'moment' is, of course, profoundly and unassailably subjective, and easily dismissed as such. But it is also, I suggest, the kind of juncture at which any credible 'Curatopia' occupies time and opens up the possibility of agency in the task of 'designing the future'. The juncture is not just a critically inert one between an individual conscious-ness and 'the times'. I think of it, rather, as the battered, inevitably anach-ronistic vehicle of thought that must be kept circulating through many 'presents' that will be at once hallucinatory and cognitively secure, abject and confident, expedient and speculative, anarchic and programmatic, ephemeral and obdurate. We will have a lot of fun in this vehicle, and we will probably be scared and uncertain sometimes, fearful of what may be about to happen and where we are going. As part of our trip we may visit a museum or historic site, such as the Sri Dalada Maligawa or Temple of the Tooth in Kandy, where one of Gautama Buddha's teeth is kept. We may receive the gift of healing holy water from the tooth's weekly bathing. The water will be scented with flowers called *Nanumura Mangalya*. We remem-ber the name of the flower. Then we catch our plane to the time when we remember this moment, and it happens.

Notes

1　See for example M. Frise, 'Preservationism in the Epistemology of Memory', *Philosophical Quarterly* (November 2016): pqw074. doi: 10.1093/pq/pqw074. Accessed 3 April 2017.

2　See for example S. Pincus and W. Novak, 'Political History after the Cultural Turn', in *Perspectives on History* (Washington, DC: American Historical Association, May 2011). Accessed 3 April 2017.

3　AHRC Heritage Futures project webpage: https://heritage-futures.org. Accessed 4 April 2017.

4 'A Note On Our Project's Rationale, Methods And Significance.', Heritage Futures webpage: https://heritage-futures.org/about/. Accessed 4 April 2017.
5 W.G. Sebald, *The Emigrants*, trans. by M. Hulse (New York: New Directions, 1996); and *Austerlitz*, trans. by A. Bell (New York: Random House/Modern Library Trade Paperback Edition, 2001).
6 Sebald, *Austerlitz*, 101.
7 M. Merleau-Ponty, *Phenomenology of Perception*, trans. by C. Smith (London: Routledge & Kegan Paul, 1965).
8 Sebald, *Austerlitz*, 101.

Virtual museums and new directions?

20

Vilsoni Hereniko

The word 'museum' for me evokes images of cultural objects in glass cases that reflect an era which is dead and gone. This has been my experience visiting most museums in different countries in Oceania. The better-funded museums in Australia and Aotearoa New Zealand as well as North America and Europe (including the United Kingdom), on the other hand, appear to be more vibrant and able to attract tourists and residents in larger numbers. The Hawaiian Hall and the Pacific Hall of the Bishop Museum in Honolulu used to reflect a bygone era until recent renovations and imaginative presentations made them more appealing to me, especially the new additions to the displays that juxtapose the present with the past.

Many museums today have valuable collections that are carefully curated and displayed for maximum enjoyment by visitors. Some of these museums house valuable cultural treasures of their country's former colonies with more cultural objects wrapped in plastic and hidden away in basements. Every now and then, if space or schedule permits, some of these hidden objects will be uncovered and displayed for a time before they are returned to hibernation. A concern is how people all over the world could gain access to valuable collections in such museums. This afterword explores some ideas that could democratise access to overseas collections of Pacific objects in this time of rapid technological change.

Nearly twenty years since the Internet opened up access to museums, many curators have yet to fully embrace the opportunities of globalisation. The kinds of changes that have been unleashed by digital technology are a reality that will not go away; it is therefore imperative that museum curators take charge of their futures by mastering the necessary skills. It is easy to protest in horror at the notion that anyone can be their own curator; it is more difficult to imagine a future in which members of the public who want to be informed and enlightened (as opposed to visitors just passing through) could find their museum experiences enhanced by new ways of learning about cultures that were previously unavailable.[1]

Two major forces that have shaped the various ways in which museums have evolved are decolonisation and globalisation. There are many examples of how specific museums have responded, some with success, to these

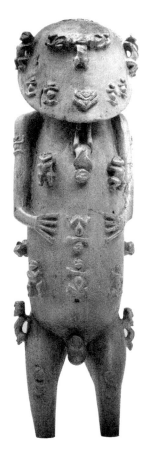

20.1 The statue of A'a from Rurutu in French Polynesia, 117 x 36 cm. British Museum, London, UK.

compelling influences. Decolonisation continues to be practised and theorised among scholars and will continue to be a source of debate and reflection. On the other hand, globalisation has not received enough attention by most museums, especially those in the Pacific. The ability to respond or not to the opportunities opened up by globalisation appears to be dependent on funding, location, focus, leadership and openness to change.

Museums today should have two presences: one physical, the other virtual. A virtual presence is recommended for relatively well-funded museums in developed countries, such as those in North America, Europe and Asia. These are countries that are most likely to have the human and financial resources to make their collection of Pacific Islands treasures housed in their exhibitions or basements available to people from Oceania. Not everyone has the means to leave the comfort of their homes in Samoa, Tonga, Fiji, the Cook Islands or French Polynesia (to name a few) and fly to the other end of the world to view cultural objects made by their ancestors. Many of these folks, however, especially those in cities or urban centres, have

Internet access. Colleges and universities in Oceania could also subscribe, making these rarely seen cultural treasures that originated in Oceania but are housed overseas become readily available to Pacific Islanders either for their viewing pleasure or for research purposes.

A number of museums, such as the Whitney Museum of American Art in New York, USA, are now making the entirety of their collections available online. The Rijksmuseum in Amsterdam, Netherlands, has taken things a step further and made its collection available on open data, 'so people can reproduce, edit, and play around with the works'. The Metropolitan Museum of Art (Met), New York, USA, the British Museum, London, UK, and the Smithsonian, Washington, DC, USA, are encouraging people to download and print 3-D-print replicas of artefacts, while the Google Art project, launched in 2011, features 'works by more than six thousand artists in more than 250 museums'. Since July 2016, people with Google Cardboard headsets can 'tour' twenty museums and historical sites. It is likely that, one day, some museums will exist online only. This suggests a future in which a curator's responsibility would be to 'curate digital exhibitions and change displays quickly to respond to global events in real time.'[2]

In May 2016, when I was screening a film I had made at the British Museum, I overheard a reference to an exhibition of the A'a, a God figure carved in anthropomorphic form with thirty small anthropomorphic figures on the surface of its body, from Rurutu, an island in French Polynesia.[3] I located the exhibition and spent time reading the accompanying literature, which suggested that this image of an ancient Polynesian religion was presented by a group of people from Rurutu to representatives of the London Missionary Society as a symbol of their conversion to Christianity (which probably accounts for the penis having been chopped off). I learned about the conflicting versions of the kind of wood that was used to create this impressive work of art that was also sacred to its creators: the people of Rurutu claimed it was made from pua keni wood (*fagraea berteriana*) that is native to the island of eastern Polynesia, while scientists claimed it was made from sandalwood. If it were the latter, then the object was made outside Rurutu and was not home-grown. Did this beautiful cultural treasure accompany people who came from beyond French Polynesia, perhaps from Hawai'i? I also learned that Pablo Picasso had two copies of this statue made (artists Roland Penrose and Henry Moore also made copies). Although I am not from Rurutu, I was proud to have seen this impressive work of sacred art from my part of the world.

How could this physical exhibition in a specific museum transcend its confinement to a building and 'travel' to the end of the world, especially to French Polynesia, the land (perhaps?) from which this unique cultural object on display originated? Given the unequal distribution of wealth between Europe and North America in comparison with the Pacific Islands, the vast majority of Pacific Islanders cannot travel to London to see an exhibition. This means that the museum would have to go to them, in a virtual sense, and via the Internet. After all, the new technologies are products as well as agents of cultural change.[4]

How could social media, especially Facebook, Instagram and Twitter, be harnessed to disseminate information about the holdings of Pacific materials in North American and European museums? How could ordinary persons who cannot travel but have access to the Internet participate in discussions and debates about these cultural treasures that are a part of their cultural heritage? How could affluent museums facilitate access beyond national borders? How could I have known about the Aʻa exhibition? The thought that I could have missed it when I was right next door raises the important question of how to easily gain access to the relevant information. In this particular instance, Facebook, Instagram and Twitter could have been deployed to get the word out to Pacific Islanders, and especially to people from French Polynesia.

The next best thing to repatriating physical cultural treasures back to their original sources is through virtual repatriation. This kind of action reconnects people with cultural treasures that had been alienated from them.[5] Usually, these alienated objects have interesting and important stories of encounters between the giver and the receiver. European versions of such exchanges may have to be revised when alternative accounts emerge after virtual repatriation. More importantly, repatriation could help make a people formerly alienated from the *mana* (spiritual power) of their ancestors whole again.[6] Until physical repatriation takes place, this way of 'giving back' demonstrates a progressive and enlightened approach to the changing role of the museum to take into account the pervasive influence of the Internet on all our lives today.

An exciting new technology being tested by museums is the use of Virtual Reality (VR) for learning about a museum's collections. The precursors to this new platform are the vast panoramic paintings of the 1800s, followed by stereoscopic photographs that produced three-dimensional effects on flat images by giving the illusion of depth. This desire to experience an alternative reality has its newest iteration in the digital format of VR, a 'user-computer interface that involves real-time simulation and interactions through multiple sensorial channels … [including visual, auditory, tactile, smell and taste]'.[7]

The British Museum, whose collection spans the whole world and forty thousand years of history, held its first VR experiment in August 2015. Visitors explored 'a virtual reality Bronze Age site, where they saw three-dimensional scans of objects placed in their original setting'.[8] Using a headset and earphones, children, young people, schools and families explored multiple interpretations of how the objects might have been used during the Bronze Age.[9] The responses to this VR experience were very positive.[10] Visitors highlighted enjoyment of the experience, its educational value, being able to see details they would have otherwise missed and the feeling of actually being there. Because the experience is non-linear with no beginning and no end point, users could interact freely with the object multiple times.

A notable finding is that the activities in an immersive VR environment left visitors with 'the lasting impression that their own ideas about the function of objects from the past can be equally valid to those of museum curators'.[11] Another outcome is helping people to remember that what they are experiencing was actually real, a way of humanising history.[12]

Since 2015, VR has given new life to museum exhibits, from guided tours to learning aids. In 2016, the Smithsonian released its first virtual app on both Apple and Android for a specific exhibition called *Wonder* that is now closed. However, this app raised important questions for museums that are constrained by real limitations of space, financial resources and staff time.[13] For example, could VR be a virtual extension of a museum's physical space and experiences? Could it be a 'sustainable way to help museums extend the life of expensive, complex and popular exhibits that can only be displayed for weeks or months at physical facilities?'[14] Also, could VR become an in-depth exhibit curated specifically and strictly for the digital realm? Regardless of the answers to the questions above, the creation of an app can achieve certain things: a longer life for important exhibits, an ability to reach a global audience and the creation of more complex and engaging experiences. The app also suggests that the curator for VR in the future can afford to have 'more audacious visions'.[15]

Recognising that cell phones have become extensions of who we are today, the Metropolitan Museum of Art made the decision about five years ago to allow visitors to use their cell phones. Rather than fighting a losing battle, museum curators could explore how to integrate Instagram-friendly exhibitions even as they use social media to market what is available. The Brooklyn Museum has an app that asks curators questions about art works in real time, and the Guggenheim and the Met have experimented with using Bluetooth to track the movements of visitors from one gallery to another as well as providing additional information. Further, an app that uses augmented reality to bring paintings to life, add flesh and skin to dinosaur bones or project images of animated beasts to follow visitors through galleries, are experiments in the use of technology to enhance a museum's offerings. A University of Southern California project is producing interactive 3-D holograms to answer visitors' questions. GPS technology, once approved, could help visitors avoid getting lost in large museums and make the experience of visiting a physical museum much more enjoyable.[16]

As the Internet broadens the reach of museums to global audiences, curators working collaboratively with the communities around them could transform their buildings into vibrant gathering places for artists and cultural practitioners. Inviting local artists to produce replicas of objects in glass boxes, or to produce contemporary versions informed by a museum's collection, are important reminders that a people's relationship to the objects on display has not been severed. In 2011, for example, the Fiji Museum in Suva had a Fijian woman producing pottery for sale just outside the museum's doors. As a recognised master potter, she affirmed her connections to a unique way of making pottery archived in the museum's collections. Selling what she was producing helped her survive economically in a capitalist economy, while those who bought from her returned home with museum-like objects that reinforced positive views of the Fiji museum.

The bringing together of people with ancestral objects reminds us of the primacy of people, over and above objects, unique and special as they are. Like 'captions' juxtaposed with cultural objects in a case, artists or cultural practitioners producing work nearby or reconnecting with their ancestors provide cultural context and complicate our perceptions of the objects on display, as well as the role of museums. They also help to stimulate cultural renewal and reinvigorate artistic and cultural production. Further, they raise new and important questions about decolonising museum practices to dispel the myth of museums exuding an air of superiority, often in a community, but not a venue that is frequented by those who live in its neighbourhoods because they are not viewed as relevant to people's lives. The ultimate goal is to work towards a time when the relationships between Euro-American museums and Indigenous peoples are 'reciprocal and symmetrical'.[17]

The restoration of lost relationships can activate mana in certain important objects that has been dormant. Such mana could be activated through touching, caressing, chanting and other associated rituals. These kinds of efforts that bring people and objects together could happen more often instead of being rare occurrences in museums. When a physical reunion is not possible, the production of digital replicas of the original is second best. Sometimes museums do not display Pacific objects because of space limitations, a problem that could be overcome by having virtual museums. Whatever the case may be, providing access (in person or through digital imagery) is an important and necessary aspect of curatorship today.[18]

How will the new technologies affect the curator of the future? This shift to a new way of viewing space as well as audience requires the museum curator of the future to be skilled in the new communication and information technologies of the present. It also requires knowledge of the conventional roles of the curator – collecting, display practices, building relationships with the relevant communities and knowledge of exhibition design to maximise the viewer's experience – as well as a flexibility and openness to experimentation with new technologies. The museum curator of the future will need to address major questions, such as how to use technology to support rather than detract from an in-person exhibit.[19] Both exhibits should complement each other, with each focusing on each medium's strengths. An exhibit that uses the new technologies requires the curator to reflect upon the ethics of repatriating or disseminating large numbers of cultural objects of value to their original homelands through digital images.[20]

It is imperative in today's technological climate that the Internet is used to make available the collections of prestigious museums to global audiences, but especially to Indigenous people who otherwise would never be able to see the cultural treasures of their ancestors. Information and communication technologies could also help to stimulate cultural production as we search for new ways of producing art that illuminates the human experience. As digital technology continues to become more sophisticated and user-friendly, it is possible that in the future 'museums will increasingly acquire artworks that aren't physical objects at all'.[21] Should this happen, the role of the museum curator will change dramatically.

One of the most interesting aspects of museums working within a virtual realm and using digital images is that this domain of exchange has the potential to shift attention away from the physical object or art work and on to the humanising experience that one could encounter through VR. For instance, it was not uncommon in Oceania and Asia for elaborate art works to be produced and used in certain rituals with the intention that at the end these creations would be destroyed or left outside to rot. The focus, after all, was not on the objects themselves, but on shared memories, feelings and emotions, as well as human connections, all of which are intangible. When visitors to Oceania – missionaries, traders, sailors, administrators, visiting dignitaries and so on – started to collect or hoard these sacred objects, attention shifted from the intangible to the tangible, resulting in these objects becoming valuable items for sale in the marketplace. Now some of them fetch millions of dollars as they are auctioned off to buyers who often have no personal connection to the original homeland or the people whose ancestors produced the object. Virtual museums could help to mitigate the capitalist impulses surrounding what is sometimes called 'tribal art' which seems to become more and more valuable as the years go by. Some of these objects are sometimes bought at auctions and make their way into museums.

Although I am a strong advocate for access to collections in museums and although I see new technologies as a necessary part of this goal, I do not think that technology and its associated impacts and benefits should be the end goal. Rather, they should exist collaboratively with physical museums that mirror the robust developments in digital technology. Physical museums need to be transformed so that their material collections can stimulate cultural production by living artists and cultural practitioners. This juxtaposition of the past and the present, the dead and the living, ensures that museums remain vibrant and vital spaces for the multicultural communities around them.

Notes

1 See the Introduction, above.
2 For all the examples in this paragraph, see S. Gilbert, 'Please Turn On Your Phone in the Museum: Cultural Institutions Learn to Love Selfies, Tailor-Made Apps, and Social Media', *The Atlantic* (October 2016), www.theatlantic.com/magazine/archive/2016/10/please-turn-on-your-phone-in-the-museum/497525/. Accessed 10 April 2017.

3 I was attending an anthropology conference organised by the Royal Anthropological Institute of the United Kingdom and Ireland. The focus was climate change. My film screening there was *Moana Rua: The Rising of the Sea*.

4 R. Parry and J. Hopwood, 'Virtual Reality and the "Soft" Museum: A Call for Further Research', *Journal of Museum Ethnography*, 16 (2004), 69–78.

5 P. Schorch, C. McCarthy and A. Hakiwai, 'Globalizing Maori Museology: Reconceptualizing Engagement, Knowledge, and Virtuality through Mana Taonga', *Journal of Museum Anthropology*, 39:1 (2016), 56.

6 *Ibid.*, 60.

7 G.C. Burdea and P. Coiffet, *Virtual Reality Technology*, Volume 1 (Hoboken, NJ: John Wiley & Sons, Inc., 2003).

8 J. Rae and L. Edwards, 'Virtual Reality at the British Museum: What Is the Value of Virtual Reality Environments for Learning by Children and Young People, Schools, and Families?' Museums and the Web Conference, Los Angeles, 6–9 April 2016, http://mw2016.museumsandtheweb.com/paper/virtual-reality-at-the-british-museum-what-is-the-value-of-virtual-reality-environments-for-learning-by-children-and-young-people-schools-and-families/. Accessed 10 April 2017. A similar experiment that this article also mentions took place in April 2015 at the Great North Museum: Hancock in Newcastle, UK, where visitors were offered the opportunity to use Oculus Rift 3D headsets to explore a virtual Greek villa populated with fifteen artefacts from the museum's pottery collection.

9 For the past three decades, virtual reality was used primarily for entertainment purposes, the gaming industry being its main user. As the quality of the hardware, related accessories and experiences with the software improved, virtual reality became more attractive to other possible users, such as the tourism sector (including time travel tourism), and the heritage sector, which uses the technology 'as a means to provide greater access provision, particularly to remote visitors'. See Rae and Edwards, 'Virtual Reality at the British Museum'.

10 See Rae and Edwards, 'Virtual Reality at the British Museum', for a detailed description of what a VR experience entails. See also A. Hill, 'Museums Embrace Virtual Reality', *Marketplace* (21 March 2017), www.marketplace.org/2017/03/20/business/american-museums-embrace-virtual-reality. Accessed 10 April 2017.

11 Rae and Edwards, 'Virtual Reality at the British Museum'. Also see Elizabeth Merritt's blog in which she writes that the most important consideration for a virtual reality experience is to '[p]ut your audience first': E. Merritt, 'Why VR? Enhancing IRL (In Real Life) Experiences for Visitors to the British Museum', Center for the Future of Museums, 28 April 2016: http://futureofmuseums.blogspot.co.nz/2016/04/. Accessed 10 April 2017.

12 Gilbert, 'Please Turn On Your Phone in the Museum'.

13 E. Alton, 'How Virtual Reality Could Give New Life to Museum Exhibits', *Entertainment Designer: Museum Design News* (10 October 2016), http://entertainmentdesigner.com/news/museum-design-news/how-virtual-reality-could-give-new-life-to-museum-exhibits/. Accessed 10 April 2017.

14 *Ibid.*

15 *Ibid.* A VR in-depth exhibit requires time and resources, which means that this medium is best reserved for very important exhibits, and is unlikely to lead to the demise of the curator altogether. However, it could lead to further training

for those curators who are not familiar with the technology, or the hiring of curators trained in this challenging medium.

16 These examples are from Gilbert, 'Please Turn On Your Phone in the Museum'.
17 Schorch, McCarthy and Hakiwai, 'Globalizing Maori Museology', 50.
18 See Lythberg, Ngata and Salmond, Chapter 14 above.
19 Alton, 'How Virtual Reality Could Give New Life to Museum Exhibits'.
20 Schorch, McCarthy and Hakiwai, 'Globalizing Maori Museology', 50.
21 Gilbert, 'Please Turn On Your Phone in the Museum'.

Index